kare kano

his and her circumstances

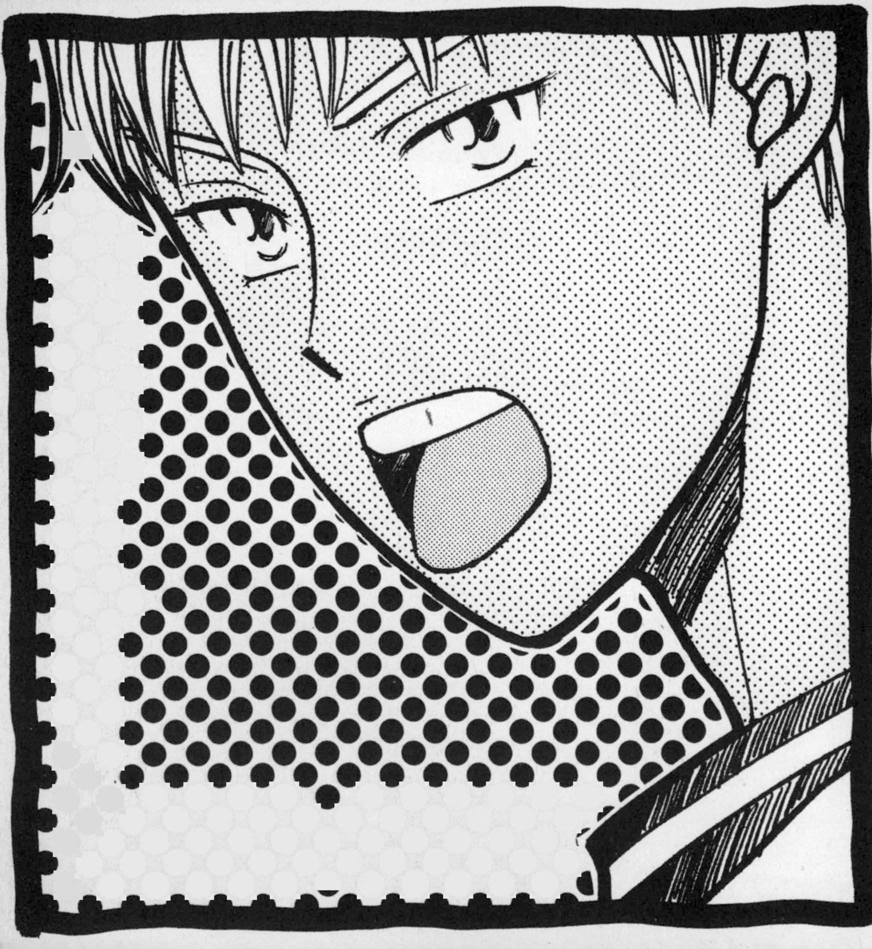

Translator - Michelle Kobayashi
English Adaptation - Darcy Lockman
Contributing Editor - Jodi Bryson
Retouch and Lettering - Jennifer Nunn
Cover Layout - Gary Shum
Graphic Designer - John Lo

Editor - Julie Taylor
Managing Editor - Jill Freshney
Production Coordinator - Antonio DePietro
Production Managers - Jennifer Miller & Mutsumi Miyazaki
Art Director - Matt Alford
Editorial Director - Jeremy Ross
VP of Production - Ron Klamert
President & C.O.O. - John Parker
Publisher & C.E.O. - Stuart Levy

Email: editor@TOKYOPOP.com
Come visit us online at www.TOKYOPOP.com

A 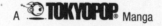 Manga

TOKYOPOP Inc.
5900 Wilshire Blvd. Suite 2000
Los Angeles, CA 90036

ISBN: 1-59182-472-9

First TOKYOPOP® printing: January 2004

10 9 8 7 6 5 4 3 2 1
Printed in the USA

kare kano

his and her circumstances

volume seven

by Masami Tsuda

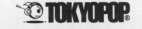

LOS ANGELES • TOKYO • LONDON

ALSO AVAILABLE FROM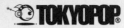

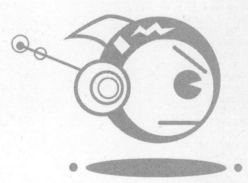

For more information visit www.TOKYOPOP.com

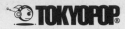
MANGA

.HACK//LEGEND OF THE TWILIGHT
@LARGE
A.I. LOVE YOU February 2004
AI YORI AOSHI January 2004
ANGELIC LAYER
BABY BIRTH
BATTLE ROYALE
BATTLE VIXENS April 2004
BIRTH May 2004
BRAIN POWERED
BRIGADOON
B'TX January 2004
CARDCAPTOR SAKURA
CARDCAPTOR SAKURA - MASTER OF THE CLOW
CARDCAPTOR SAKURA: BOXED SET COLLECTION 1
CARDCAPTOR SAKURA: BOXED SET COLLECTION 2
  March 2004
CHOBITS
CHRONICLES OF THE CURSED SWORD
CLAMP SCHOOL DETECTIVES
CLOVER
COMIC PARTY June 2004
CONFIDENTIAL CONFESSIONS
CORRECTOR YUI
COWBOY BEBOP: BOXED SET THE COMPLETE
  COLLECTION
CRESCENT MOON May 2004
CREST OF THE STARS June 2004
CYBORG 009
DEMON DIARY
DIGIMON
DIGIMON SERIES 3 April 2004
DIGIMON ZERO TWO February 2004
DNANGEL April 2004
DOLL May 2004
DRAGON HUNTER
DRAGON KNIGHTS
DUKLYON: CLAMP SCHOOL DEFENDERS:
DV June 2004
ERICA SAKURAZAWA
FAERIES' LANDING January 2004
FAKE
FLCL
FORBIDDEN DANCE
FRUITS BASKET February 2004
G GUNDAM
GATEKEEPERS
GETBACKERS February 2004
GHOST! March 2004
GIRL GOT GAME January 2004
GRAVITATION
GTO

GUNDAM WING
GUNDAM WING: BATTLEFIELD OF PACIFISTS
GUNDAM WING: ENDLESS WALTZ
GUNDAM WING: THE LAST OUTPOST
HAPPY MANIA
HARLEM BEAT
I.N.V.U.
INITIAL D
ISLAND
JING: KING OF BANDITS
JULINE
JUROR 13 March 2004
KARE KANO
KILL ME, KISS ME February 2004
KINDAICHI CASE FILES, THE
KING OF HELL
KODOCHA: SANA'S STAGE
LAMENT OF THE LAMB May 2004
LES BIJOUX February 2004
LIZZIE MCGUIRE
LOVE HINA
LUPIN III
LUPIN III SERIES 2
MAGIC KNIGHT RAYEARTH I
MAGIC KNIGHT RAYEARTH II February 2004
MAHOROMATIC: AUTOMATIC MAIDEN May 2004
MAN OF MANY FACES
MARMALADE BOY
MARS
METEOR METHUSELA June 2004
METROID June 2004
MINK April 2004
MIRACLE GIRLS
MIYUKI-CHAN IN WONDERLAND
MODEL May 2004
NELLY MUSIC MANGA April 2004
ONE April 2004
PARADISE KISS
PARASYTE
PEACH GIRL
PEACH GIRL CHANGE OF HEART
PEACH GIRL RELAUNCH BOX SET
PET SHOP OF HORRORS
PITA-TEN January 2004
PLANET LADDER February 2004
PLANETES
PRIEST
PRINCESS AI April 2004
PSYCHIC ACADEMY March 2004
RAGNAROK
RAGNAROK: BOXED SET COLLECTION 1
RAVE MASTER
RAVE MASTER: BOXED SET March 2004

KARE KANO: THE STORY SO FAR

Yukino Miyazawa is the perfect student: kind, athletic, smart. But she's not all she seems. She is really the self-professed "queen of vanity," and her only goal in life is winning the praise and admiration of everyone around her. Therefore, she makes it her business to always look and act perfect during school hours. At home, however, she lets her guard down and lets her true self show.

When Yukino enters high school, she finally meets her match: Soichiro Arima, a handsome, popular, ultra-intelligent guy. Once he steals the top seat in class away from her, Yukino sees him as a bitter rival. Over time, her anger turns to amazement when she discovers she and Soichiro have more in common than she ever imagined. As their love blossoms, they promise to stop pretending to be perfect and just be true to themselves.

But they have plenty of obstacles in their way. First, Hideaki, the school's token pretty boy, tries to come between them. Then, Yukino and Soichiro's grades drop because they've been spending so much time together, and their teacher pressures them to break up. Once that's resolved, two more speed bumps are encountered on their road to romance. Maho, a jealous classmate, is convinced that Yukino is deceiving everyone and vows to turn everyone against her. Then an old friend of Soichiro's from junior high tries to steal Soichiro's affections. Somehow, Yukino and Soichiro's love manages to persevere...but then Soichiro unexpectedly announces he will be away at a kendo tournament all summer. Yukino decides to spend her free time hanging out with her gal pals, but soon her friend Tsubasa announces she's leaving home. Yukino tries to be there for her friend while waiting for Soichiro to return. When Soichiro comes home Yukino is delighted to find that he has matured a great deal, causing her love for him to grow even more. However, Soichiro continues to struggle with personal and family issues of his own.

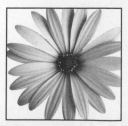

GERBERA DAISY = INNOCENCE

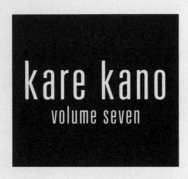

kare kano
volume seven

TABLE OF CONTENTS

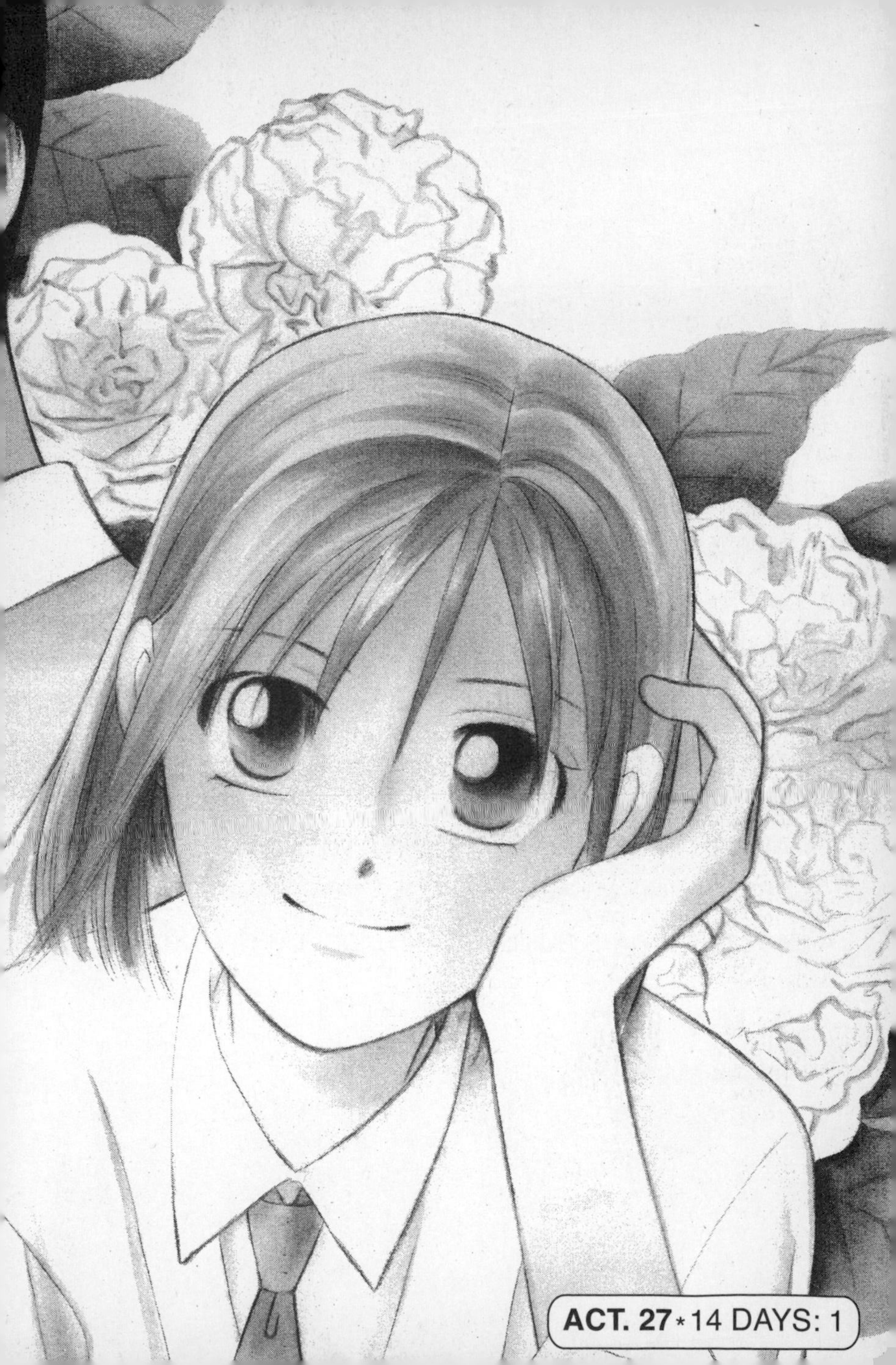
ACT. 27 * 14 DAYS: 1

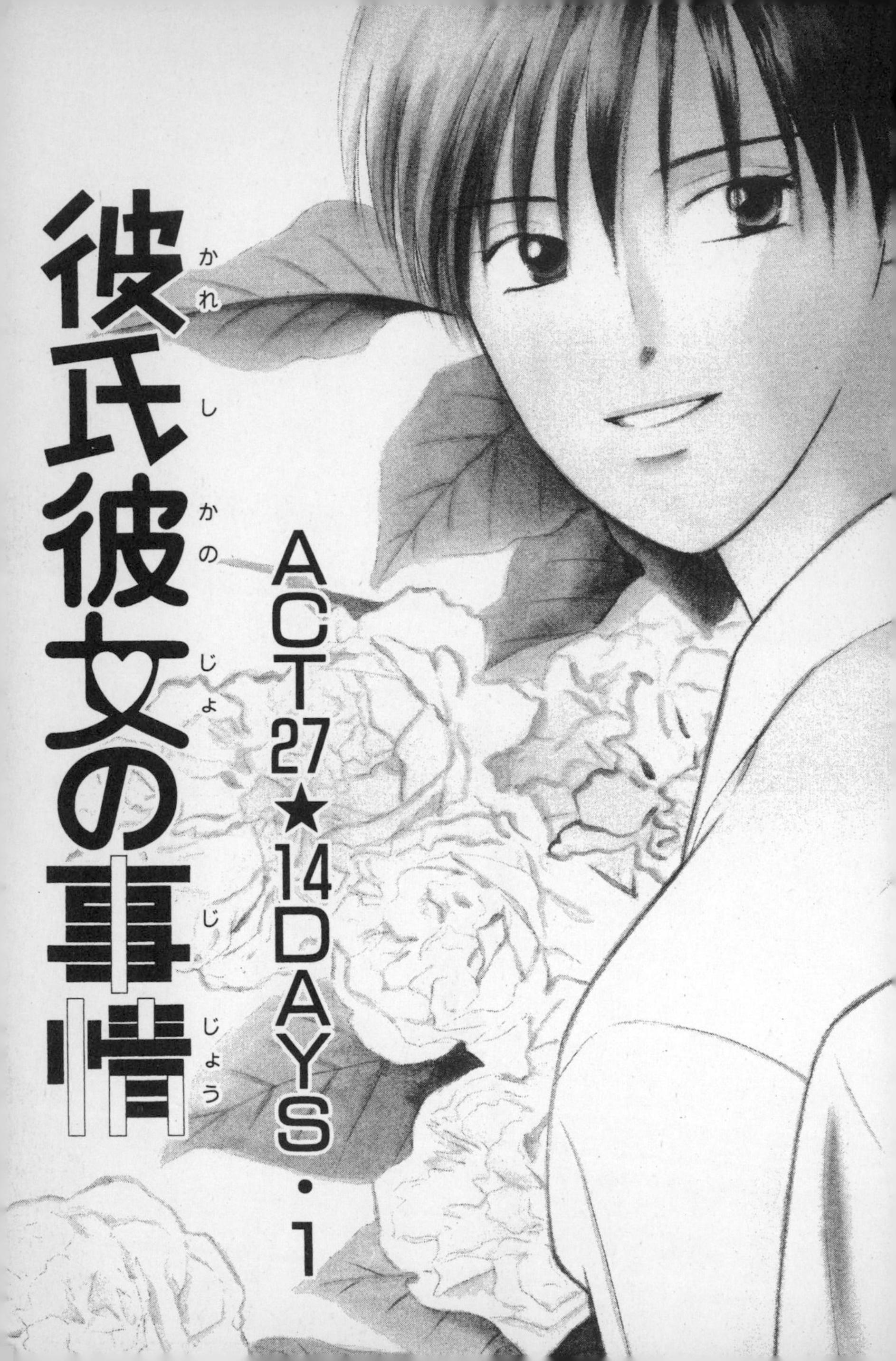
ACT 27★14 DAYS・1
彼氏彼女の事情
かれしかのじょじじょう

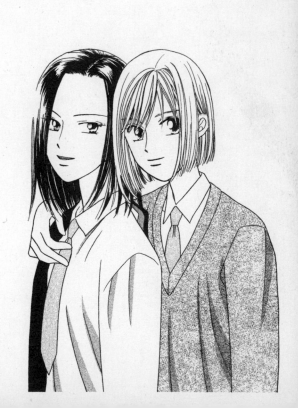

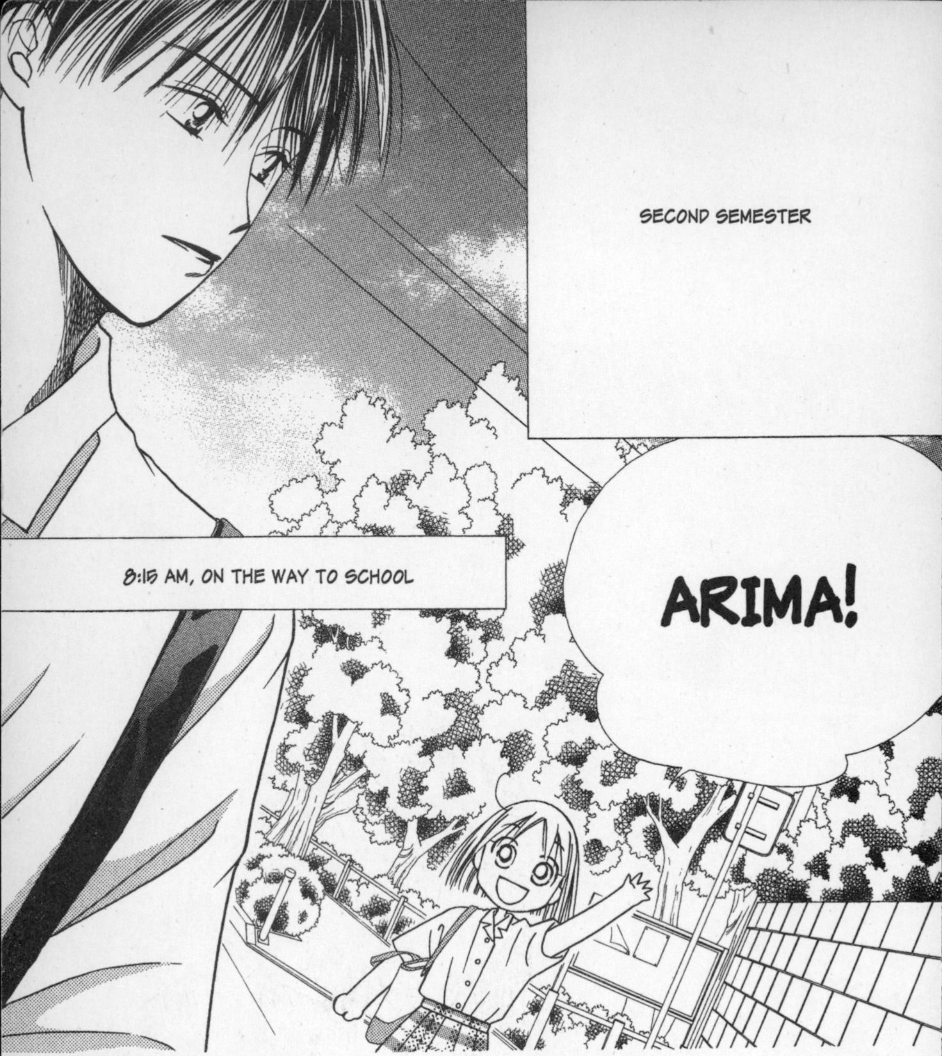
SECOND SEMESTER
8:15 AM, ON THE WAY TO SCHOOL
ARIMA!

Reminiscing...

LATELY I'VE BEEN IN THE MOOD TO LISTEN TO CLASSICAL MUSIC AGAIN. RIGHT NOW, IT'S BACH.

I LISTENED TO IT A LOT EIGHT YEARS AGO, BUT EVER SINCE THEN I JUST HAVEN'T BEEN IN THE MOOD, SO I HAVEN'T BEEN LISTENING TO IT MUCH AT ALL UNTIL NOW.

I LOVE THE MUSICIAN'S WAY OF LIFE.

I STILL HAVE VIDEO TAPES OF THAT "MAESTRO" PROGRAM THAT USED TO RUN ON FUJI TV LATE AT NIGHT.

BUT WHEN I LISTEN TO THIS MUSIC NOW THAT I'M EIGHT YEARS OLDER, I FEEL IT A LOT MORE DEEPLY. THE OLDER I GET, THE MORE MEANING IT HAS FOR ME.

I GUESS I'LL ENJOY IT EVEN MORE 10 YEARS FROM NOW.

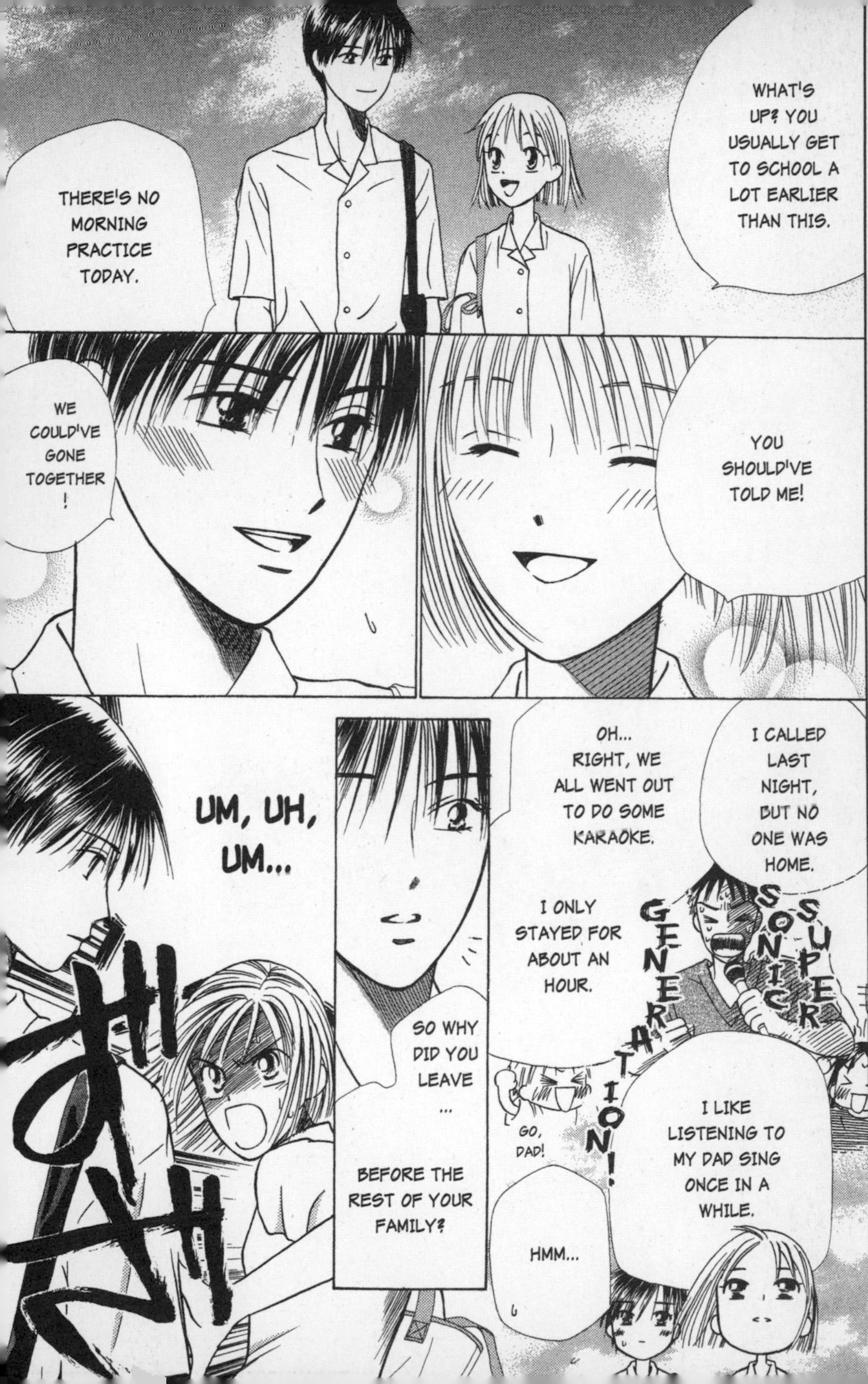
WHAT'S UP? YOU USUALLY GET TO SCHOOL A LOT EARLIER THAN THIS.
THERE'S NO MORNING PRACTICE TODAY.
YOU SHOULD'VE TOLD ME!
WE COULD'VE GONE TOGETHER!
I CALLED LAST NIGHT, BUT NO ONE WAS HOME.
OH... RIGHT, WE ALL WENT OUT TO DO SOME KARAOKE.
I ONLY STAYED FOR ABOUT AN HOUR.
SUPER SONIC GENERATION!
GO, DAD!
I LIKE LISTENING TO MY DAD SING ONCE IN A WHILE.
HMM...
SO WHY DID YOU LEAVE ...
BEFORE THE REST OF YOUR FAMILY?
UM, UH, UM...

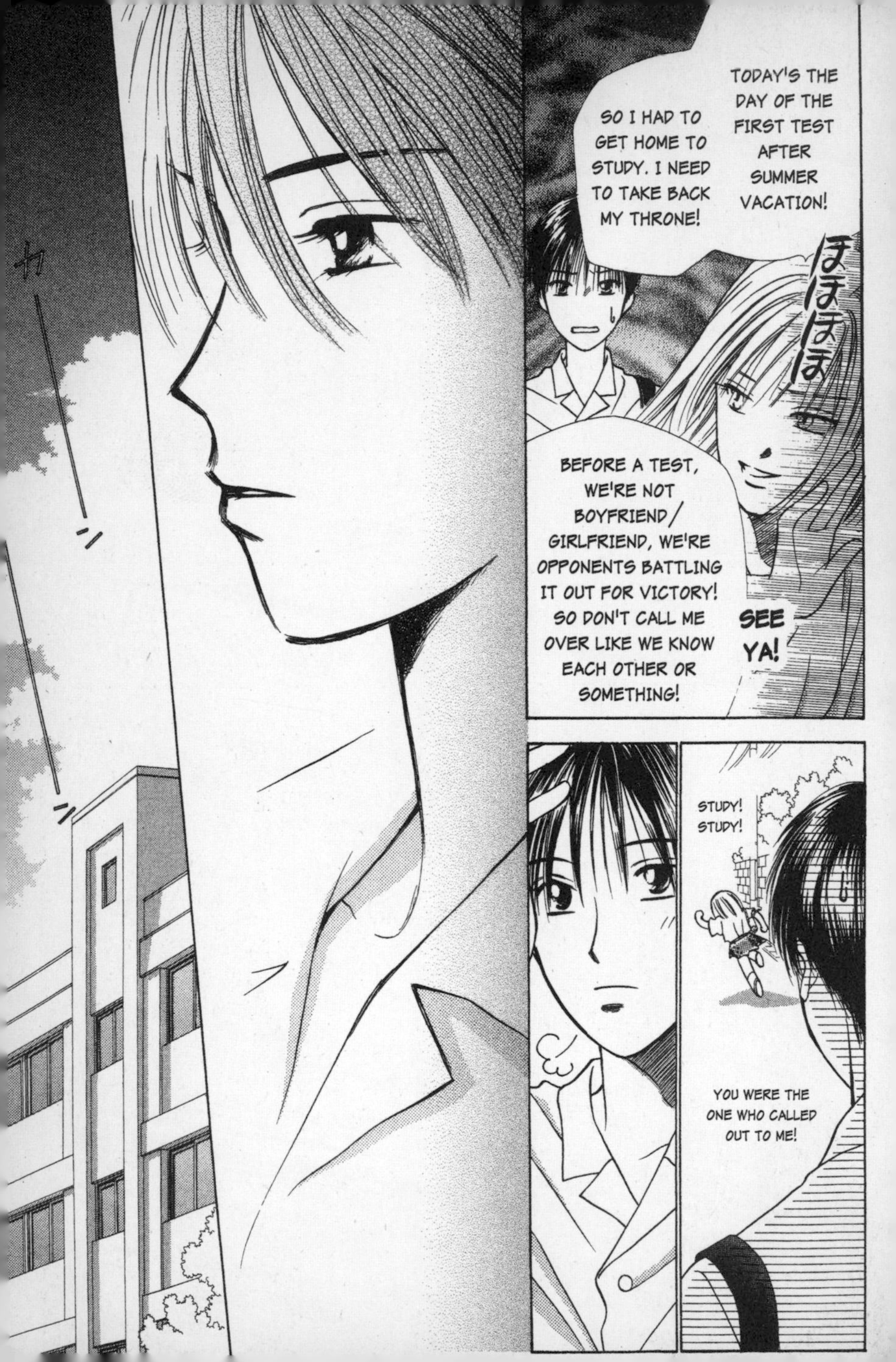
TODAY'S THE DAY OF THE FIRST TEST AFTER SUMMER VACATION!
SO I HAD TO GET HOME TO STUDY. I NEED TO TAKE BACK MY THRONE!
ほほほほ
BEFORE A TEST, WE'RE NOT BOYFRIEND/ GIRLFRIEND, WE'RE OPPONENTS BATTLING IT OUT FOR VICTORY! SO DON'T CALL ME OVER LIKE WE KNOW EACH OTHER OR SOMETHING!
SEE YA!
STUDY! STUDY!
YOU WERE THE ONE WHO CALLED OUT TO ME!
カ

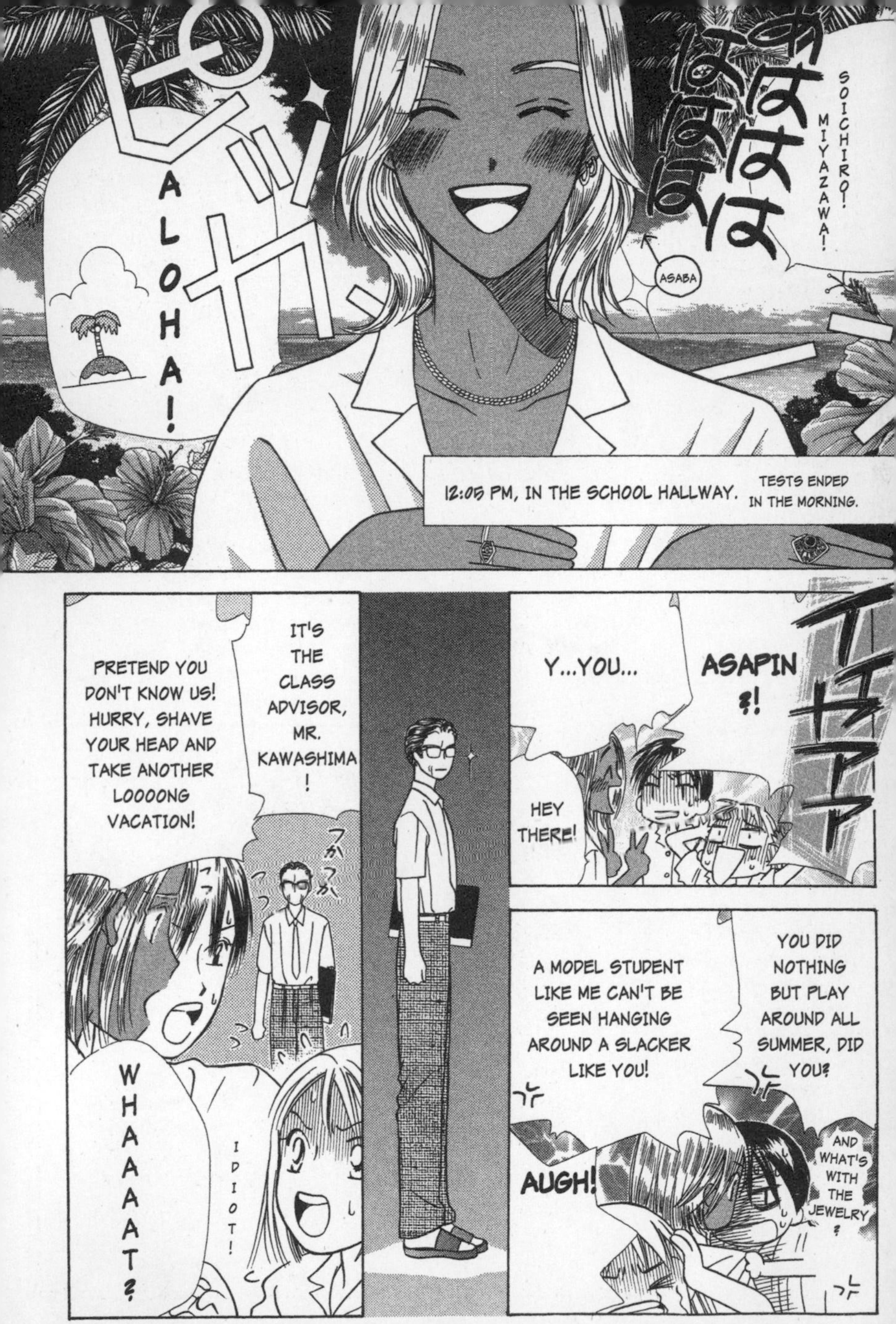

あはははははは
SOICHIRO! MIYAZAWA!
ASABA
ALOHA!
TESTS ENDED IN THE MORNING.
12:05 PM, IN THE SCHOOL HALLWAY.
ASAPIN?!
Y...YOU...
HEY THERE!
YOU DID NOTHING BUT PLAY AROUND ALL SUMMER, DID YOU?
A MODEL STUDENT LIKE ME CAN'T BE SEEN HANGING AROUND A SLACKER LIKE YOU!
AND WHAT'S WITH THE JEWELRY?
AUGH!
IT'S THE CLASS ADVISOR, MR. KAWASHIMA!
PRETEND YOU DON'T KNOW US! HURRY, SHAVE YOUR HEAD AND TAKE ANOTHER LOOOONG VACATION!
WHAAAAAT?
IDIOT!

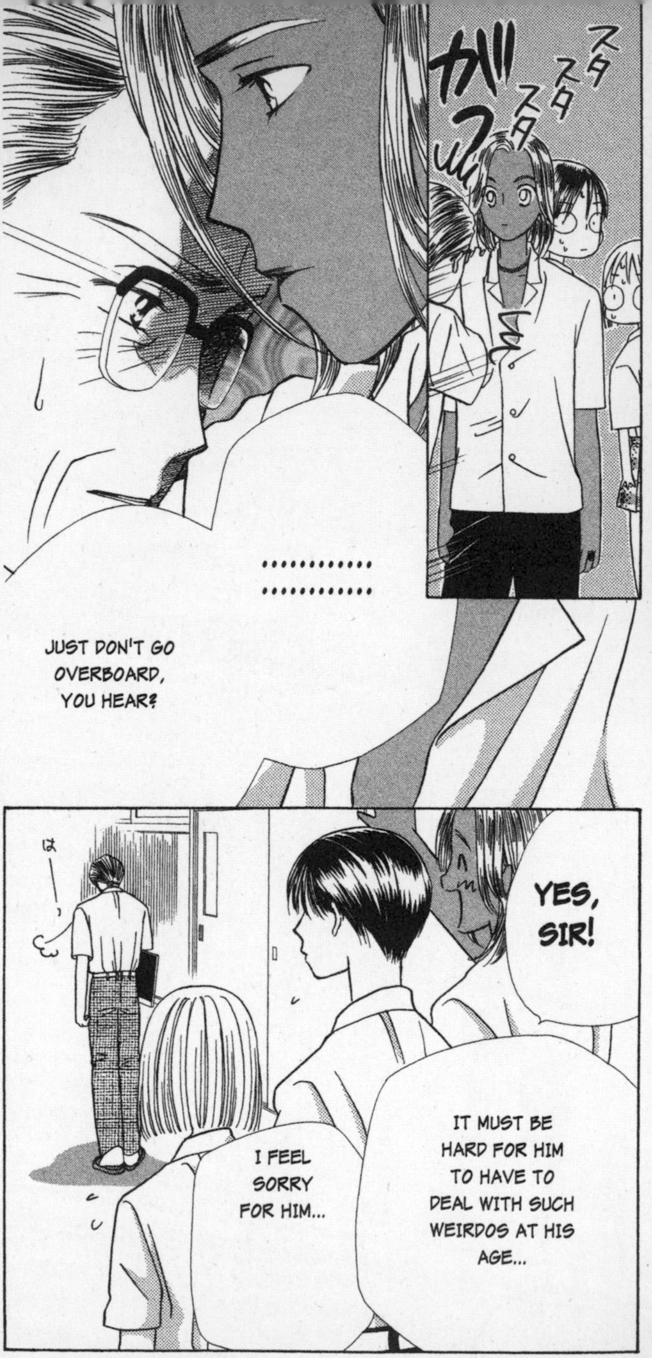

スタスタスタ
ガラッ
....
....
JUST DON'T GO OVERBOARD, YOU HEAR?
YES, SIR!
は—
IT MUST BE HARD FOR HIM TO HAVE TO DEAL WITH SUCH WEIRDOS AT HIS AGE...
I FEEL SORRY FOR HIM...

1

Hello and welcome to <u>Kare Kano</u> Volume 7!

I was looking at an old ad and it said "Volume 4 about to start!" And I realized how far I've come...

I never really thought that far ahead.

The stories I'm writing now are stories I wanted to write two years ago, so when I think that I've finally made it this far, I get really emotional.

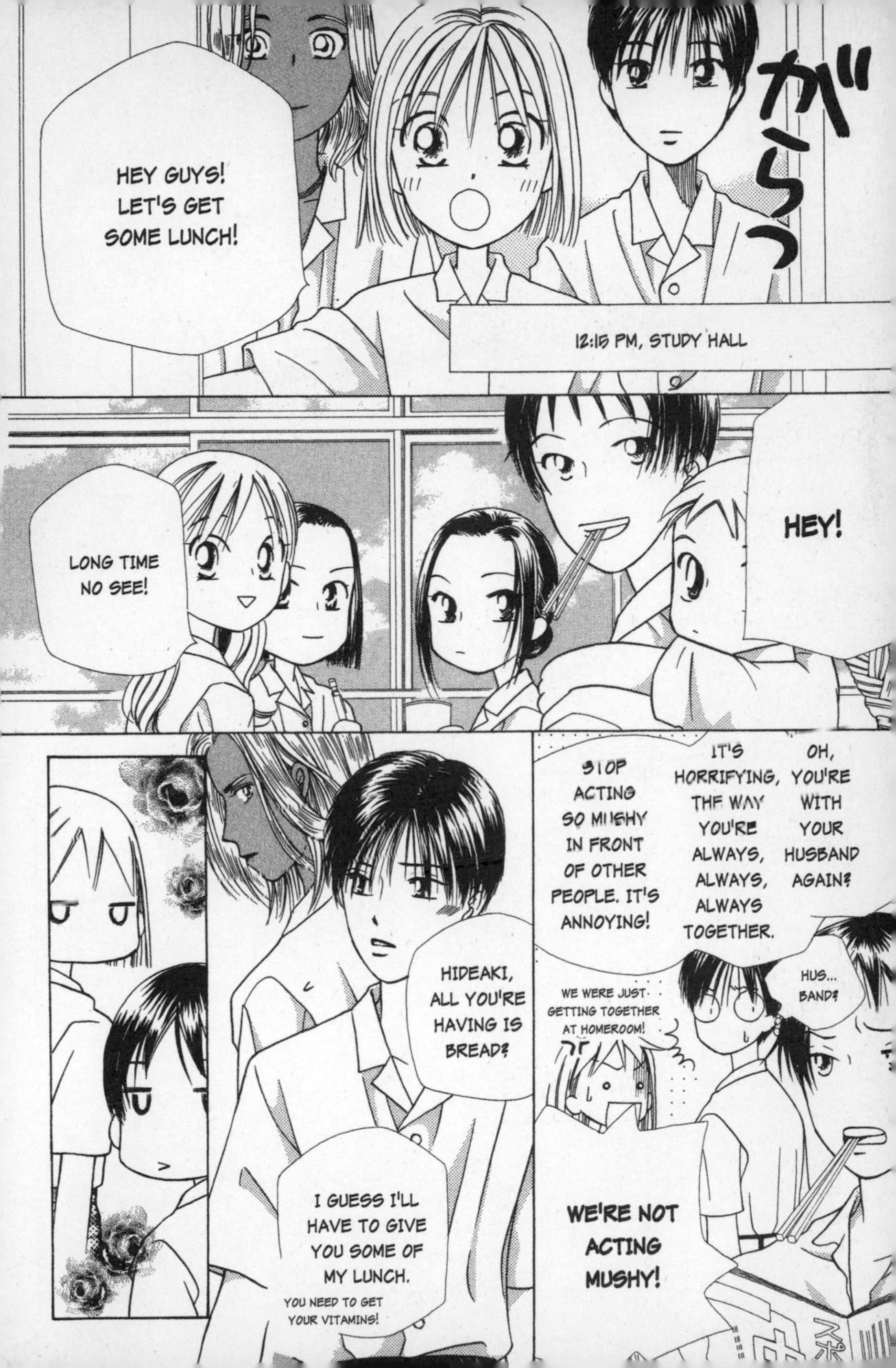
がらっ
HEY GUYS! LET'S GET SOME LUNCH!
12:15 PM, STUDY HALL
HEY!
LONG TIME NO SEE!
OH, YOU'RE WITH YOUR HUSBAND AGAIN?
IT'S HORRIFYING, THE WAY YOU'RE ALWAYS, ALWAYS, ALWAYS TOGETHER.
STOP ACTING SO MUSHY IN FRONT OF OTHER PEOPLE. IT'S ANNOYING!
HUS... BAND?
WE WERE JUST GETTING TOGETHER AT HOMEROOM!
WE'RE NOT ACTING MUSHY!
HIDEAKI, ALL YOU'RE HAVING IS BREAD?
I GUESS I'LL HAVE TO GIVE YOU SOME OF MY LUNCH.
YOU NEED TO GET YOUR VITAMINS!

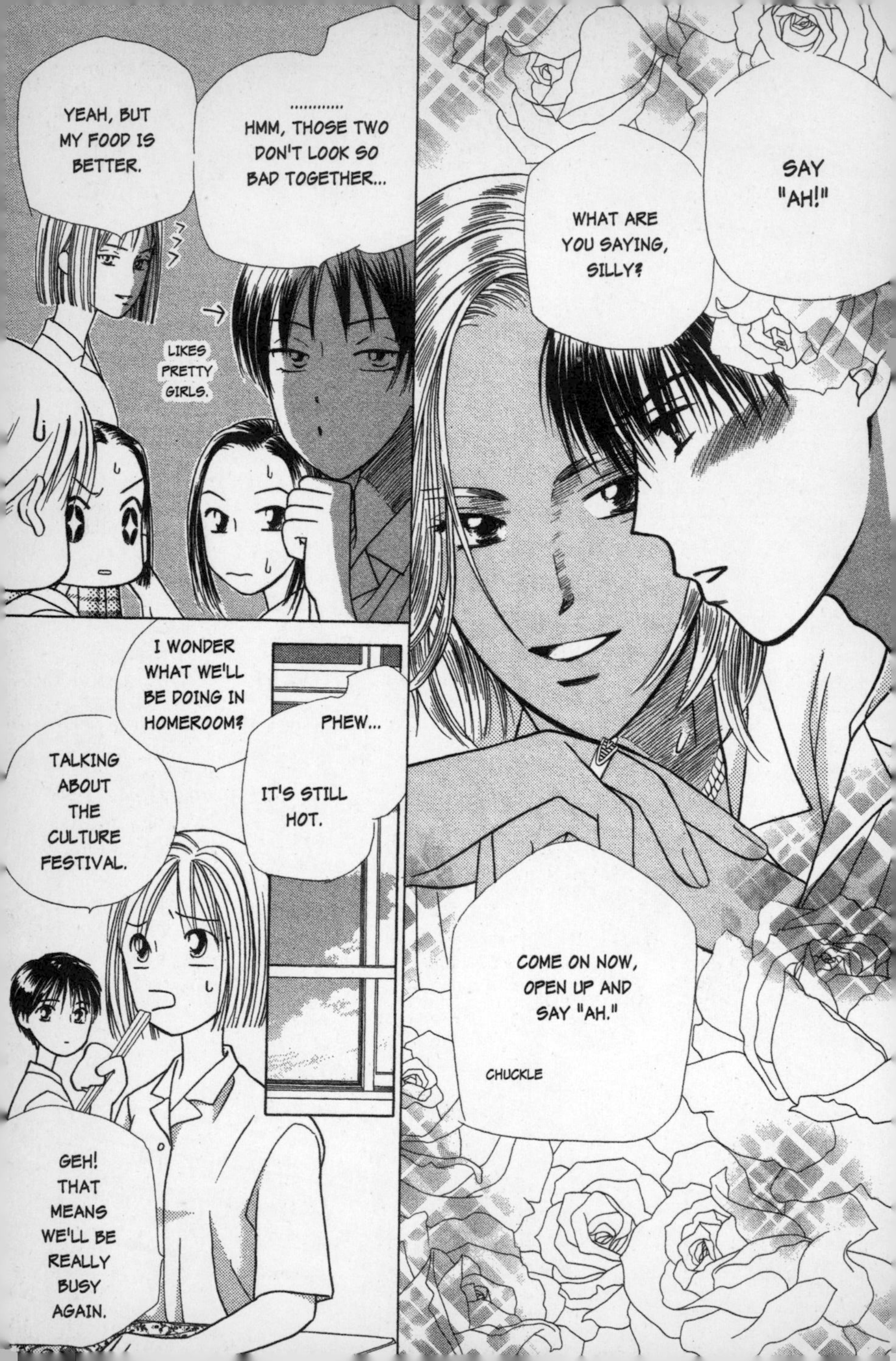
SAY "AH!"
WHAT ARE YOU SAYING, SILLY?
COME ON NOW, OPEN UP AND SAY "AH."
CHUCKLE
.... HMM, THOSE TWO DON'T LOOK SO BAD TOGETHER...
YEAH, BUT MY FOOD IS BETTER.
LIKES PRETTY GIRLS.
PHEW... IT'S STILL HOT.
I WONDER WHAT WE'LL BE DOING IN HOMEROOM?
TALKING ABOUT THE CULTURE FESTIVAL.
GEH! THAT MEANS WE'LL BE REALLY BUSY AGAIN.

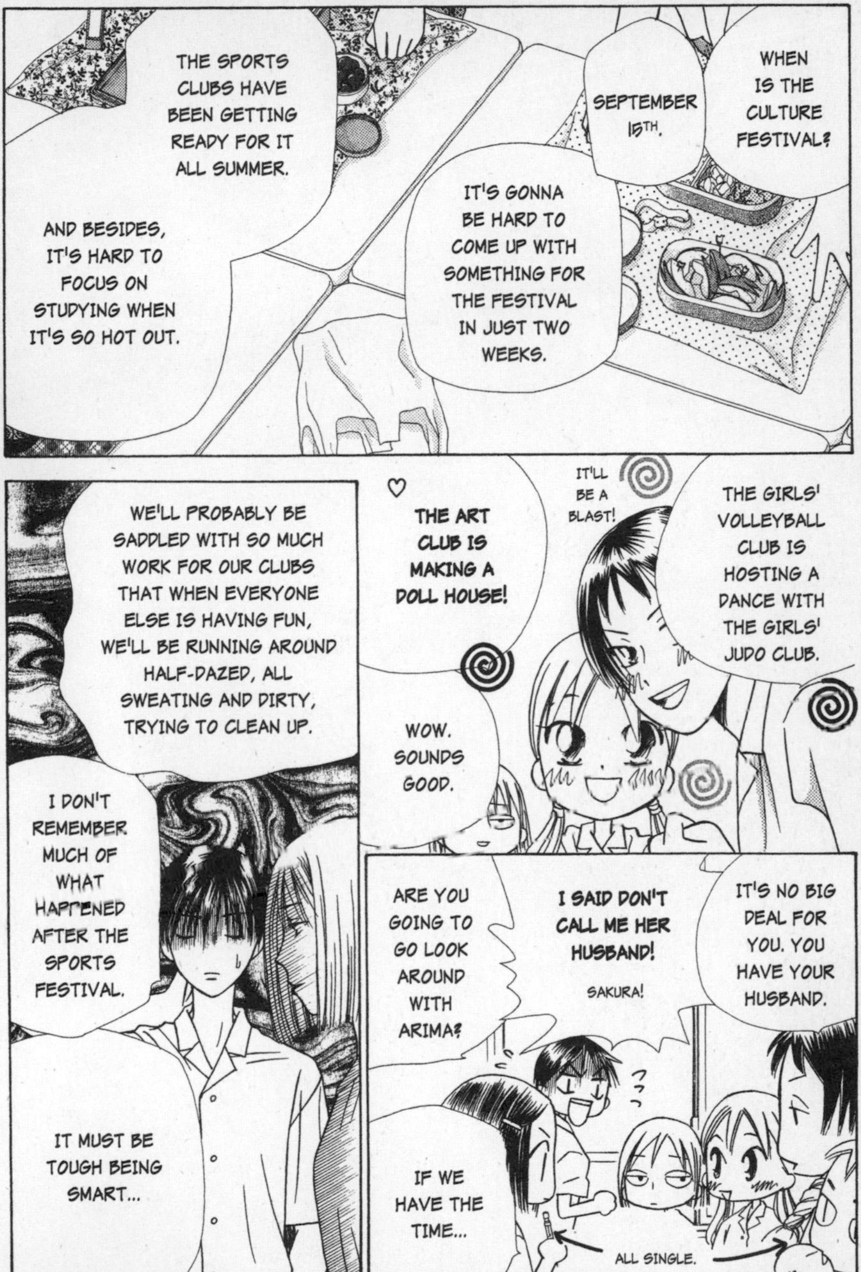
WHEN IS THE CULTURE FESTIVAL?
SEPTEMBER 15TH.
IT'S GONNA BE HARD TO COME UP WITH SOMETHING FOR THE FESTIVAL IN JUST TWO WEEKS.
THE SPORTS CLUBS HAVE BEEN GETTING READY FOR IT ALL SUMMER.
AND BESIDES, IT'S HARD TO FOCUS ON STUDYING WHEN IT'S SO HOT OUT.
THE GIRLS' VOLLEYBALL CLUB IS HOSTING A DANCE WITH THE GIRLS' JUDO CLUB.
IT'LL BE A BLAST!
THE ART CLUB IS MAKING A DOLL HOUSE!
WOW. SOUNDS GOOD.
IT'S NO BIG DEAL FOR YOU. YOU HAVE YOUR HUSBAND.
I SAID DON'T CALL ME HER HUSBAND!
SAKURA!
ARE YOU GOING TO GO LOOK AROUND WITH ARIMA?
IF WE HAVE THE TIME...
ALL SINGLE.
WE'LL PROBABLY BE SADDLED WITH SO MUCH WORK FOR OUR CLUBS THAT WHEN EVERYONE ELSE IS HAVING FUN, WE'LL BE RUNNING AROUND HALF-DAZED, ALL SWEATING AND DIRTY, TRYING TO CLEAN UP.
I DON'T REMEMBER MUCH OF WHAT HAPPENED AFTER THE SPORTS FESTIVAL.
IT MUST BE TOUGH BEING SMART...

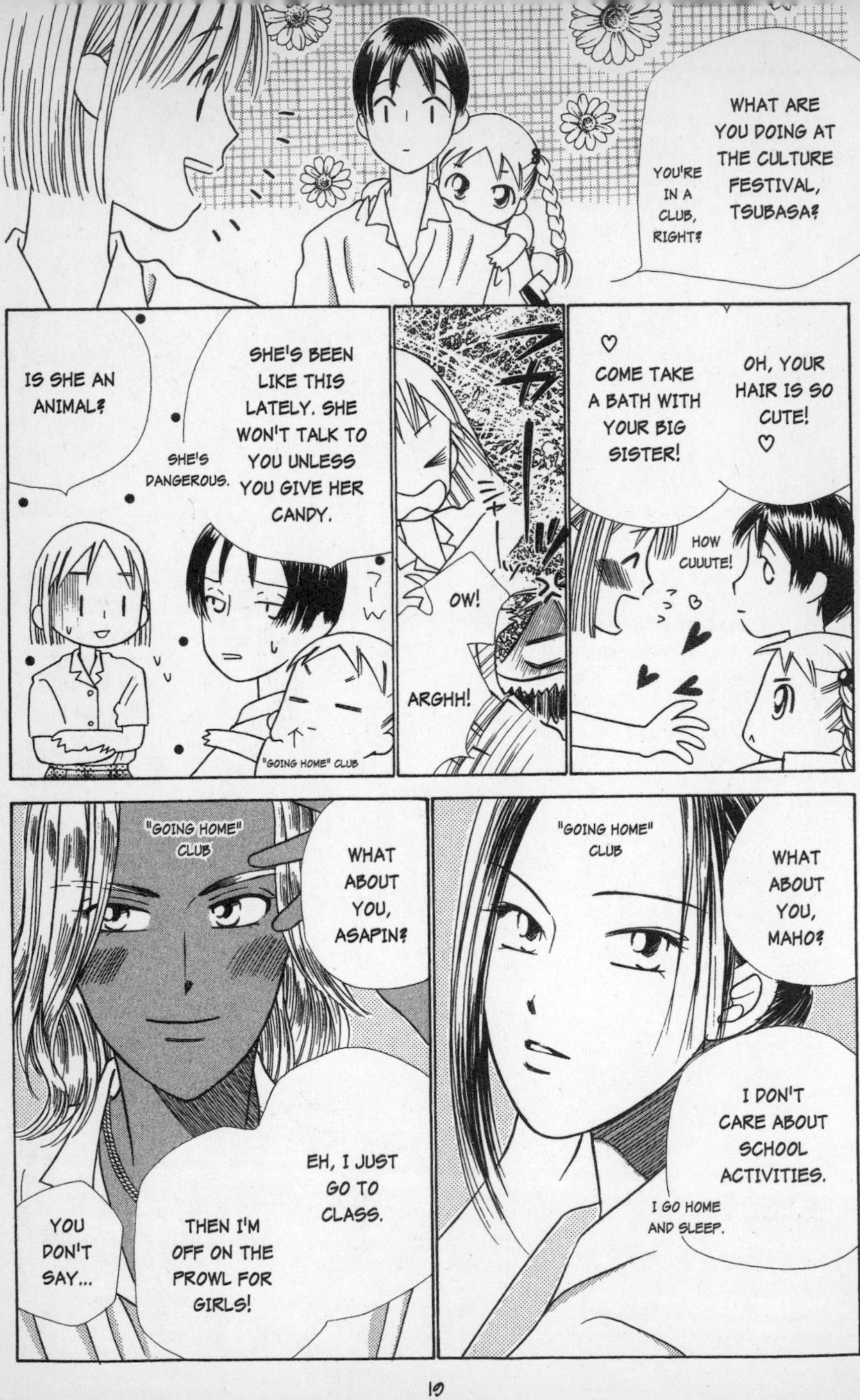
WHAT ARE YOU DOING AT THE CULTURE FESTIVAL, TSUBASA?
YOU'RE IN A CLUB, RIGHT?
OH, YOUR HAIR IS SO CUTE! ♡
♡ COME TAKE A BATH WITH YOUR BIG SISTER!
HOW CUUUTE!
OW!
ARGHH!
SHE'S BEEN LIKE THIS LATELY. SHE WON'T TALK TO YOU UNLESS YOU GIVE HER CANDY.
SHE'S DANGEROUS.
IS SHE AN ANIMAL?
"GOING HOME" CLUB
WHAT ABOUT YOU, MAHO?
"GOING HOME" CLUB
I DON'T CARE ABOUT SCHOOL ACTIVITIES.
I GO HOME AND SLEEP.
WHAT ABOUT YOU, ASAPIN?
"GOING HOME" CLUB
EH, I JUST GO TO CLASS.
THEN I'M OFF ON THE PROWL FOR GIRLS!
YOU DON'T SAY...

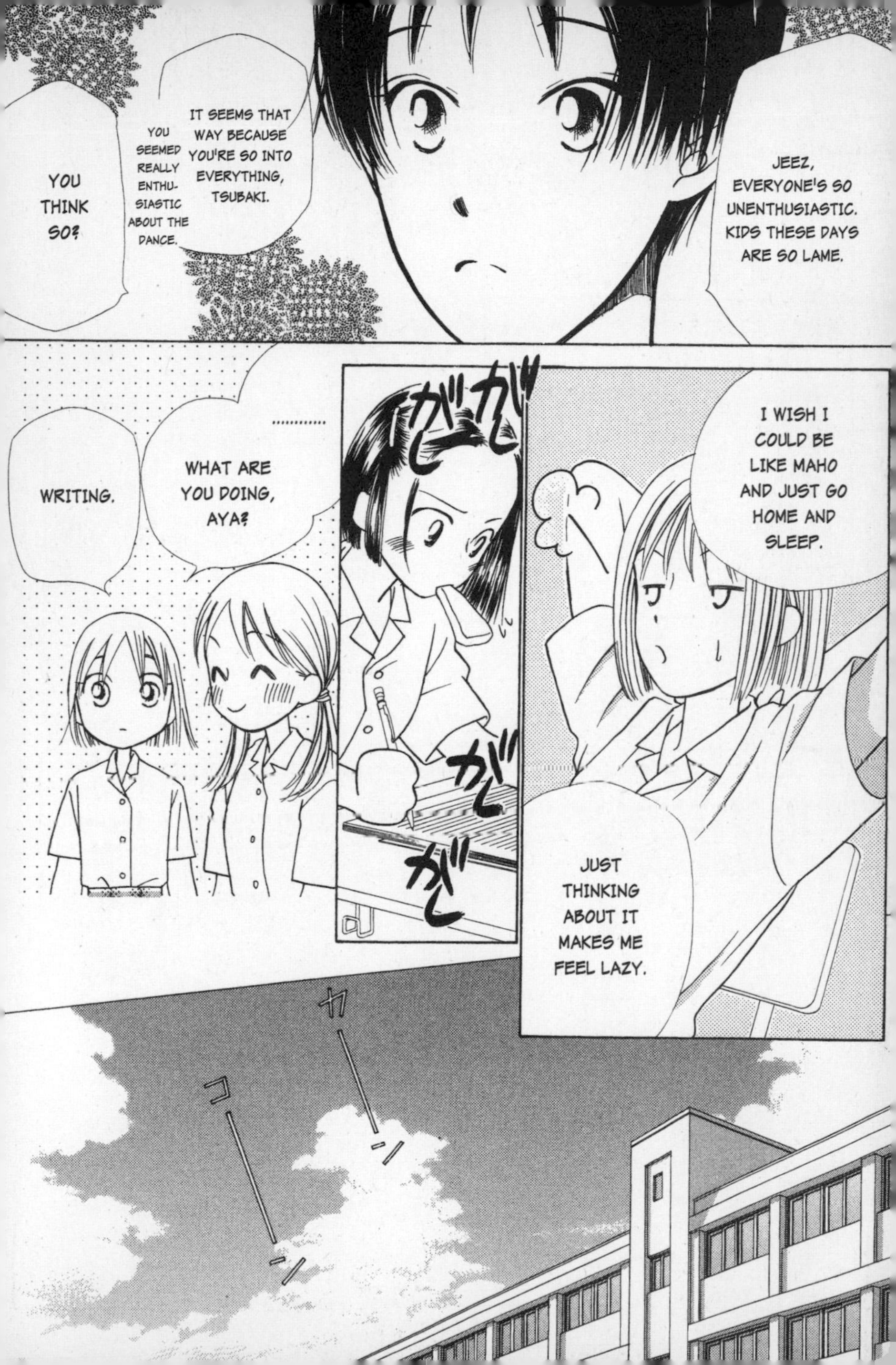
JEEZ, EVERYONE'S SO UNENTHUSIASTIC. KIDS THESE DAYS ARE SO LAME.
IT SEEMS THAT WAY BECAUSE YOU'RE SO INTO EVERYTHING, TSUBAKI.
YOU SEEMED REALLY ENTHUSIASTIC ABOUT THE DANCE.
YOU THINK SO?
I WISH I COULD BE LIKE MAHO AND JUST GO HOME AND SLEEP.
JUST THINKING ABOUT IT MAKES ME FEEL LAZY.
....
WHAT ARE YOU DOING, AYA?
WRITING.
カーン
コーン

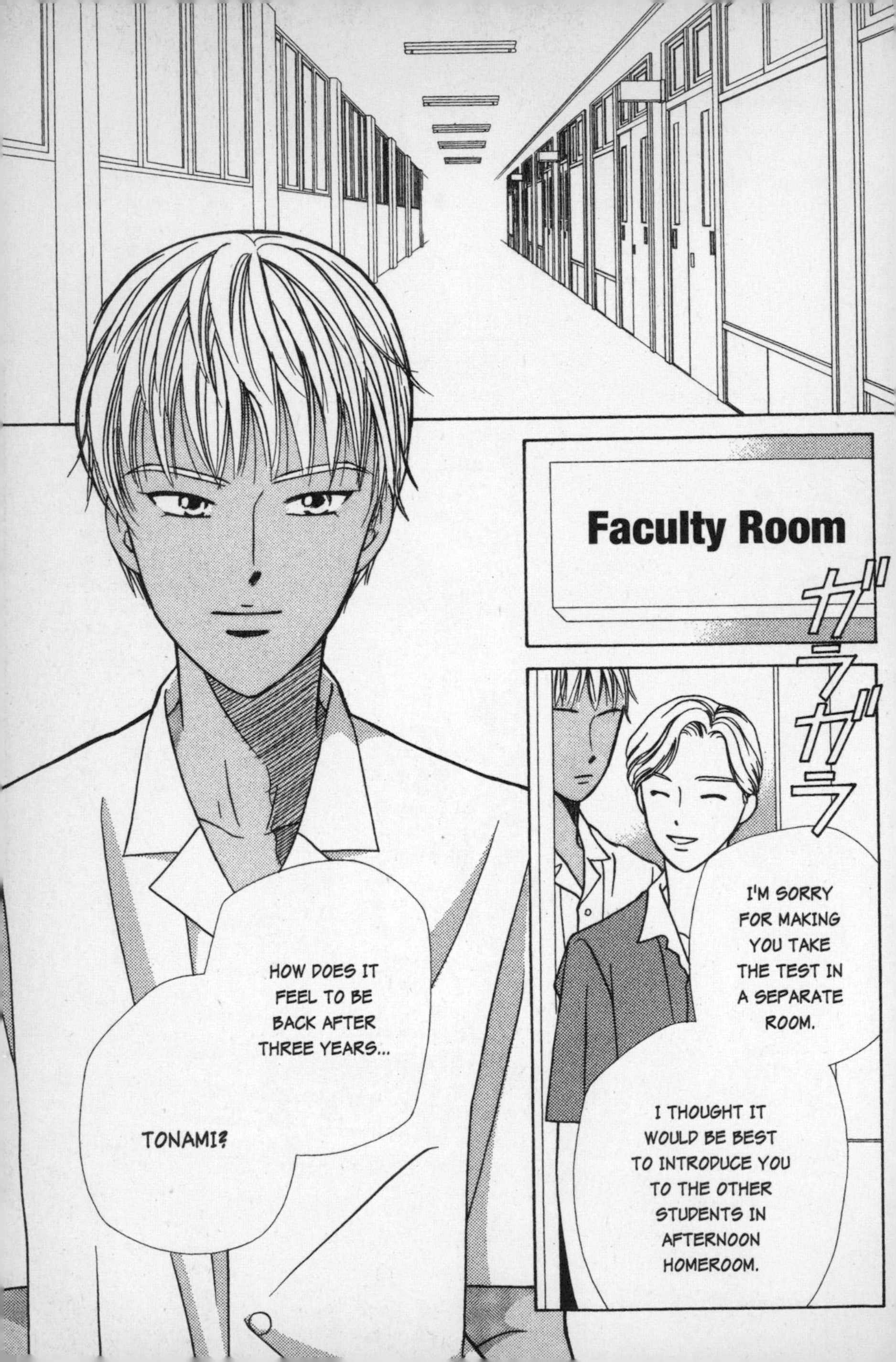
Faculty Room
ガラガラ
I'M SORRY FOR MAKING YOU TAKE THE TEST IN A SEPARATE ROOM.
I THOUGHT IT WOULD BE BEST TO INTRODUCE YOU TO THE OTHER STUDENTS IN AFTERNOON HOMEROOM.
HOW DOES IT FEEL TO BE BACK AFTER THREE YEARS...
TONAMI?

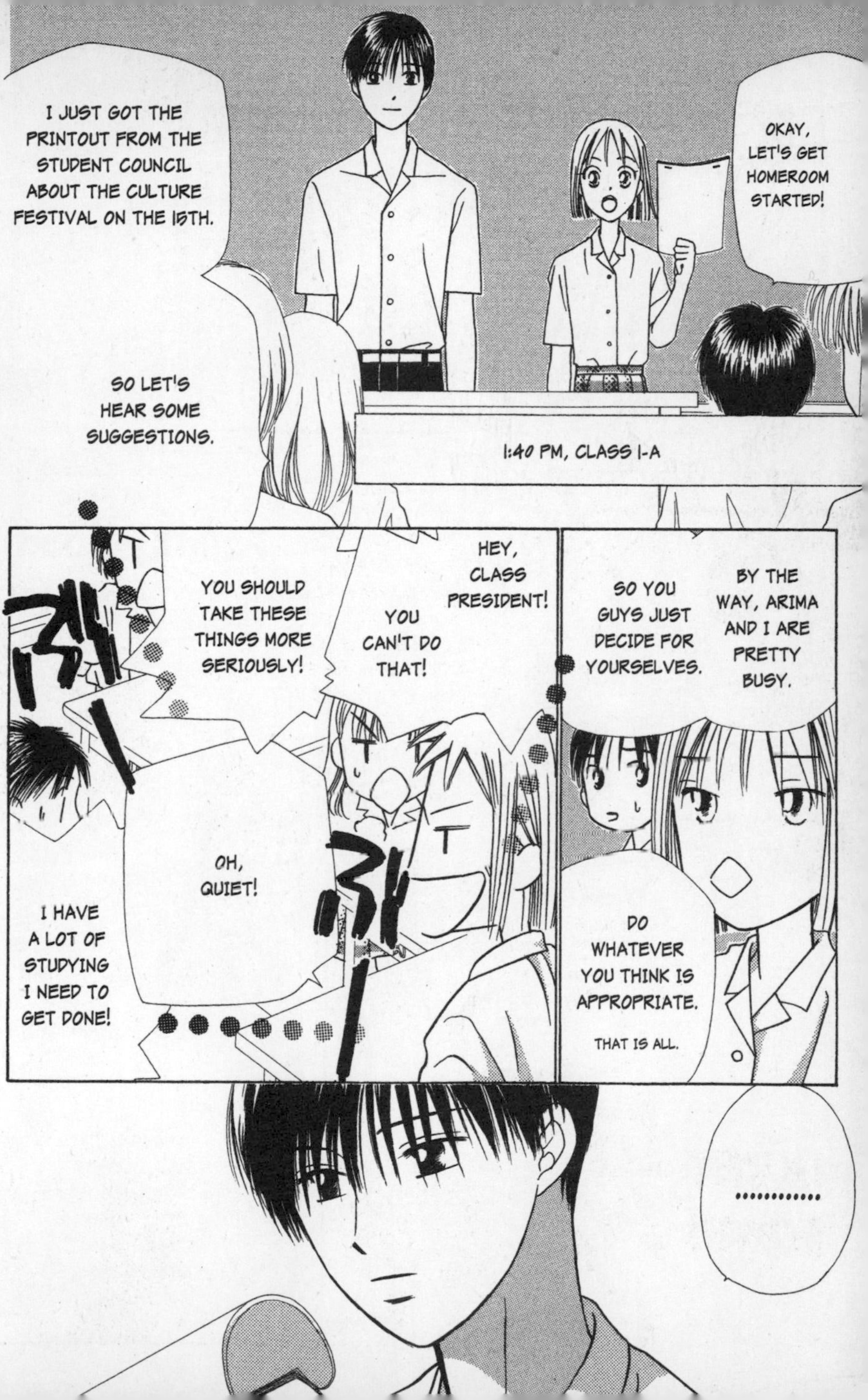
OKAY, LET'S GET HOMEROOM STARTED!
I JUST GOT THE PRINTOUT FROM THE STUDENT COUNCIL ABOUT THE CULTURE FESTIVAL ON THE 15TH.
SO LET'S HEAR SOME SUGGESTIONS.
1:40 PM, CLASS 1-A
BY THE WAY, ARIMA AND I ARE PRETTY BUSY.
SO YOU GUYS JUST DECIDE FOR YOURSELVES.
DO WHATEVER YOU THINK IS APPROPRIATE.
THAT IS ALL.
HEY, CLASS PRESIDENT!
YOU CAN'T DO THAT!
YOU SHOULD TAKE THESE THINGS MORE SERIOUSLY!
OH, QUIET!
I HAVE A LOT OF STUDYING I NEED TO GET DONE!
....

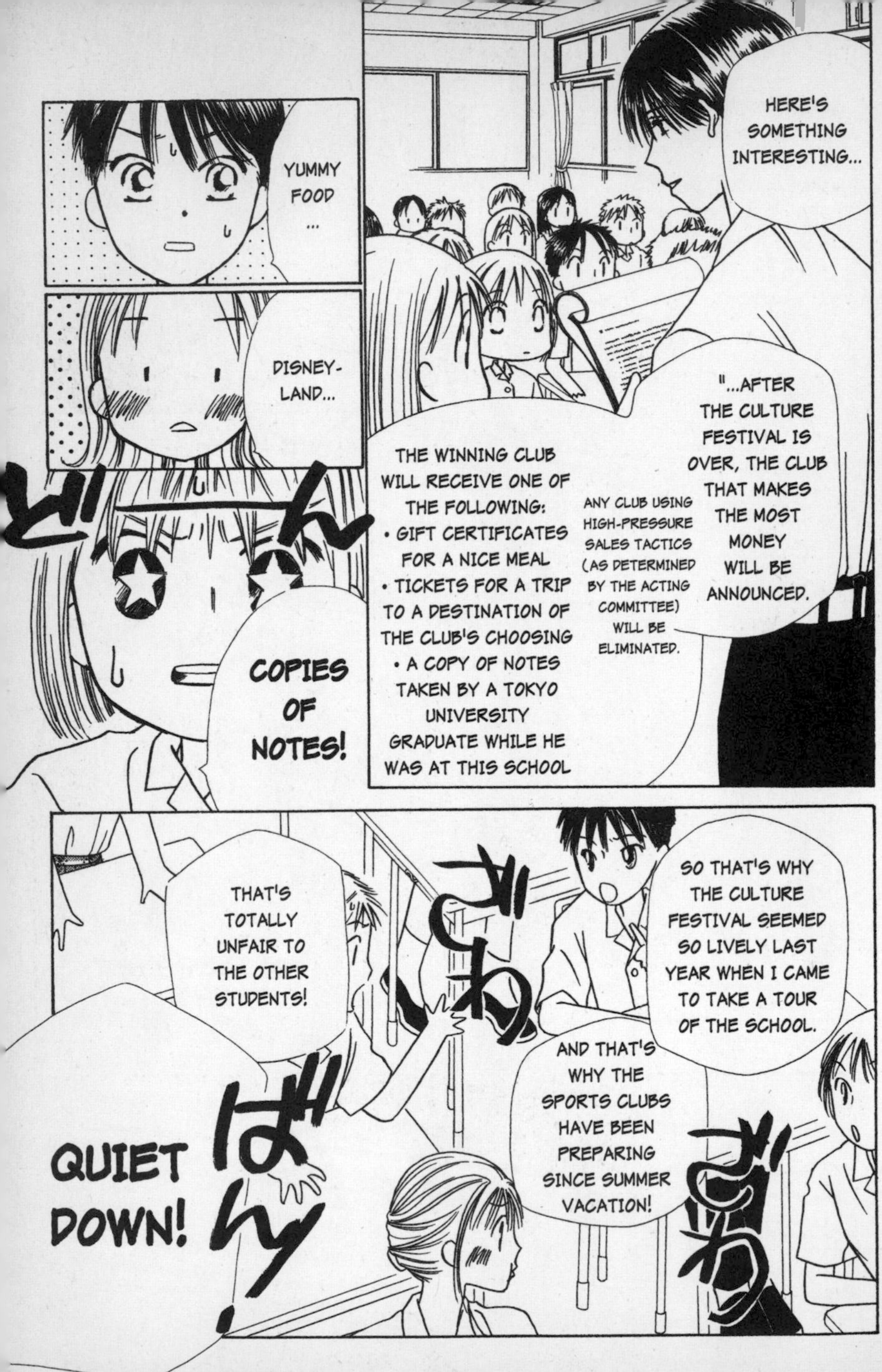

HERE'S SOMETHING INTERESTING...
"...AFTER THE CULTURE FESTIVAL IS OVER, THE CLUB THAT MAKES THE MOST MONEY WILL BE ANNOUNCED.
ANY CLUB USING HIGH-PRESSURE SALES TACTICS (AS DETERMINED BY THE ACTING COMMITTEE) WILL BE ELIMINATED.
THE WINNING CLUB WILL RECEIVE ONE OF THE FOLLOWING:
• GIFT CERTIFICATES FOR A NICE MEAL
• TICKETS FOR A TRIP TO A DESTINATION OF THE CLUB'S CHOOSING
• A COPY OF NOTES TAKEN BY A TOKYO UNIVERSITY GRADUATE WHILE HE WAS AT THIS SCHOOL
YUMMY FOOD ...
DISNEY-LAND...
どーん
COPIES OF NOTES!
ざわ
SO THAT'S WHY THE CULTURE FESTIVAL SEEMED SO LIVELY LAST YEAR WHEN I CAME TO TAKE A TOUR OF THE SCHOOL.
ざわ
AND THAT'S WHY THE SPORTS CLUBS HAVE BEEN PREPARING SINCE SUMMER VACATION!
THAT'S TOTALLY UNFAIR TO THE OTHER STUDENTS!
ばん
QUIET DOWN!

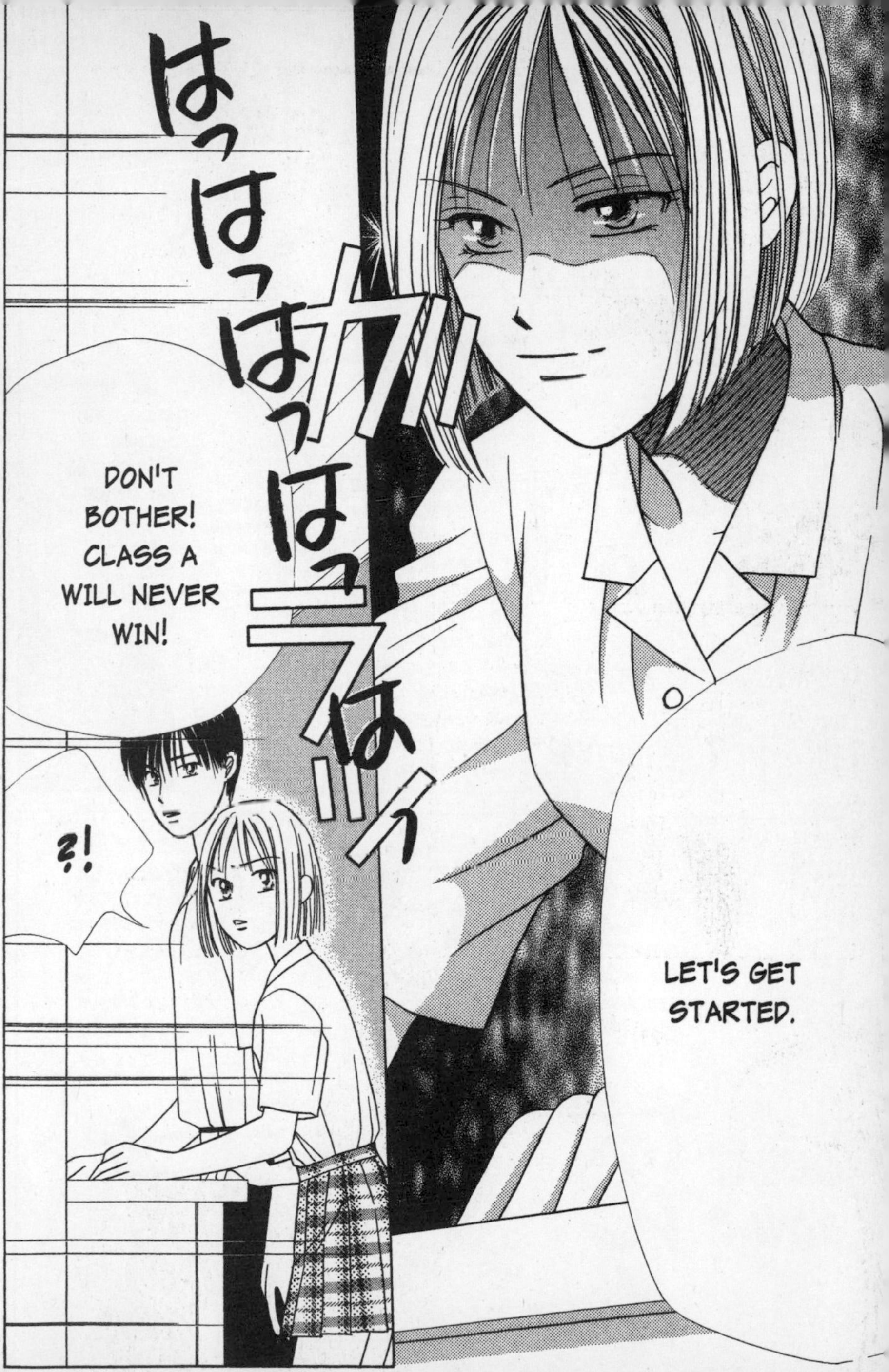
LET'S GET STARTED.
はっはっはっはっ
DON'T BOTHER! CLASS A WILL NEVER WIN!
?!

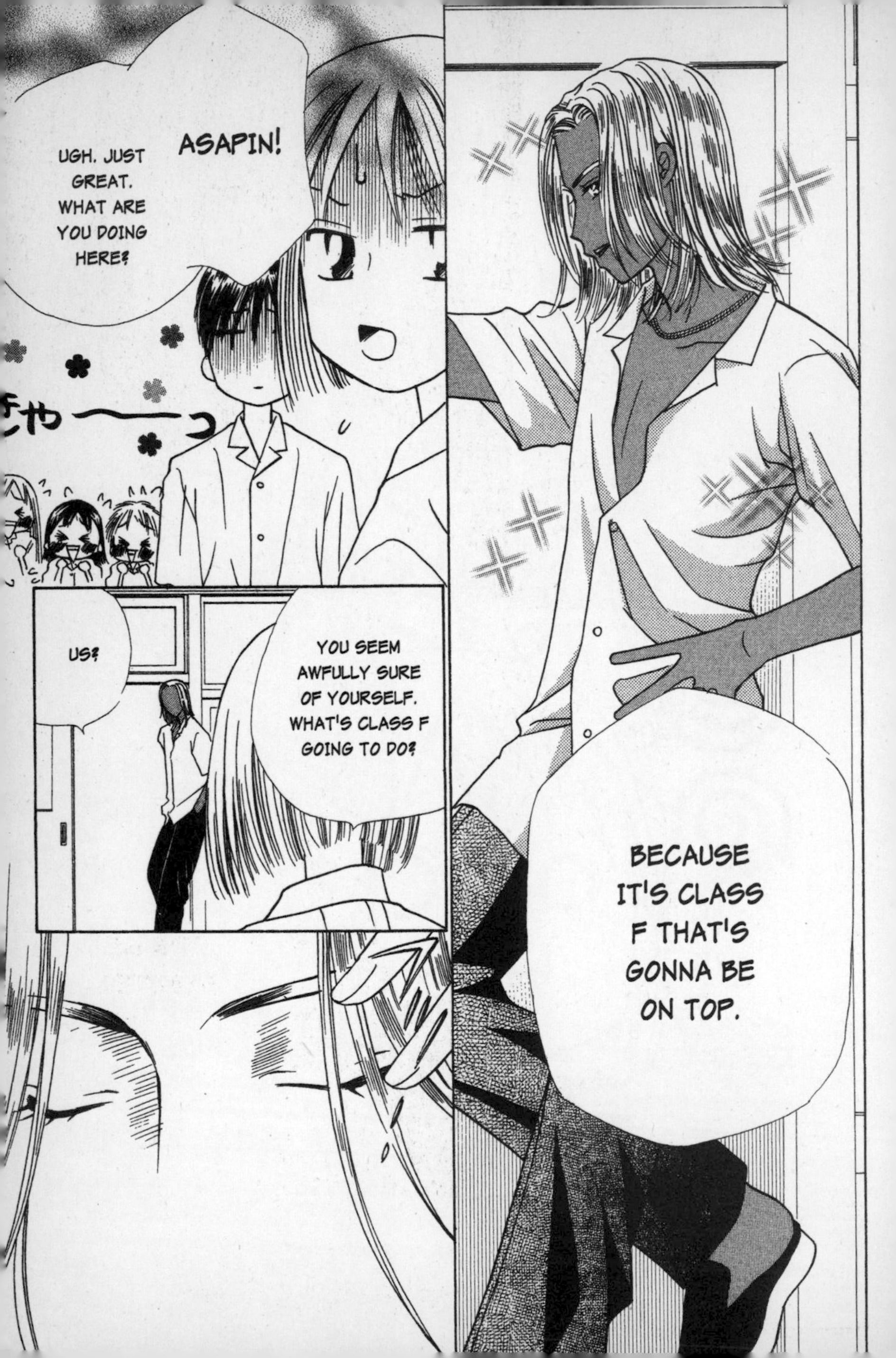
BECAUSE IT'S CLASS F THAT'S GONNA BE ON TOP.
ASAPIN!
UGH. JUST GREAT. WHAT ARE YOU DOING HERE?
やーーっ
YOU SEEM AWFULLY SURE OF YOURSELF. WHAT'S CLASS F GOING TO DO?
US?

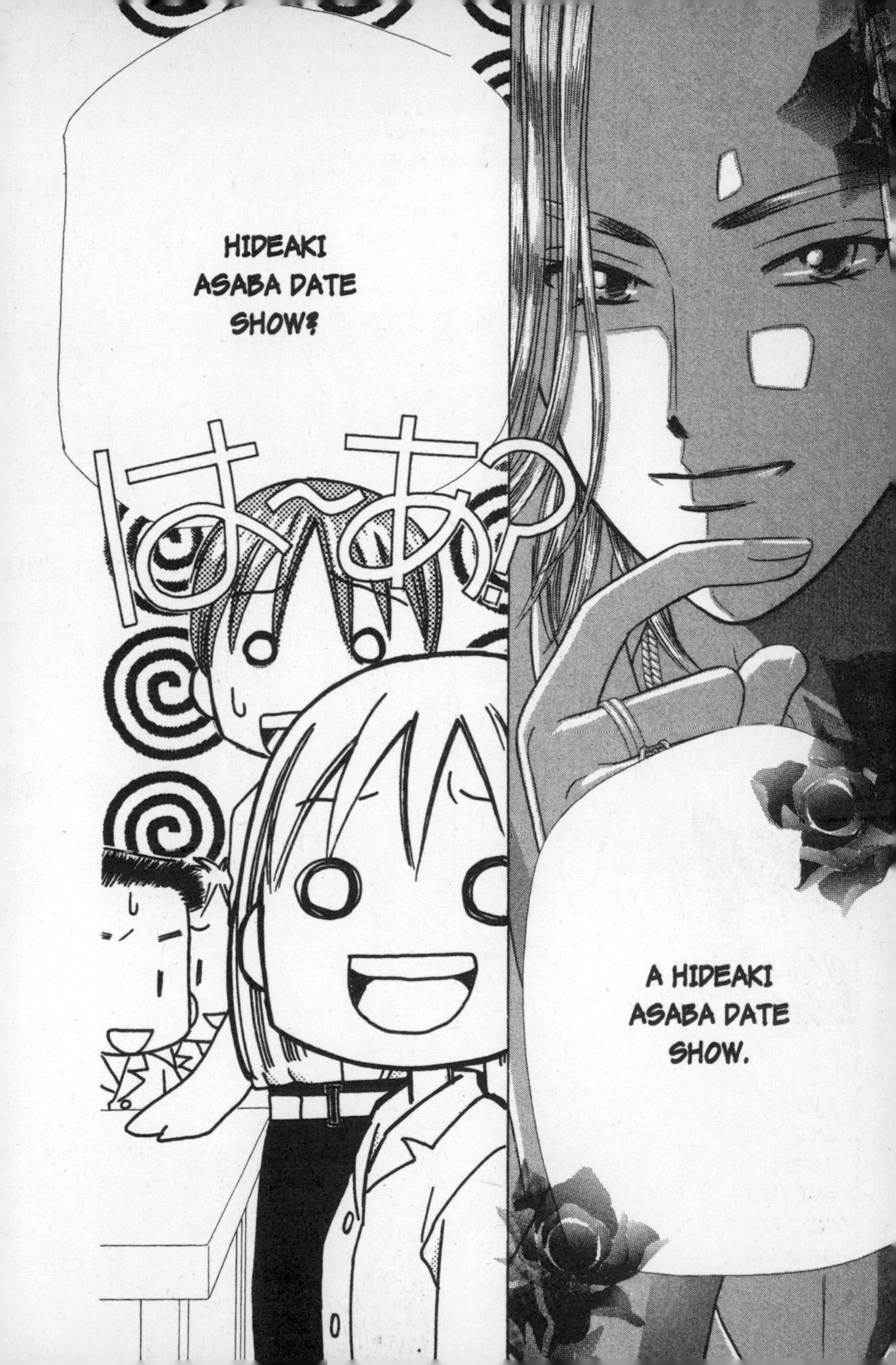
A HIDEAKI ASABA DATE SHOW.
HIDEAKI ASABA DATE SHOW?
は〜あ?!

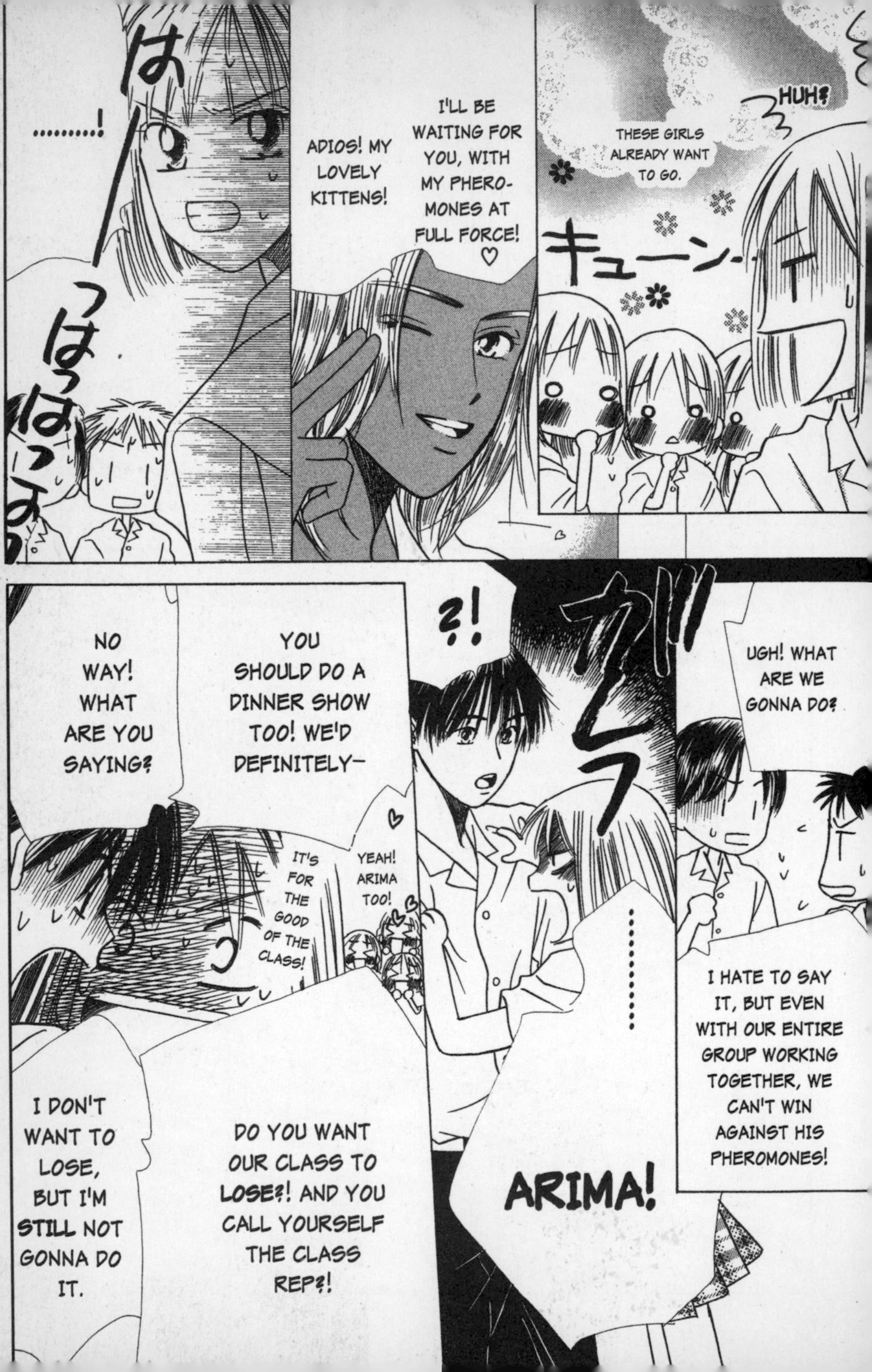
HUH?
THESE GIRLS ALREADY WANT TO GO.
キューン
I'LL BE WAITING FOR YOU, WITH MY PHERO-MONES AT FULL FORCE! ♡
ADIOS! MY LOVELY KITTENS!
.........!
UGH! WHAT ARE WE GONNA DO?
I HATE TO SAY IT, BUT EVEN WITH OUR ENTIRE GROUP WORKING TOGETHER, WE CAN'T WIN AGAINST HIS PHEROMONES!
?!
ARIMA!
....
YOU SHOULD DO A DINNER SHOW TOO! WE'D DEFINITELY—
NO WAY! WHAT ARE YOU SAYING?
YEAH! ARIMA TOO!
IT'S FOR THE GOOD OF THE CLASS!
DO YOU WANT OUR CLASS TO LOSE?! AND YOU CALL YOURSELF THE CLASS REP?!
I DON'T WANT TO LOSE, BUT I'M STILL NOT GONNA DO IT.

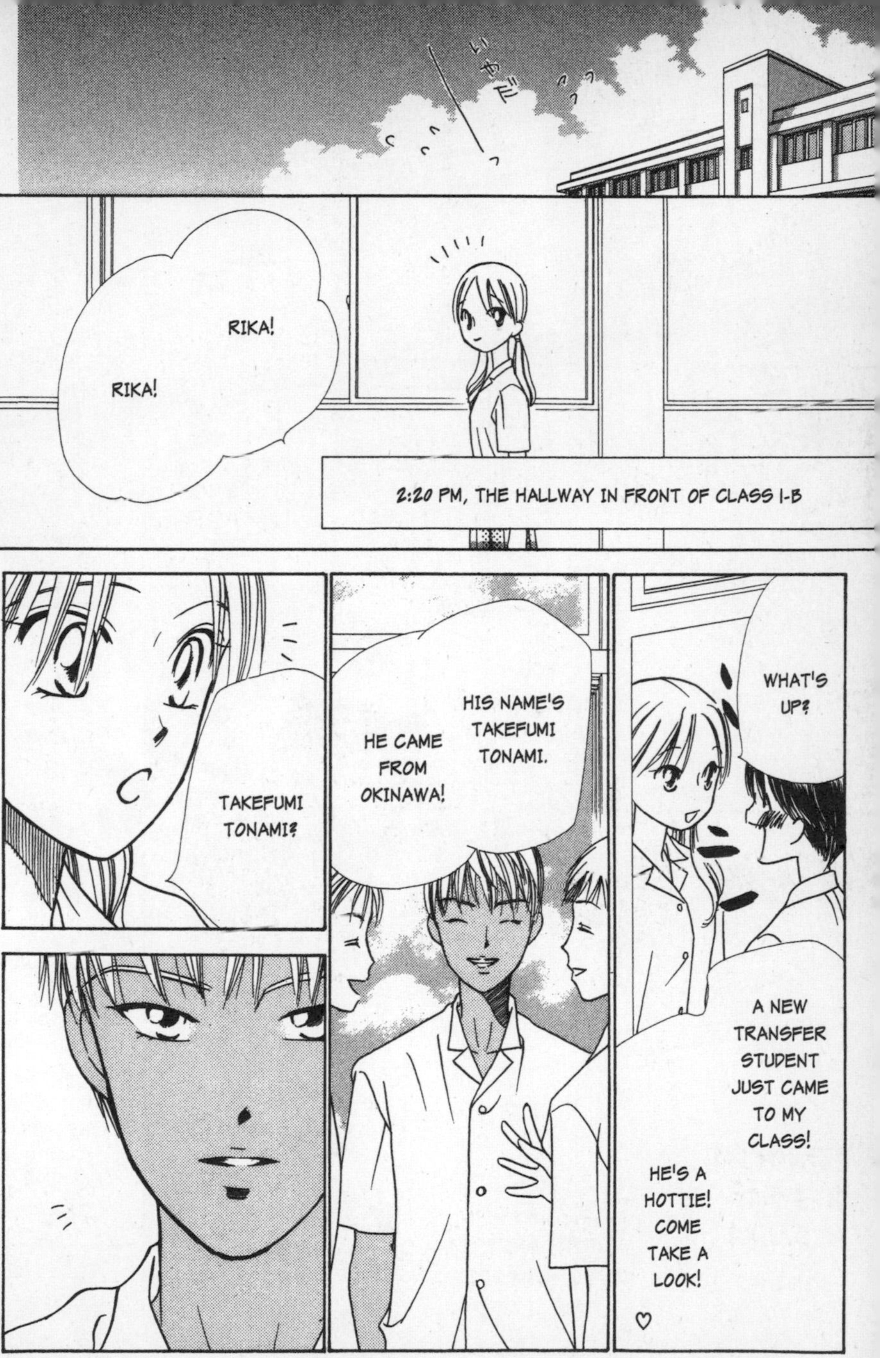
いやだ
RIKA!
RIKA!
2:20 PM, THE HALLWAY IN FRONT OF CLASS 1-B
WHAT'S UP?
A NEW TRANSFER STUDENT JUST CAME TO MY CLASS!
HE'S A HOTTIE! COME TAKE A LOOK! ♡
HIS NAME'S TAKEFUMI TONAMI.
HE CAME FROM OKINAWA!
TAKEFUMI TONAMI?

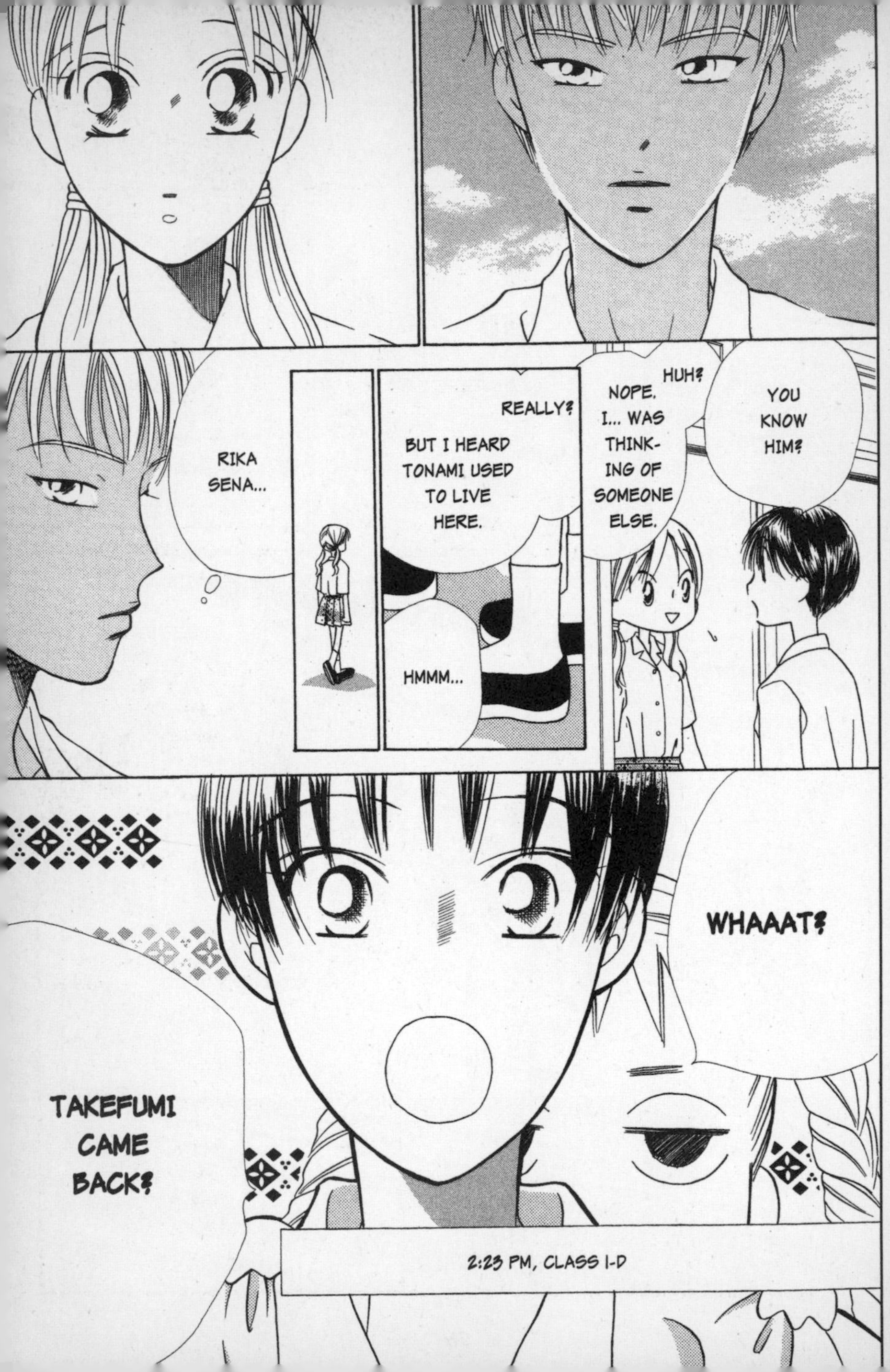
YOU KNOW HIM?
HUH?
NOPE. I... WAS THINKING OF SOMEONE ELSE.
REALLY?
BUT I HEARD TONAMI USED TO LIVE HERE.
HMMM...
RIKA SENA...
WHAAAT?
TAKEFUMI CAME BACK?
2:23 PM, CLASS 1-D

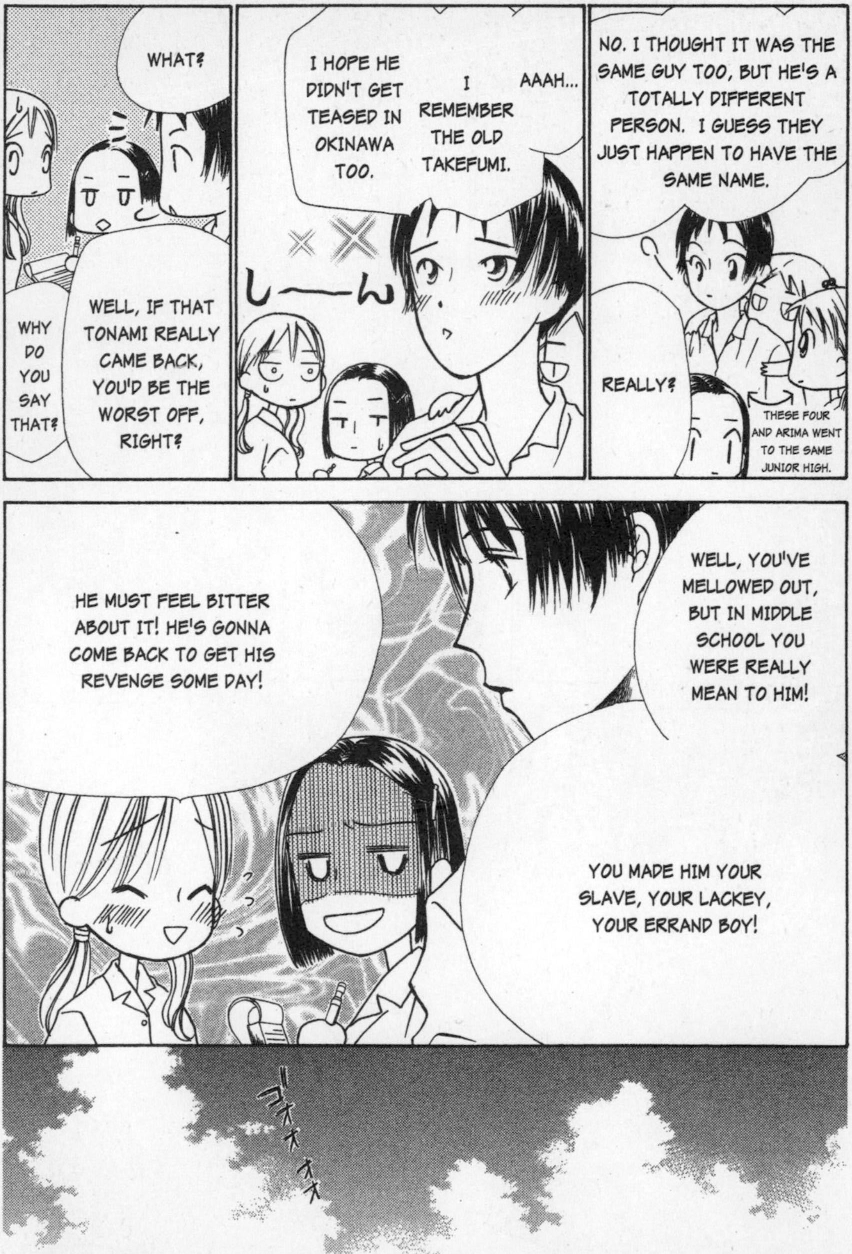
NO. I THOUGHT IT WAS THE SAME GUY TOO, BUT HE'S A TOTALLY DIFFERENT PERSON. I GUESS THEY JUST HAPPEN TO HAVE THE SAME NAME.
REALLY?
THESE FOUR AND ARIMA WENT TO THE SAME JUNIOR HIGH.
AAAH...
I REMEMBER THE OLD TAKEFUMI.
I HOPE HE DIDN'T GET TEASED IN OKINAWA TOO.
しーん
WHAT?
WELL, IF THAT TONAMI REALLY CAME BACK, YOU'D BE THE WORST OFF, RIGHT?
WHY DO YOU SAY THAT?
WELL, YOU'VE MELLOWED OUT, BUT IN MIDDLE SCHOOL YOU WERE REALLY MEAN TO HIM!
YOU MADE HIM YOUR SLAVE, YOUR LACKEY, YOUR ERRAND BOY!
HE MUST FEEL BITTER ABOUT IT! HE'S GONNA COME BACK TO GET HIS REVENGE SOME DAY!
ゴオオオオ

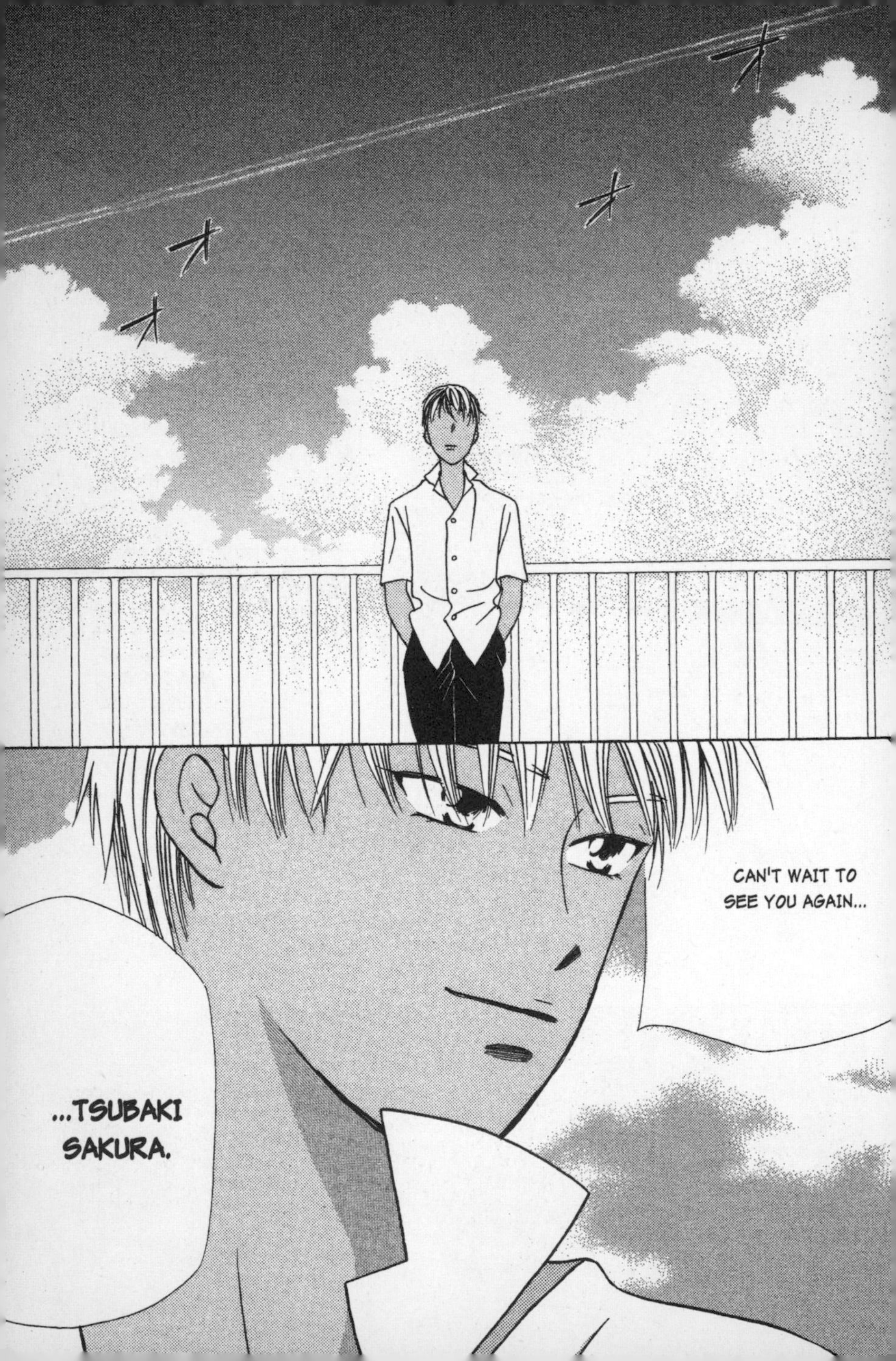
オ
オ
オ
オ
CAN'T WAIT TO SEE YOU AGAIN...
...TSUBAKI SAKURA.

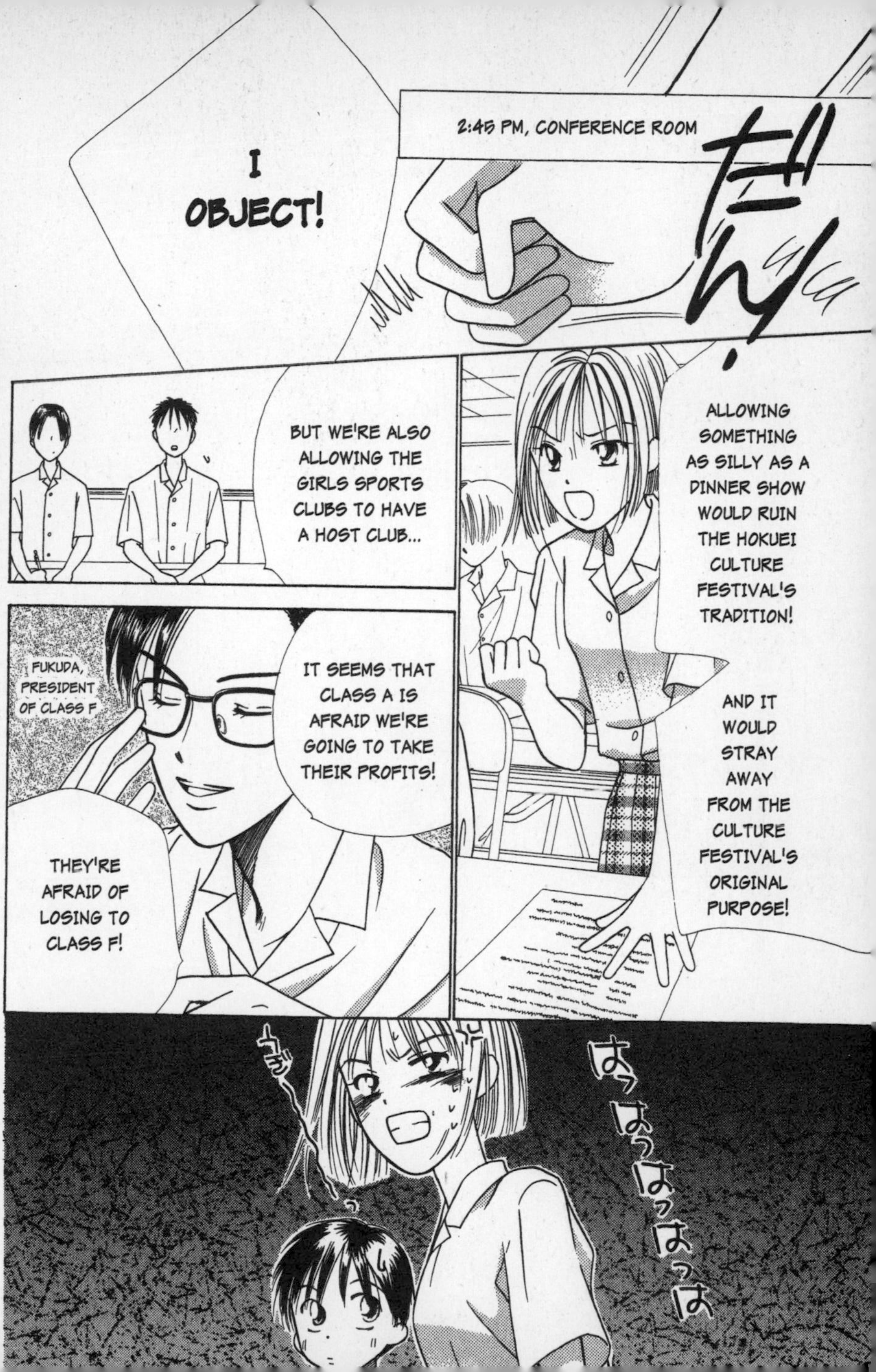
2:45 PM, CONFERENCE ROOM
だん!
I OBJECT!
ALLOWING SOMETHING AS SILLY AS A DINNER SHOW WOULD RUIN THE HOKUEI CULTURE FESTIVAL'S TRADITION!
AND IT WOULD STRAY AWAY FROM THE CULTURE FESTIVAL'S ORIGINAL PURPOSE!
BUT WE'RE ALSO ALLOWING THE GIRLS SPORTS CLUBS TO HAVE A HOST CLUB...
IT SEEMS THAT CLASS A IS AFRAID WE'RE GOING TO TAKE THEIR PROFITS!
FUKUDA, PRESIDENT OF CLASS F
THEY'RE AFRAID OF LOSING TO CLASS F!
はっはっはっはっは

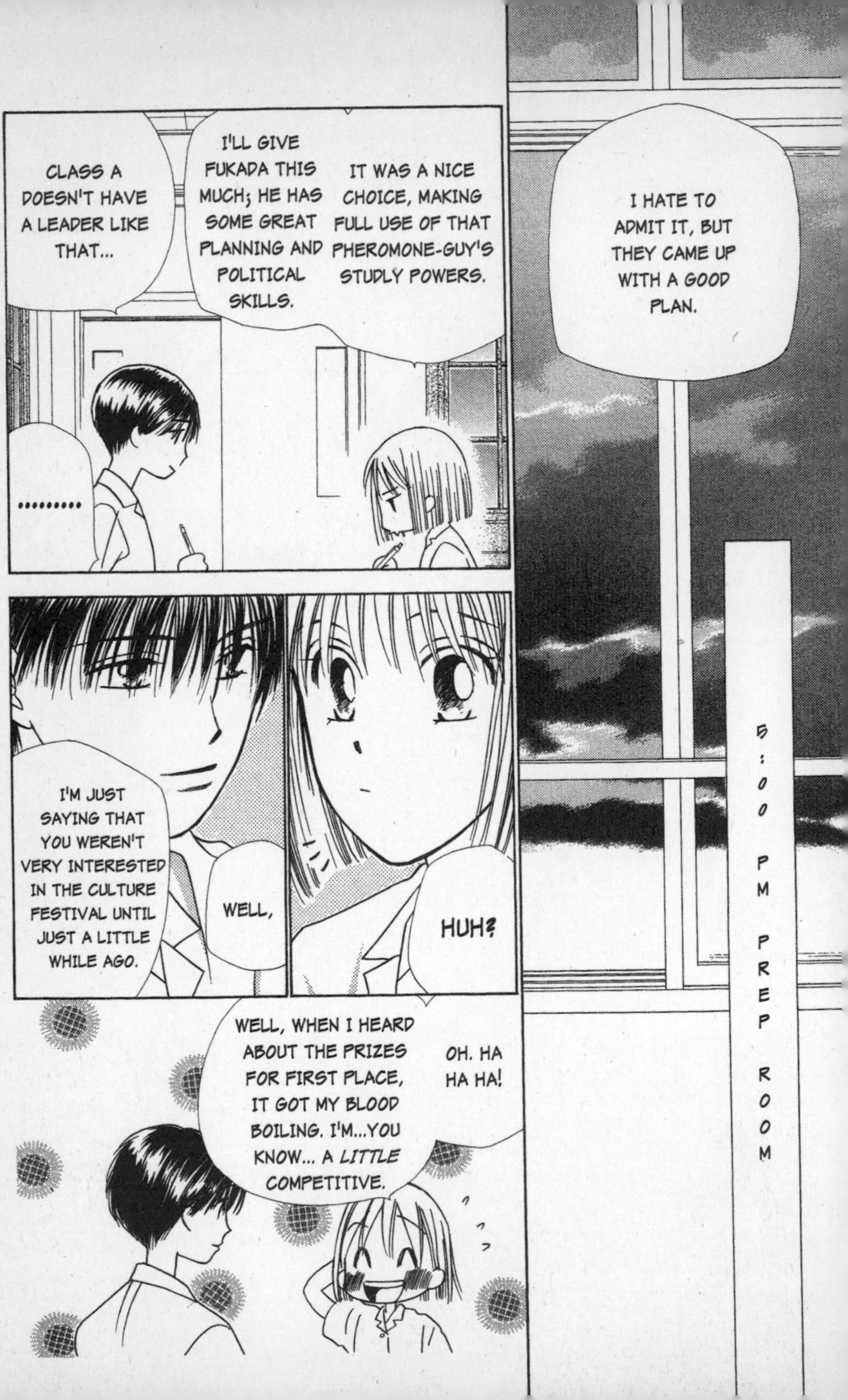
I HATE TO ADMIT IT, BUT THEY CAME UP WITH A GOOD PLAN.
5:00 PM PREP ROOM
IT WAS A NICE CHOICE, MAKING FULL USE OF THAT PHEROMONE-GUY'S STUDLY POWERS.
I'LL GIVE FUKADA THIS MUCH; HE HAS SOME GREAT PLANNING AND POLITICAL SKILLS.
CLASS A DOESN'T HAVE A LEADER LIKE THAT...
....
HUH?
I'M JUST SAYING THAT YOU WEREN'T VERY INTERESTED IN THE CULTURE FESTIVAL UNTIL JUST A LITTLE WHILE AGO.
WELL,
WELL, WHEN I HEARD ABOUT THE PRIZES FOR FIRST PLACE, IT GOT MY BLOOD BOILING. I'M...YOU KNOW... A *LITTLE* COMPETITIVE.
OH. HA HA HA!

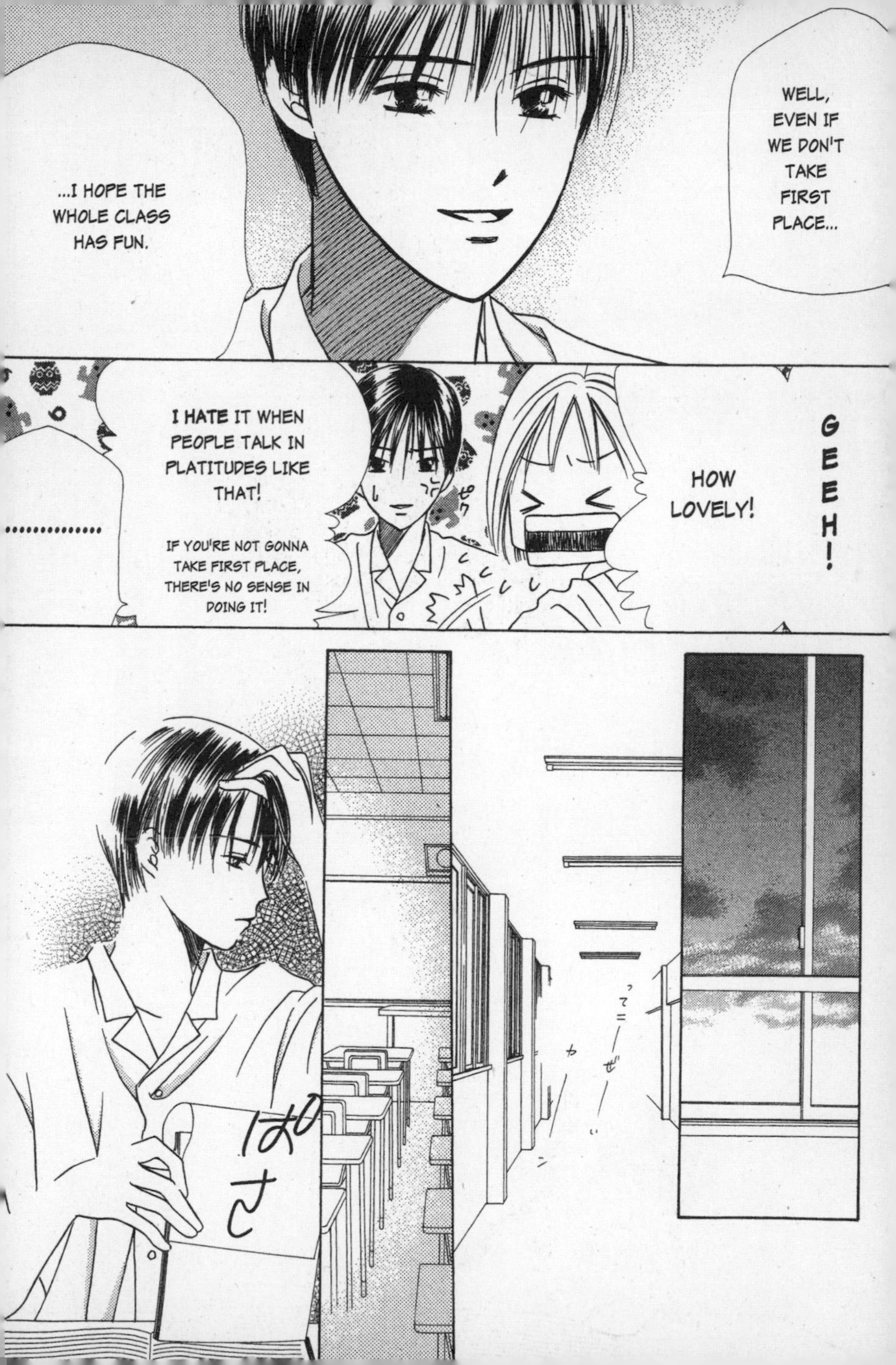
WELL, EVEN IF WE DON'T TAKE FIRST PLACE...
...I HOPE THE WHOLE CLASS HAS FUN.
GEEH!
HOW LOVELY!
I HATE IT WHEN PEOPLE TALK IN PLATITUDES LIKE THAT!
IF YOU'RE NOT GONNA TAKE FIRST PLACE, THERE'S NO SENSE IN DOING IT!
....
ぱさ

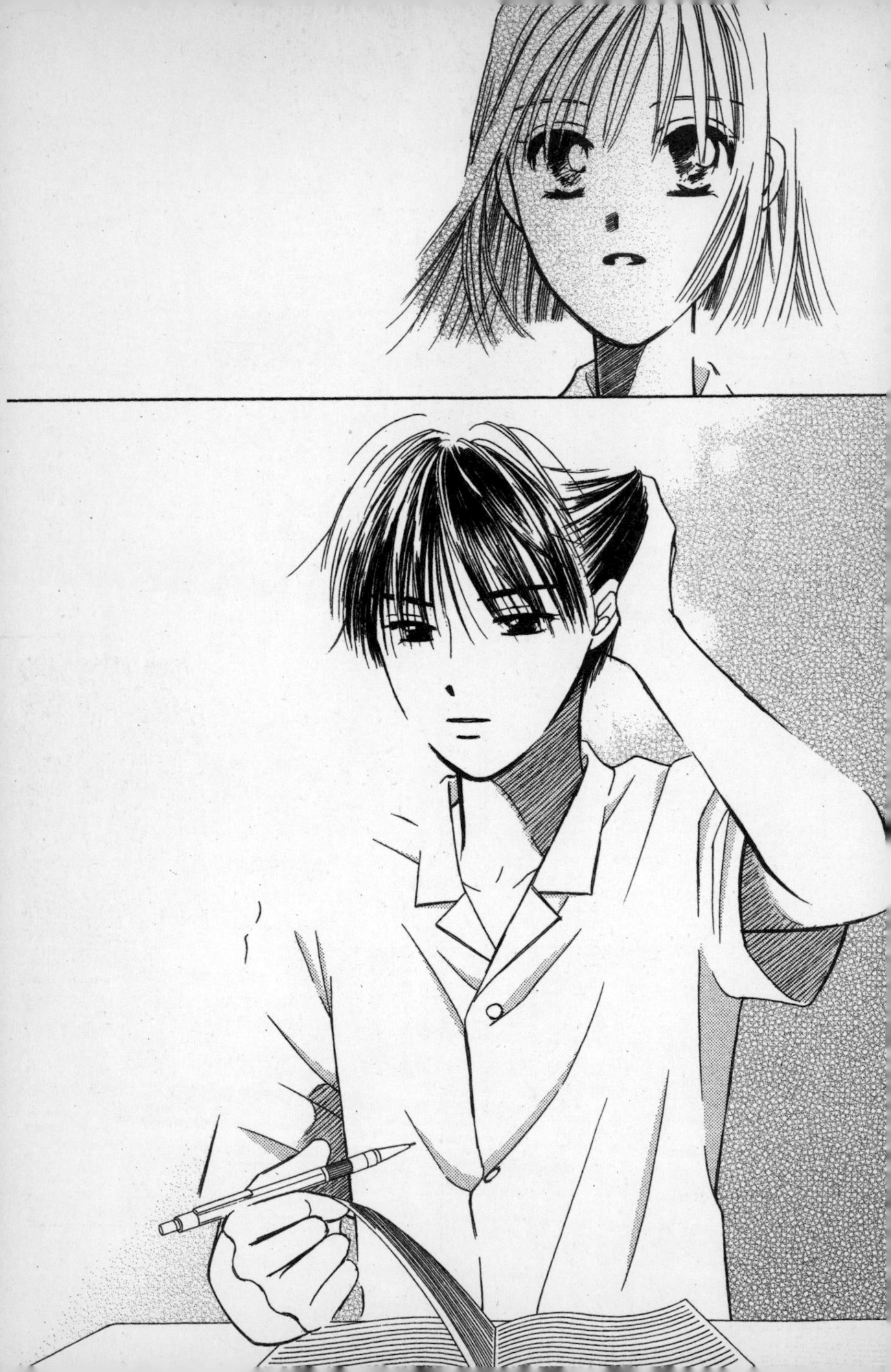

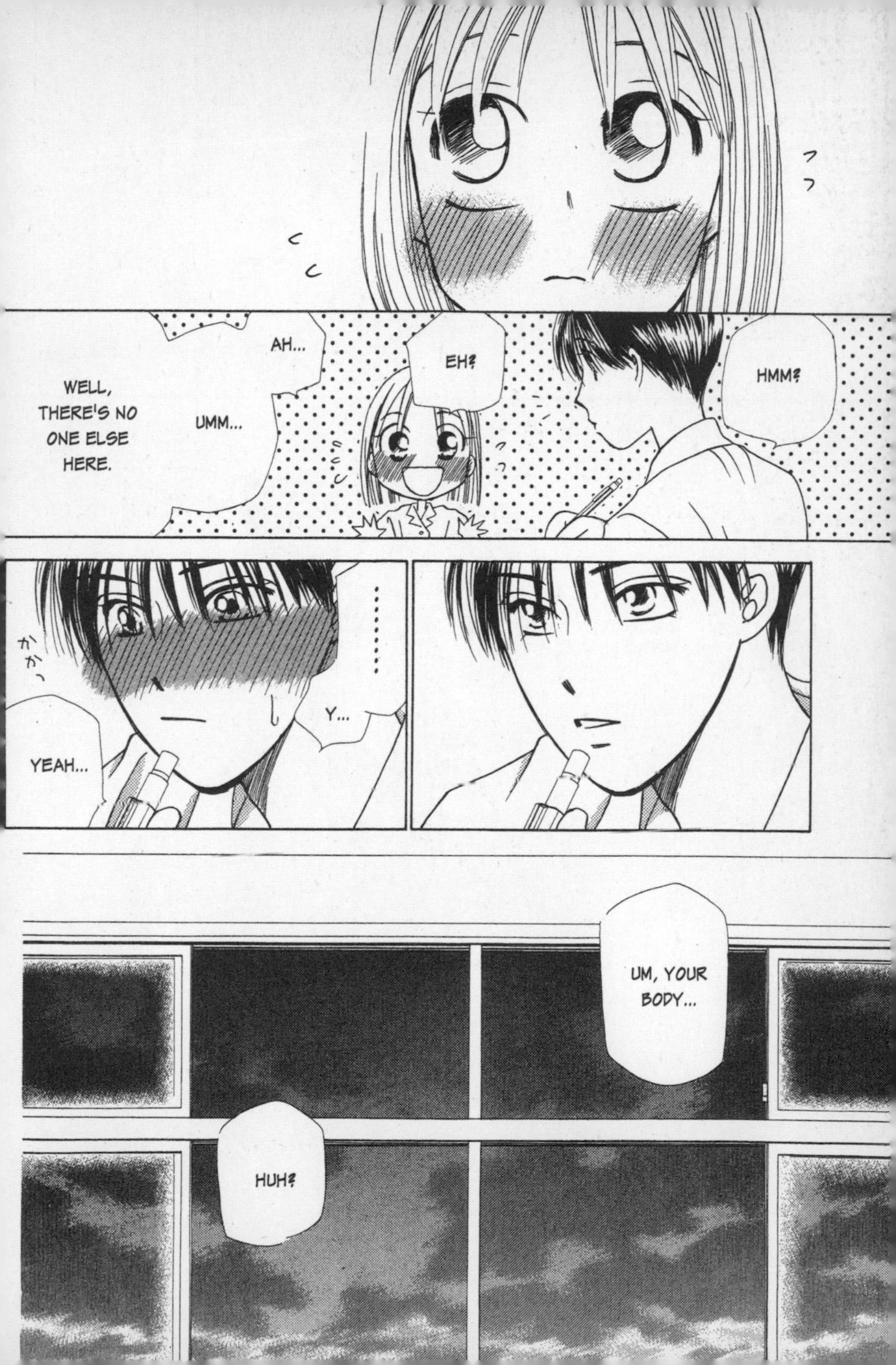
HMM?
EH?
AH...
UMM...
WELL, THERE'S NO ONE ELSE HERE.
......
Y...
YEAH...
UM, YOUR BODY...
HUH?

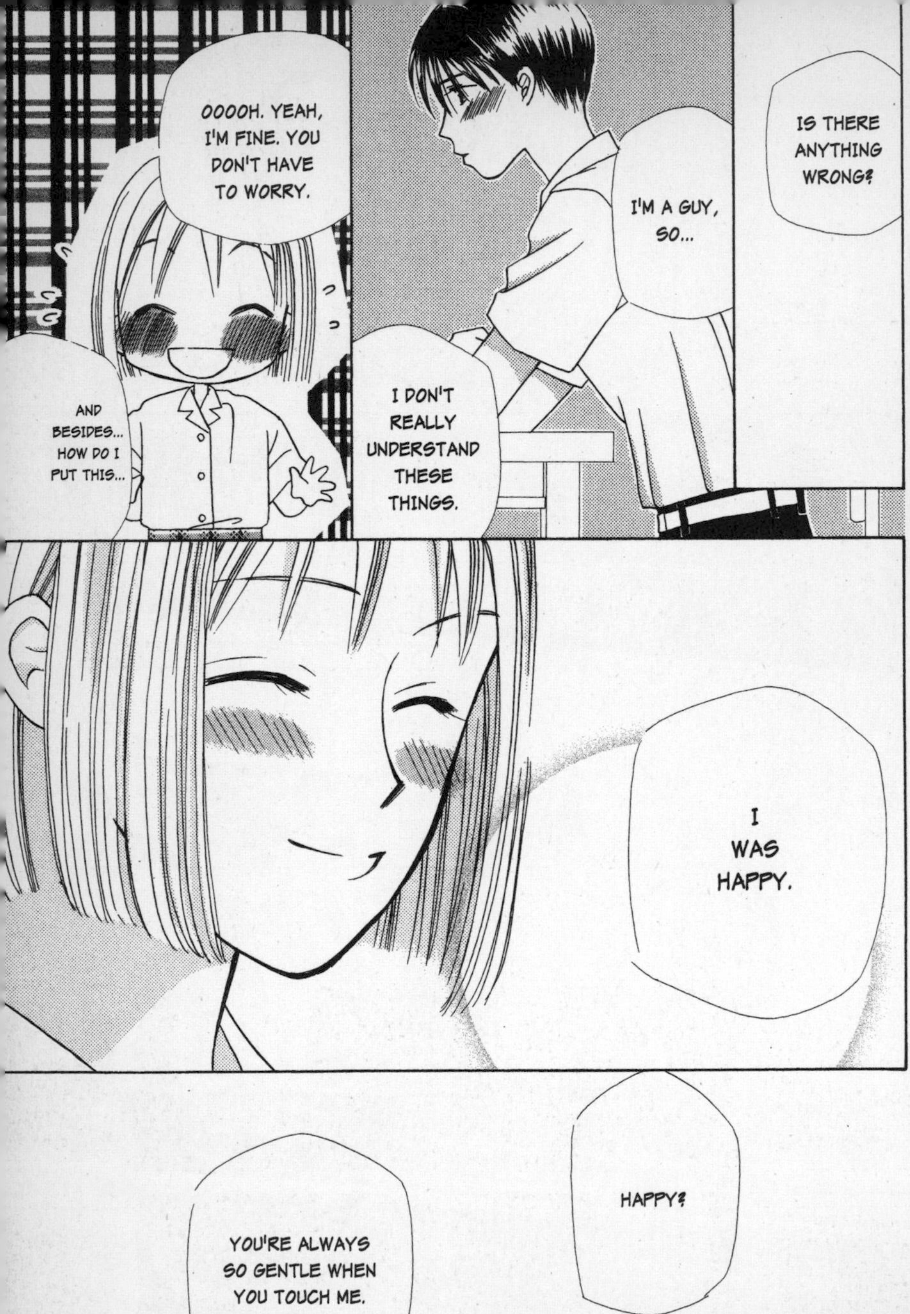
IS THERE ANYTHING WRONG?
I'M A GUY, SO...
I DON'T REALLY UNDERSTAND THESE THINGS.
OOOOH. YEAH, I'M FINE. YOU DON'T HAVE TO WORRY.
AND BESIDES... HOW DO I PUT THIS...
I WAS HAPPY.
HAPPY?
YOU'RE ALWAYS SO GENTLE WHEN YOU TOUCH ME.

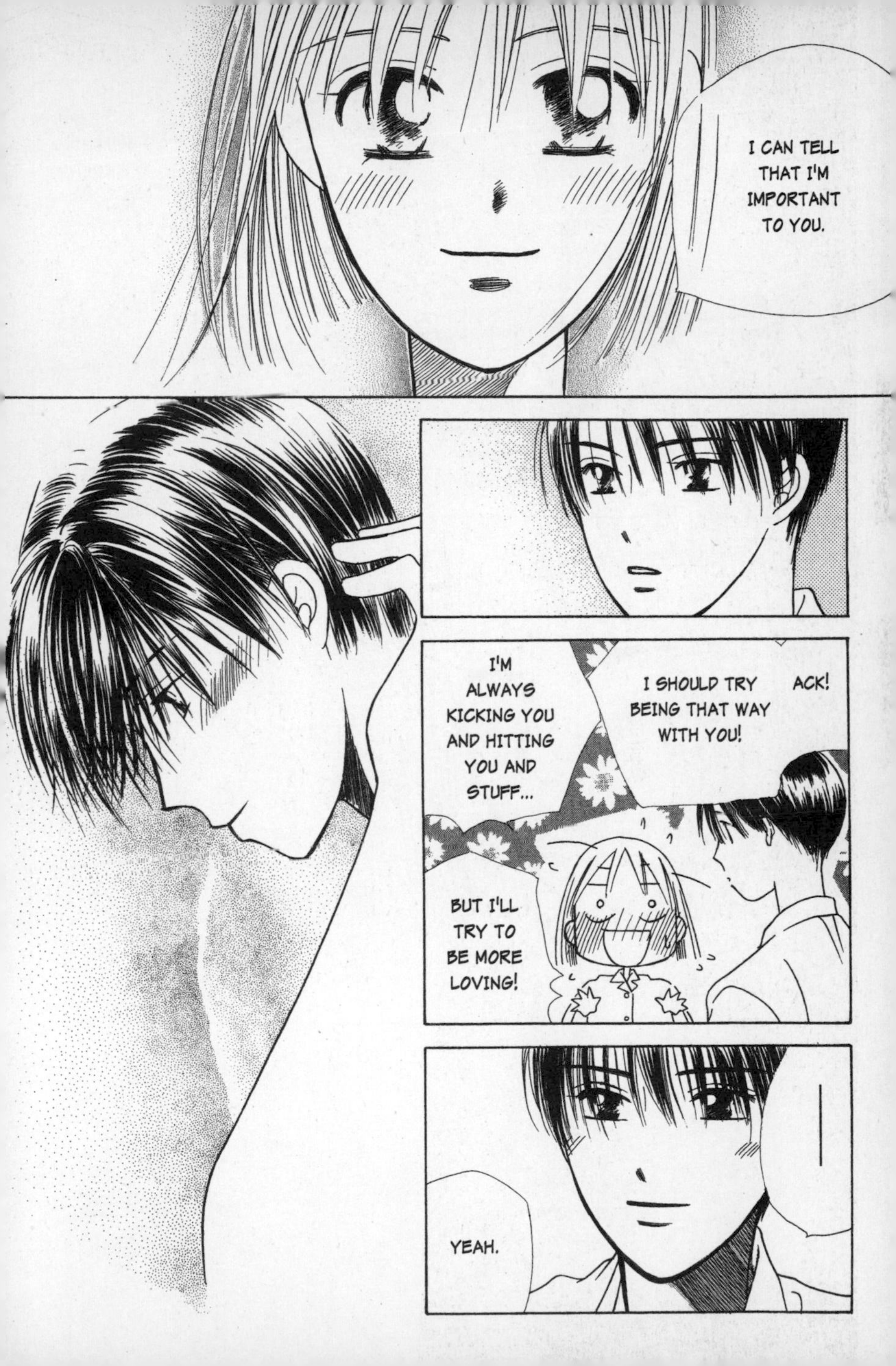
I CAN TELL THAT I'M IMPORTANT TO YOU.
ACK!
I SHOULD TRY BEING THAT WAY WITH YOU!
I'M ALWAYS KICKING YOU AND HITTING YOU AND STUFF...
BUT I'LL TRY TO BE MORE LOVING!
YEAH.

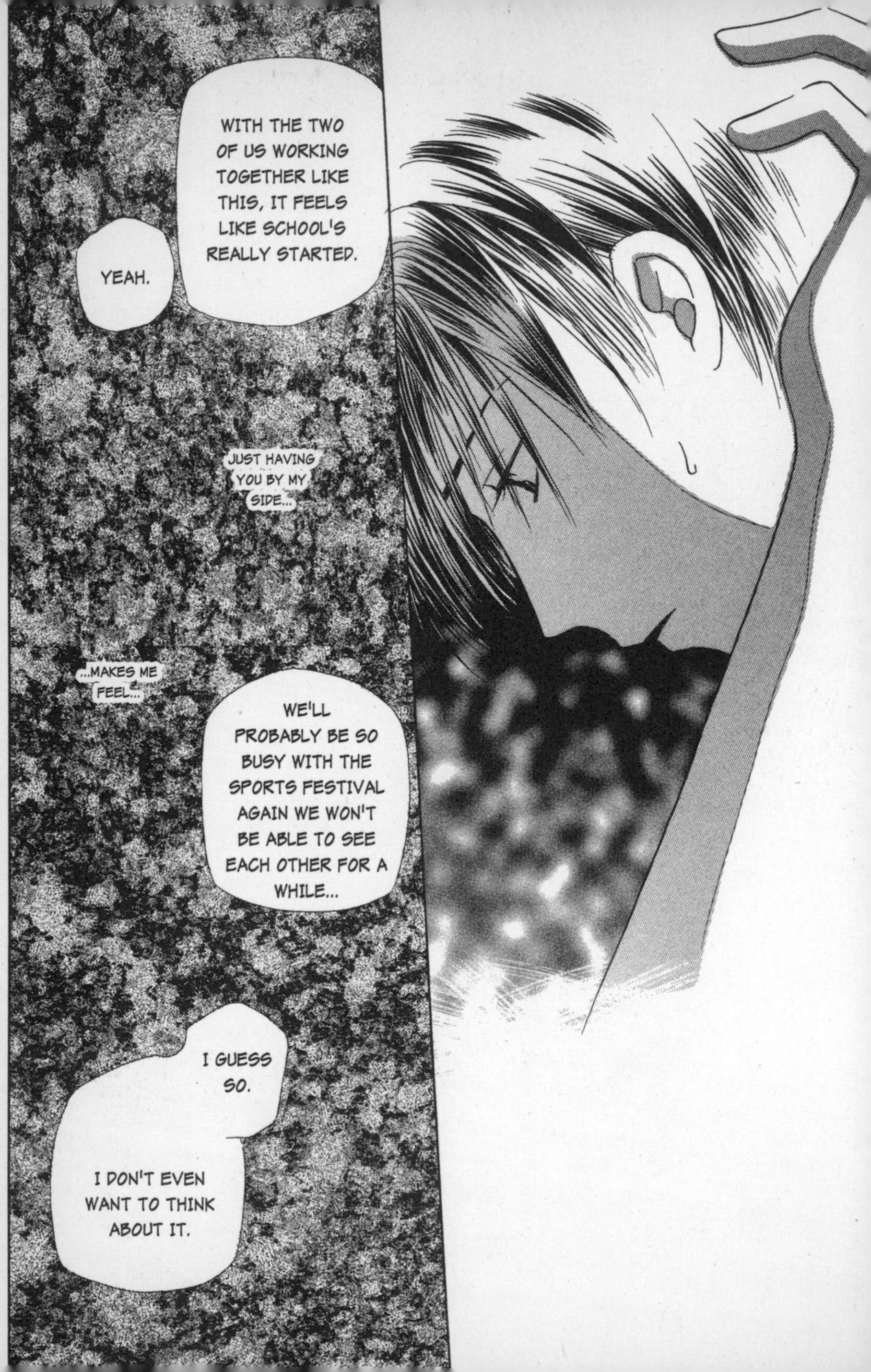
WITH THE TWO OF US WORKING TOGETHER LIKE THIS, IT FEELS LIKE SCHOOL'S REALLY STARTED.
YEAH.
JUST HAVING YOU BY MY SIDE...
...MAKES ME FEEL...
WE'LL PROBABLY BE SO BUSY WITH THE SPORTS FESTIVAL AGAIN WE WON'T BE ABLE TO SEE EACH OTHER FOR A WHILE...
I GUESS SO.
I DON'T EVEN WANT TO THINK ABOUT IT.

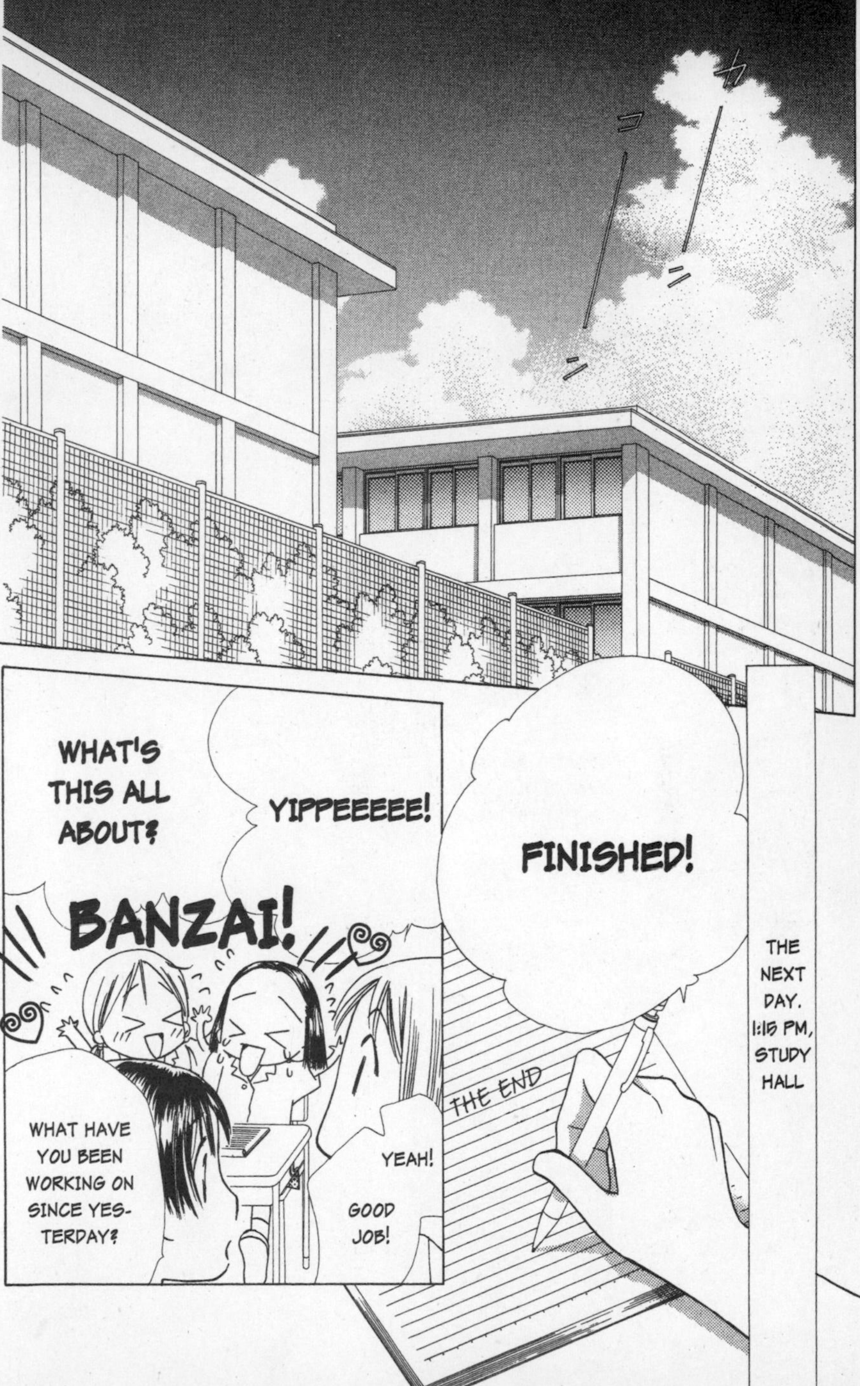
THE NEXT DAY. 1:15 PM, STUDY HALL
FINISHED!
THE END
YIPPEEEEE!
WHAT'S THIS ALL ABOUT?
BANZAI!
YEAH!
GOOD JOB!
WHAT HAVE YOU BEEN WORKING ON SINCE YES-TERDAY?

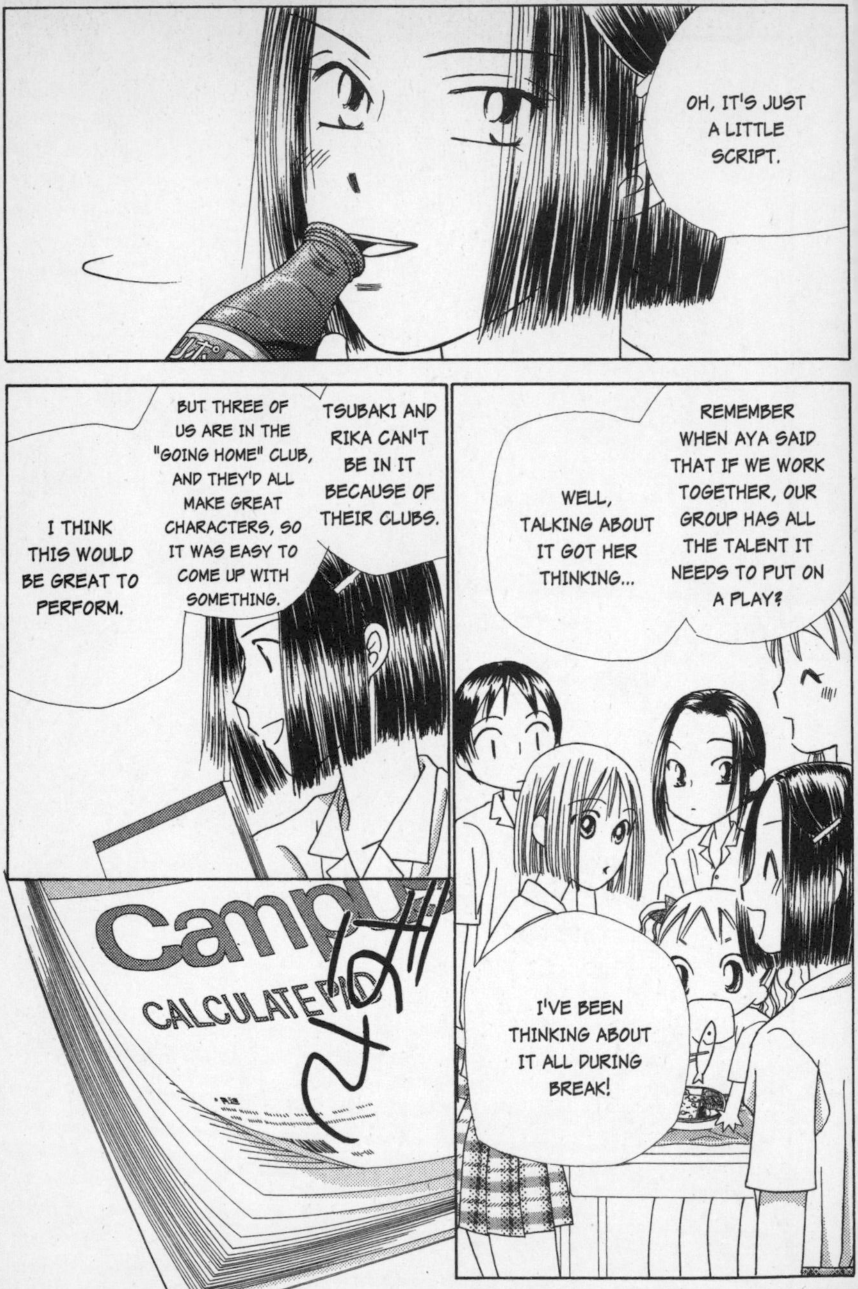
OH, IT'S JUST A LITTLE SCRIPT.
REMEMBER WHEN AYA SAID THAT IF WE WORK TOGETHER, OUR GROUP HAS ALL THE TALENT IT NEEDS TO PUT ON A PLAY?
WELL, TALKING ABOUT IT GOT HER THINKING...
I'VE BEEN THINKING ABOUT IT ALL DURING BREAK!
TSUBAKI AND RIKA CAN'T BE IN IT BECAUSE OF THEIR CLUBS.
BUT THREE OF US ARE IN THE "GOING HOME" CLUB, AND THEY'D ALL MAKE GREAT CHARACTERS, SO IT WAS EASY TO COME UP WITH SOMETHING.
I THINK THIS WOULD BE GREAT TO PERFORM.

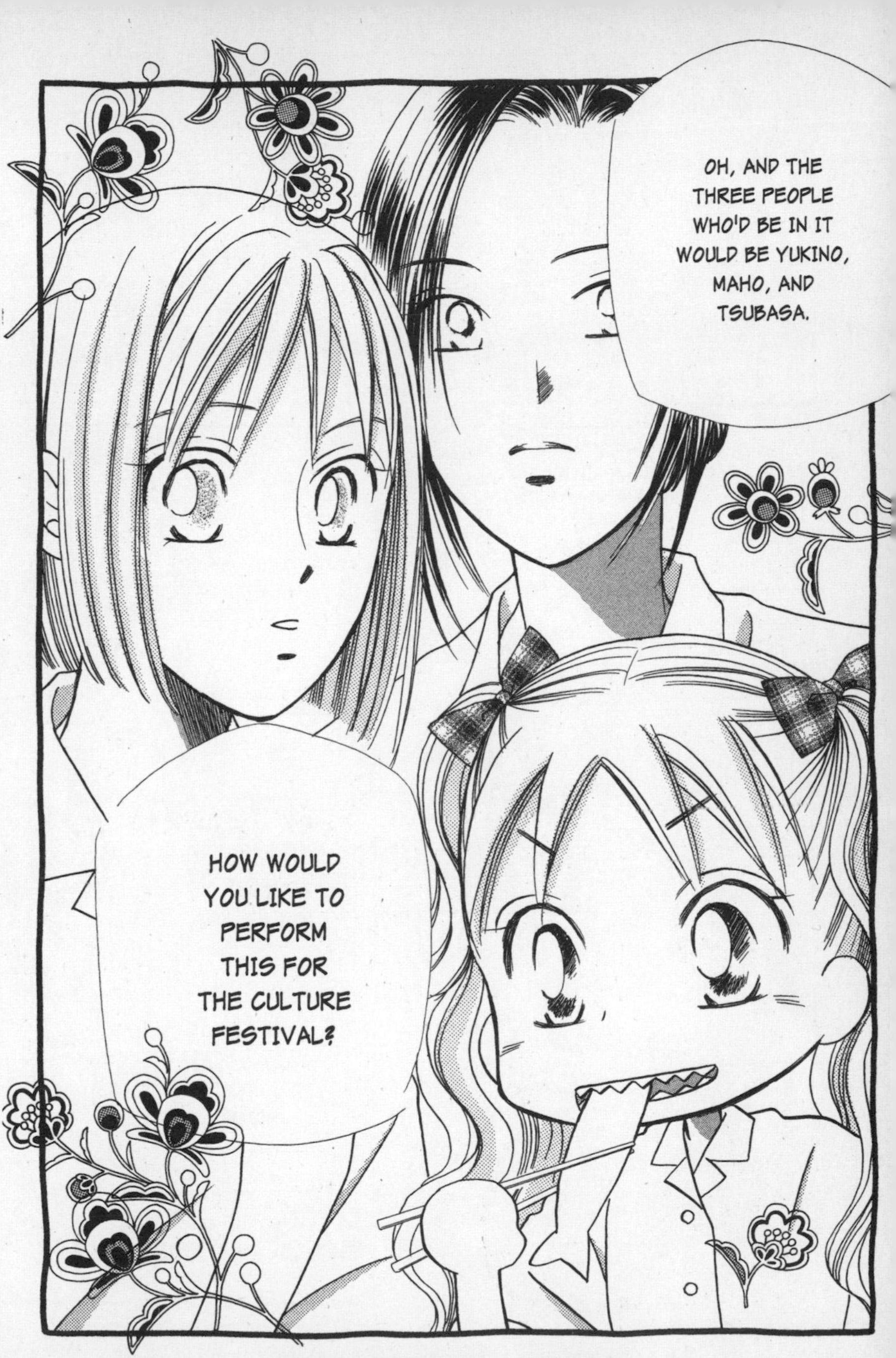
OH, AND THE THREE PEOPLE WHO'D BE IN IT WOULD BE YUKINO, MAHO, AND TSUBASA.
HOW WOULD YOU LIKE TO PERFORM THIS FOR THE CULTURE FESTIVAL?

ACT 27 * 14 DAYS I —THE END

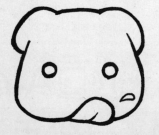

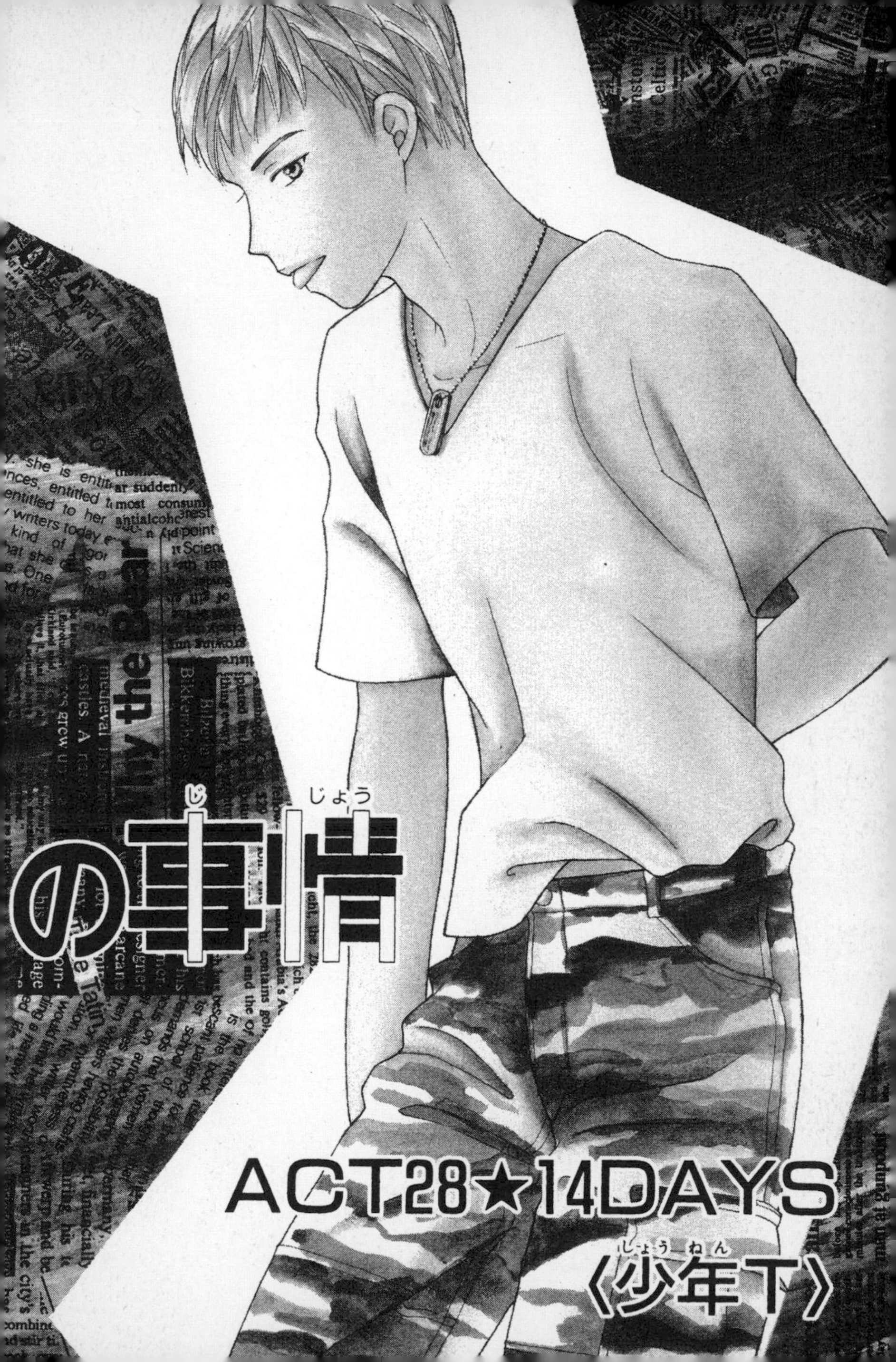
の事情
ACT28★14DAYS
〈少年T〉

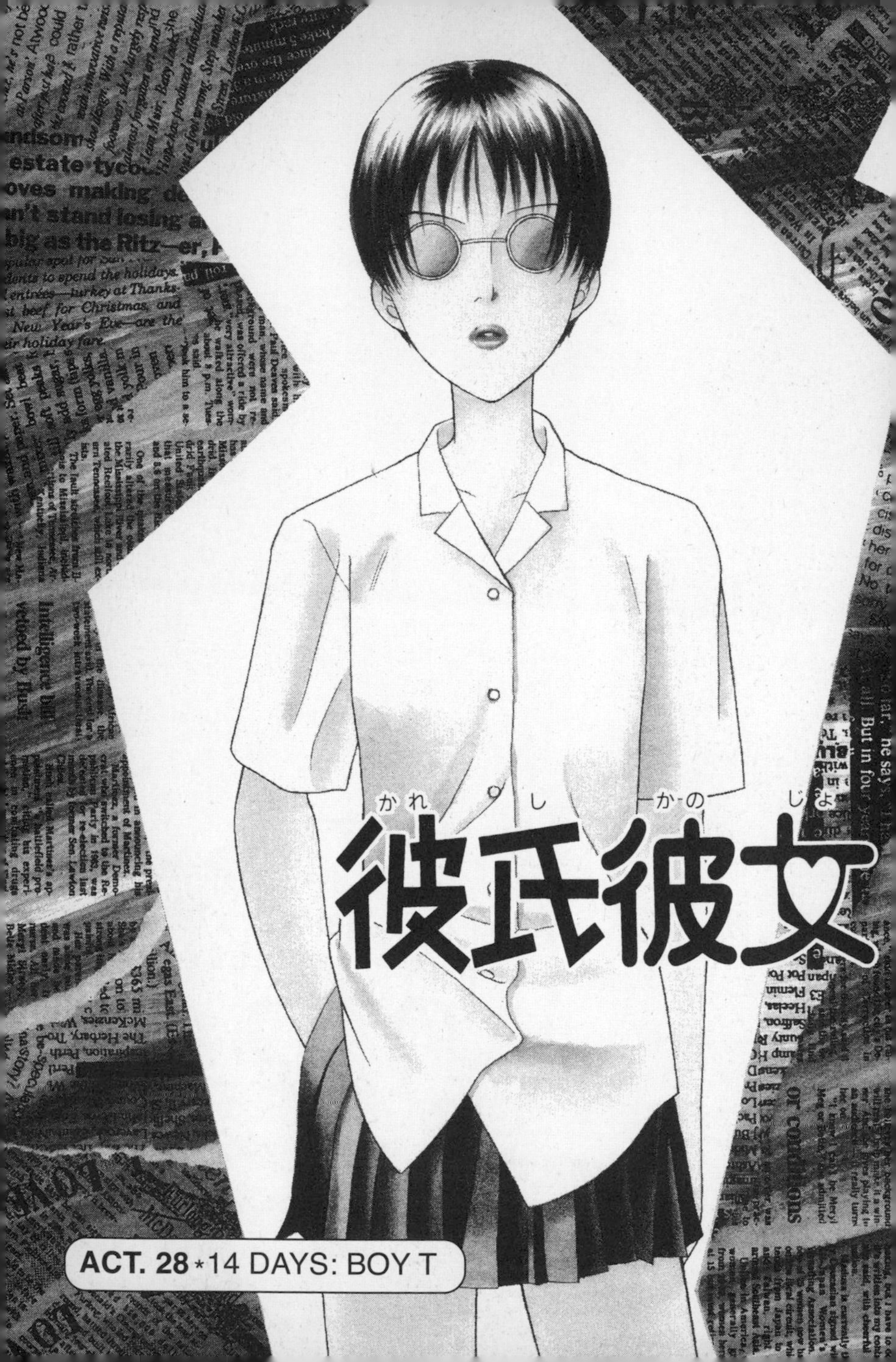
かれ し かの じょ
彼氏彼女
ACT. 28 * 14 DAYS: BOY T

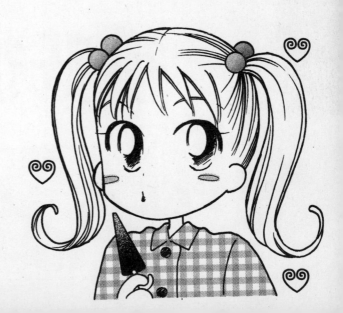

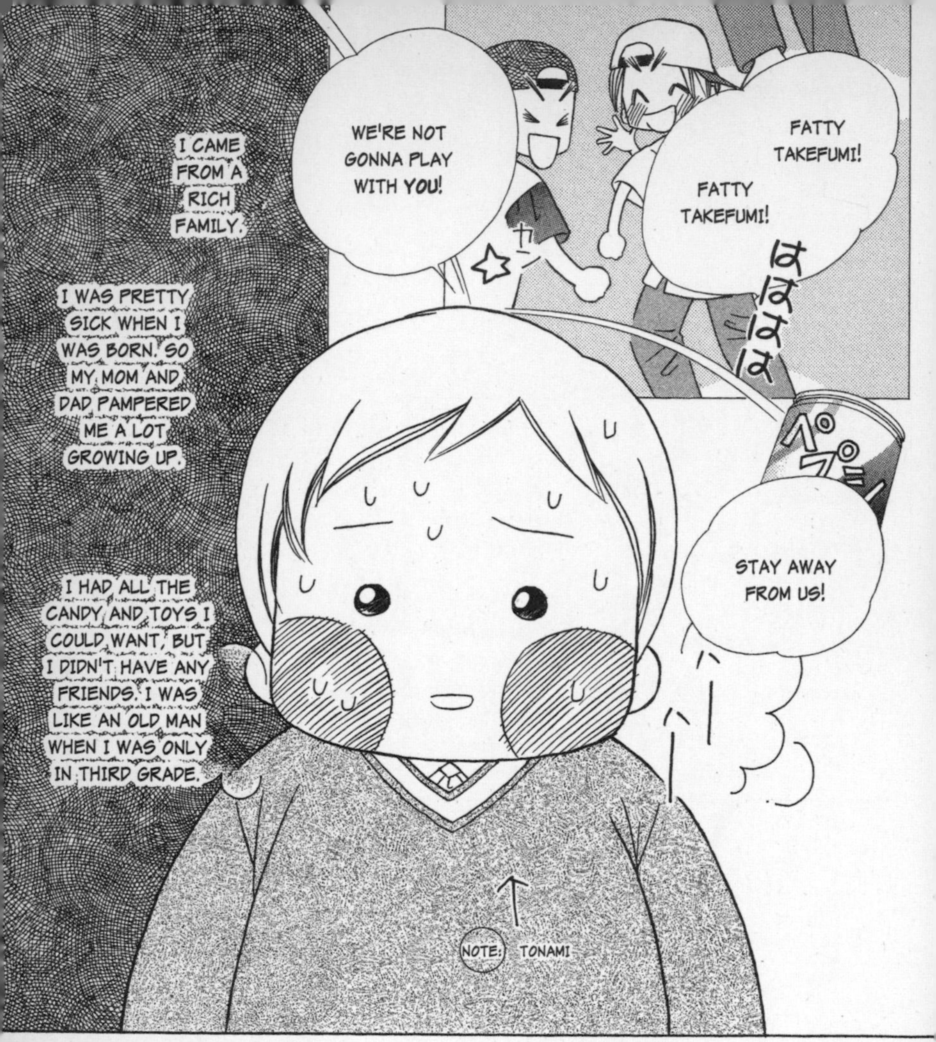
FATTY TAKEFUMI!
FATTY TAKEFUMI!
WE'RE NOT GONNA PLAY WITH YOU!
はははは
STAY AWAY FROM US!
I CAME FROM A RICH FAMILY.
I WAS PRETTY SICK WHEN I WAS BORN. SO MY MOM AND DAD PAMPERED ME A LOT GROWING UP.
I HAD ALL THE CANDY AND TOYS I COULD WANT, BUT I DIDN'T HAVE ANY FRIENDS. I WAS LIKE AN OLD MAN WHEN I WAS ONLY IN THIRD GRADE.
NOTE: TONAMI

Reminiscing... Part 2

I HATED LITERATURE. I THOUGHT IT WAS TOO DULL AND DEPRESSING. AND I HATED THE ATTITUDE OF THE AUTHORS.

IT SEEMED THEY DIDN'T CARE IF ORDINARY PEOPLE COULDN'T UNDERSTAND THEIR BOOKS WITHOUT EXPLANATIONS.

(LIKE K'S REALLY DISGUSTING METHOD OF SUICIDE IN KOKORO.)

BUT LATELY, I'VE BEEN LOOKING FORWARD TO READING BOOKS BY MISHIMA AND AKUTAGAWA.

(AND I SHOULD READ THE TALE OF GENJI, TOO, WHILE I'M STILL YOUNG...)

WHEN I FIRST READ KUSA NO HANA BY TAKEHIKO FUKUNAGA, I COULDN'T UNDERSTAND IT AT ALL, BUT WHEN I READ IT A SECOND TIME, I COULD REALLY FEEL THE LONELINESS EXPRESSED IN THE BOOK. IT WAS SO SAD...

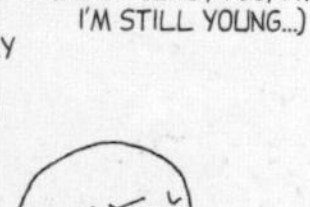

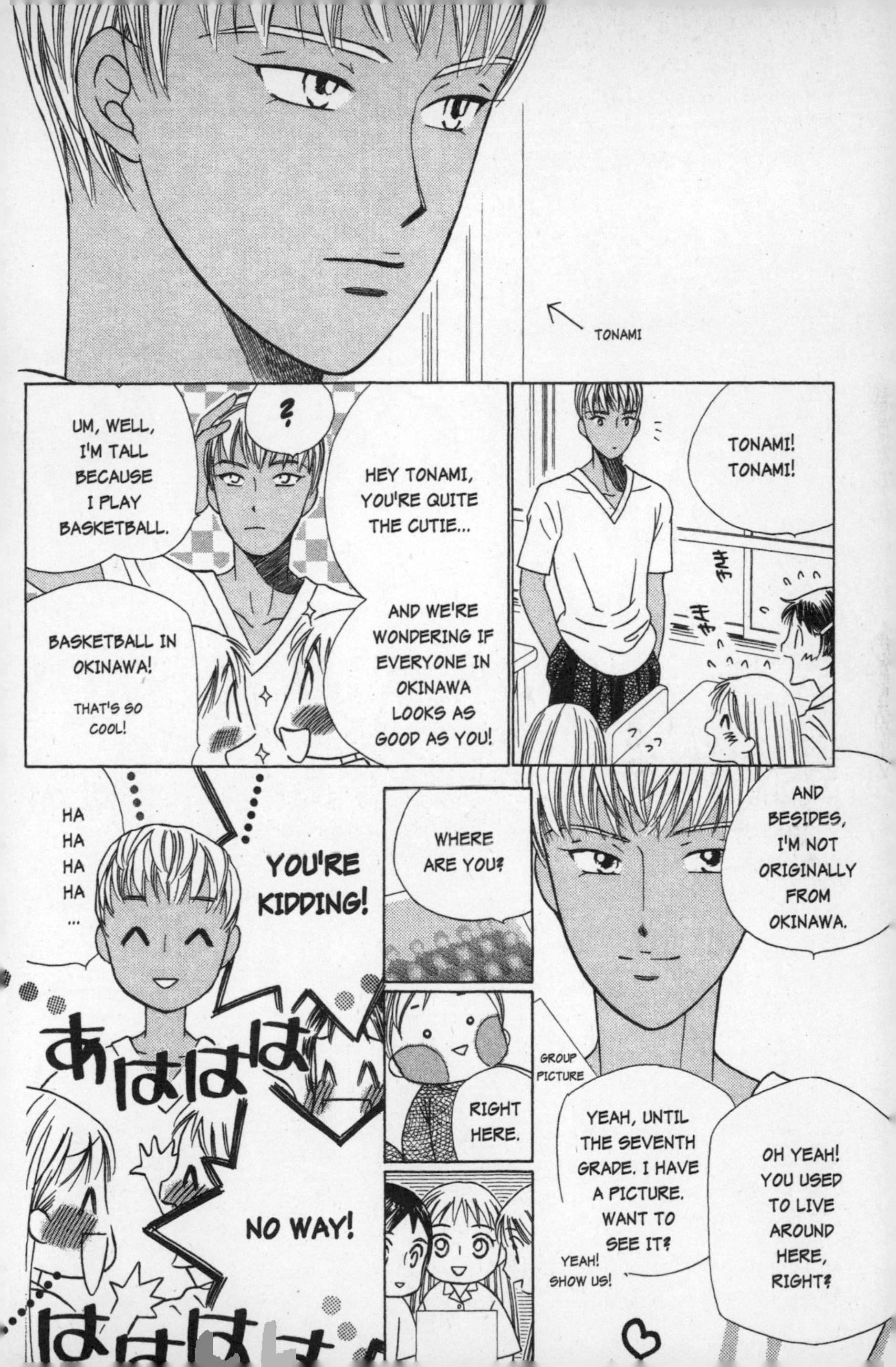
TONAMI
TONAMI! TONAMI!
HEY TONAMI, YOU'RE QUITE THE CUTIE...
AND WE'RE WONDERING IF EVERYONE IN OKINAWA LOOKS AS GOOD AS YOU!
?
UM, WELL, I'M TALL BECAUSE I PLAY BASKETBALL.
BASKETBALL IN OKINAWA!
THAT'S SO COOL!
AND BESIDES, I'M NOT ORIGINALLY FROM OKINAWA.
OH YEAH! YOU USED TO LIVE AROUND HERE, RIGHT?
YEAH, UNTIL THE SEVENTH GRADE. I HAVE A PICTURE. WANT TO SEE IT?
YEAH! SHOW US!
WHERE ARE YOU?
GROUP PICTURE
RIGHT HERE.
YOU'RE KIDDING!
NO WAY!
HA HA HA HA ...
あははは

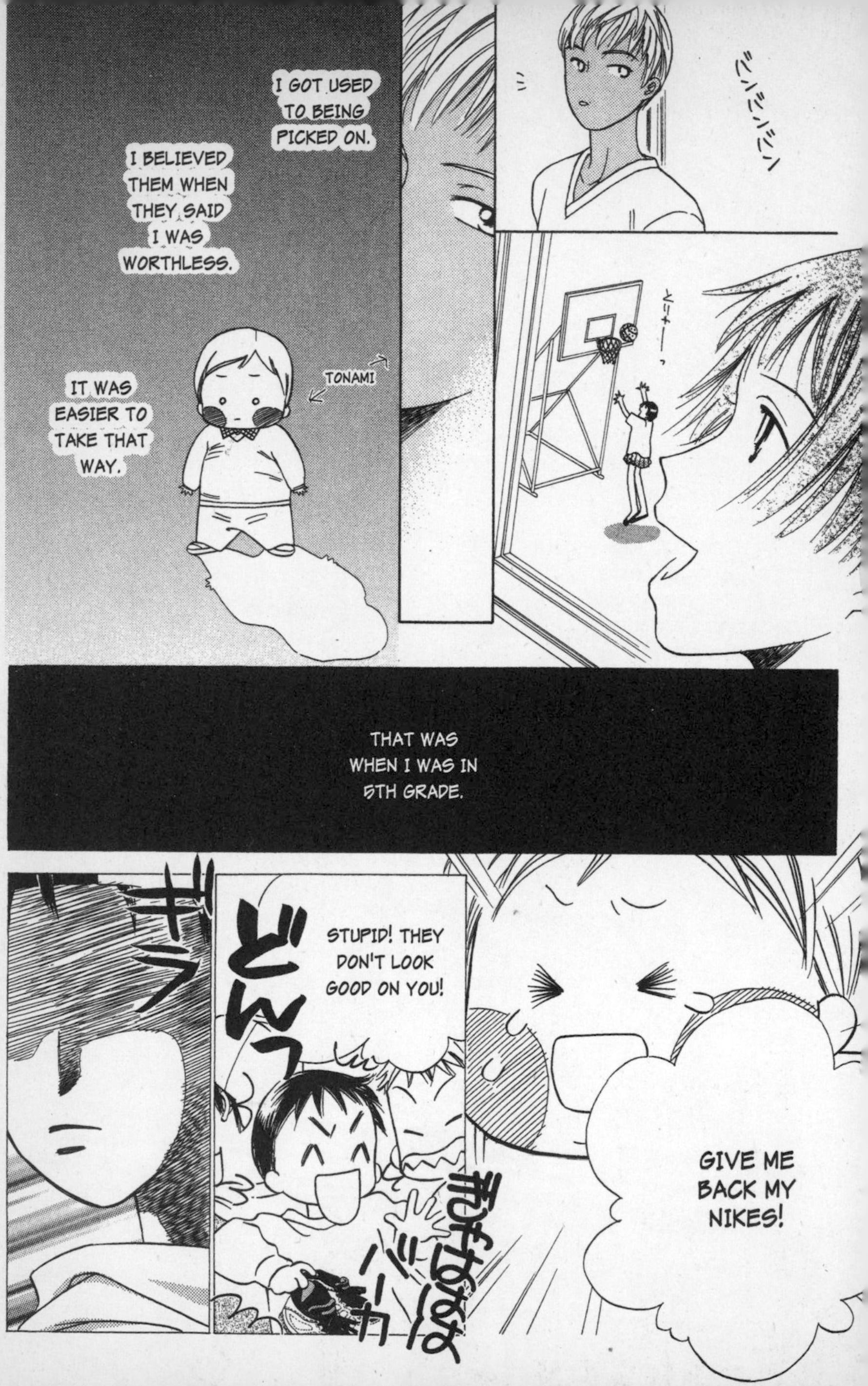
I GOT USED TO BEING PICKED ON.
I BELIEVED THEM WHEN THEY SAID I WAS WORTHLESS.
TONAMI
IT WAS EASIER TO TAKE THAT WAY.
THAT WAS WHEN I WAS IN 5TH GRADE.
GIVE ME BACK MY NIKES!
STUPID! THEY DON'T LOOK GOOD ON YOU!
どんっ
ぎゃははは
バーカ
ギラ

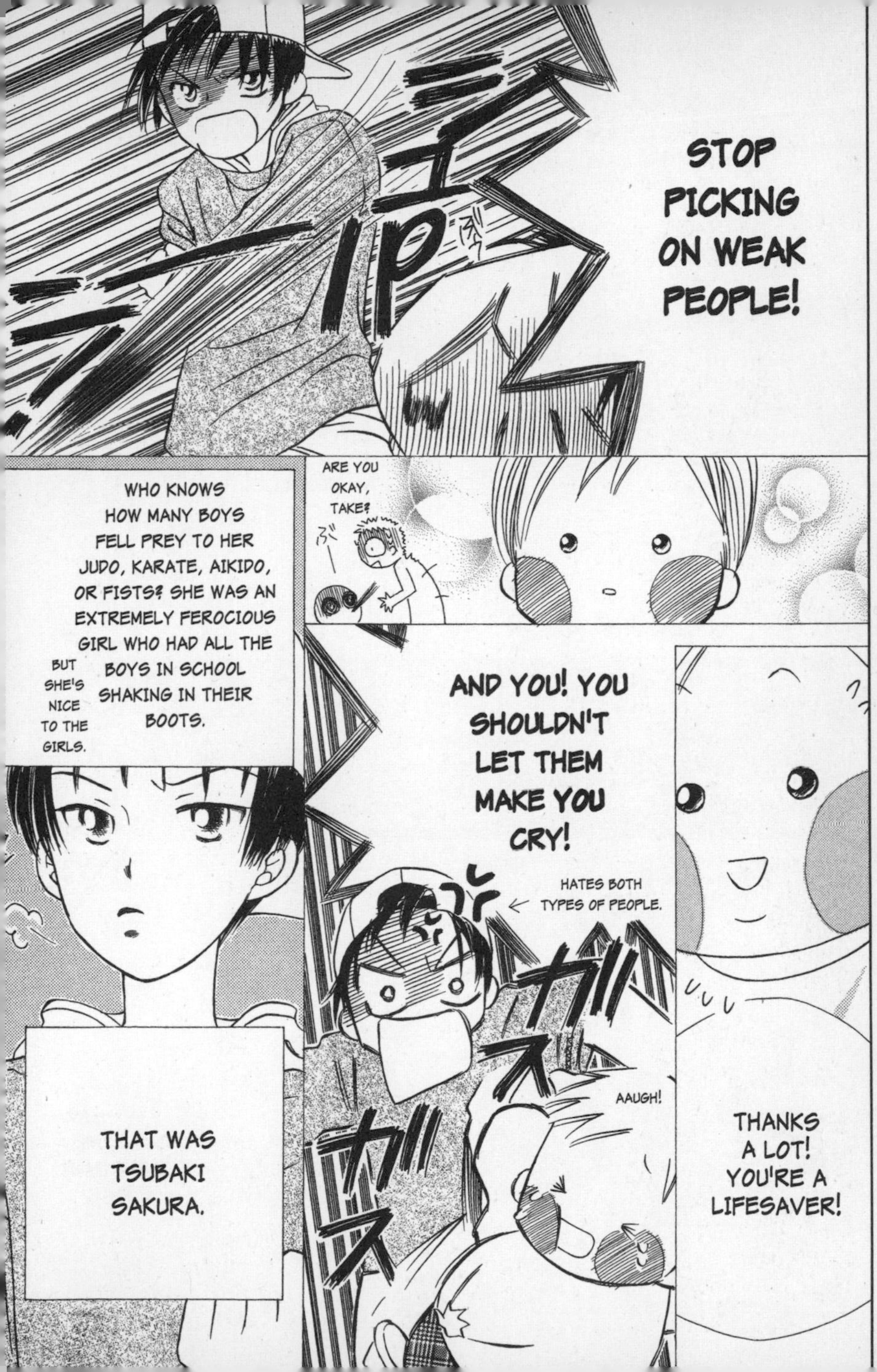
STOP PICKING ON WEAK PEOPLE!
ARE YOU OKAY, TAKE?
THANKS A LOT! YOU'RE A LIFESAVER!
AND YOU! YOU SHOULDN'T LET THEM MAKE YOU CRY!
HATES BOTH TYPES OF PEOPLE.
AAUGH!
WHO KNOWS HOW MANY BOYS FELL PREY TO HER JUDO, KARATE, AIKIDO, OR FISTS? SHE WAS AN EXTREMELY FEROCIOUS GIRL WHO HAD ALL THE BOYS IN SCHOOL SHAKING IN THEIR BOOTS.
BUT SHE'S NICE TO THE GIRLS.
THAT WAS TSUBAKI SAKURA.

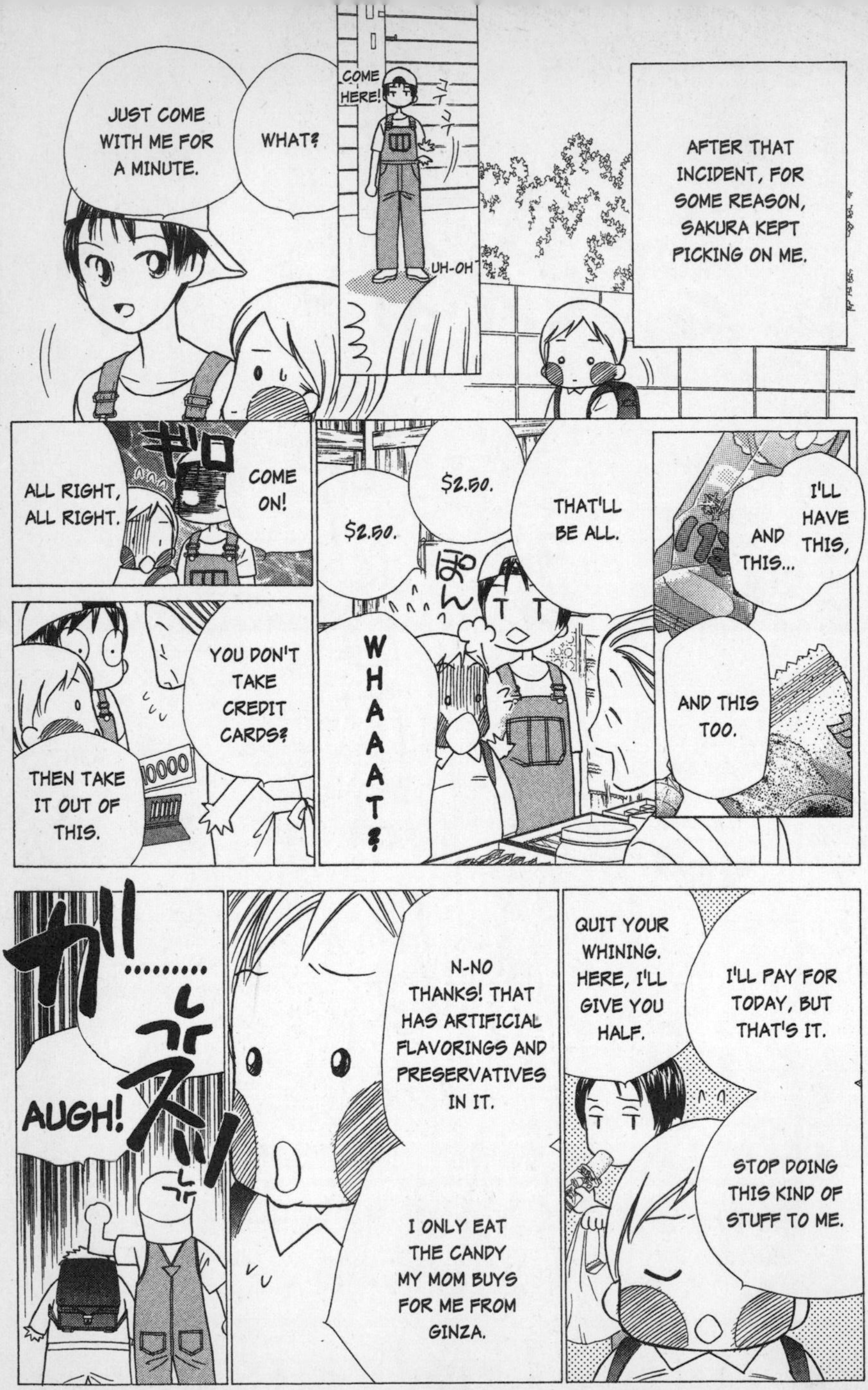

AFTER THAT INCIDENT, FOR SOME REASON, SAKURA KEPT PICKING ON ME.
COME HERE!
UH-OH
JUST COME WITH ME FOR A MINUTE.
WHAT?
I'LL HAVE THIS,
AND THIS...
AND THIS TOO.
THAT'LL BE ALL.
$2.50.
$2.50.
WHAAAT?
COME ON!
ALL RIGHT, ALL RIGHT.
YOU DON'T TAKE CREDIT CARDS?
10000
THEN TAKE IT OUT OF THIS.
I'LL PAY FOR TODAY, BUT THAT'S IT.
QUIT YOUR WHINING. HERE, I'LL GIVE YOU HALF.
STOP DOING THIS KIND OF STUFF TO ME.
N-NO THANKS! THAT HAS ARTIFICIAL FLAVORINGS AND PRESERVATIVES IN IT.
I ONLY EAT THE CANDY MY MOM BUYS FOR ME FROM GINZA.
AUGH!

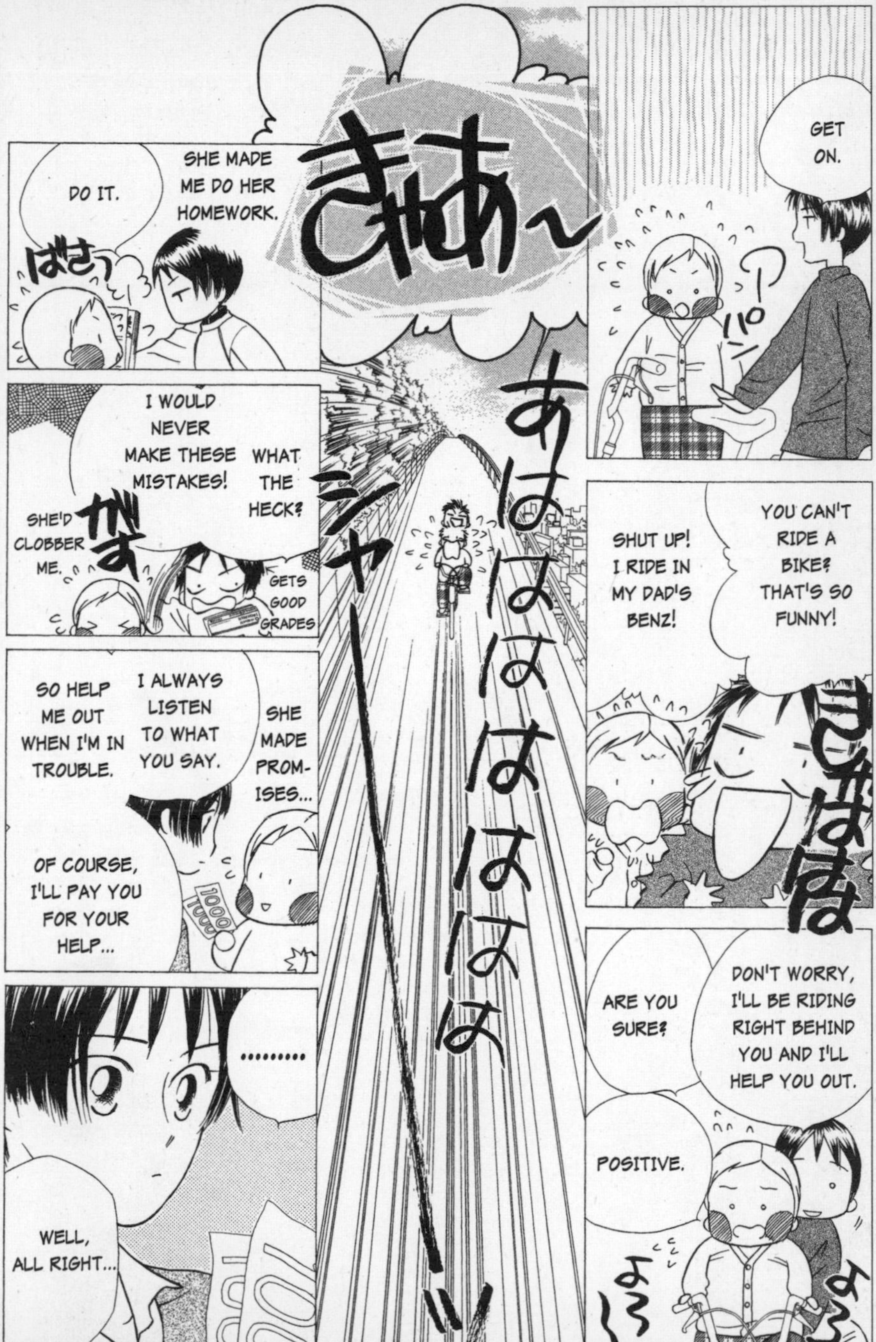
GET ON.
YOU CAN'T RIDE A BIKE? THAT'S SO FUNNY!
SHUT UP! I RIDE IN MY DAD'S BENZ!
きゃはは
DON'T WORRY, I'LL BE RIDING RIGHT BEHIND YOU AND I'LL HELP YOU OUT.
ARE YOU SURE?
POSITIVE.
よろ~
よろ~
きゃあ~
あははははは
シャー
SHE MADE ME DO HER HOMEWORK.
DO IT.
ばさっ
WHAT THE HECK?
I WOULD NEVER MAKE THESE MISTAKES!
がす
SHE'D CLOBBER ME.
GETS GOOD GRADES
SHE MADE PROMISES...
I ALWAYS LISTEN TO WHAT YOU SAY.
SO HELP ME OUT WHEN I'M IN TROUBLE.
OF COURSE, I'LL PAY YOU FOR YOUR HELP...
1000
....
WELL, ALL RIGHT...

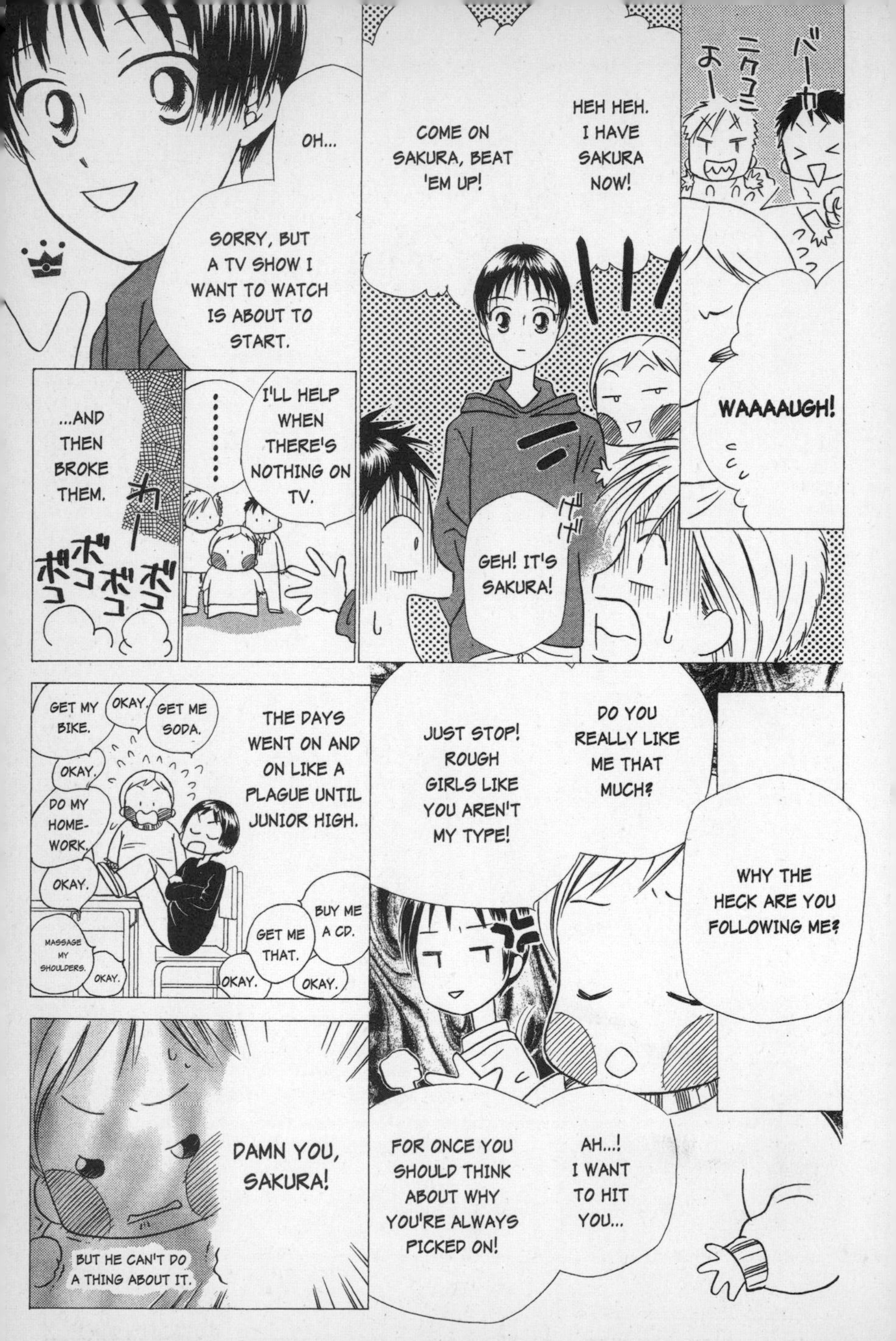
バーカ
WAAAAUGH!
HEH HEH. I HAVE SAKURA NOW!
COME ON SAKURA, BEAT 'EM UP!
GEH! IT'S SAKURA!
OH...
SORRY, BUT A TV SHOW I WANT TO WATCH IS ABOUT TO START.
......
I'LL HELP WHEN THERE'S NOTHING ON TV.
...AND THEN BROKE THEM.
DO YOU REALLY LIKE ME THAT MUCH?
JUST STOP! ROUGH GIRLS LIKE YOU AREN'T MY TYPE!
WHY THE HECK ARE YOU FOLLOWING ME?
AH...! I WANT TO HIT YOU...
FOR ONCE YOU SHOULD THINK ABOUT WHY YOU'RE ALWAYS PICKED ON!
THE DAYS WENT ON AND ON LIKE A PLAGUE UNTIL JUNIOR HIGH.
GET ME SODA.
OKAY.
GET MY BIKE.
OKAY.
DO MY HOME-WORK.
OKAY.
BUY ME A CD.
GET ME THAT.
OKAY.
OKAY.
MASSAGE MY SHOULDERS.
OKAY.
DAMN YOU, SAKURA!
BUT HE CAN'T DO A THING ABOUT IT.

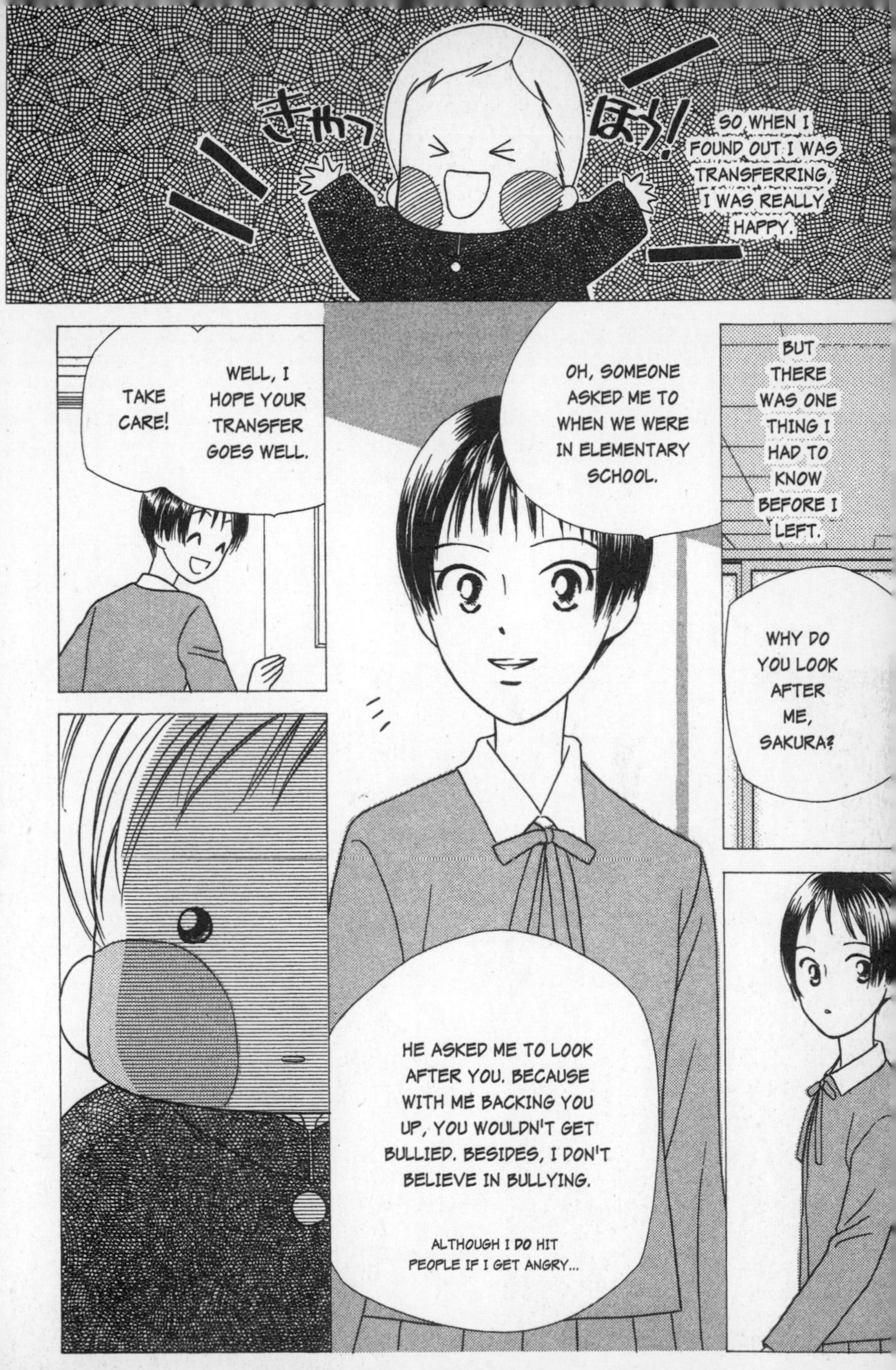

きゃっ
ほぅ!
SO WHEN I FOUND OUT I WAS TRANSFERRING, I WAS REALLY HAPPY.
BUT THERE WAS ONE THING I HAD TO KNOW BEFORE I LEFT.
WHY DO YOU LOOK AFTER ME, SAKURA?
OH, SOMEONE ASKED ME TO WHEN WE WERE IN ELEMENTARY SCHOOL.
HE ASKED ME TO LOOK AFTER YOU. BECAUSE WITH ME BACKING YOU UP, YOU WOULDN'T GET BULLIED. BESIDES, I DON'T BELIEVE IN BULLYING.
ALTHOUGH I DO HIT PEOPLE IF I GET ANGRY...
WELL, I HOPE YOUR TRANSFER GOES WELL.
TAKE CARE!

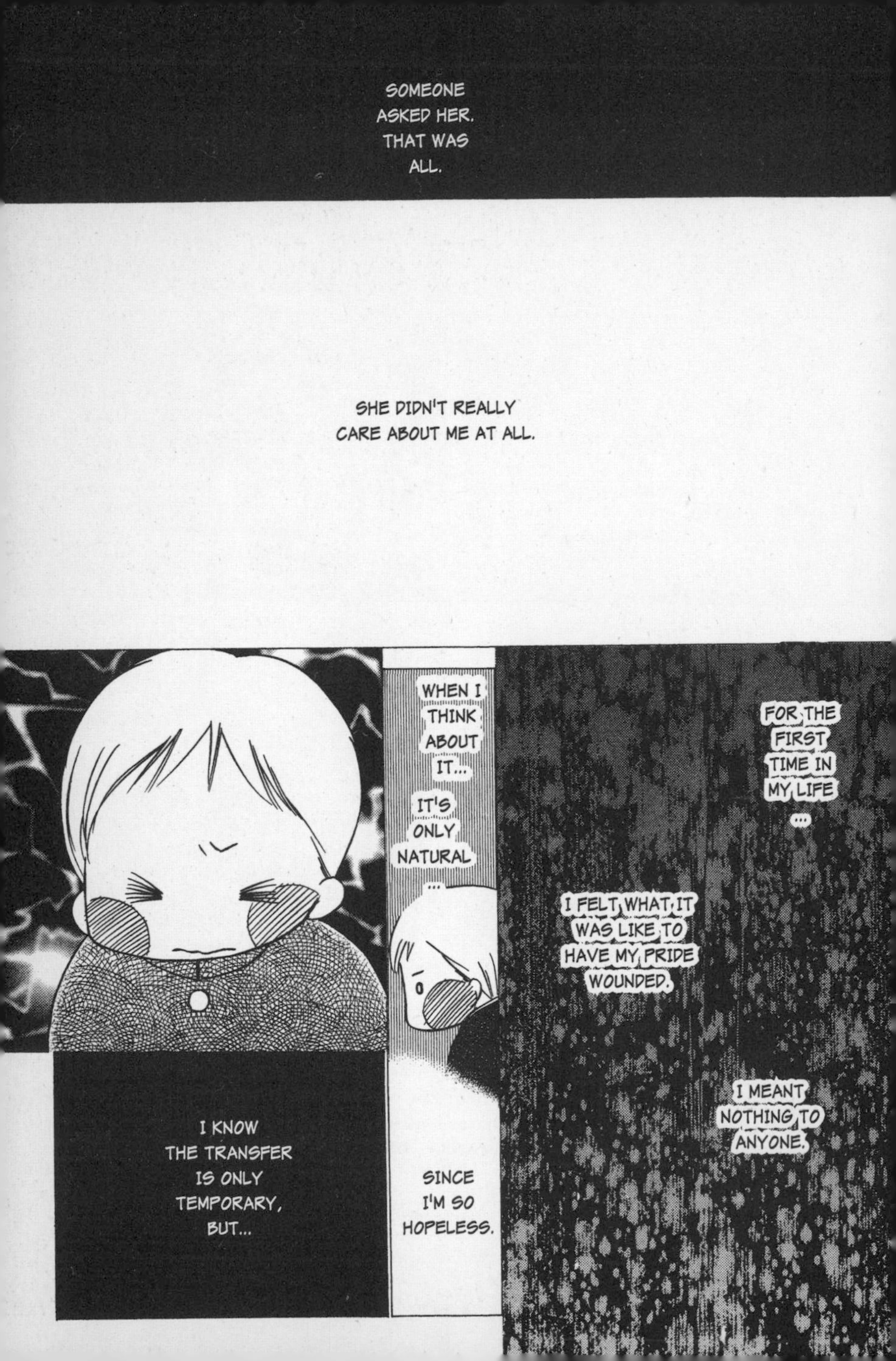
SOMEONE ASKED HER. THAT WAS ALL.
SHE DIDN'T REALLY CARE ABOUT ME AT ALL.
FOR THE FIRST TIME IN MY LIFE...
I FELT WHAT IT WAS LIKE TO HAVE MY PRIDE WOUNDED.
I MEANT NOTHING TO ANYONE.
WHEN I THINK ABOUT IT...
IT'S ONLY NATURAL...
SINCE I'M SO HOPELESS.
I KNOW THE TRANSFER IS ONLY TEMPORARY, BUT...

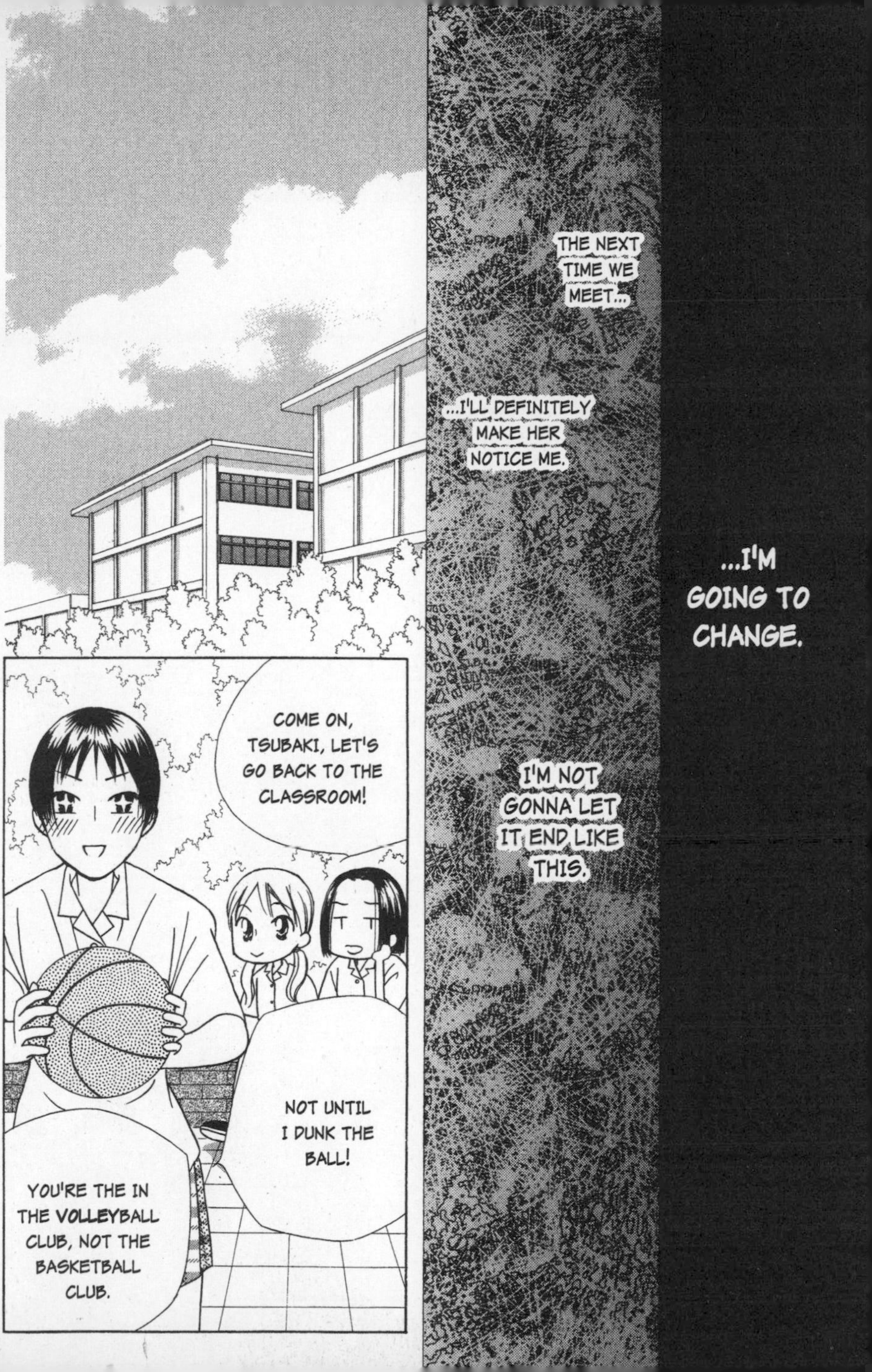
THE NEXT TIME WE MEET...
...I'LL DEFINITELY MAKE HER NOTICE ME.
I'M NOT GONNA LET IT END LIKE THIS.
...I'M GOING TO CHANGE.
COME ON, TSUBAKI, LET'S GO BACK TO THE CLASSROOM!
NOT UNTIL I DUNK THE BALL!
YOU'RE THE IN THE VOLLEYBALL CLUB, NOT THE BASKETBALL CLUB.

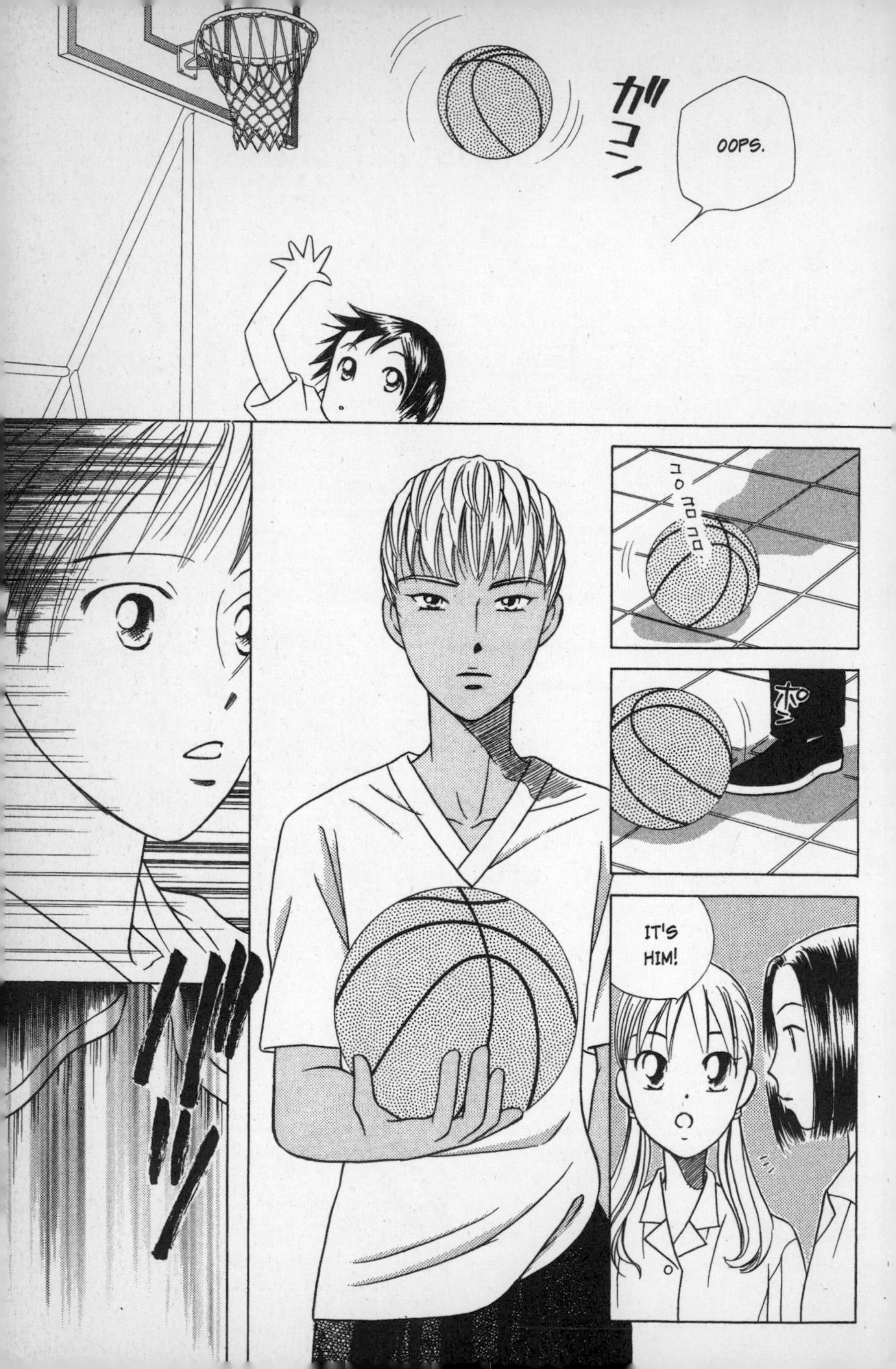
ガコン
OOPS.
コロコロコロ
ポン
IT'S HIM!

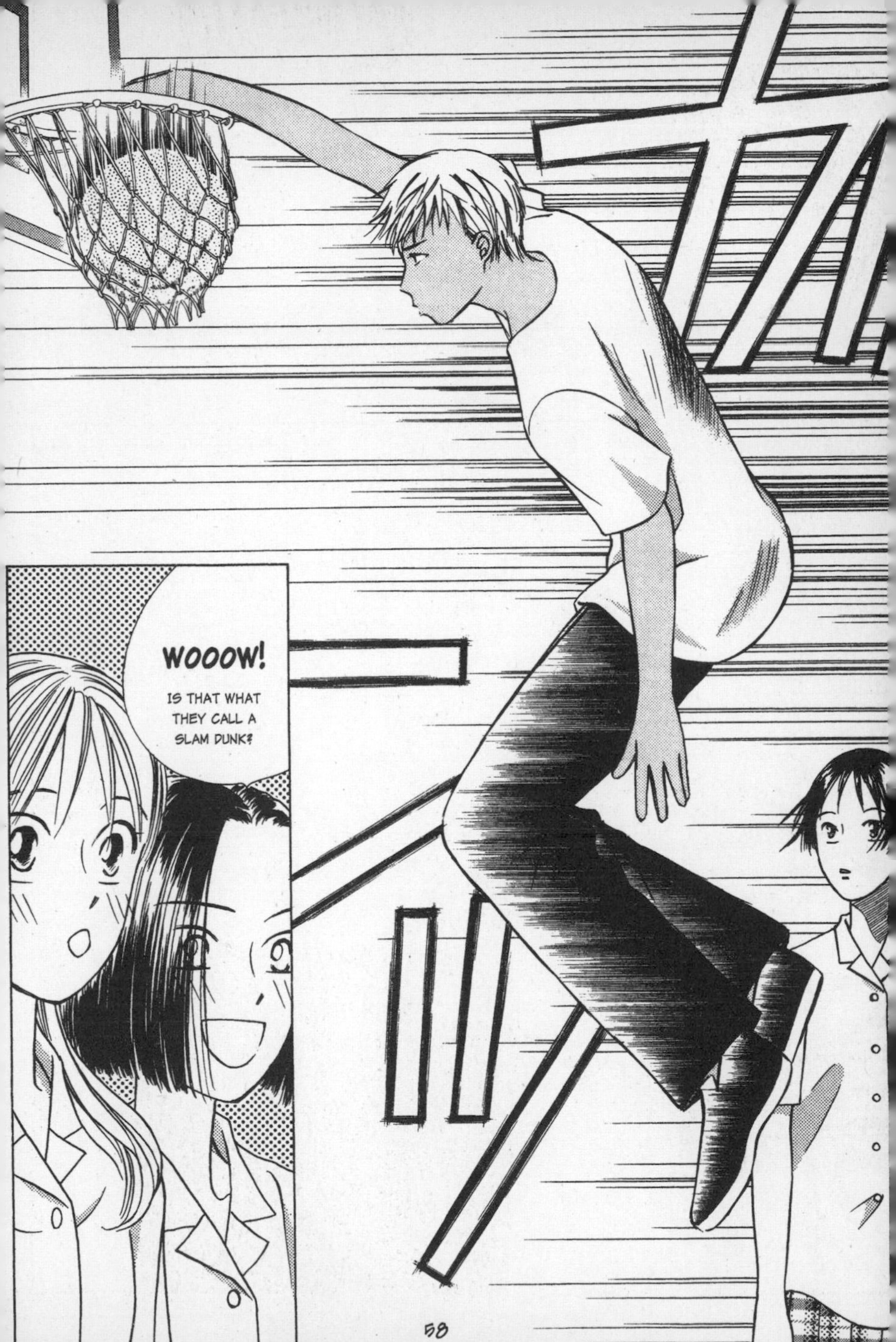
WOOOW!
IS THAT WHAT THEY CALL A SLAM DUNK?

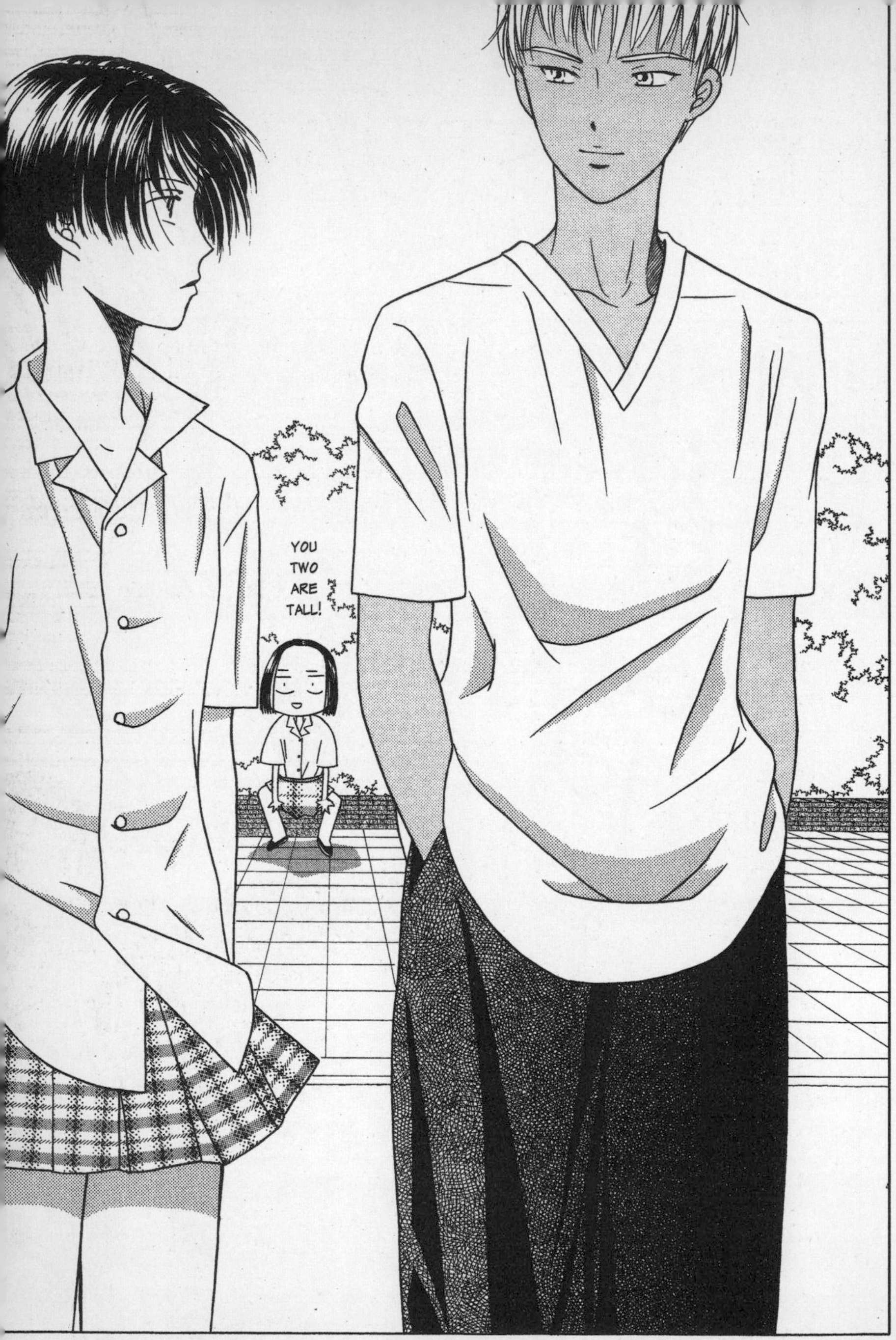
YOU TWO ARE TALL!

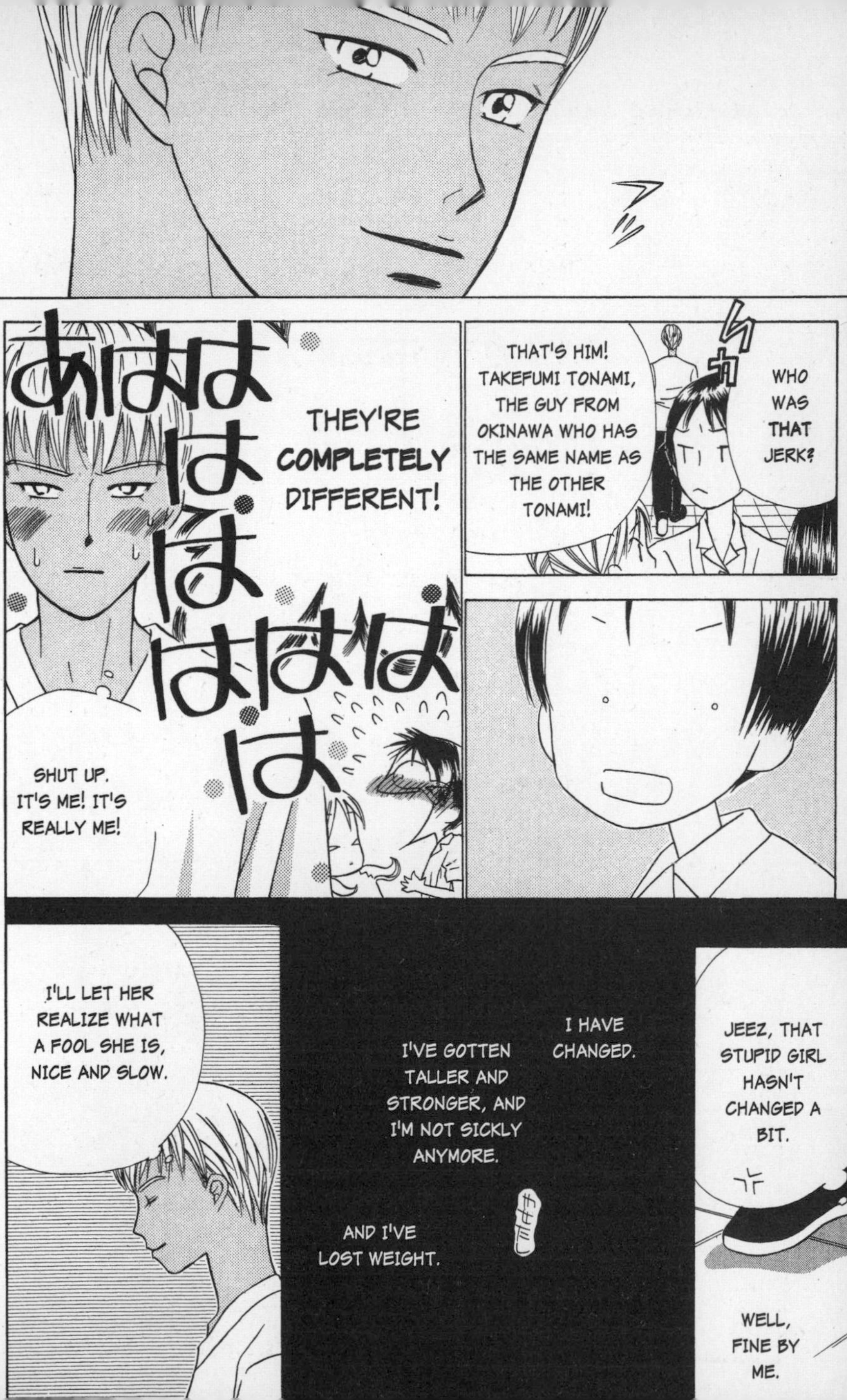
WHO WAS THAT JERK?
THAT'S HIM! TAKEFUMI TONAMI, THE GUY FROM OKINAWA WHO HAS THE SAME NAME AS THE OTHER TONAMI!
THEY'RE COMPLETELY DIFFERENT!
あははははははははは
SHUT UP. IT'S ME! IT'S REALLY ME!
JEEZ, THAT STUPID GIRL HASN'T CHANGED A BIT.
WELL, FINE BY ME.
I HAVE CHANGED.
I'VE GOTTEN TALLER AND STRONGER, AND I'M NOT SICKLY ANYMORE.
やせたし
AND I'VE LOST WEIGHT.
I'LL LET HER REALIZE WHAT A FOOL SHE IS, NICE AND SLOW.

BEGINNING OF SEMESTER EXAMS: TOP STUDENT RANKING (10TH GRADE)

RANK	STUDENT NAME	CLASS	POINTS
1	ARIMA, SOICHIRO	A	394
1	TONAMI, TAKEFUMI	B	394
1	MIYAZAWA, YUKINO	A	394
4	FUKUDA, KOHEI	F	387

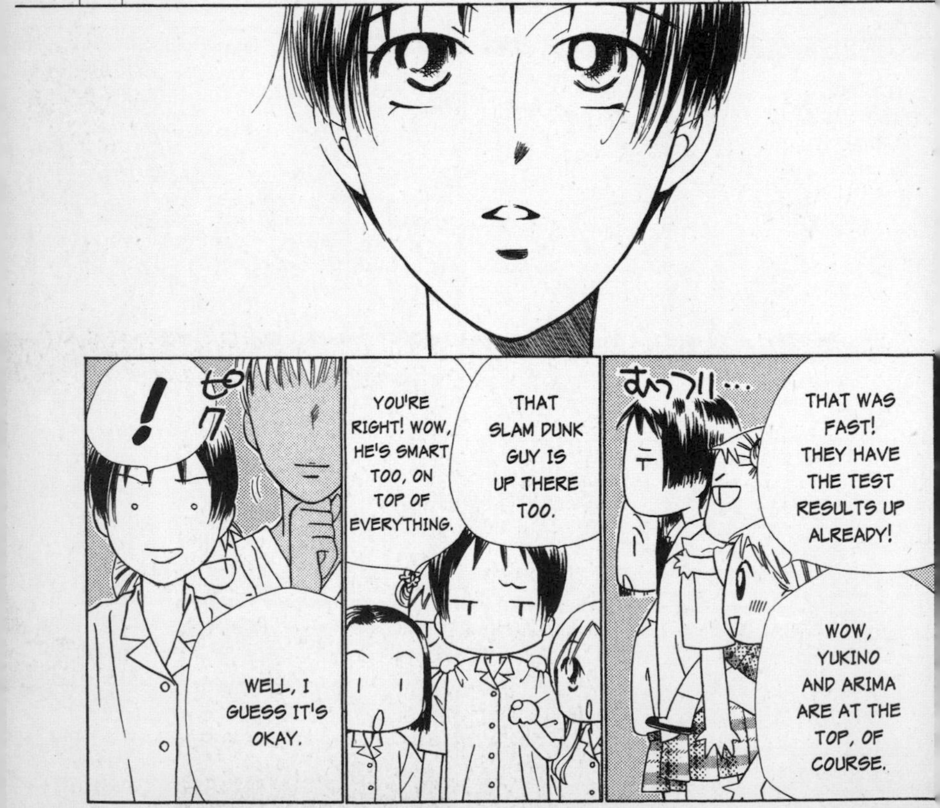
むっ!!...
THAT WAS FAST! THEY HAVE THE TEST RESULTS UP ALREADY!
WOW, YUKINO AND ARIMA ARE AT THE TOP, OF COURSE.
THAT SLAM DUNK GUY IS UP THERE TOO.
YOU'RE RIGHT! WOW, HE'S SMART TOO, ON TOP OF EVERYTHING.
!
ピク
WELL, I GUESS IT'S OKAY.

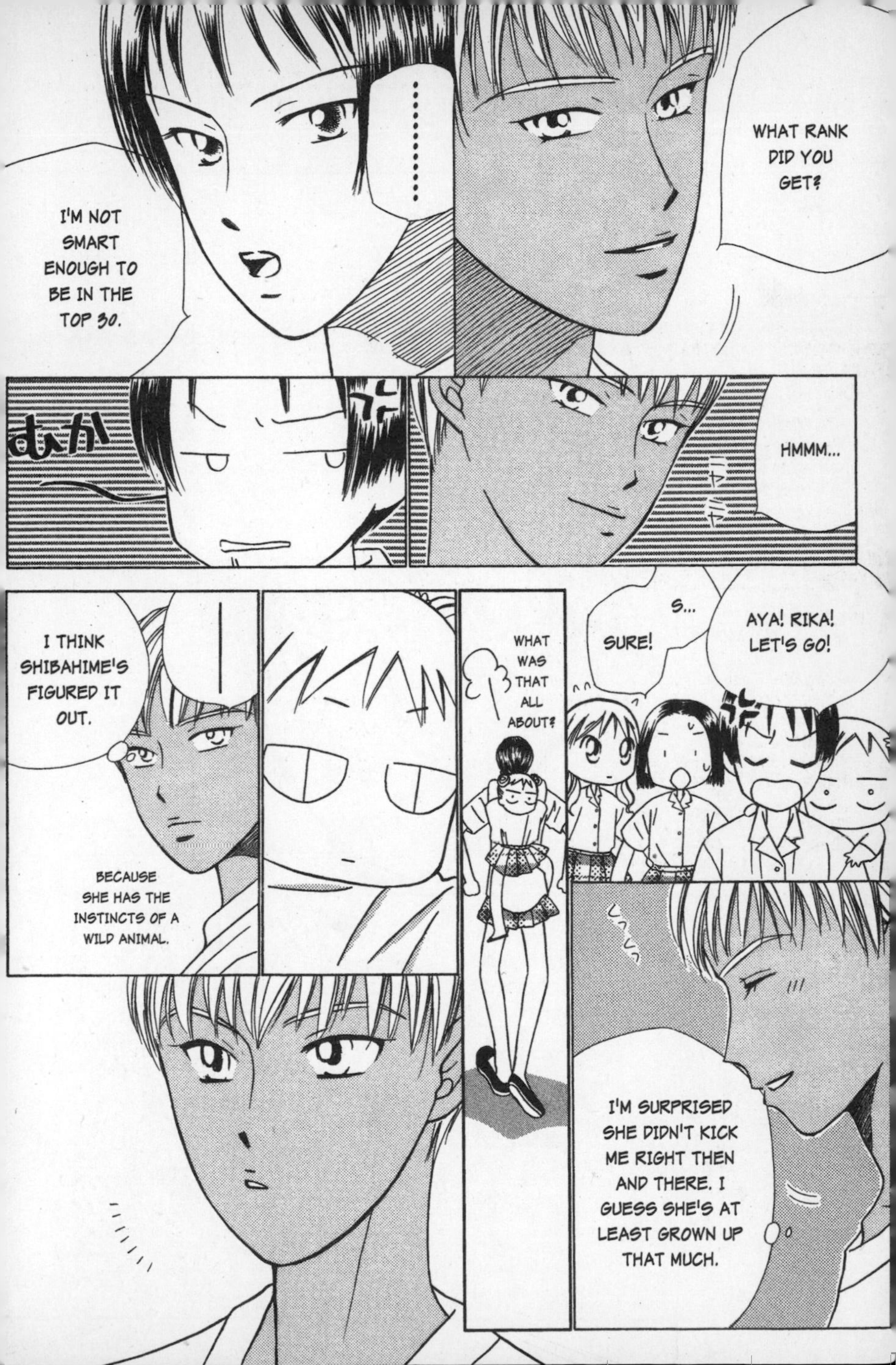
WHAT RANK DID YOU GET?
I'M NOT SMART ENOUGH TO BE IN THE TOP 30.
HMMM...
むか
AYA! RIKA! LET'S GO!
S... SURE!
WHAT WAS THAT ALL ABOUT?
I THINK SHIBAHIME'S FIGURED IT OUT.
BECAUSE SHE HAS THE INSTINCTS OF A WILD ANIMAL.
I'M SURPRISED SHE DIDN'T KICK ME RIGHT THEN AND THERE. I GUESS SHE'S AT LEAST GROWN UP THAT MUCH.

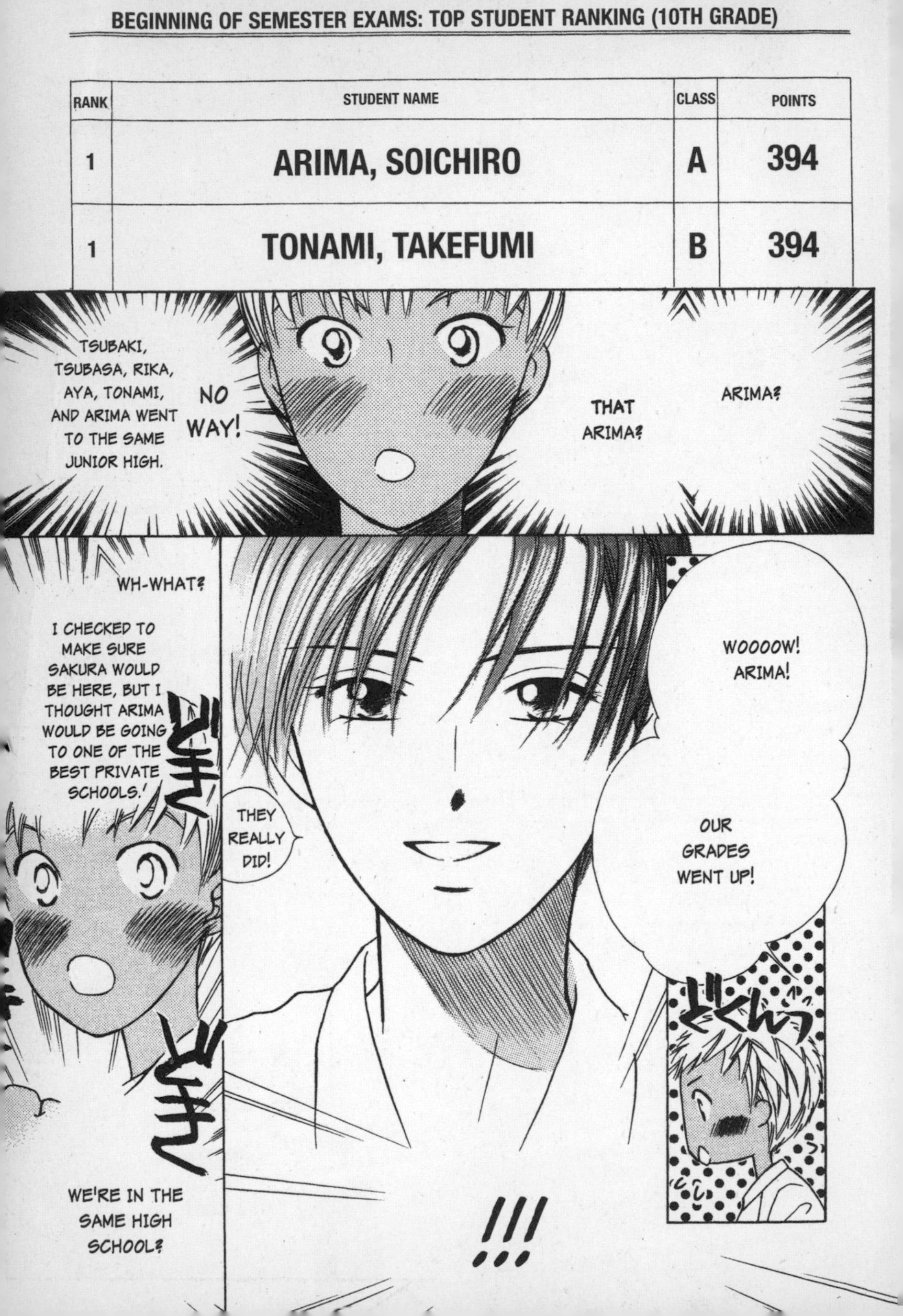
BEGINNING OF SEMESTER EXAMS: TOP STUDENT RANKING (10TH GRADE)
RANK
STUDENT NAME
CLASS
POINTS
1 ARIMA, SOICHIRO A 394
1 TONAMI, TAKEFUMI B 394
ARIMA?
THAT ARIMA?
NO WAY!
TSUBAKI, TSUBASA, RIKA, AYA, TONAMI, AND ARIMA WENT TO THE SAME JUNIOR HIGH.
WOOOOW! ARIMA!
OUR GRADES WENT UP!
THEY REALLY DID!
!!!
WH-WHAT?
I CHECKED TO MAKE SURE SAKURA WOULD BE HERE, BUT I THOUGHT ARIMA WOULD BE GOING TO ONE OF THE BEST PRIVATE SCHOOLS.'
WE'RE IN THE SAME HIGH SCHOOL?

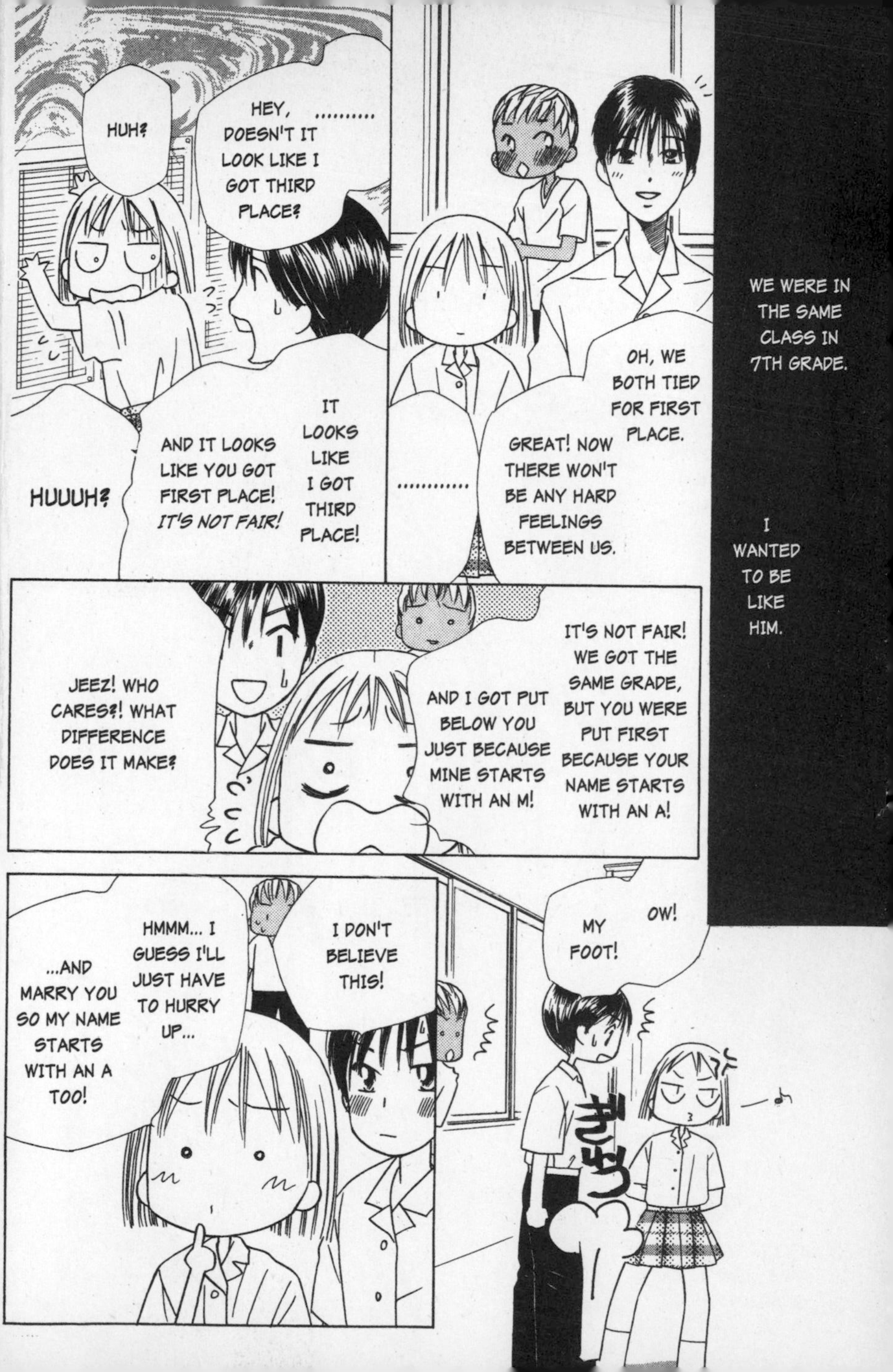

WE WERE IN THE SAME CLASS IN 7TH GRADE.
I WANTED TO BE LIKE HIM.
OH, WE BOTH TIED FOR FIRST PLACE.
GREAT! NOW THERE WON'T BE ANY HARD FEELINGS BETWEEN US.
....
HEY, DOESN'T IT LOOK LIKE I GOT THIRD PLACE?
....
HUH?
IT LOOKS LIKE I GOT THIRD PLACE!
AND IT LOOKS LIKE YOU GOT FIRST PLACE! *IT'S NOT FAIR!*
HUUUH?
IT'S NOT FAIR! WE GOT THE SAME GRADE, BUT YOU WERE PUT FIRST BECAUSE YOUR NAME STARTS WITH AN A!
AND I GOT PUT BELOW YOU JUST BECAUSE MINE STARTS WITH AN M!
JEEZ! WHO CARES?! WHAT DIFFERENCE DOES IT MAKE?
OW!
MY FOOT!
I DON'T BELIEVE THIS!
HMMM... I GUESS I'LL JUST HAVE TO HURRY UP...
...AND MARRY YOU SO MY NAME STARTS WITH AN A TOO!

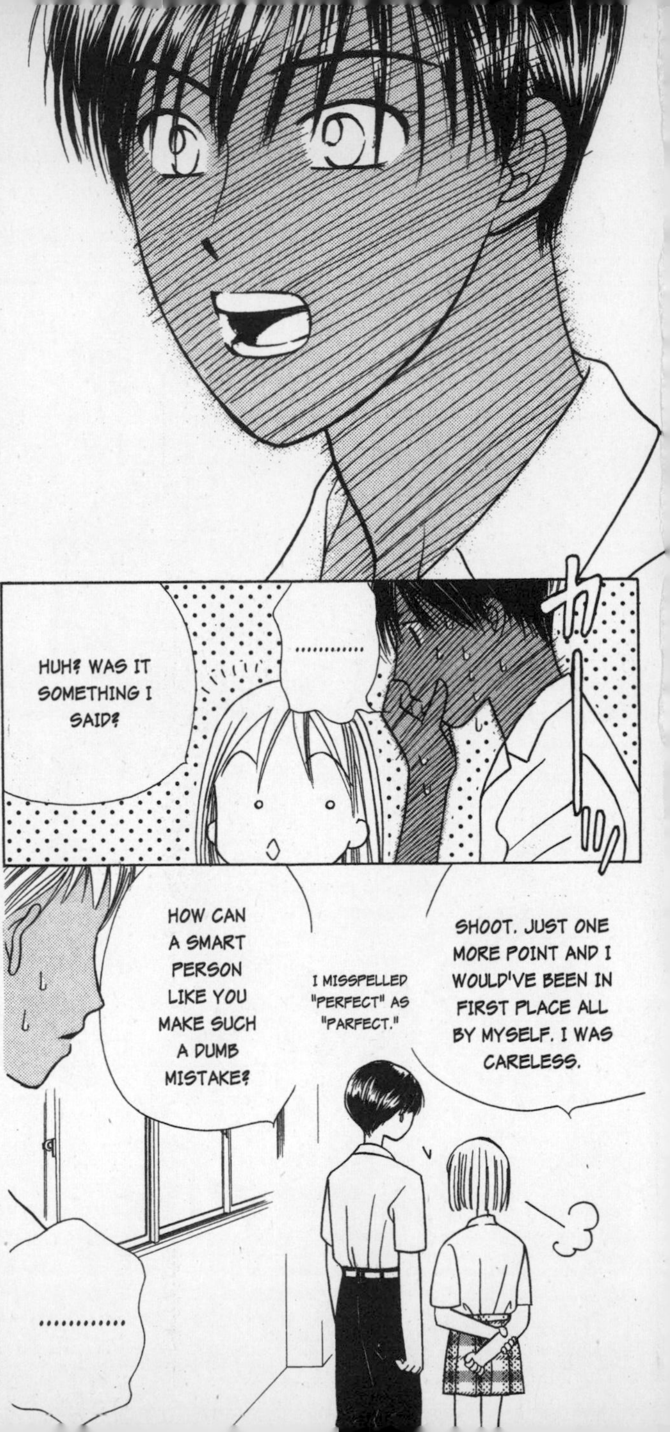

....
HUH? WAS IT SOMETHING I SAID?
SHOOT. JUST ONE MORE POINT AND I WOULD'VE BEEN IN FIRST PLACE ALL BY MYSELF. I WAS CARELESS.
I MISSPELLED "PERFECT" AS "PARFECT."
HOW CAN A SMART PERSON LIKE YOU MAKE SUCH A DUMB MISTAKE?
....

2

Ever since last year, my cooking has suddenly started getting better and better. I'm messing up less and less.

I haven't been doing too much at once.

For example, when I had eggs, sausage, and tomato for breakfast, on the first day, I'd make something pretty normal and simple, like this:

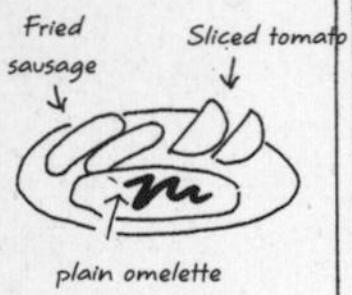

Fried sausage
Sliced tomato
plain omelette

The next day, I took the seeds out of the tomato, diced it, cut the sausage and mixed it with the eggs, then mixed in some dry parsley and scrambled it all up!

On the next day, I combined the leftovers with some vegetables and made some soup out of it!

And then on the next day, I was out of sausage so I made bacon.

To be continued ↓

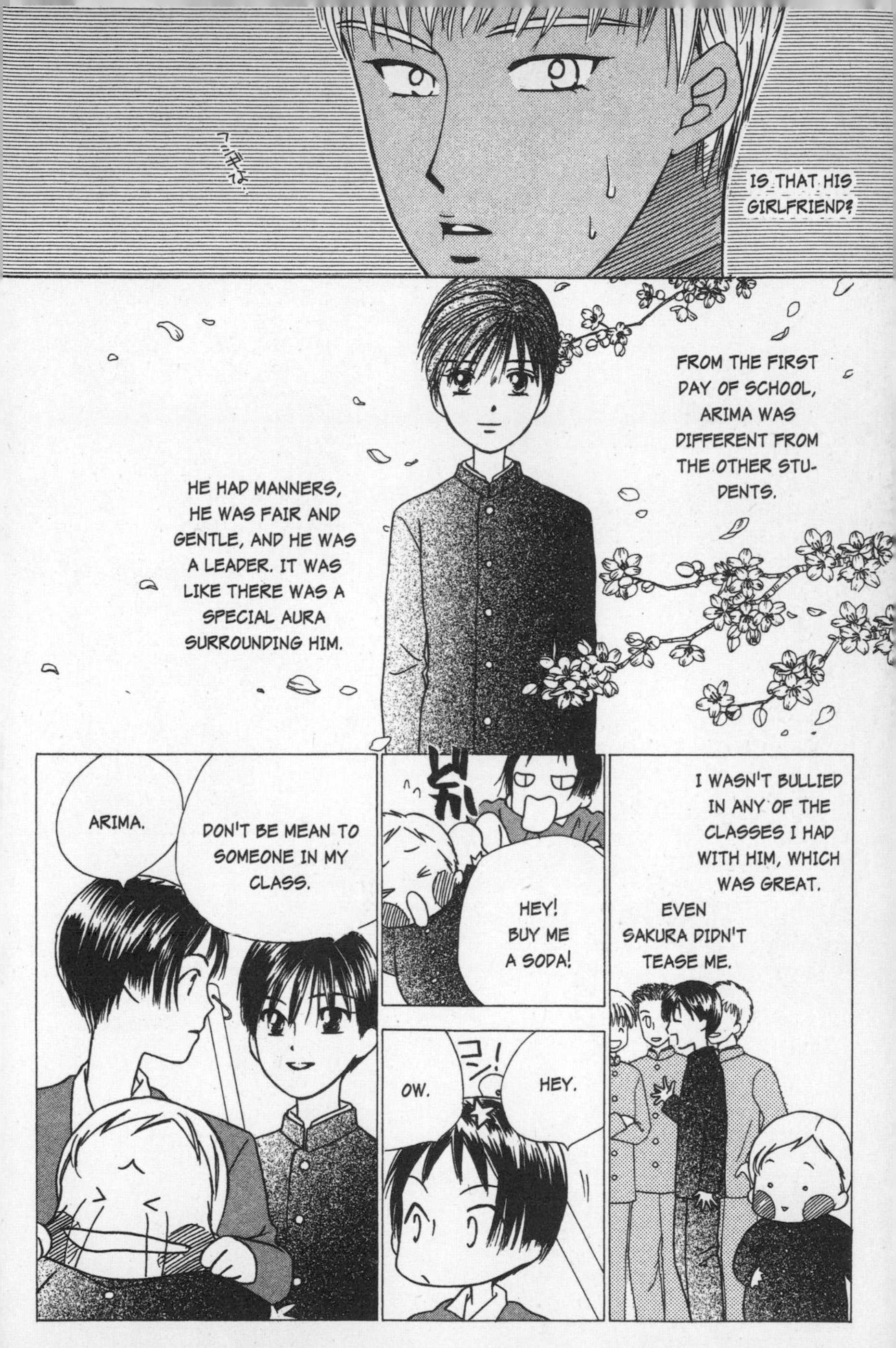
IS THAT HIS GIRLFRIEND?
FROM THE FIRST DAY OF SCHOOL, ARIMA WAS DIFFERENT FROM THE OTHER STU-DENTS.
HE HAD MANNERS, HE WAS FAIR AND GENTLE, AND HE WAS A LEADER. IT WAS LIKE THERE WAS A SPECIAL AURA SURROUNDING HIM.
I WASN'T BULLIED IN ANY OF THE CLASSES I HAD WITH HIM, WHICH WAS GREAT.
EVEN SAKURA DIDN'T TEASE ME.
HEY! BUY ME A SODA!
HEY.
OW.
ARIMA.
DON'T BE MEAN TO SOMEONE IN MY CLASS.

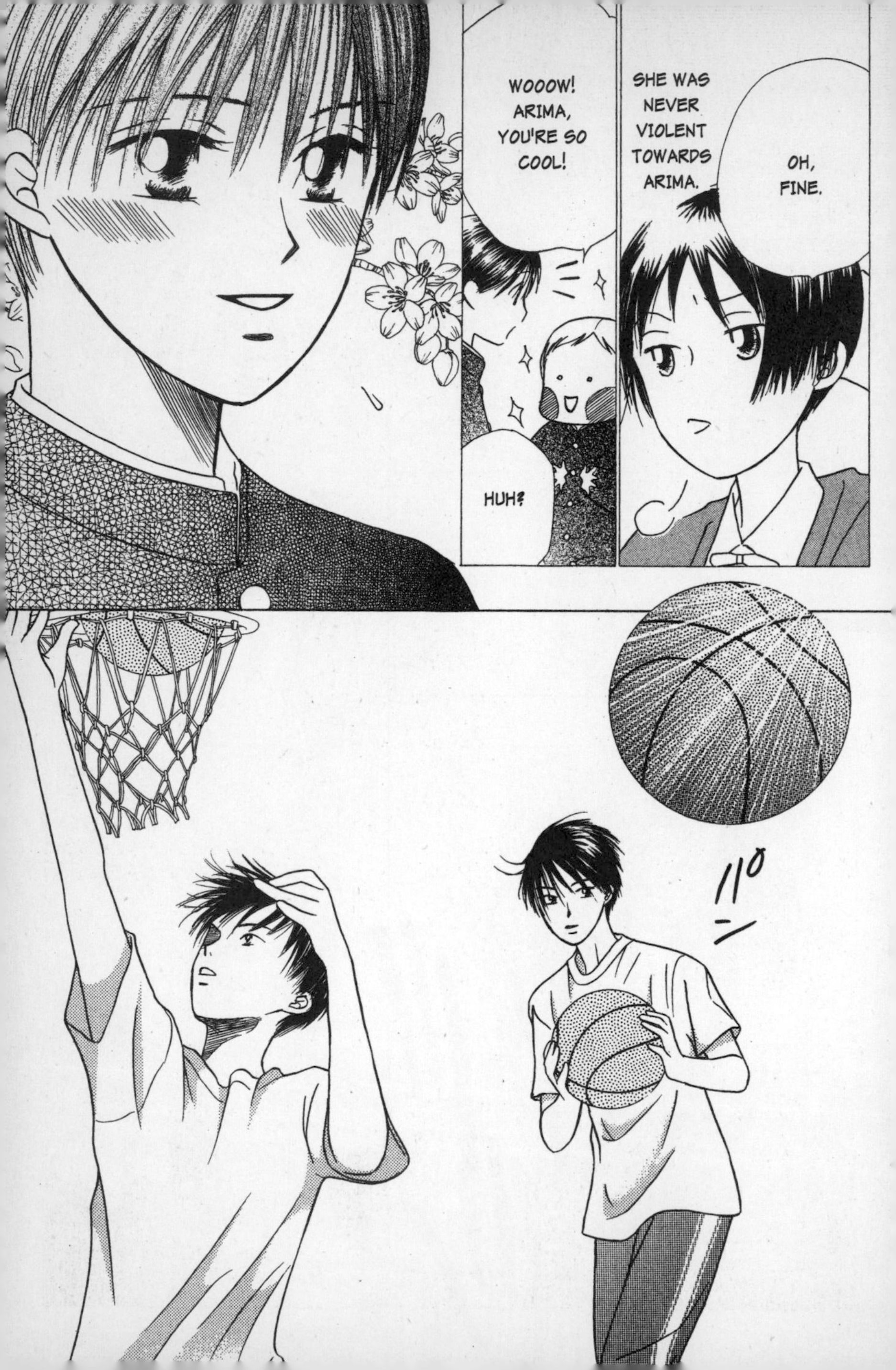
OH, FINE.
SHE WAS NEVER VIOLENT TOWARDS ARIMA.
WOOOW! ARIMA, YOU'RE SO COOL!
HUH?

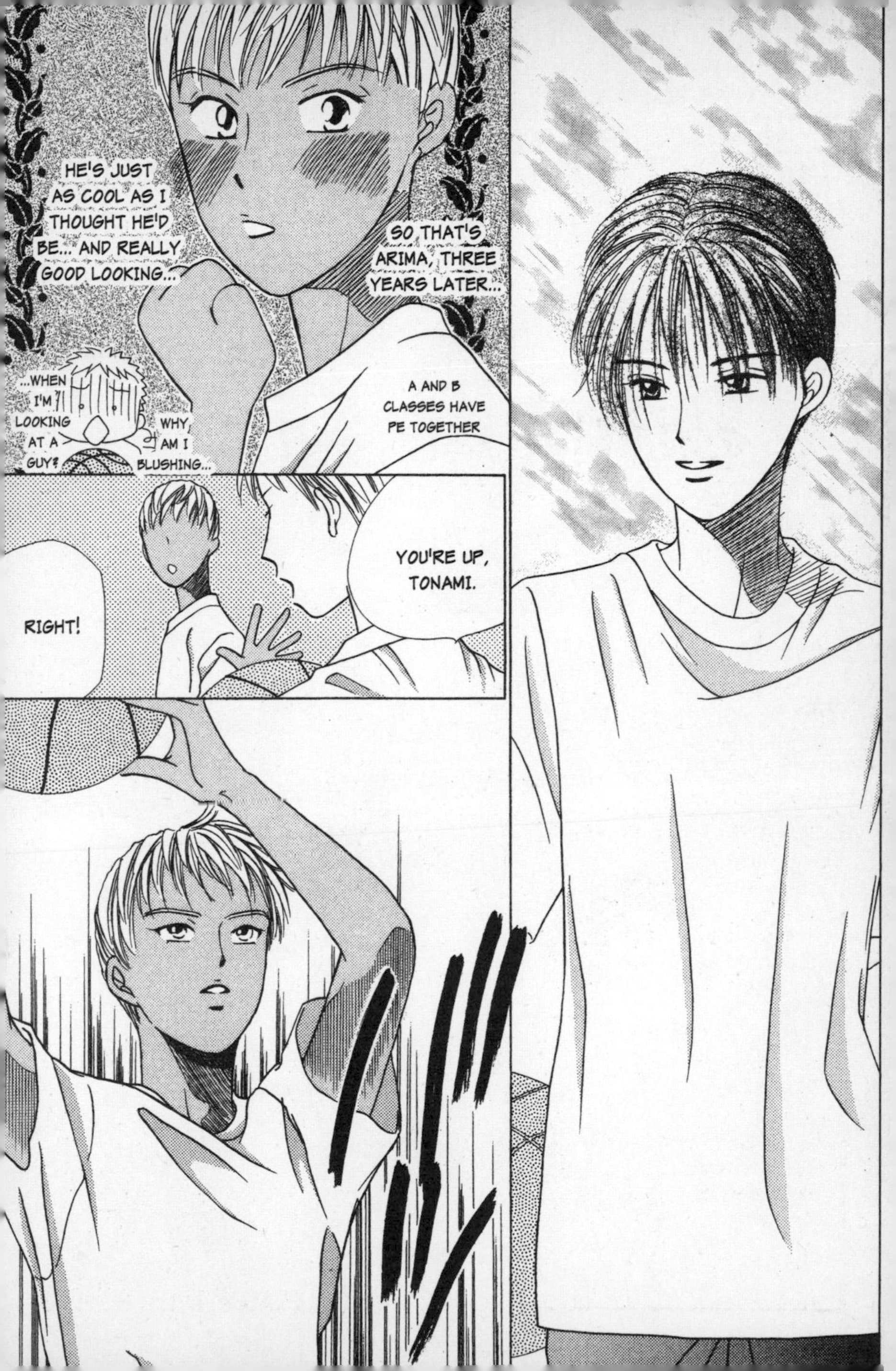
SO THAT'S ARIMA, THREE YEARS LATER...
HE'S JUST AS COOL AS I THOUGHT HE'D BE... AND REALLY GOOD LOOKING...
A AND B CLASSES HAVE PE TOGETHER
WHY AM I BLUSHING...
...WHEN I'M LOOKING AT A GUY?
YOU'RE UP, TONAMI.
RIGHT!

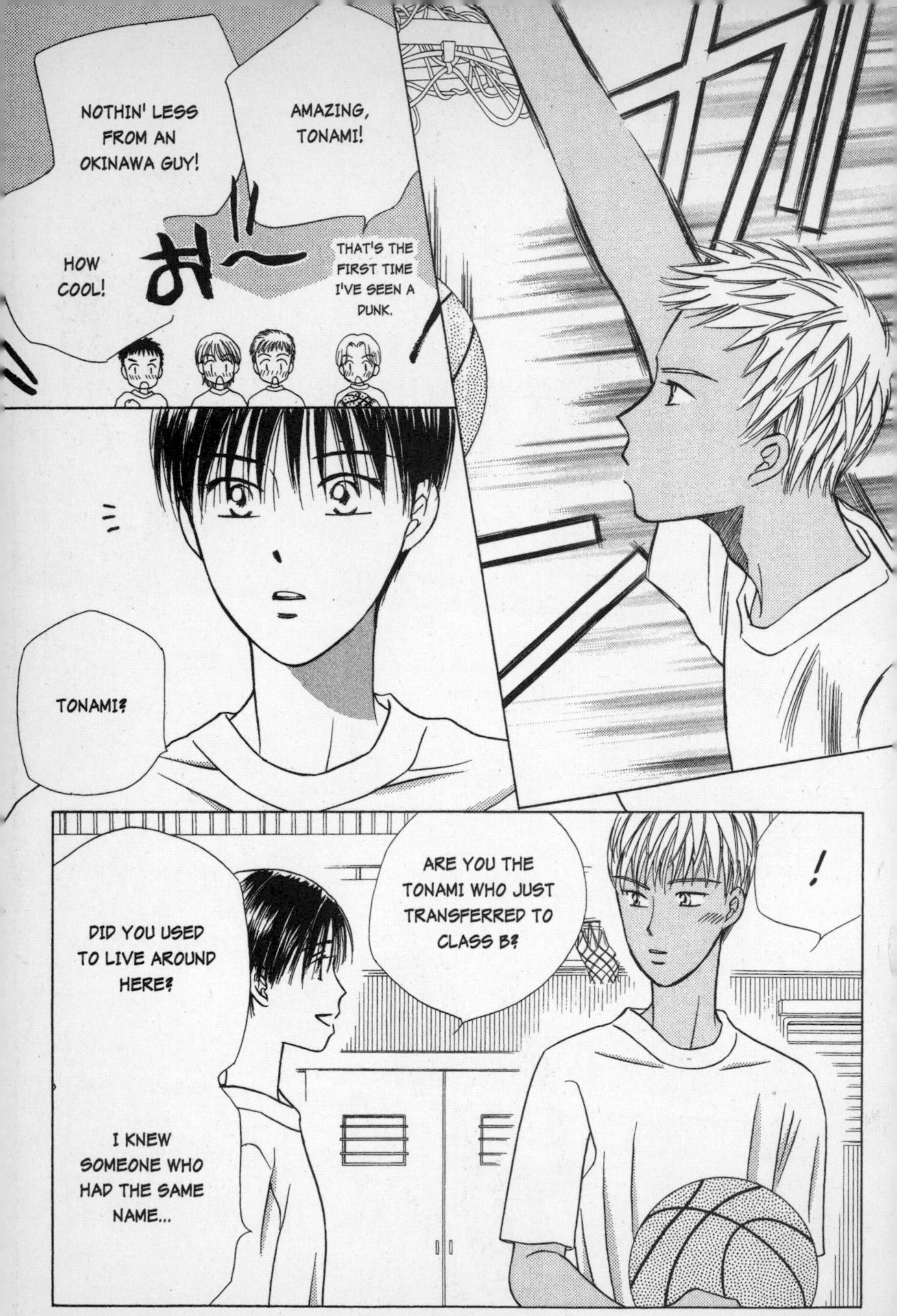
THAT'S THE FIRST TIME I'VE SEEN A DUNK.
AMAZING, TONAMI!
お~!!
NOTHIN' LESS FROM AN OKINAWA GUY!
HOW COOL!
TONAMI?
!
ARE YOU THE TONAMI WHO JUST TRANSFERRED TO CLASS B?
DID YOU USED TO LIVE AROUND HERE?
I KNEW SOMEONE WHO HAD THE SAME NAME...

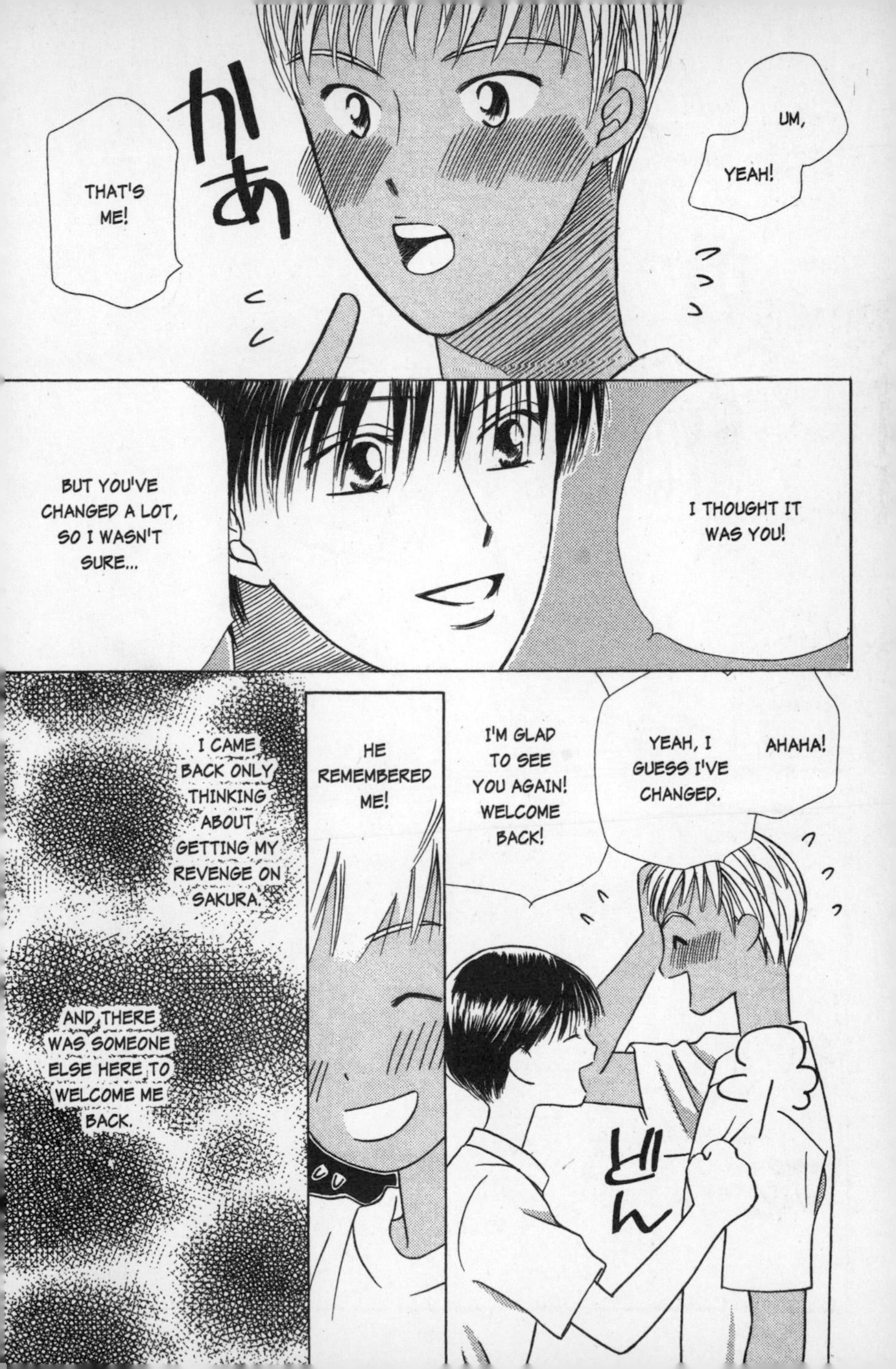
UM, YEAH!
かあ
THAT'S ME!
I THOUGHT IT WAS YOU!
BUT YOU'VE CHANGED A LOT, SO I WASN'T SURE...
AHAHA!
YEAH, I GUESS I'VE CHANGED.
I'M GLAD TO SEE YOU AGAIN! WELCOME BACK!
びん
HE REMEMBERED ME!
I CAME BACK ONLY THINKING ABOUT GETTING MY REVENGE ON SAKURA.
AND THERE WAS SOMEONE ELSE HERE TO WELCOME ME BACK.

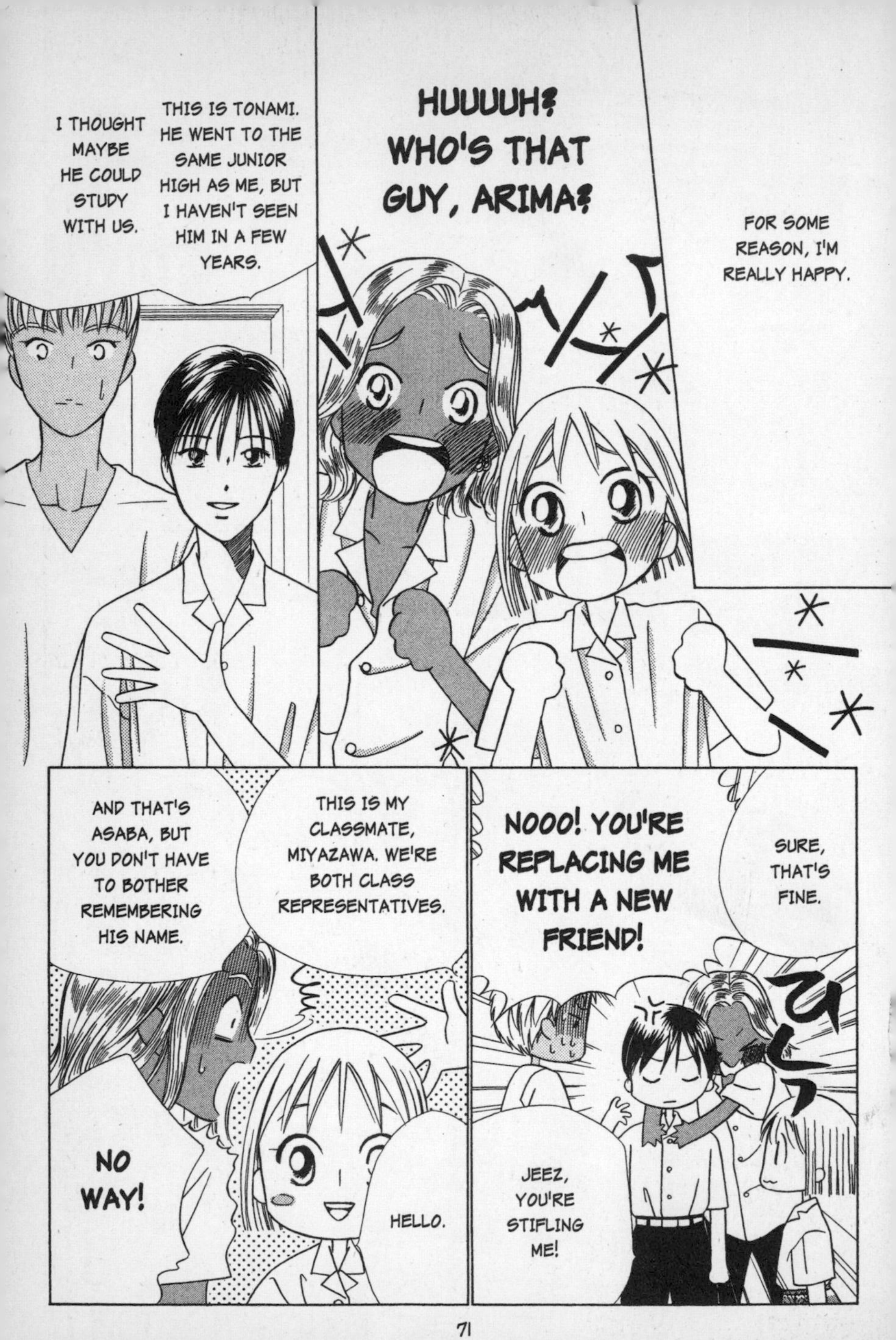
FOR SOME REASON, I'M REALLY HAPPY.
HUUUUH? WHO'S THAT GUY, ARIMA?
THIS IS TONAMI. HE WENT TO THE SAME JUNIOR HIGH AS ME, BUT I HAVEN'T SEEN HIM IN A FEW YEARS.
I THOUGHT MAYBE HE COULD STUDY WITH US.
SURE, THAT'S FINE.
NOOO! YOU'RE REPLACING ME WITH A NEW FRIEND!
JEEZ, YOU'RE STIFLING ME!
THIS IS MY CLASSMATE, MIYAZAWA. WE'RE BOTH CLASS REPRESENTATIVES.
AND THAT'S ASABA, BUT YOU DON'T HAVE TO BOTHER REMEMBERING HIS NAME.
HELLO.
NO WAY!

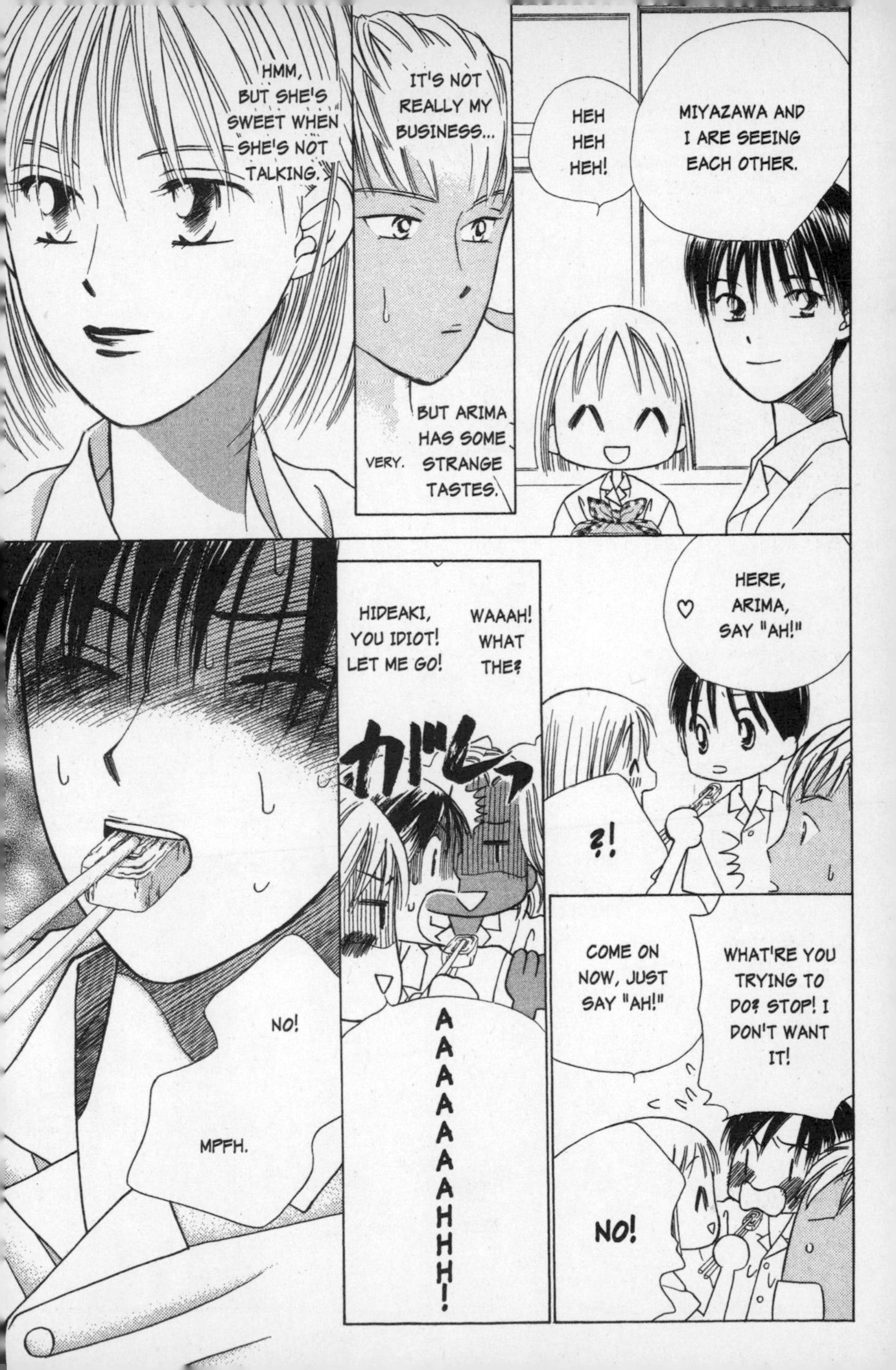
MIYAZAWA AND I ARE SEEING EACH OTHER.
HEH HEH HEH!
IT'S NOT REALLY MY BUSINESS...
BUT ARIMA HAS SOME STRANGE TASTES.
VERY.
HMM, BUT SHE'S SWEET WHEN SHE'S NOT TALKING.
HERE, ARIMA, SAY "AH!" ♡
?!
WHAT'RE YOU TRYING TO DO? STOP! I DON'T WANT IT!
COME ON NOW, JUST SAY "AH!"
NO!
WAAAH! WHAT THE?
HIDEAKI, YOU IDIOT! LET ME GO!
AAAAAAAAAHHH!
NO!
MPFH.

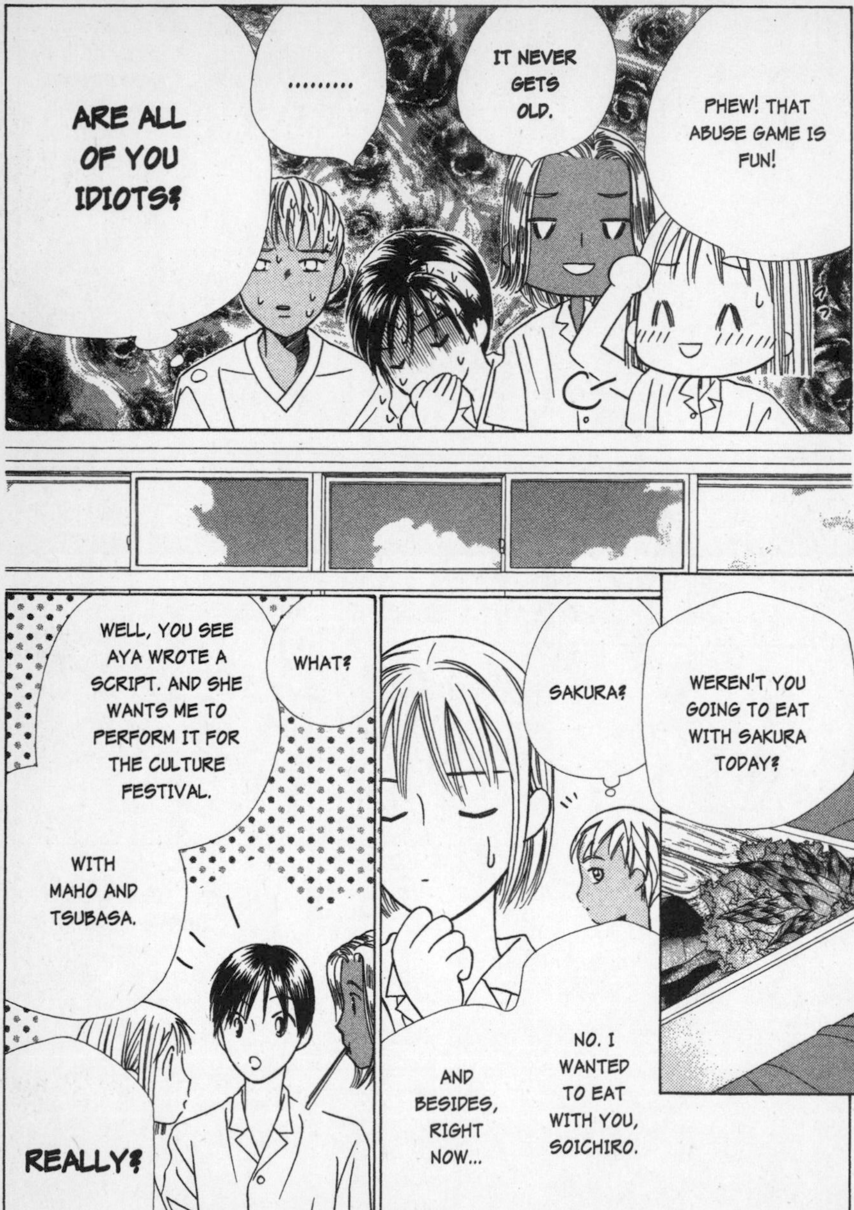
PHEW! THAT ABUSE GAME IS FUN!
IT NEVER GETS OLD.
....
ARE ALL OF YOU IDIOTS?
WEREN'T YOU GOING TO EAT WITH SAKURA TODAY?
SAKURA?
NO. I WANTED TO EAT WITH YOU, SOICHIRO.
AND BESIDES, RIGHT NOW...
WHAT?
WELL, YOU SEE AYA WROTE A SCRIPT. AND SHE WANTS ME TO PERFORM IT FOR THE CULTURE FESTIVAL.
WITH MAHO AND TSUBASA.
REALLY?

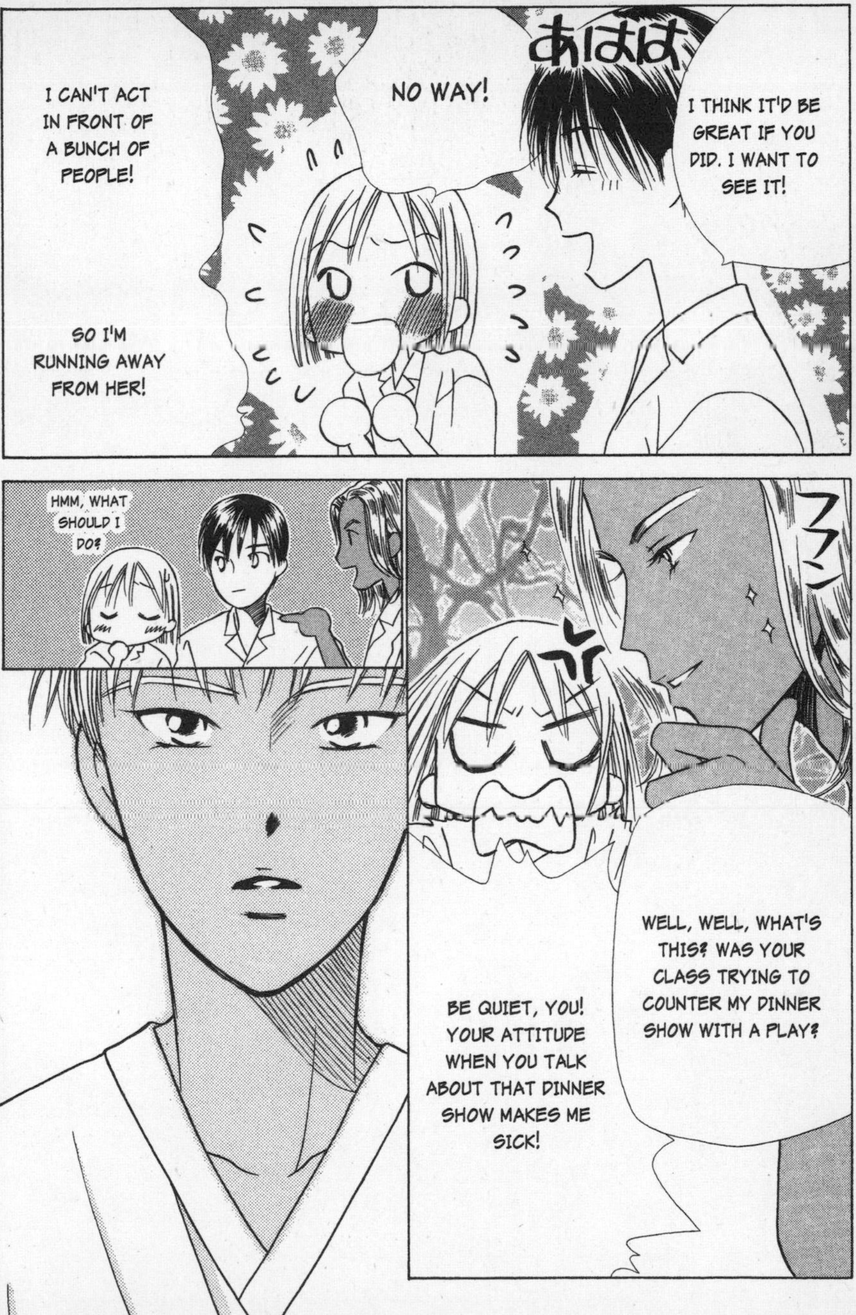
あはは
I THINK IT'D BE GREAT IF YOU DID. I WANT TO SEE IT!
NO WAY!
I CAN'T ACT IN FRONT OF A BUNCH OF PEOPLE!
SO I'M RUNNING AWAY FROM HER!
フフン
WELL, WELL, WHAT'S THIS? WAS YOUR CLASS TRYING TO COUNTER MY DINNER SHOW WITH A PLAY?
BE QUIET, YOU! YOUR ATTITUDE WHEN YOU TALK ABOUT THAT DINNER SHOW MAKES ME SICK!
HMM, WHAT SHOULD I DO?

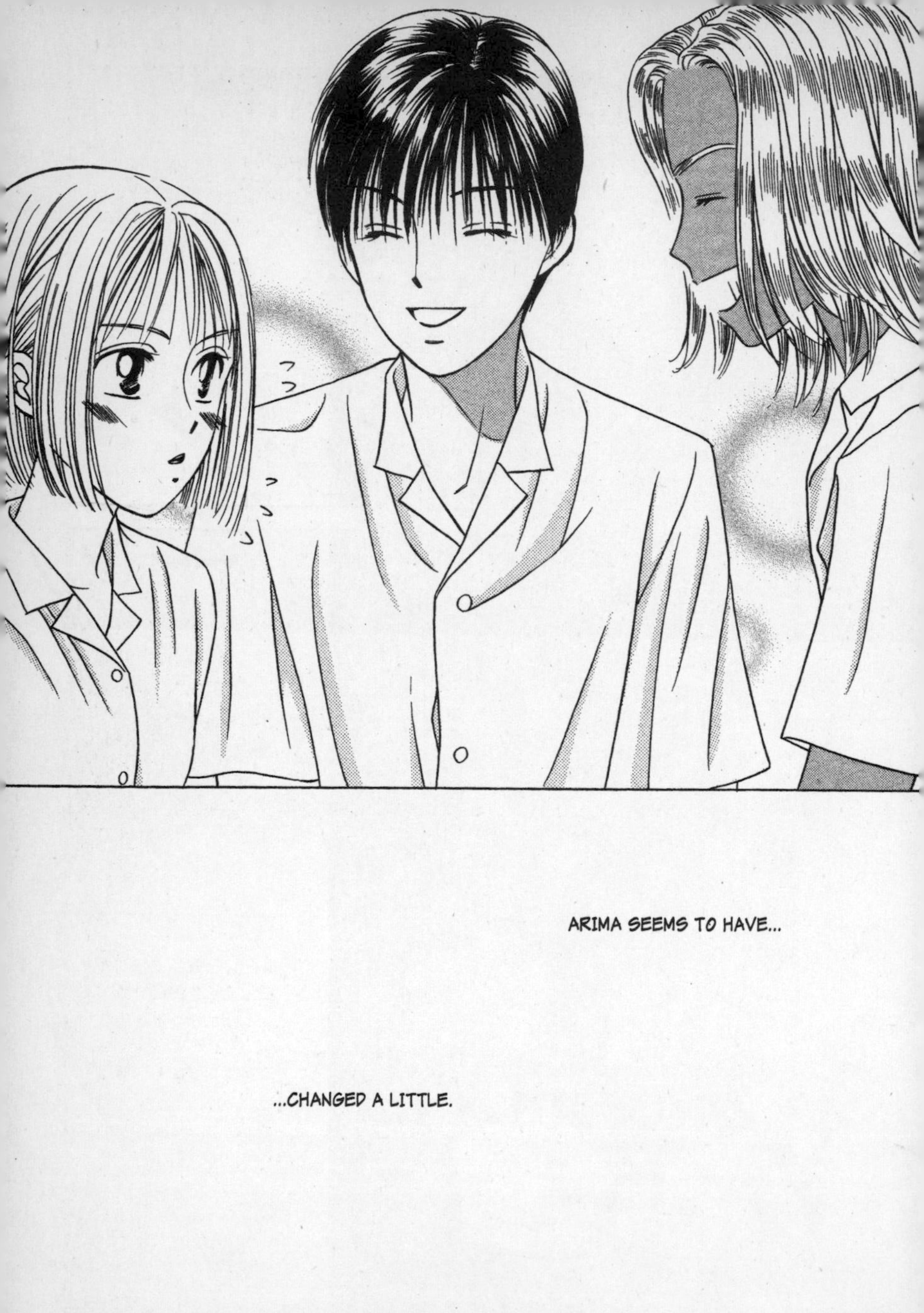
ARIMA SEEMS TO HAVE...
...CHANGED A LITTLE.

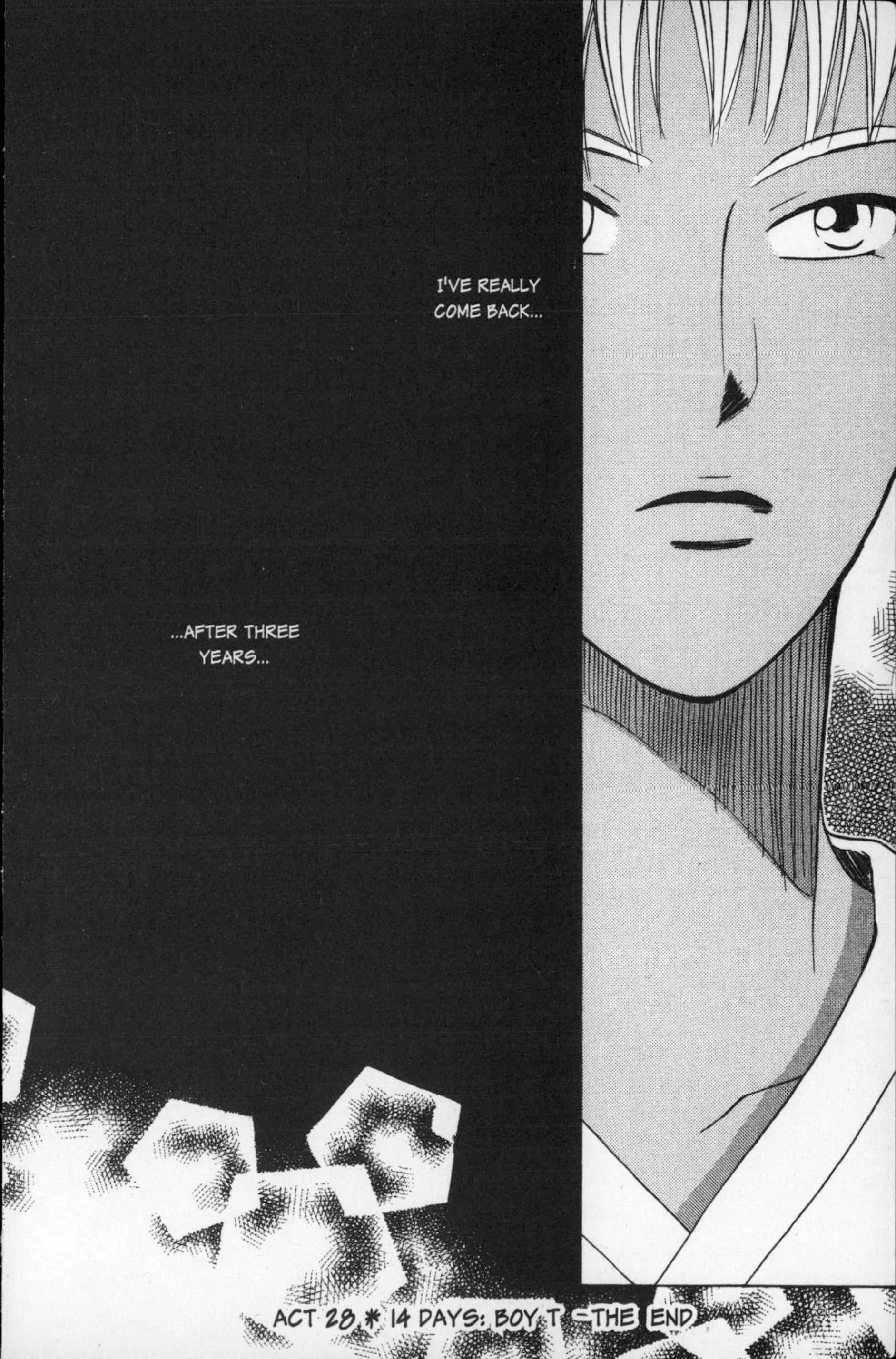
I'VE REALLY COME BACK...
...AFTER THREE YEARS...
ACT 28 * 14 DAYS: BOY T -THE END

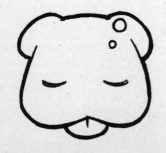

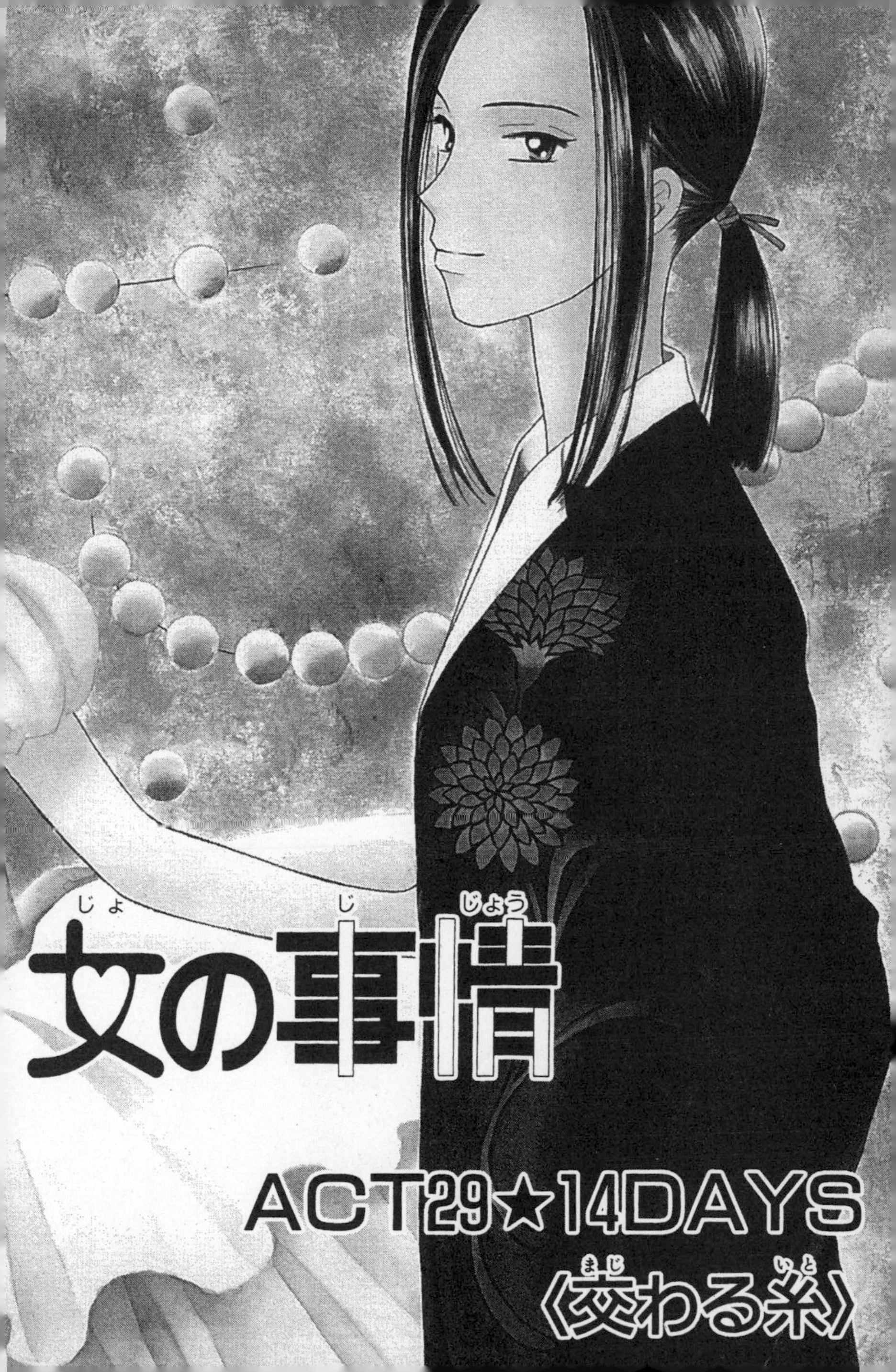
女の事情
ACT29★14DAYS
《交わる糸》

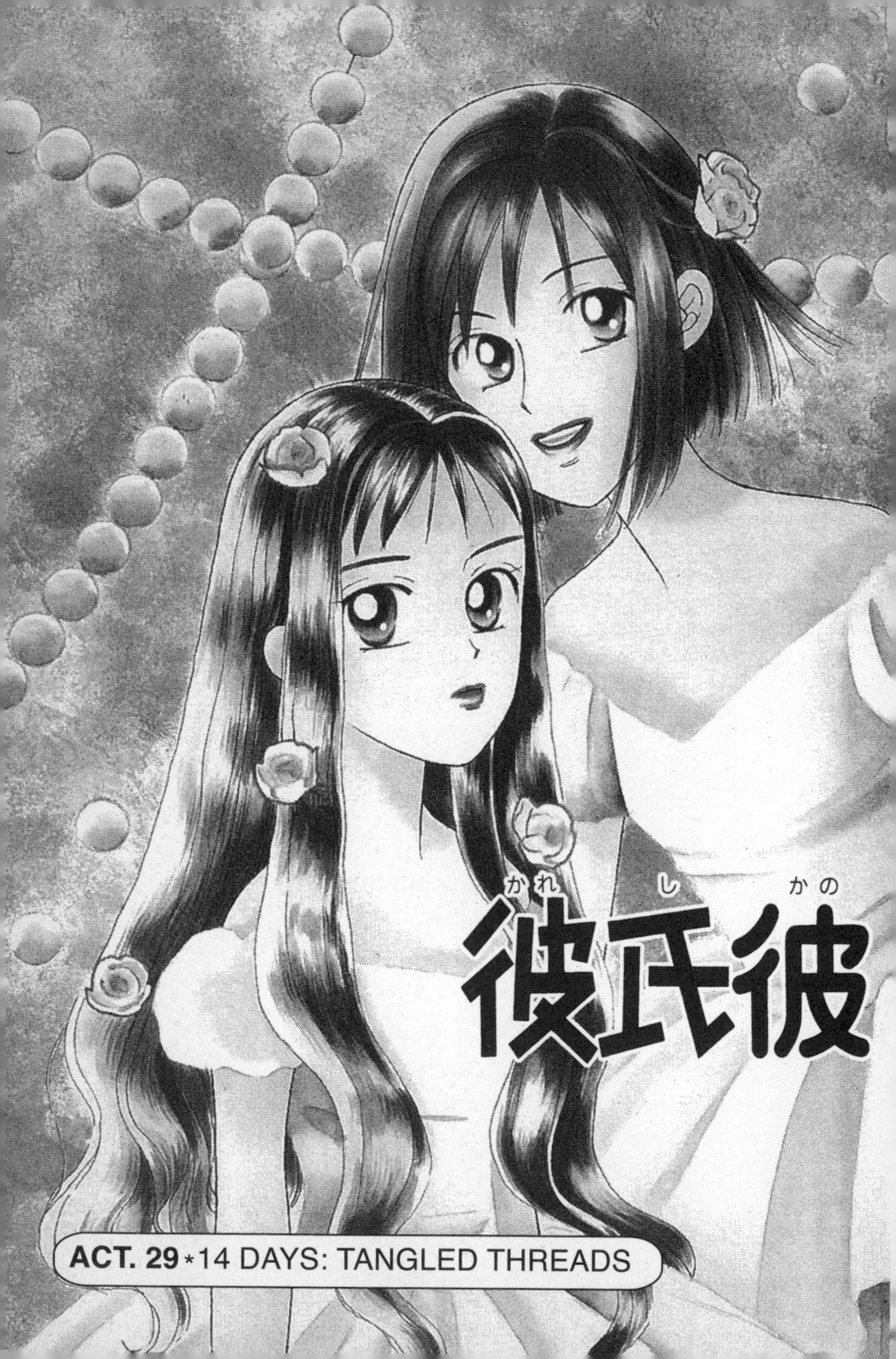
かれ し かの
彼氏彼
ACT. 29 * 14 DAYS: TANGLED THREADS

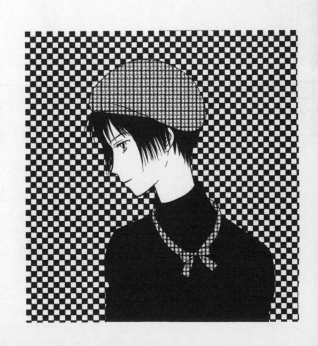

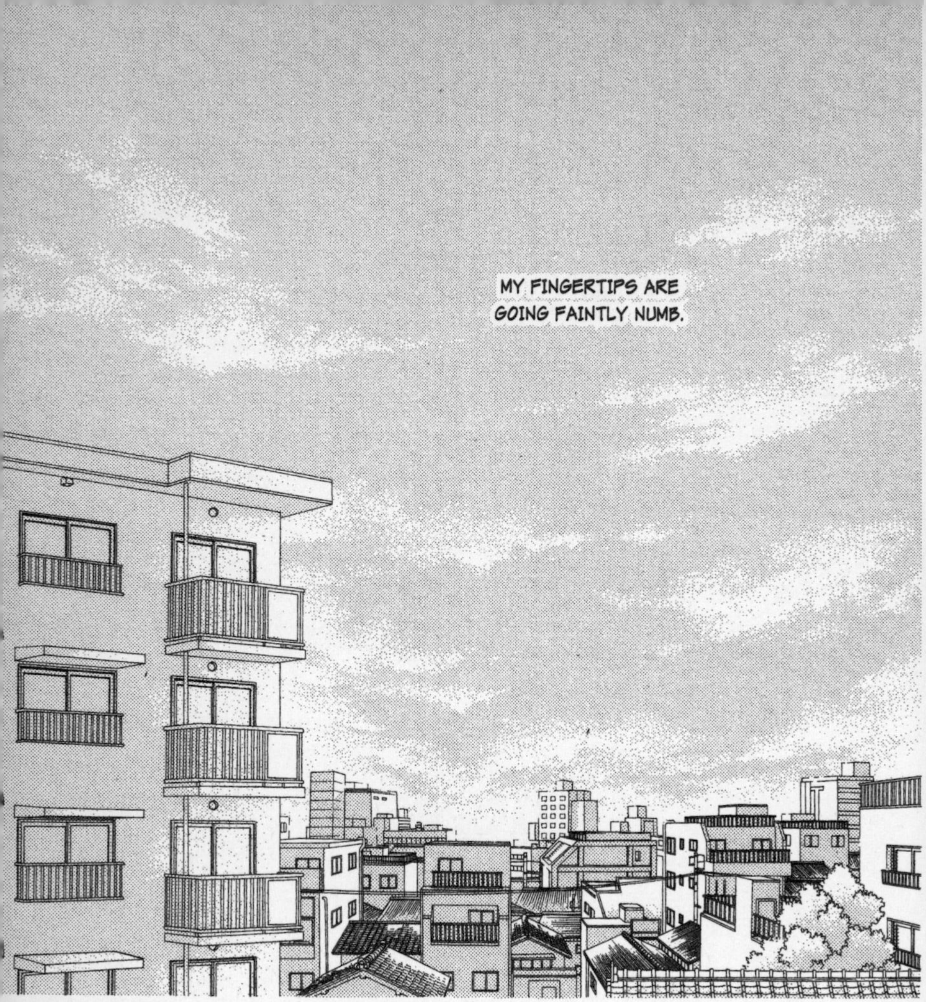
MY FINGERTIPS ARE GOING FAINTLY NUMB.

About Music...

I SEEM TO REALLY LIKE ELECTRIC GROOVE. IT'S SO COOL! JUST AMAZING! REALLY COOL!

I LOVE THE ALBUMS "ORANGE" AND "KARATEKA."

AND THERE'S A CERTAIN OTHER BAND THAT I LIKE SO MUCH...

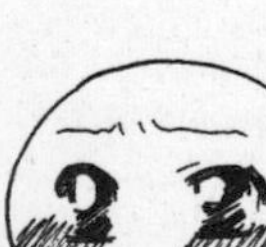

...THAT I GET LIKE THIS PICTURE!

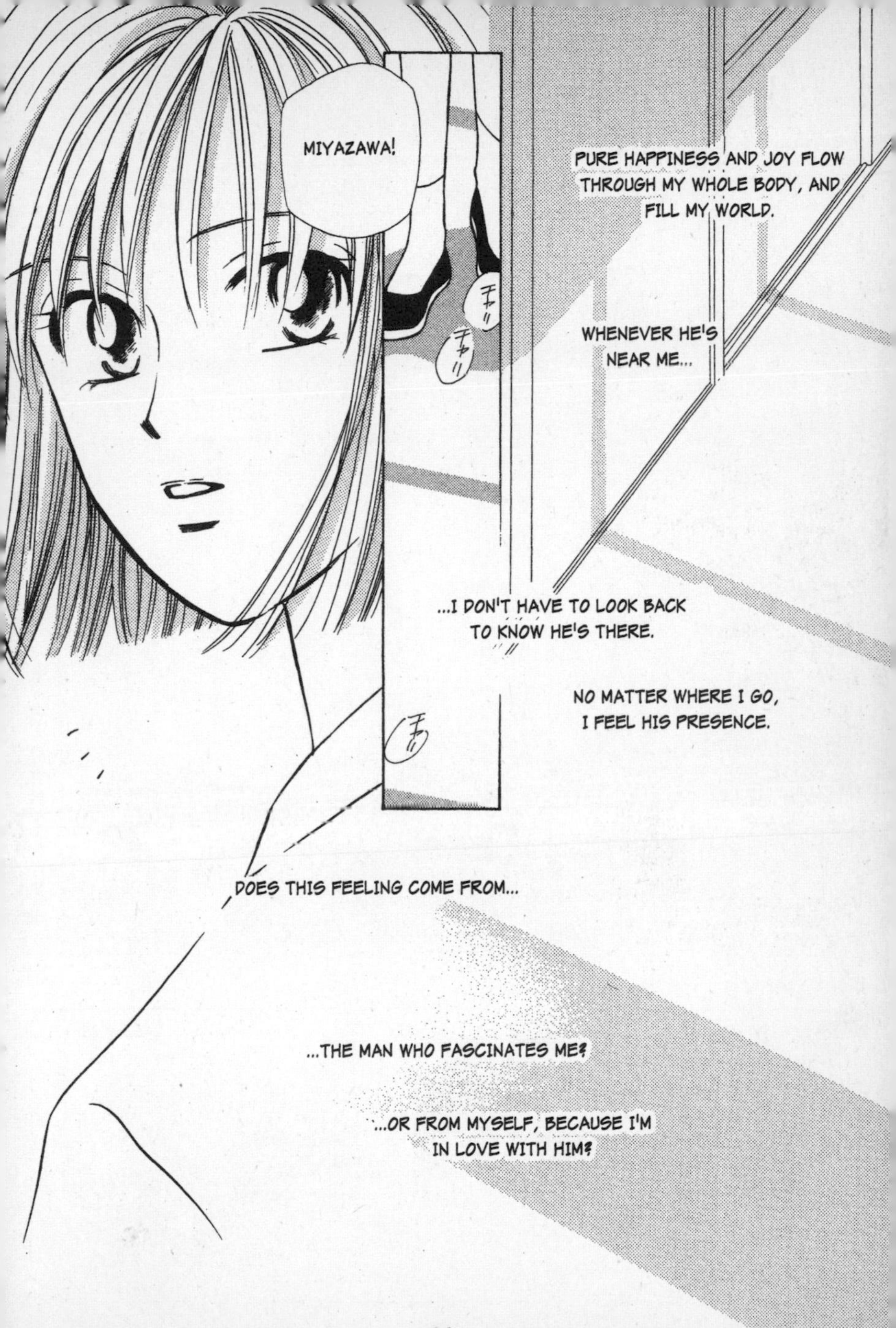
PURE HAPPINESS AND JOY FLOW THROUGH MY WHOLE BODY, AND FILL MY WORLD.
MIYAZAWA!
WHENEVER HE'S NEAR ME...
...I DON'T HAVE TO LOOK BACK TO KNOW HE'S THERE.
NO MATTER WHERE I GO, I FEEL HIS PRESENCE.
DOES THIS FEELING COME FROM...
...THE MAN WHO FASCINATES ME?
...OR FROM MYSELF, BECAUSE I'M IN LOVE WITH HIM?

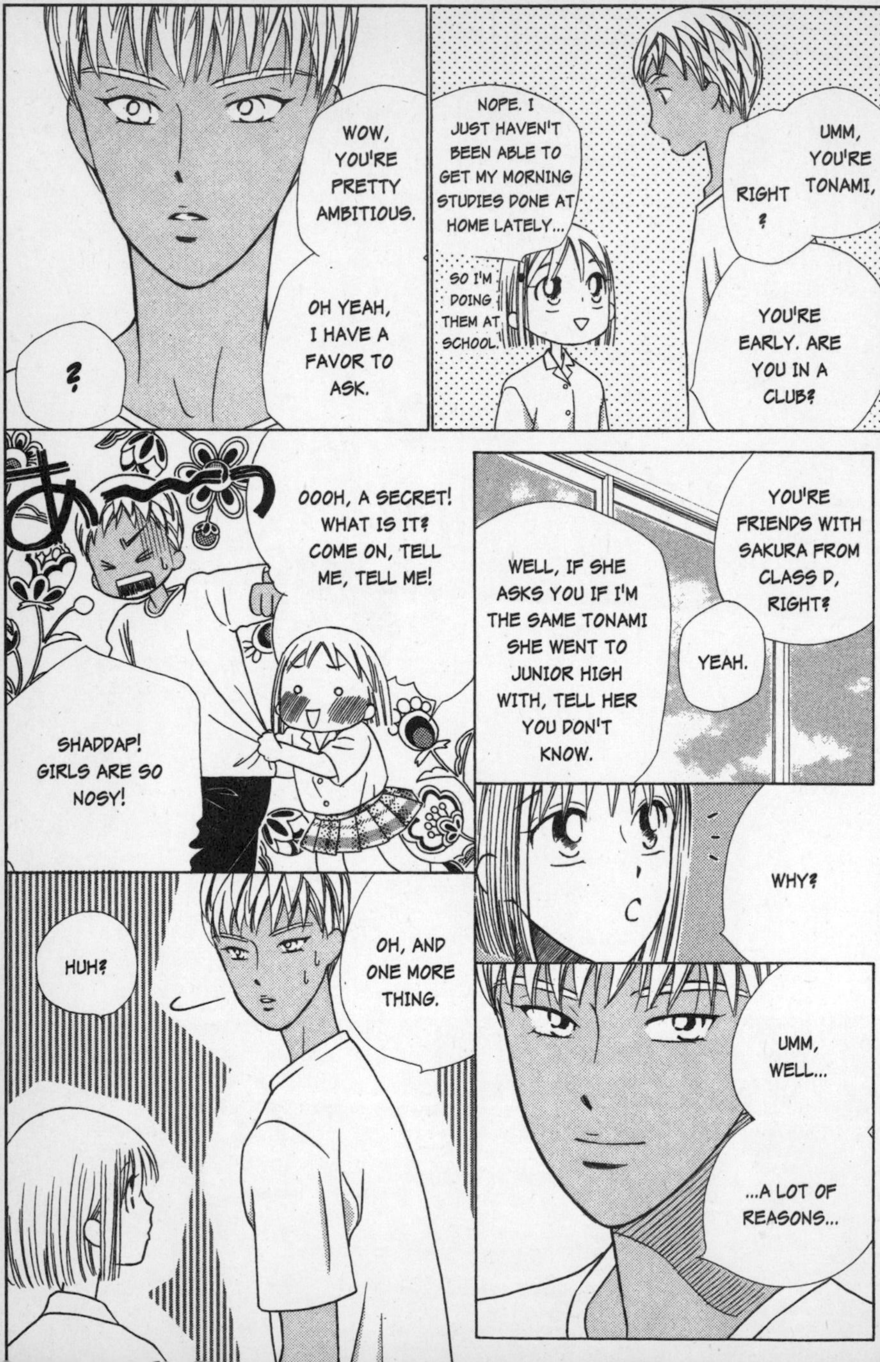
UMM, YOU'RE TONAMI, RIGHT?
YOU'RE EARLY. ARE YOU IN A CLUB?
NOPE. I JUST HAVEN'T BEEN ABLE TO GET MY MORNING STUDIES DONE AT HOME LATELY...
SO I'M DOING THEM AT SCHOOL.
WOW, YOU'RE PRETTY AMBITIOUS.
OH YEAH, I HAVE A FAVOR TO ASK.
?
YOU'RE FRIENDS WITH SAKURA FROM CLASS D, RIGHT?
YEAH.
WELL, IF SHE ASKS YOU IF I'M THE SAME TONAMI SHE WENT TO JUNIOR HIGH WITH, TELL HER YOU DON'T KNOW.
WHY?
UMM, WELL...
...A LOT OF REASONS...
あ〜っ
OOOH, A SECRET! WHAT IS IT? COME ON, TELL ME, TELL ME!
SHADDAP! GIRLS ARE SO NOSY!
OH, AND ONE MORE THING.
HUH?

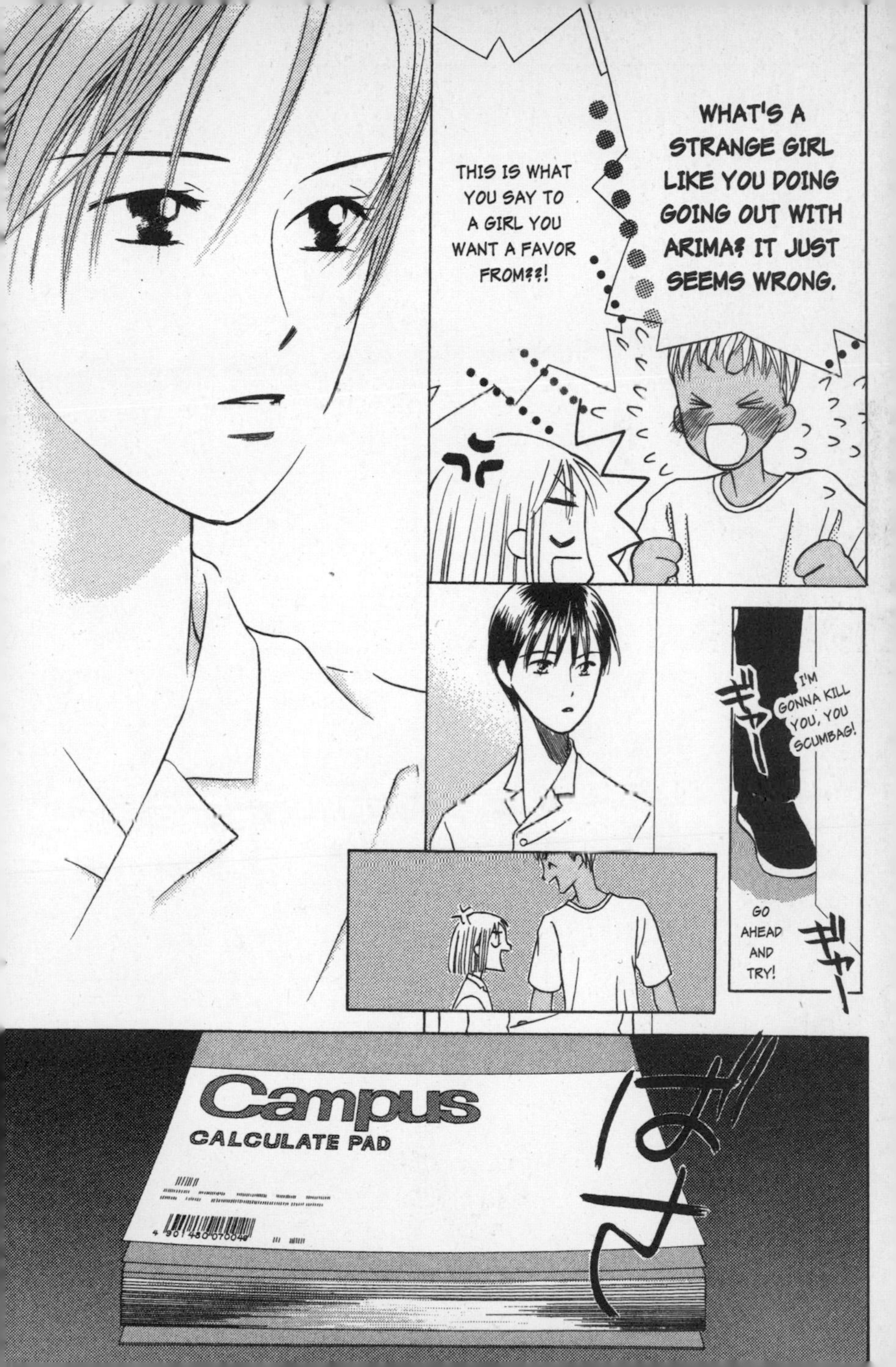
WHAT'S A STRANGE GIRL LIKE YOU DOING GOING OUT WITH ARIMA? IT JUST SEEMS WRONG.
THIS IS WHAT YOU SAY TO A GIRL YOU WANT A FAVOR FROM??!
ギャー
I'M GONNA KILL YOU, YOU SCUMBAG!
ギャー
GO AHEAD AND TRY!
Campus
CALCULATE PAD
ばさ

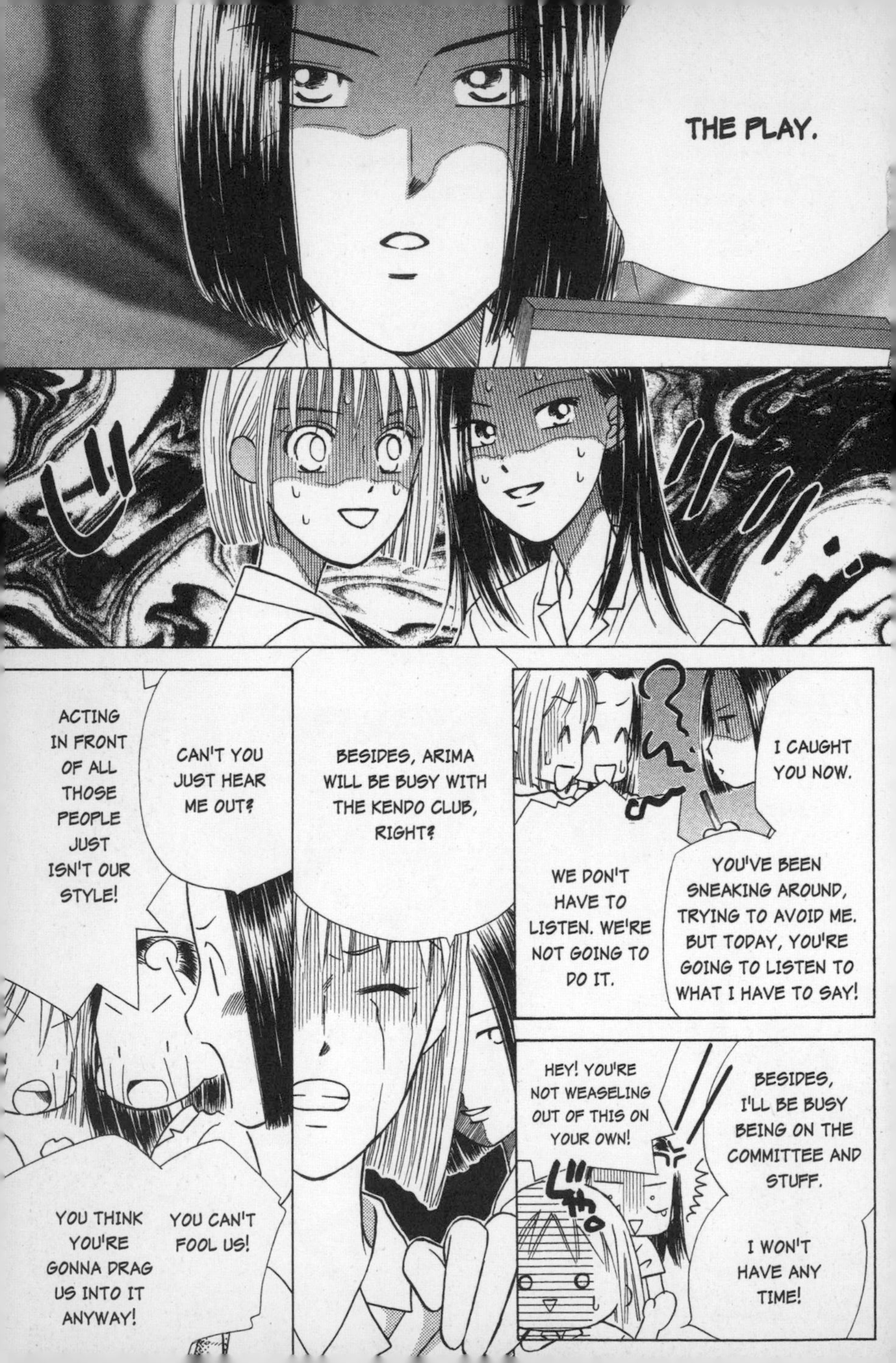
THE PLAY.
I CAUGHT YOU NOW.
YOU'VE BEEN SNEAKING AROUND, TRYING TO AVOID ME. BUT TODAY, YOU'RE GOING TO LISTEN TO WHAT I HAVE TO SAY!
WE DON'T HAVE TO LISTEN. WE'RE NOT GOING TO DO IT.
BESIDES, I'LL BE BUSY BEING ON THE COMMITTEE AND STUFF.
I WON'T HAVE ANY TIME!
HEY! YOU'RE NOT WEASELING OUT OF THIS ON YOUR OWN!
BESIDES, ARIMA WILL BE BUSY WITH THE KENDO CLUB, RIGHT?
CAN'T YOU JUST HEAR ME OUT?
ACTING IN FRONT OF ALL THOSE PEOPLE JUST ISN'T OUR STYLE!
YOU CAN'T FOOL US!
YOU THINK YOU'RE GONNA DRAG US INTO IT ANYWAY!

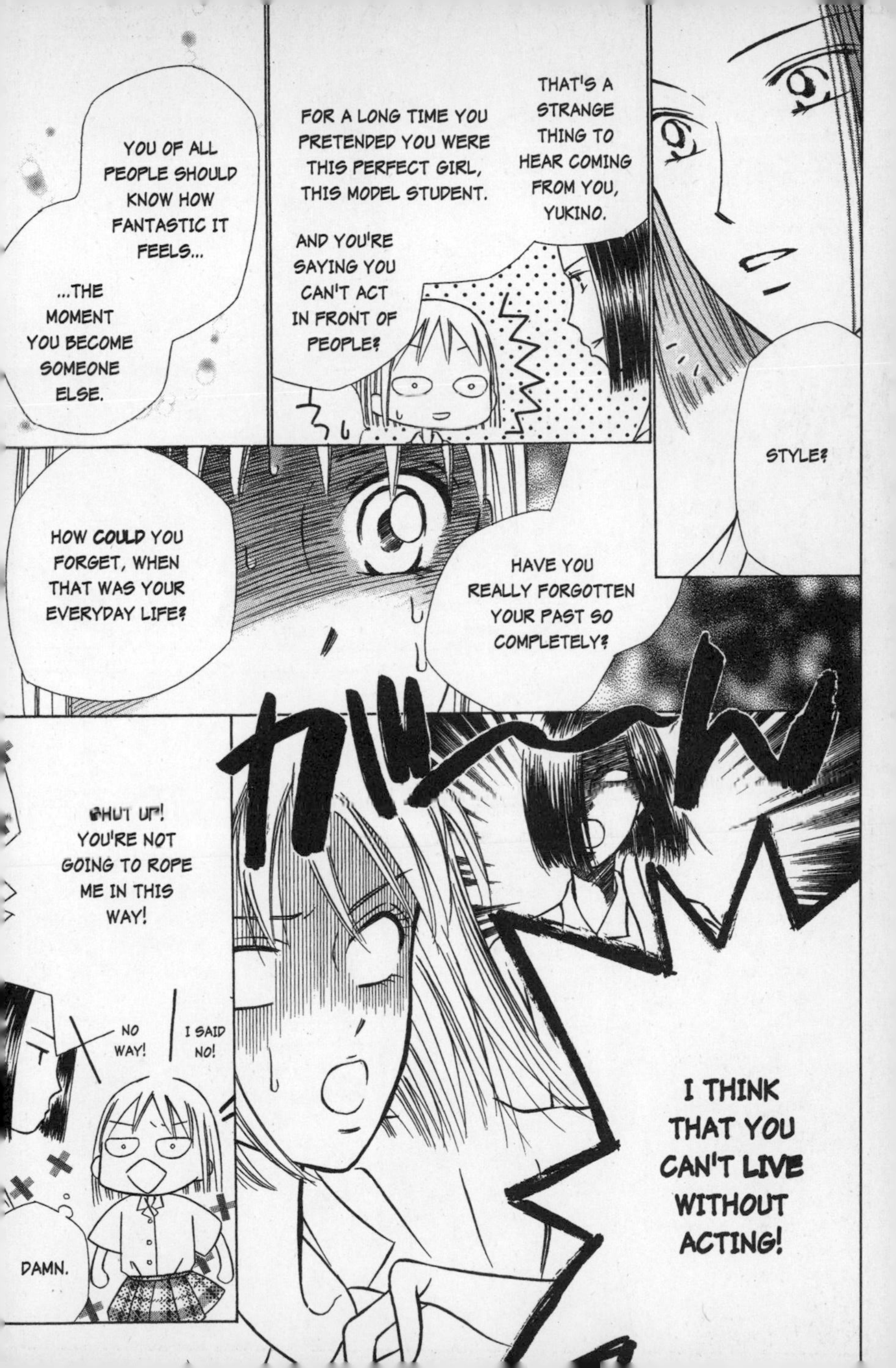
STYLE?
THAT'S A STRANGE THING TO HEAR COMING FROM YOU, YUKINO.
FOR A LONG TIME YOU PRETENDED YOU WERE THIS PERFECT GIRL, THIS MODEL STUDENT.
AND YOU'RE SAYING YOU CAN'T ACT IN FRONT OF PEOPLE?
YOU OF ALL PEOPLE SHOULD KNOW HOW FANTASTIC IT FEELS...
...THE MOMENT YOU BECOME SOMEONE ELSE.
HAVE YOU REALLY FORGOTTEN YOUR PAST SO COMPLETELY?
HOW COULD YOU FORGET, WHEN THAT WAS YOUR EVERYDAY LIFE?
I THINK THAT YOU CAN'T LIVE WITHOUT ACTING!
SHUT UP! YOU'RE NOT GOING TO ROPE ME IN THIS WAY!
I SAID NO!
NO WAY!
DAMN.

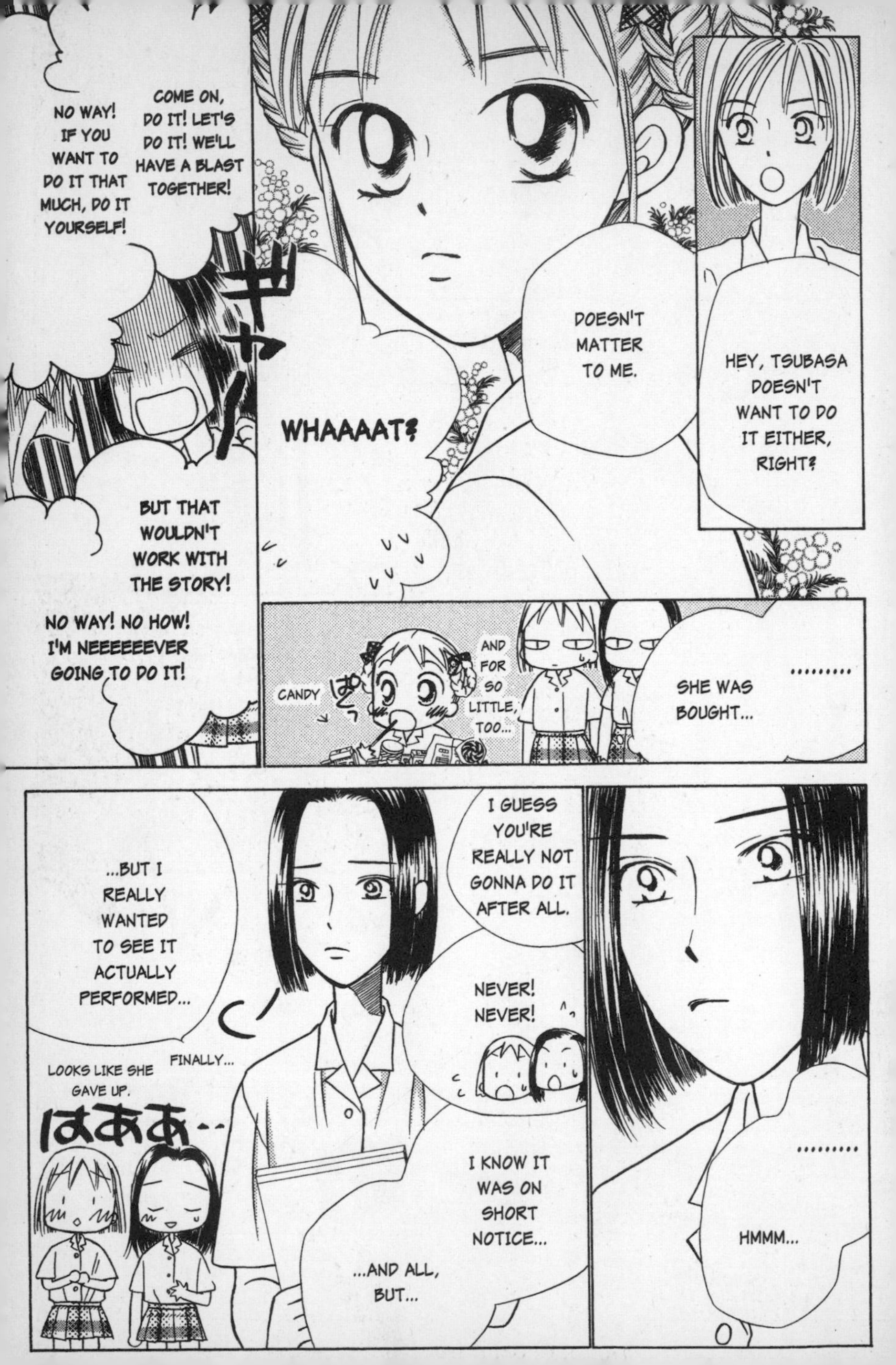
HEY, TSUBASA DOESN'T WANT TO DO IT EITHER, RIGHT?
DOESN'T MATTER TO ME.
WHAAAAT?
....
SHE WAS BOUGHT...
AND FOR SO LITTLE, TOO...
CANDY
COME ON, DO IT! LET'S DO IT! WE'LL HAVE A BLAST TOGETHER!
NO WAY! IF YOU WANT TO DO IT THAT MUCH, DO IT YOURSELF!
BUT THAT WOULDN'T WORK WITH THE STORY!
NO WAY! NO HOW! I'M NEEEEEEVER GOING TO DO IT!
....
HMMM...
I GUESS YOU'RE REALLY NOT GONNA DO IT AFTER ALL.
NEVER! NEVER!
...BUT I REALLY WANTED TO SEE IT ACTUALLY PERFORMED...
I KNOW IT WAS ON SHORT NOTICE...
...AND ALL, BUT...
FINALLY...
LOOKS LIKE SHE GAVE UP.
はあぁ‥

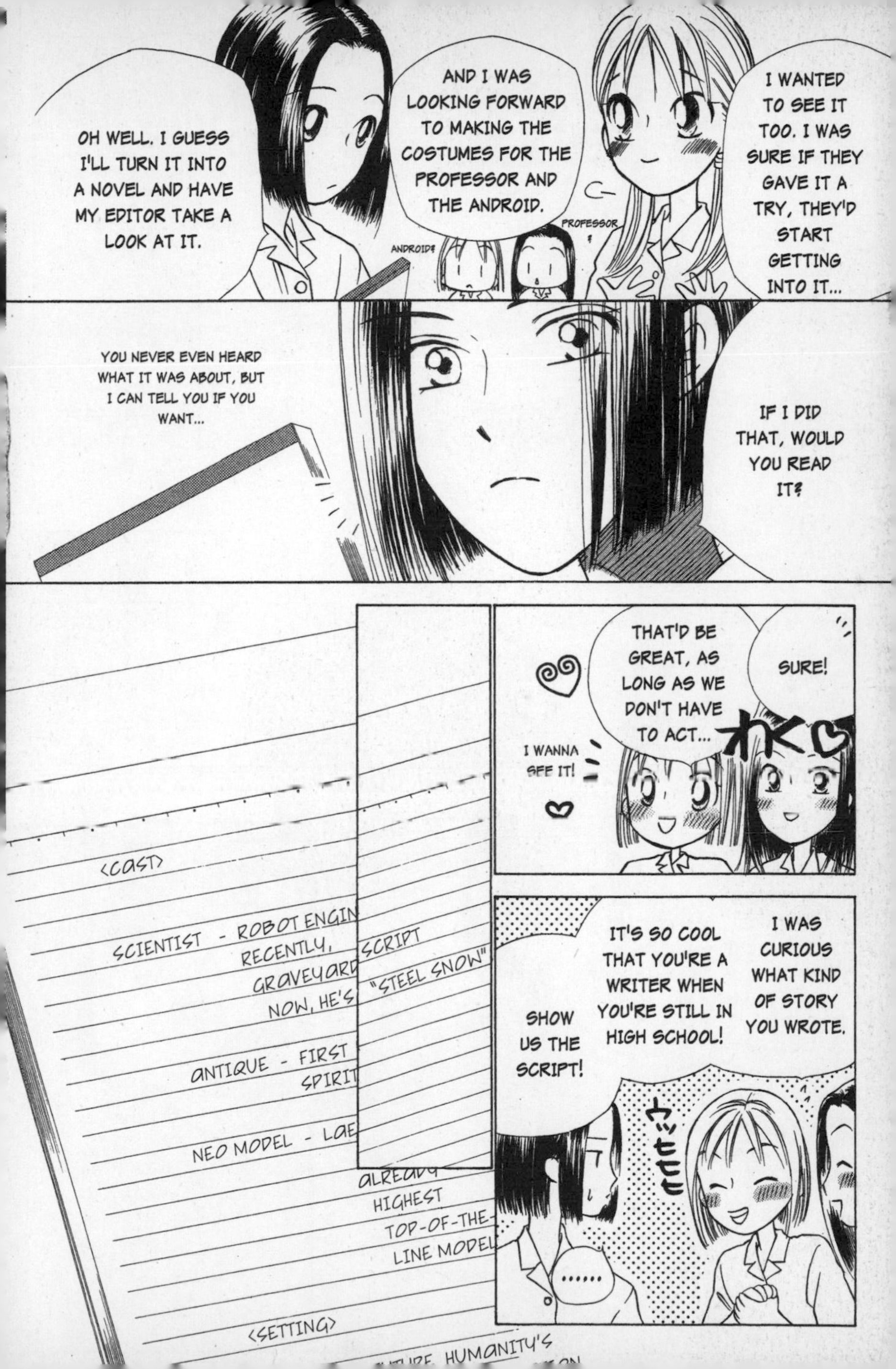

I WANTED TO SEE IT TOO. I WAS SURE IF THEY GAVE IT A TRY, THEY'D START GETTING INTO IT...
PROFESSOR?
AND I WAS LOOKING FORWARD TO MAKING THE COSTUMES FOR THE PROFESSOR AND THE ANDROID.
ANDROID?
OH WELL. I GUESS I'LL TURN IT INTO A NOVEL AND HAVE MY EDITOR TAKE A LOOK AT IT.
IF I DID THAT, WOULD YOU READ IT?
YOU NEVER EVEN HEARD WHAT IT WAS ABOUT, BUT I CAN TELL YOU IF YOU WANT...
SURE!
わく
THAT'D BE GREAT, AS LONG AS WE DON'T HAVE TO ACT...
I WANNA SEE IT!
I WAS CURIOUS WHAT KIND OF STORY YOU WROTE.
IT'S SO COOL THAT YOU'RE A WRITER WHEN YOU'RE STILL IN HIGH SCHOOL!
SHOW US THE SCRIPT!
ウッヒヒヒ
......
SCRIPT
"STEEL SNOW"
<CAST>
SCIENTIST - ROBOT ENGIN
RECENTLY,
GRAVEYARD
NOW, HE'S
ANTIQUE - FIRST
SPIRIT
NEO MODEL - LAE
ALREADY
HIGHEST
TOP-OF-THE-LINE MODEL
<SETTING>
HUMANITY'S

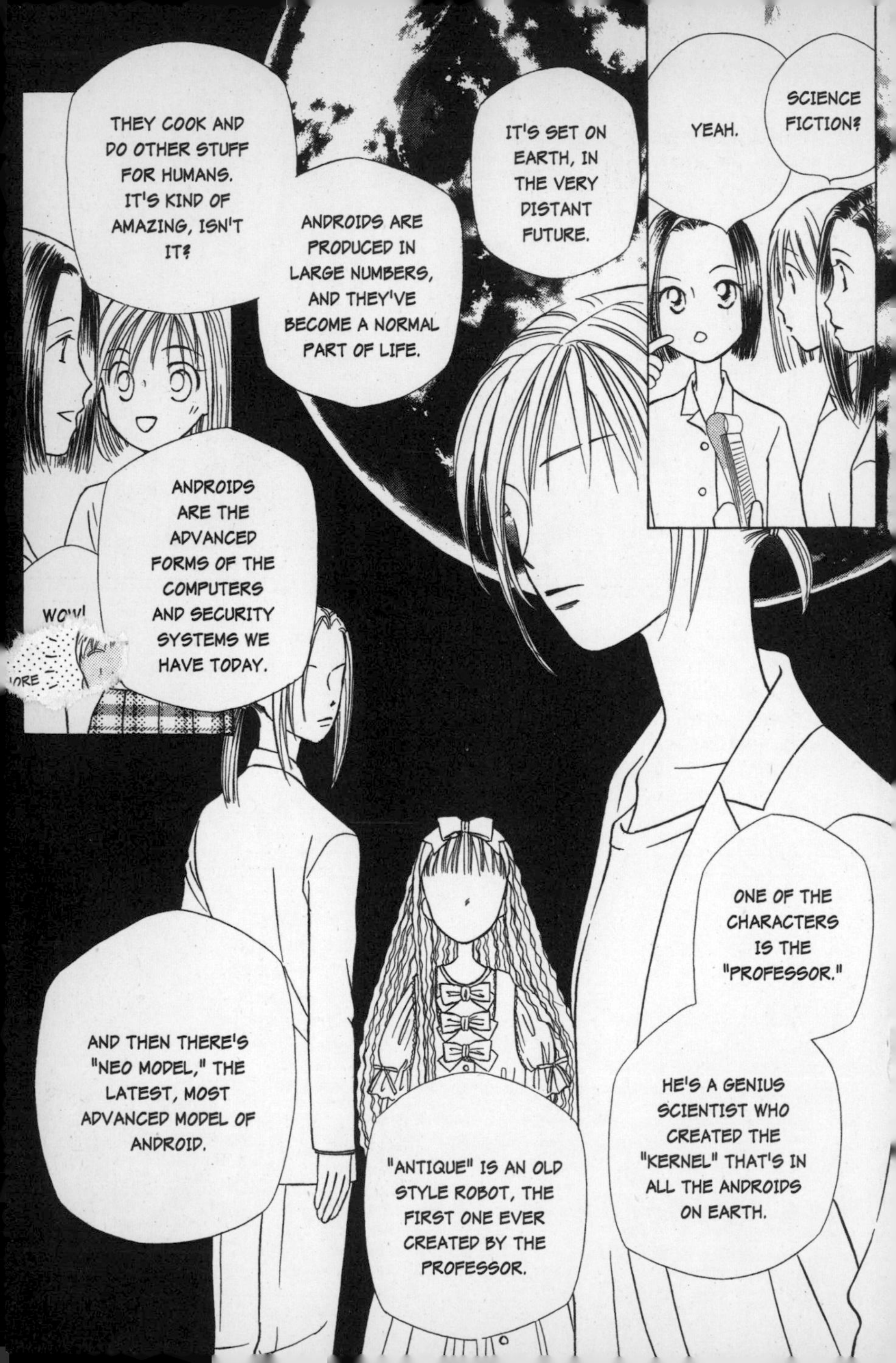
SCIENCE FICTION?
YEAH.
IT'S SET ON EARTH, IN THE VERY DISTANT FUTURE.
ANDROIDS ARE PRODUCED IN LARGE NUMBERS, AND THEY'VE BECOME A NORMAL PART OF LIFE.
ANDROIDS ARE THE ADVANCED FORMS OF THE COMPUTERS AND SECURITY SYSTEMS WE HAVE TODAY.
THEY COOK AND DO OTHER STUFF FOR HUMANS. IT'S KIND OF AMAZING, ISN'T IT?
WOW!
ONE OF THE CHARACTERS IS THE "PROFESSOR."
HE'S A GENIUS SCIENTIST WHO CREATED THE "KERNEL" THAT'S IN ALL THE ANDROIDS ON EARTH.
"ANTIQUE" IS AN OLD STYLE ROBOT, THE FIRST ONE EVER CREATED BY THE PROFESSOR.
AND THEN THERE'S "NEO MODEL," THE LATEST, MOST ADVANCED MODEL OF ANDROID.

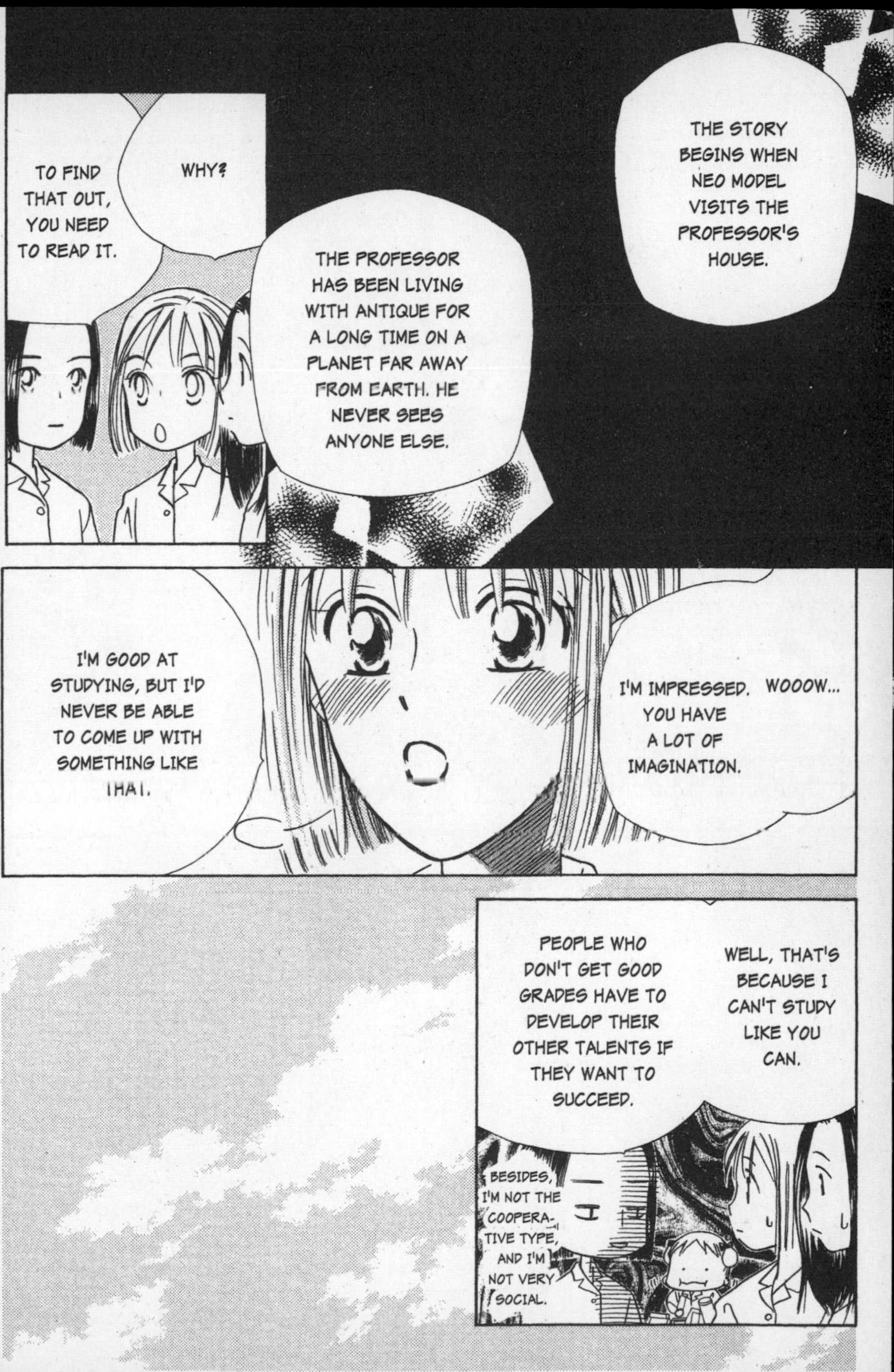
THE STORY BEGINS WHEN NEO MODEL VISITS THE PROFESSOR'S HOUSE.
THE PROFESSOR HAS BEEN LIVING WITH ANTIQUE FOR A LONG TIME ON A PLANET FAR AWAY FROM EARTH. HE NEVER SEES ANYONE ELSE.
WHY?
TO FIND THAT OUT, YOU NEED TO READ IT.
WOOOW...
I'M IMPRESSED. YOU HAVE A LOT OF IMAGINATION.
I'M GOOD AT STUDYING, BUT I'D NEVER BE ABLE TO COME UP WITH SOMETHING LIKE THAT.
WELL, THAT'S BECAUSE I CAN'T STUDY LIKE YOU CAN.
PEOPLE WHO DON'T GET GOOD GRADES HAVE TO DEVELOP THEIR OTHER TALENTS IF THEY WANT TO SUCCEED.
BESIDES, I'M NOT THE COOPERA-TIVE TYPE, AND I'M NOT VERY SOCIAL.

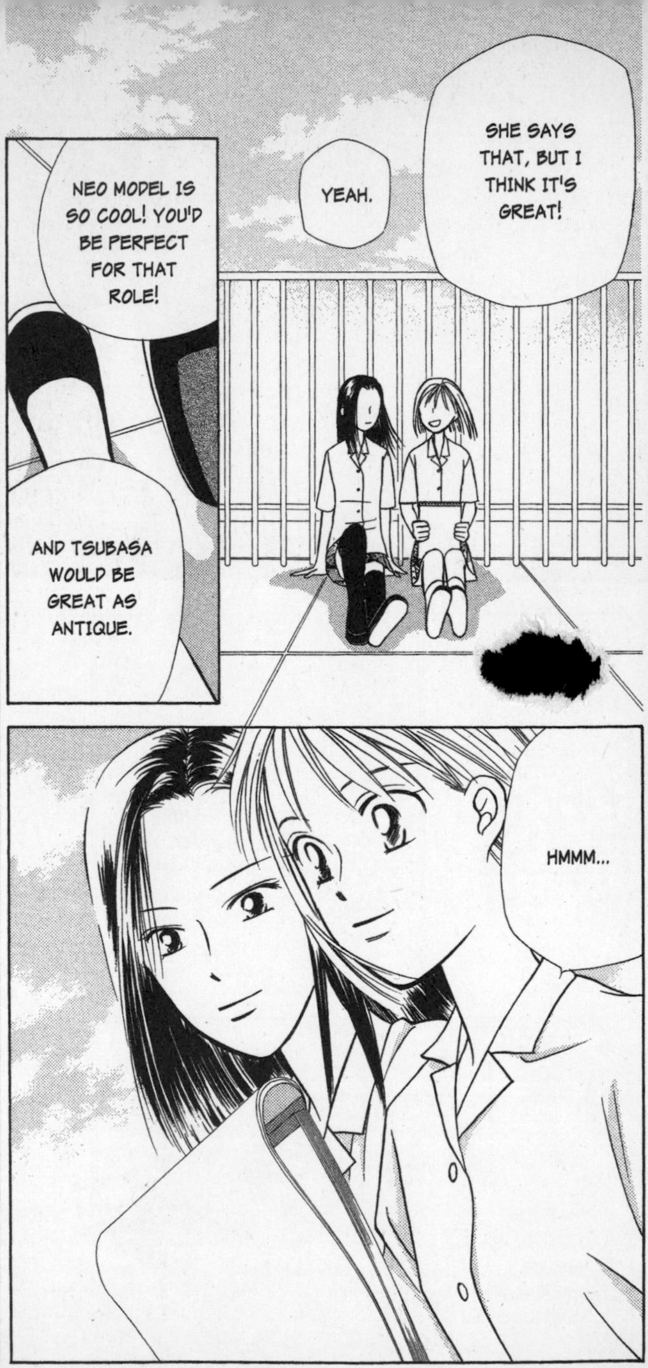
SHE SAYS THAT, BUT I THINK IT'S GREAT!
YEAH.
NEO MODEL IS SO COOL! YOU'D BE PERFECT FOR THAT ROLE!
AND TSUBASA WOULD BE GREAT AS ANTIQUE.
HMMM...

3

Whenever I eat bread, whether it's white bread or rice bread, or that kind with fruit in it, I put honey or sugar-free jelly on it.

And sometimes I'll take some leftover fried pork out of the refrigerator, slice it up in small pieces, and mix it in fried rice. It's delicious!

I really love thinking up things to cook like that.

I've become a real glutton lately, but...

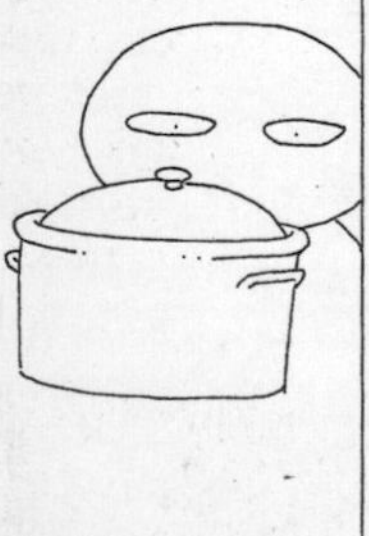

I just love eating delicious things!

♡

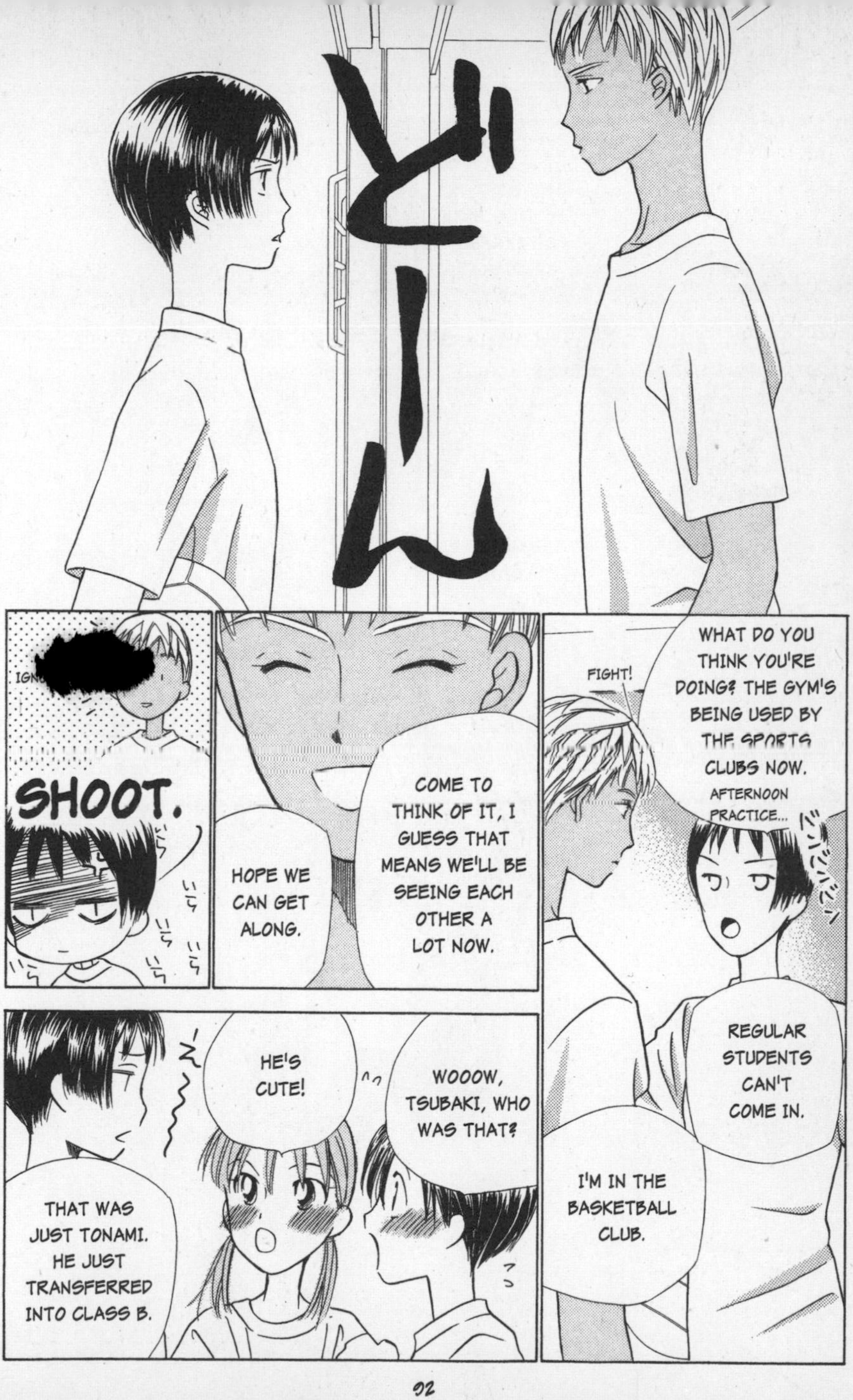
どーん
FIGHT!
WHAT DO YOU THINK YOU'RE DOING? THE GYM'S BEING USED BY THE SPORTS CLUBS NOW.
AFTERNOON PRACTICE...
REGULAR STUDENTS CAN'T COME IN.
I'M IN THE BASKETBALL CLUB.
COME TO THINK OF IT, I GUESS THAT MEANS WE'LL BE SEEING EACH OTHER A LOT NOW.
HOPE WE CAN GET ALONG.
IGN[redacted]
SHOOT.
WOOOW, TSUBAKI, WHO WAS THAT?
HE'S CUTE!
THAT WAS JUST TONAMI. HE JUST TRANSFERRED INTO CLASS B.

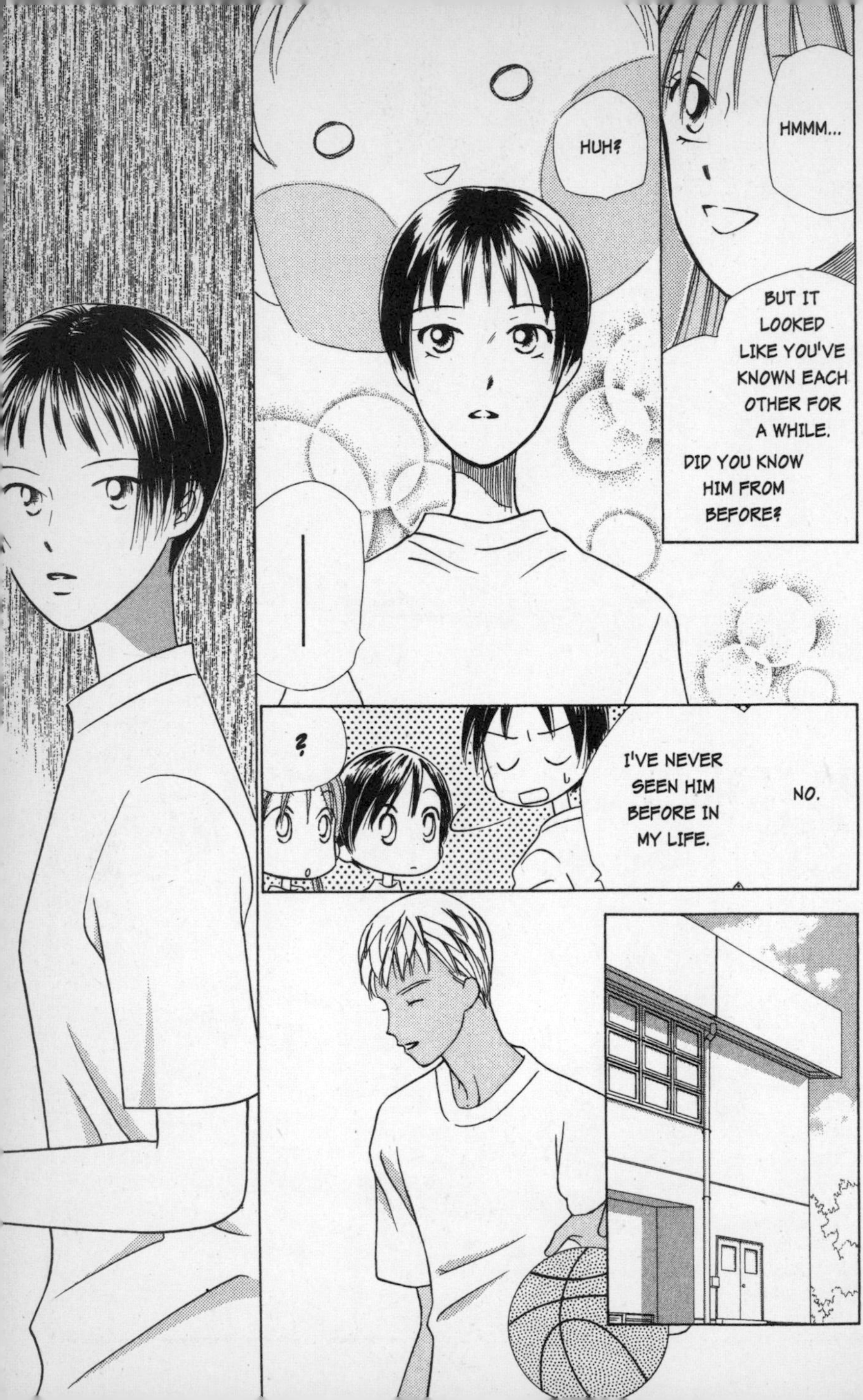
HMMM...
BUT IT LOOKED LIKE YOU'VE KNOWN EACH OTHER FOR A WHILE.
DID YOU KNOW HIM FROM BEFORE?
HUH?
NO.
I'VE NEVER SEEN HIM BEFORE IN MY LIFE.
?

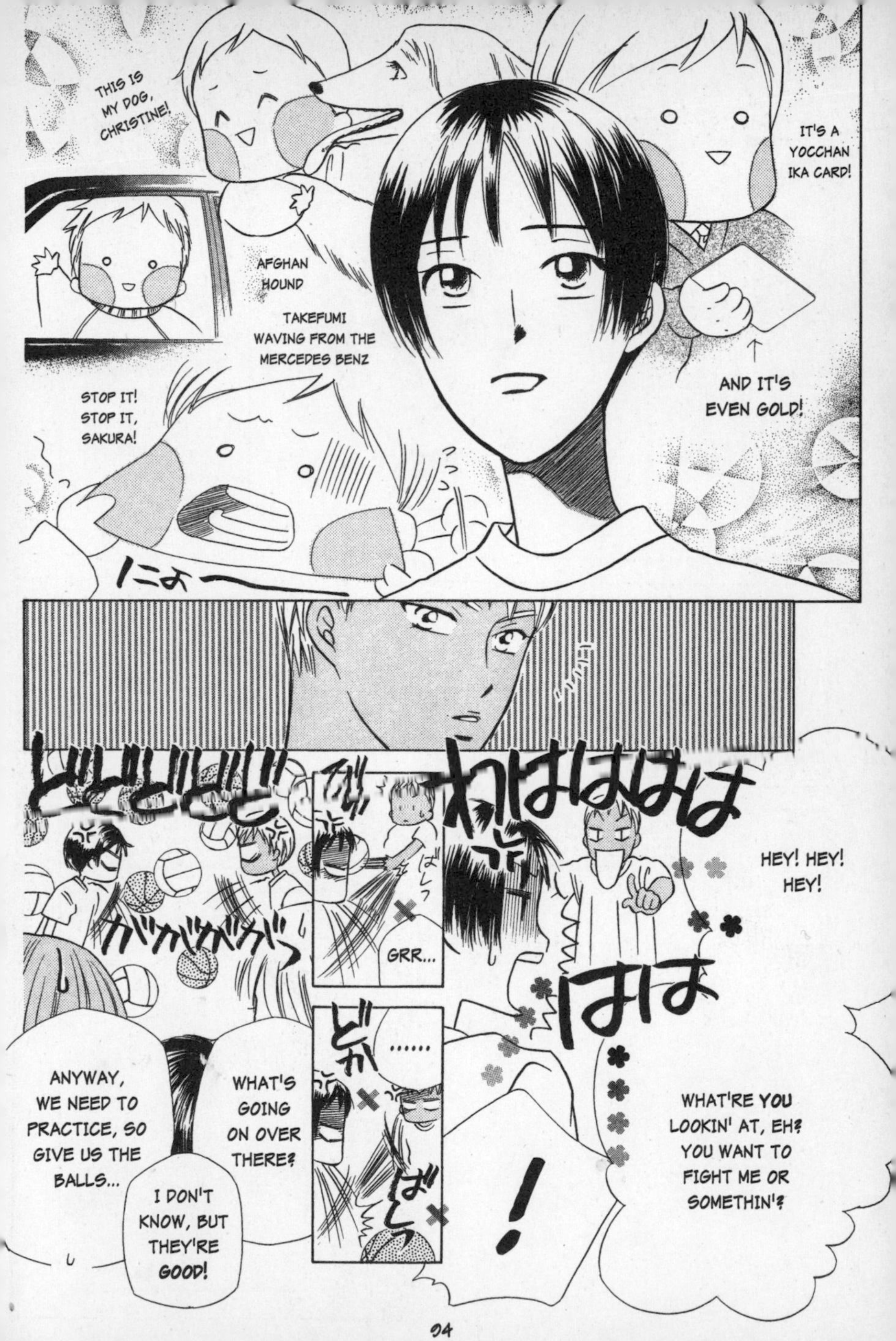
IT'S A YOCCHAN IKA CARD!
AND IT'S EVEN GOLD!
THIS IS MY DOG, CHRISTINE!
AFGHAN HOUND
TAKEFUMI WAVING FROM THE MERCEDES BENZ
STOP IT! STOP IT, SAKURA!
にょー
わはははは
HEY! HEY! HEY!
はは
WHAT'RE YOU LOOKIN' AT, EH? YOU WANT TO FIGHT ME OR SOMETHIN'?
!
ばしっ
GRR...
どが
......
ばしっ
WHAT'S GOING ON OVER THERE?
I DON'T KNOW, BUT THEY'RE GOOD!
ANYWAY, WE NEED TO PRACTICE, SO GIVE US THE BALLS...

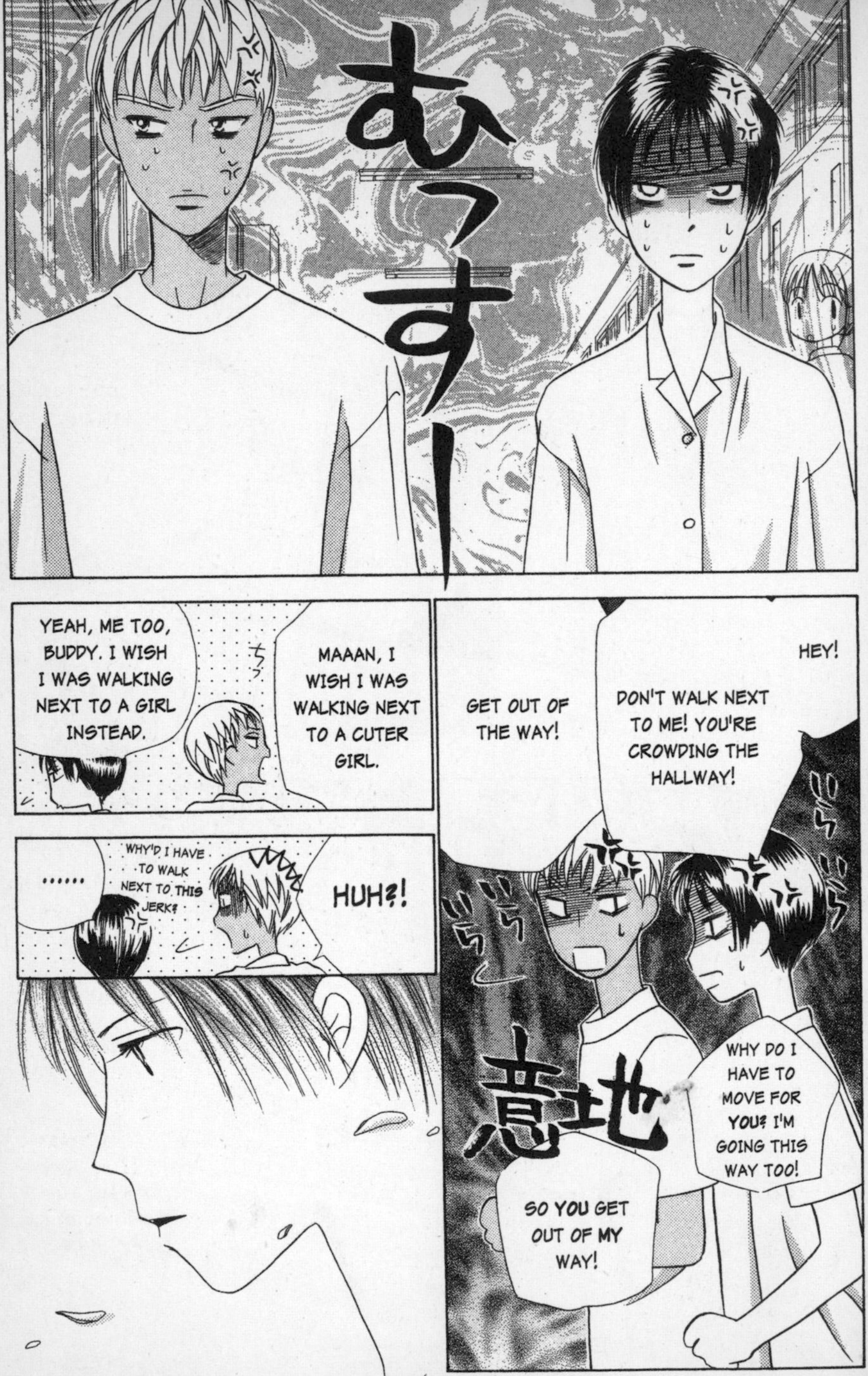
あつすー
HEY!
DON'T WALK NEXT TO ME! YOU'RE CROWDING THE HALLWAY!
GET OUT OF THE WAY!
いらいら
意地
WHY DO I HAVE TO MOVE FOR YOU? I'M GOING THIS WAY TOO!
SO YOU GET OUT OF MY WAY!
MAAAN, I WISH I WAS WALKING NEXT TO A CUTER GIRL.
YEAH, ME TOO, BUDDY. I WISH I WAS WALKING NEXT TO A GIRL INSTEAD.
HUH?!
WHY'D I HAVE TO WALK NEXT TO THIS JERK?
......

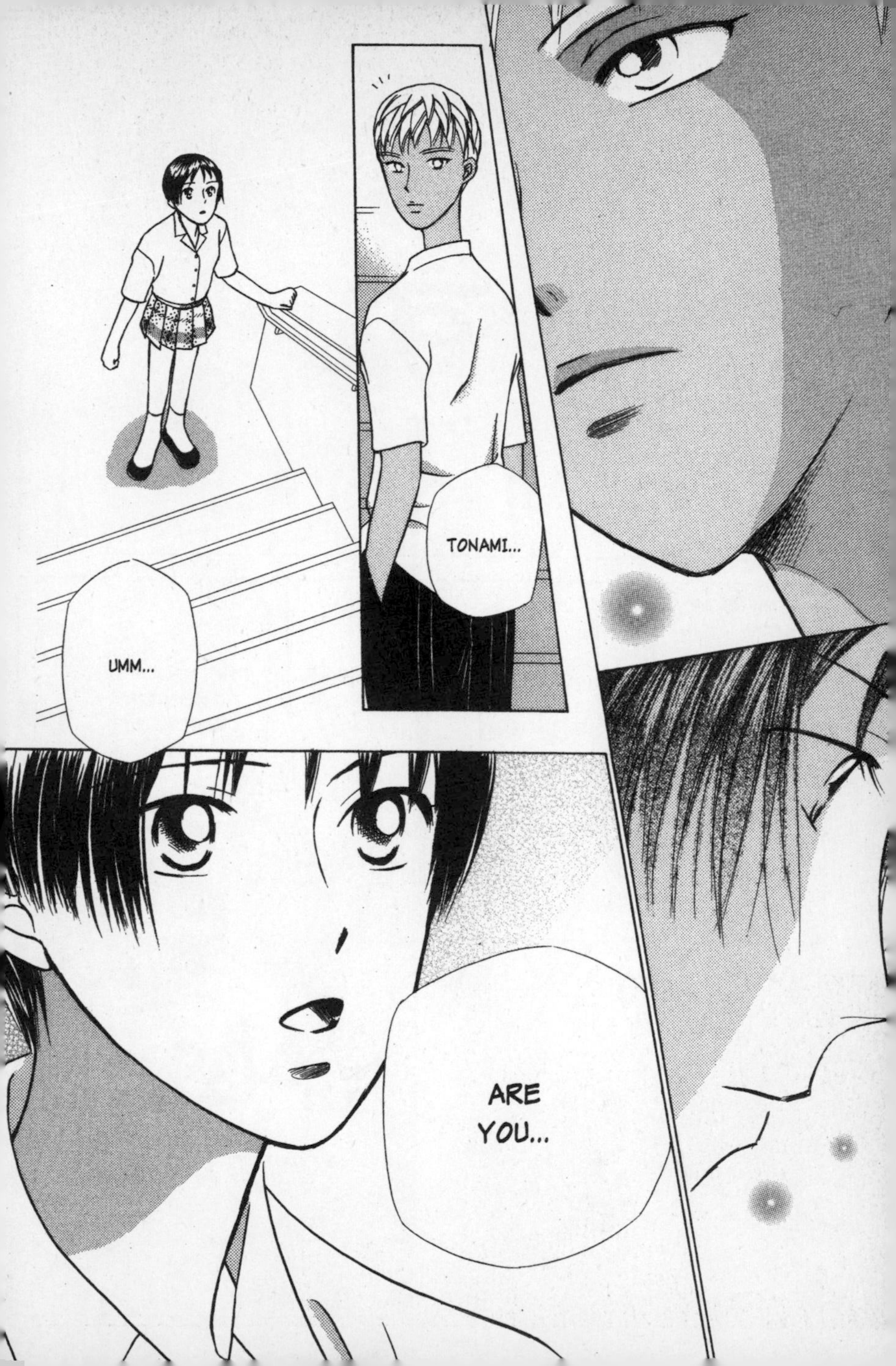
TONAMI...
UMM...
ARE YOU...

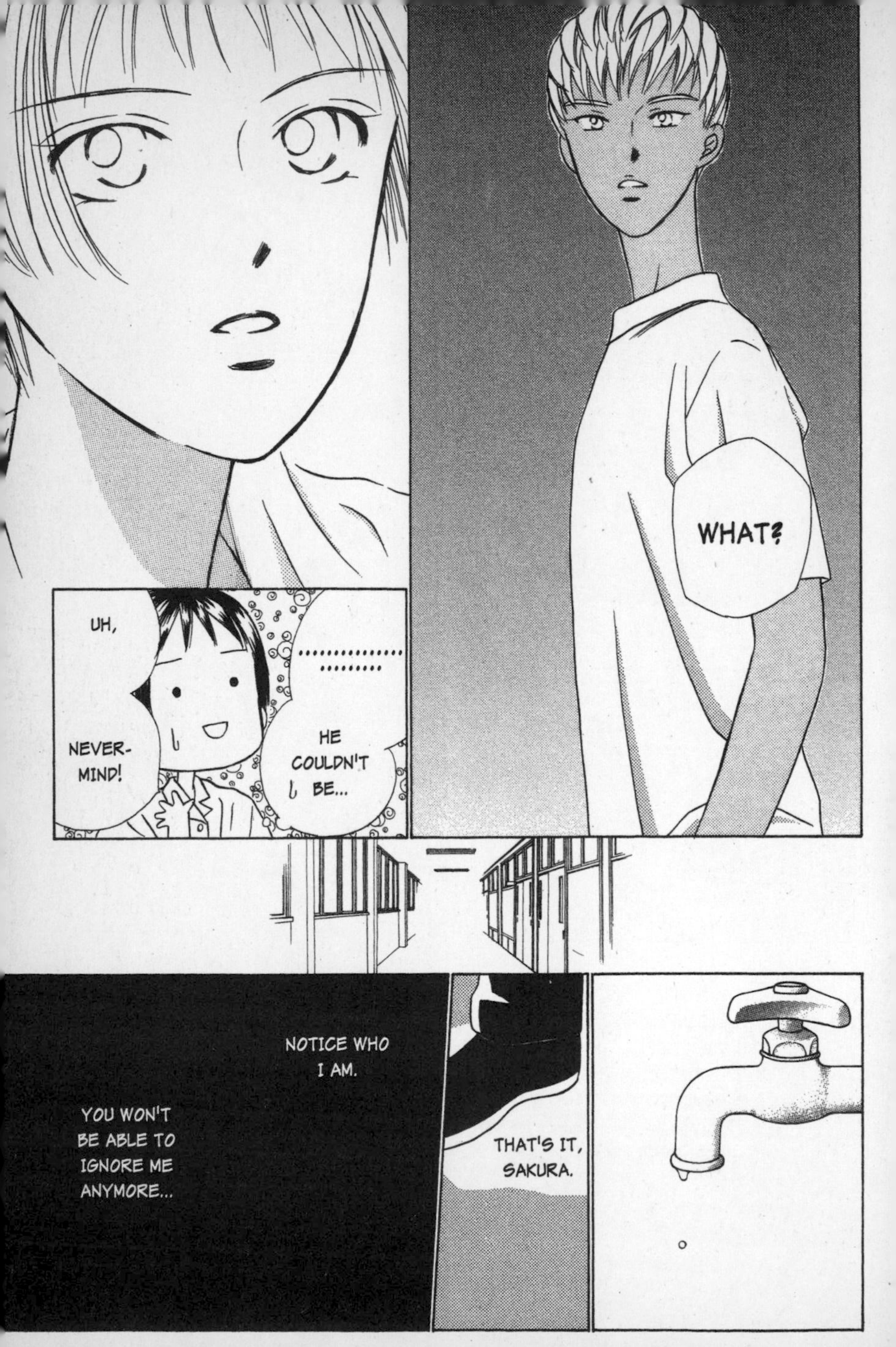
WHAT?
....
....
HE COULDN'T BE...
UH,
NEVER-MIND!
THAT'S IT, SAKURA.
NOTICE WHO I AM.
YOU WON'T BE ABLE TO IGNORE ME ANYMORE...

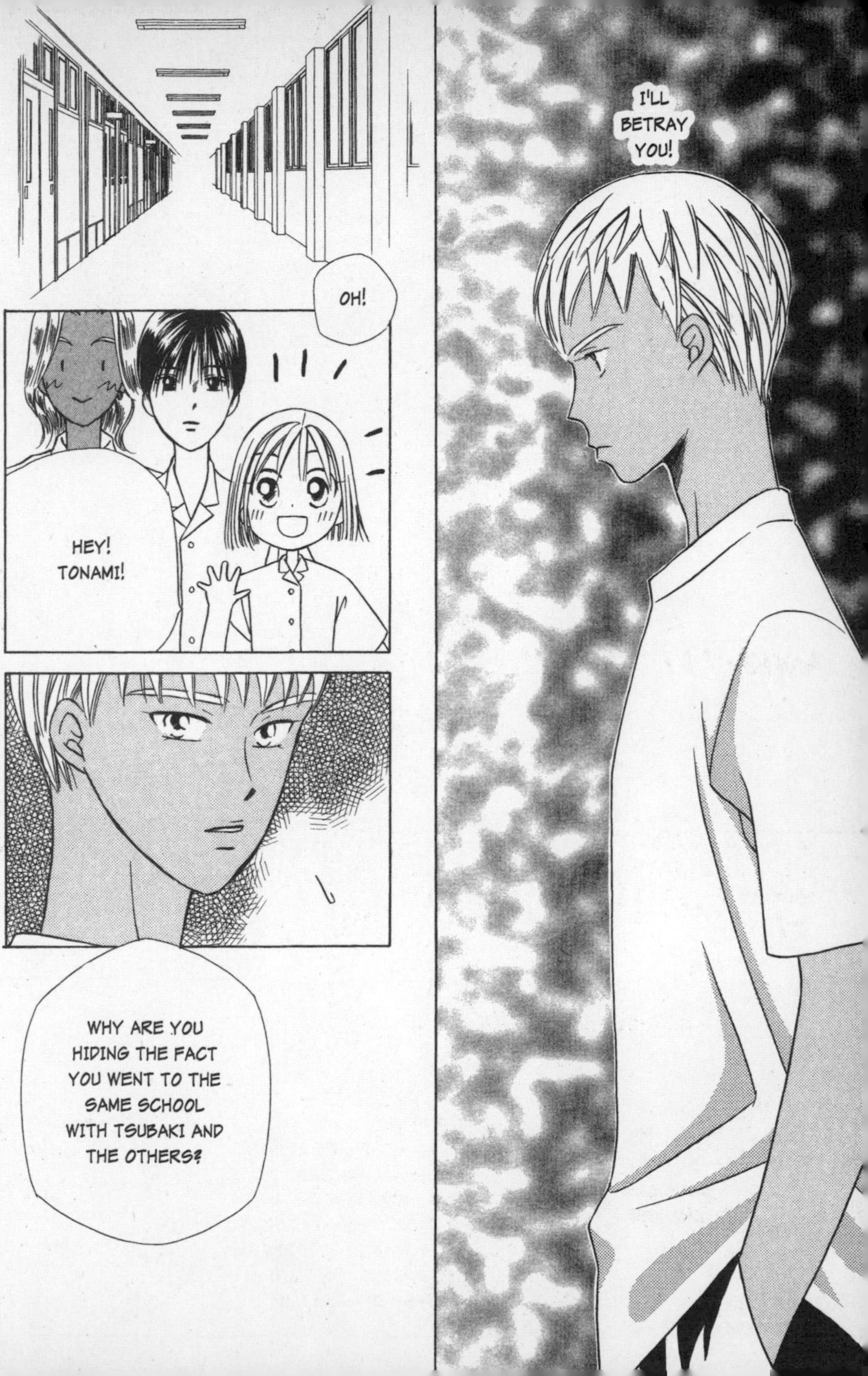
I'LL BETRAY YOU!
OH!
HEY! TONAMI!
WHY ARE YOU HIDING THE FACT YOU WENT TO THE SAME SCHOOL WITH TSUBAKI AND THE OTHERS?

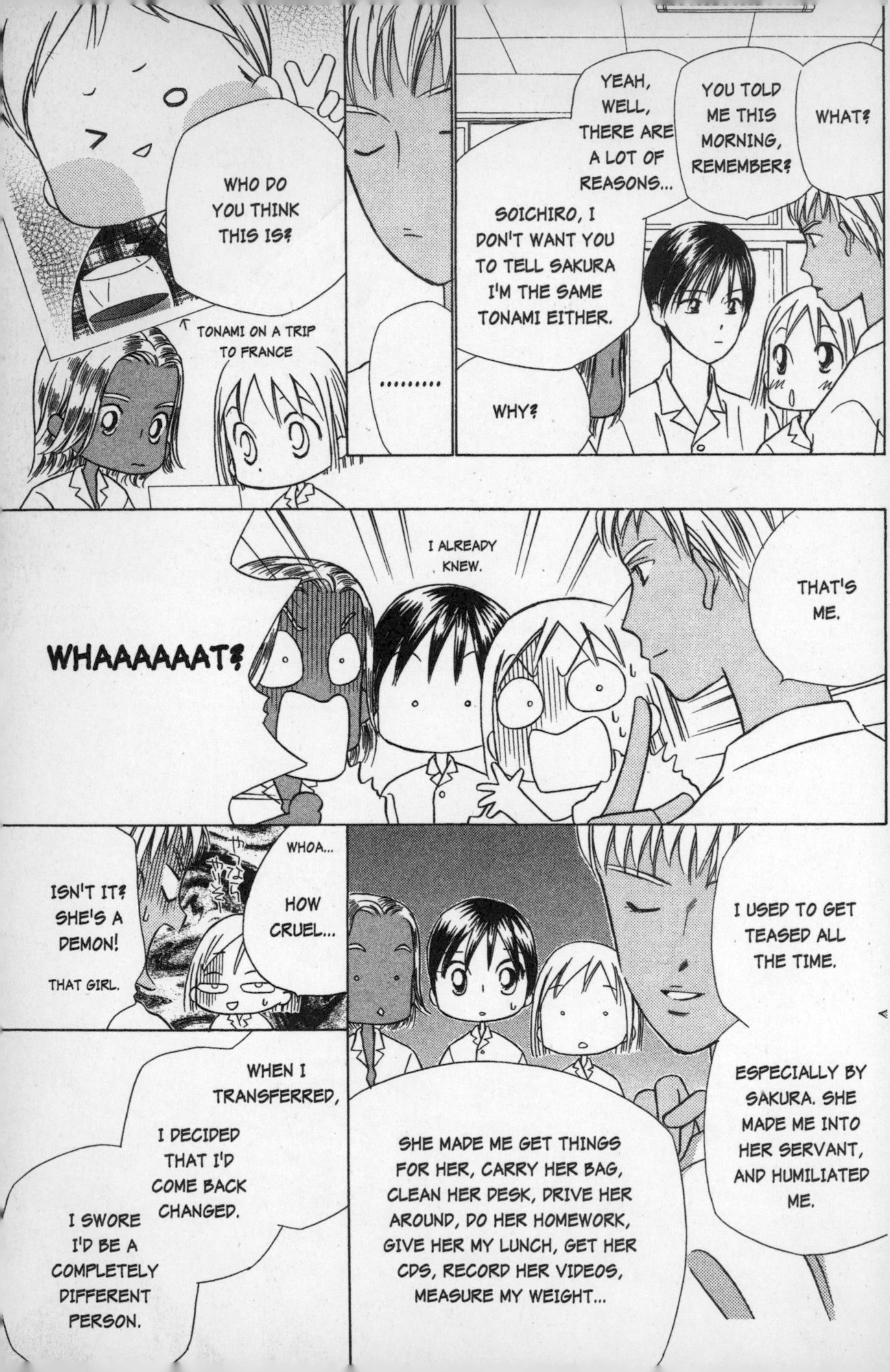
WHAT?
YOU TOLD ME THIS MORNING, REMEMBER?
YEAH, WELL, THERE ARE A LOT OF REASONS...
SOICHIRO, I DON'T WANT YOU TO TELL SAKURA I'M THE SAME TONAMI EITHER.
WHY?
....
WHO DO YOU THINK THIS IS?
TONAMI ON A TRIP TO FRANCE
THAT'S ME.
I ALREADY KNEW.
WHAAAAAAT?
I USED TO GET TEASED ALL THE TIME.
ESPECIALLY BY SAKURA. SHE MADE ME INTO HER SERVANT, AND HUMILIATED ME.
SHE MADE ME GET THINGS FOR HER, CARRY HER BAG, CLEAN HER DESK, DRIVE HER AROUND, DO HER HOMEWORK, GIVE HER MY LUNCH, GET HER CDS, RECORD HER VIDEOS, MEASURE MY WEIGHT...
WHOA...
HOW CRUEL...
ISN'T IT? SHE'S A DEMON!
THAT GIRL.
WHEN I TRANSFERRED,
I DECIDED THAT I'D COME BACK CHANGED.
I SWORE I'D BE A COMPLETELY DIFFERENT PERSON.

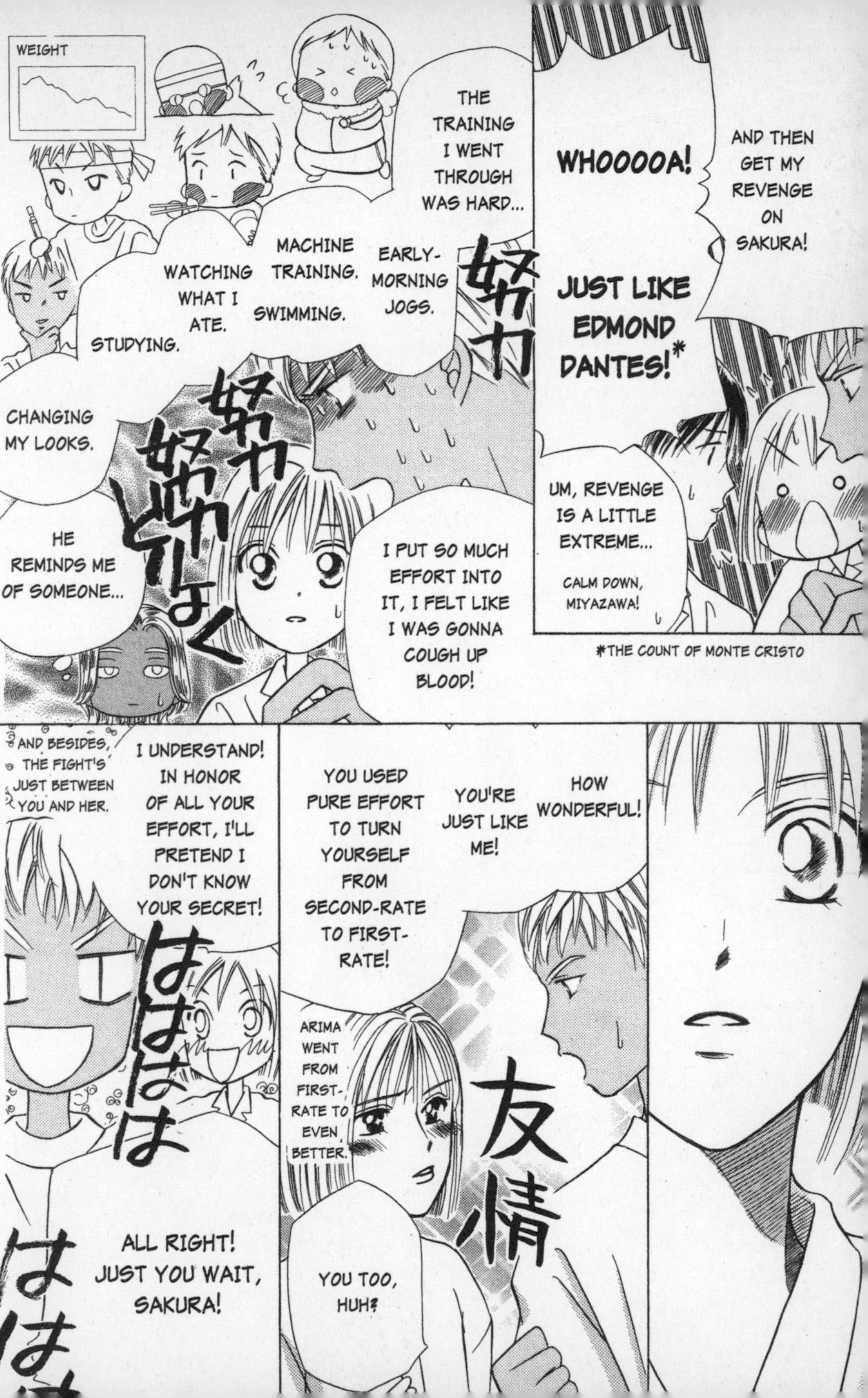
AND THEN GET MY REVENGE ON SAKURA!
WHOOOOA!
JUST LIKE EDMOND DANTES!*
UM, REVENGE IS A LITTLE EXTREME...
CALM DOWN, MIYAZAWA!
THE TRAINING I WENT THROUGH WAS HARD...
WEIGHT
EARLY-MORNING JOGS.
MACHINE TRAINING.
SWIMMING.
WATCHING WHAT I ATE.
STUDYING.
CHANGING MY LOOKS.
努力
努力
努力
どりょく
I PUT SO MUCH EFFORT INTO IT, I FELT LIKE I WAS GONNA COUGH UP BLOOD!
HE REMINDS ME OF SOMEONE...
HOW WONDERFUL!
YOU'RE JUST LIKE ME!
YOU USED PURE EFFORT TO TURN YOURSELF FROM SECOND-RATE TO FIRST-RATE!
友情
ARIMA WENT FROM FIRST-RATE TO EVEN BETTER.
YOU TOO, HUH?
I UNDERSTAND! IN HONOR OF ALL YOUR EFFORT, I'LL PRETEND I DON'T KNOW YOUR SECRET!
AND BESIDES, THE FIGHT'S JUST BETWEEN YOU AND HER.
ははは
ALL RIGHT! JUST YOU WAIT, SAKURA!
はは

*THE COUNT OF MONTE CRISTO

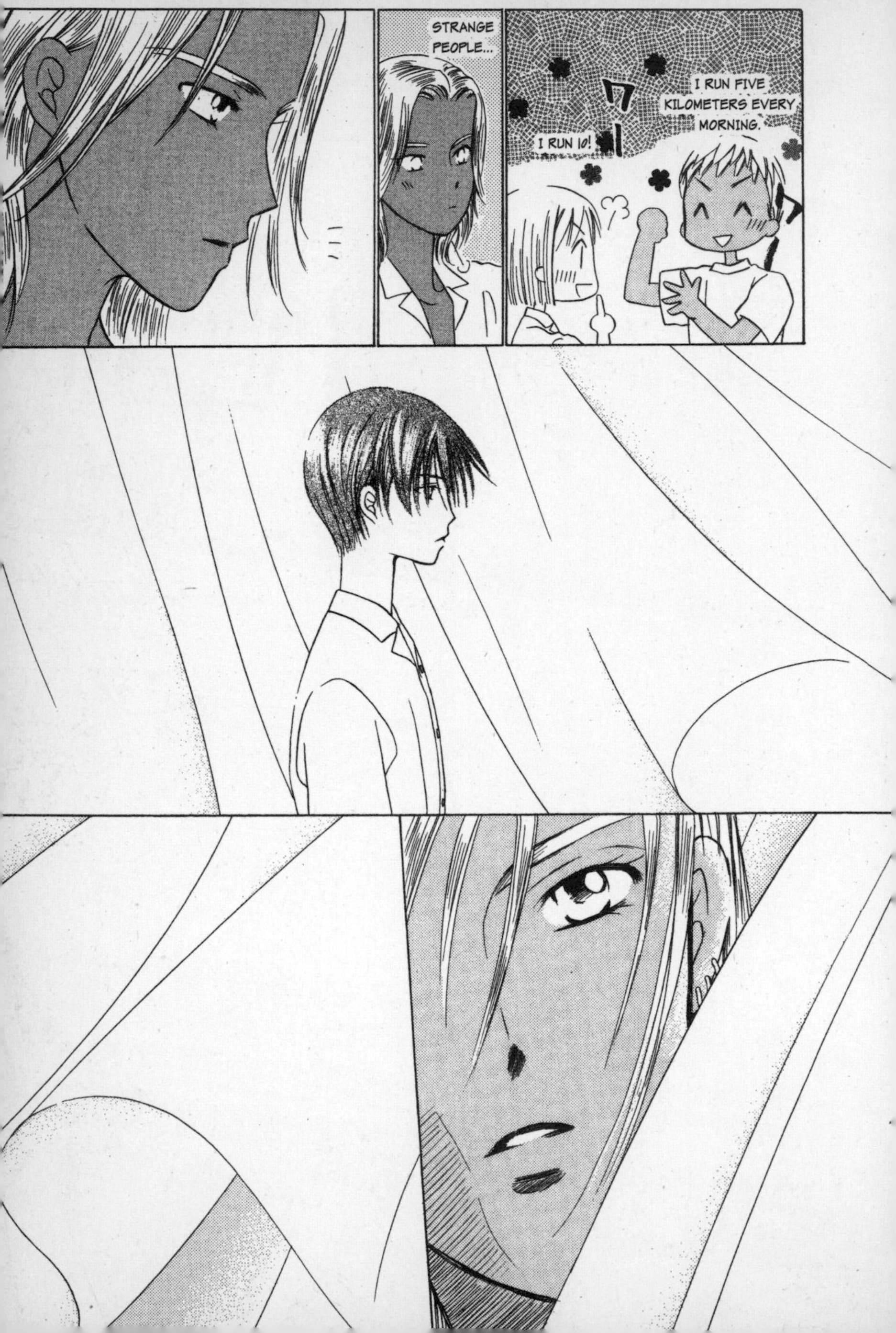
I RUN FIVE KILOMETERS EVERY MORNING.
I RUN 10!
STRANGE PEOPLE...

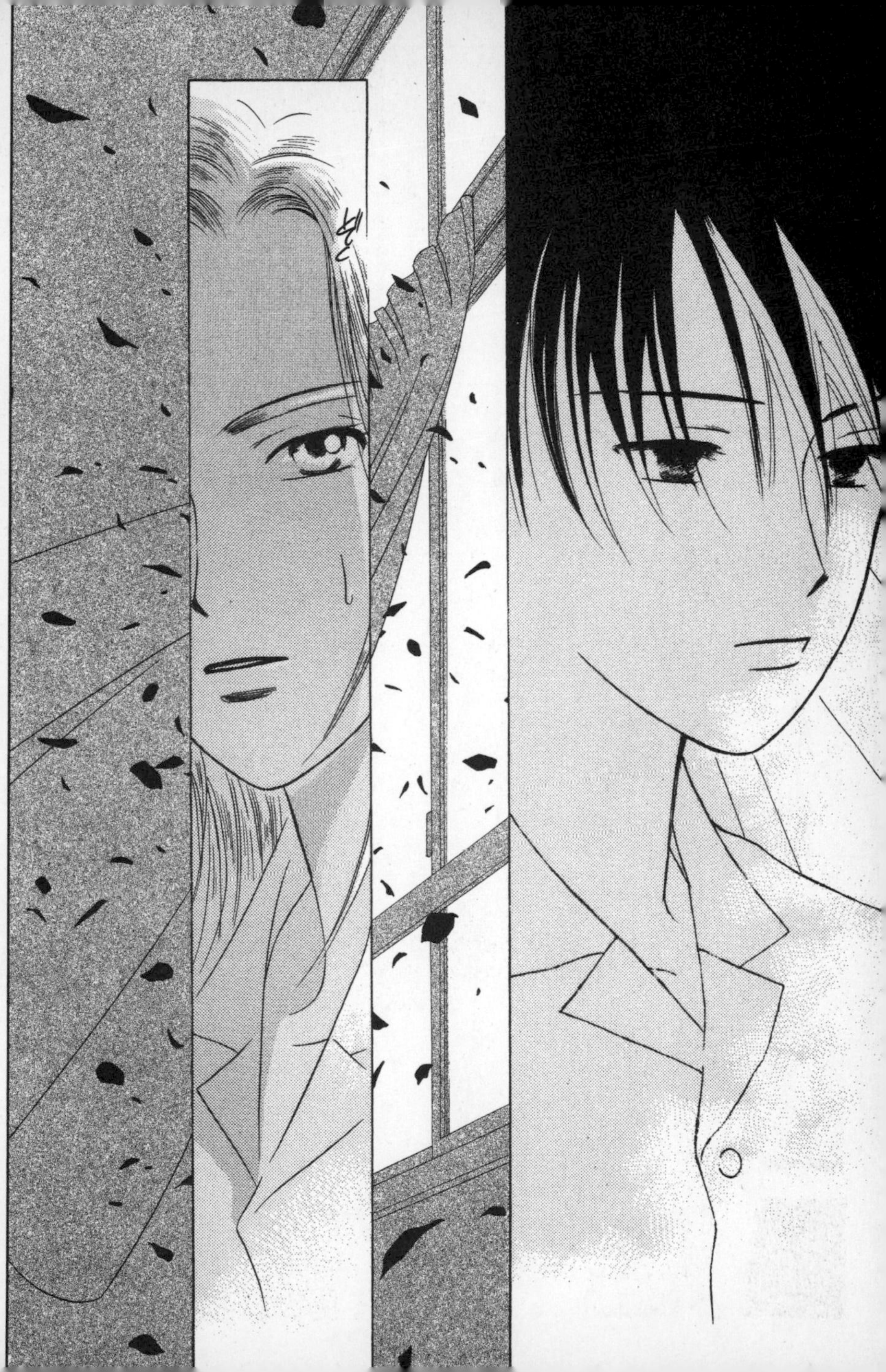
どく

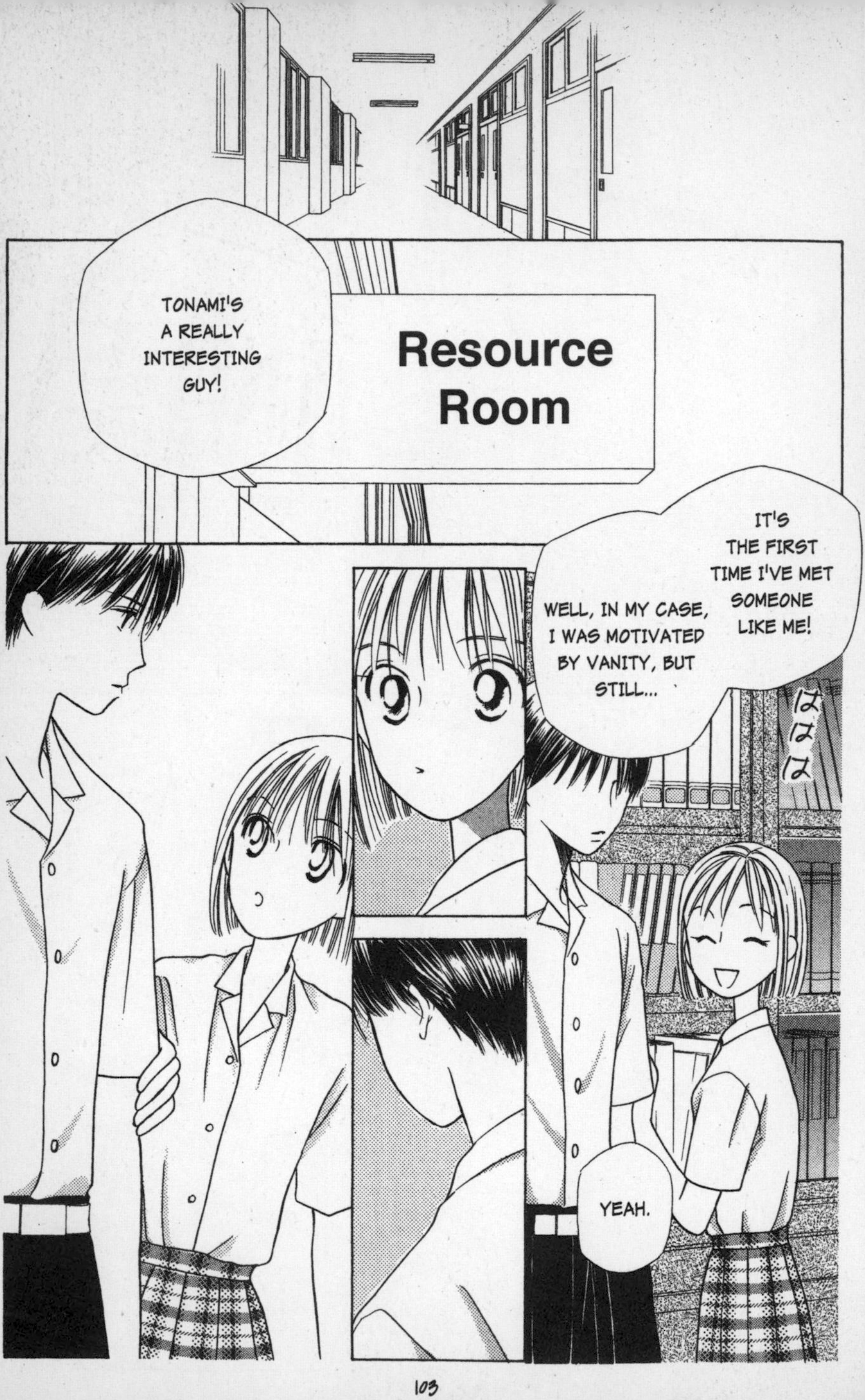

Resource Room
TONAMI'S A REALLY INTERESTING GUY!
IT'S THE FIRST TIME I'VE MET SOMEONE LIKE ME!
WELL, IN MY CASE, I WAS MOTIVATED BY VANITY, BUT STILL...
ははは
YEAH.

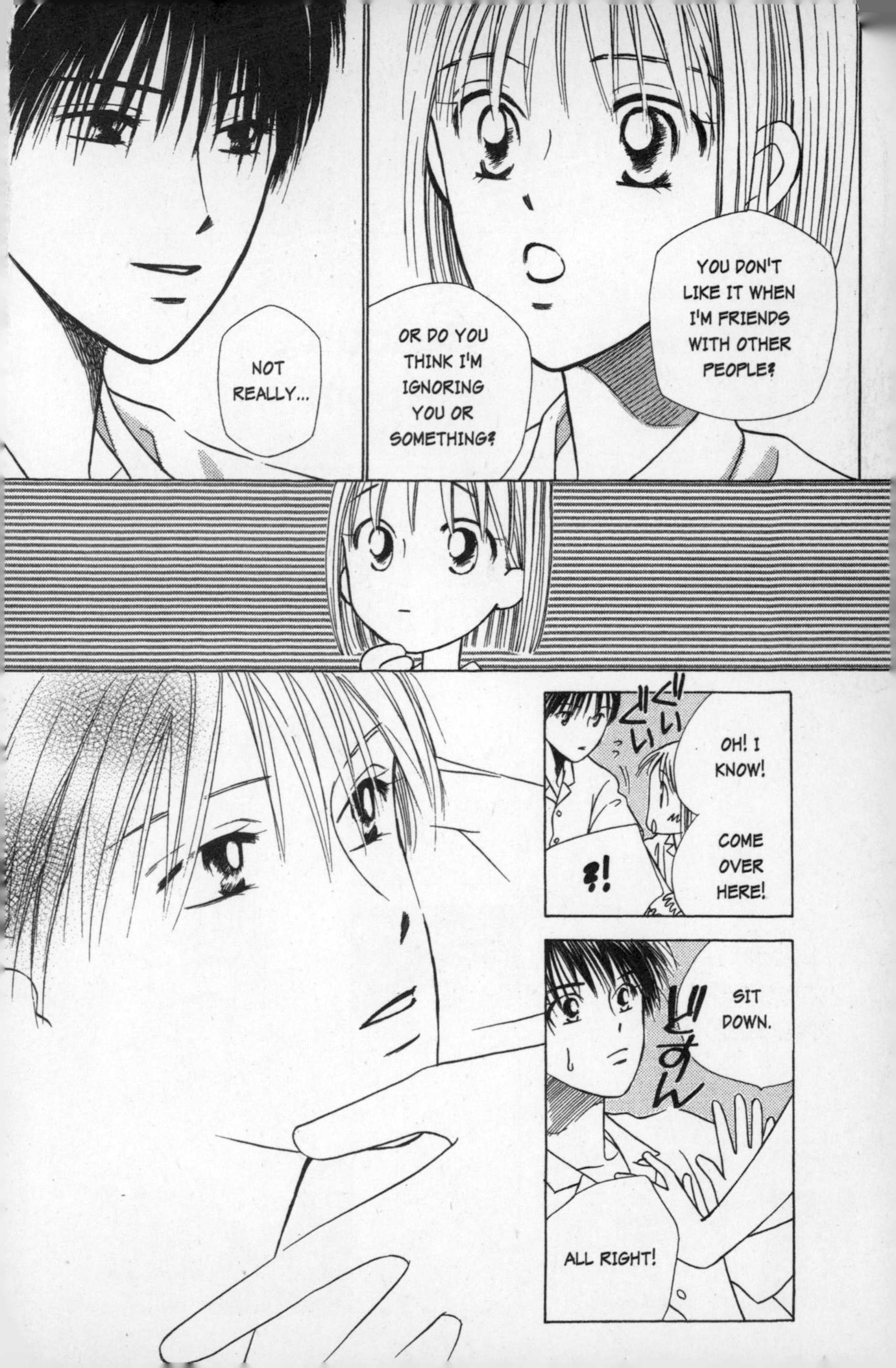
YOU DON'T LIKE IT WHEN I'M FRIENDS WITH OTHER PEOPLE?
OR DO YOU THINK I'M IGNORING YOU OR SOMETHING?
NOT REALLY...
ぐいぐい
OH! I KNOW!
COME OVER HERE!
?!
どすん
SIT DOWN.
ALL RIGHT!

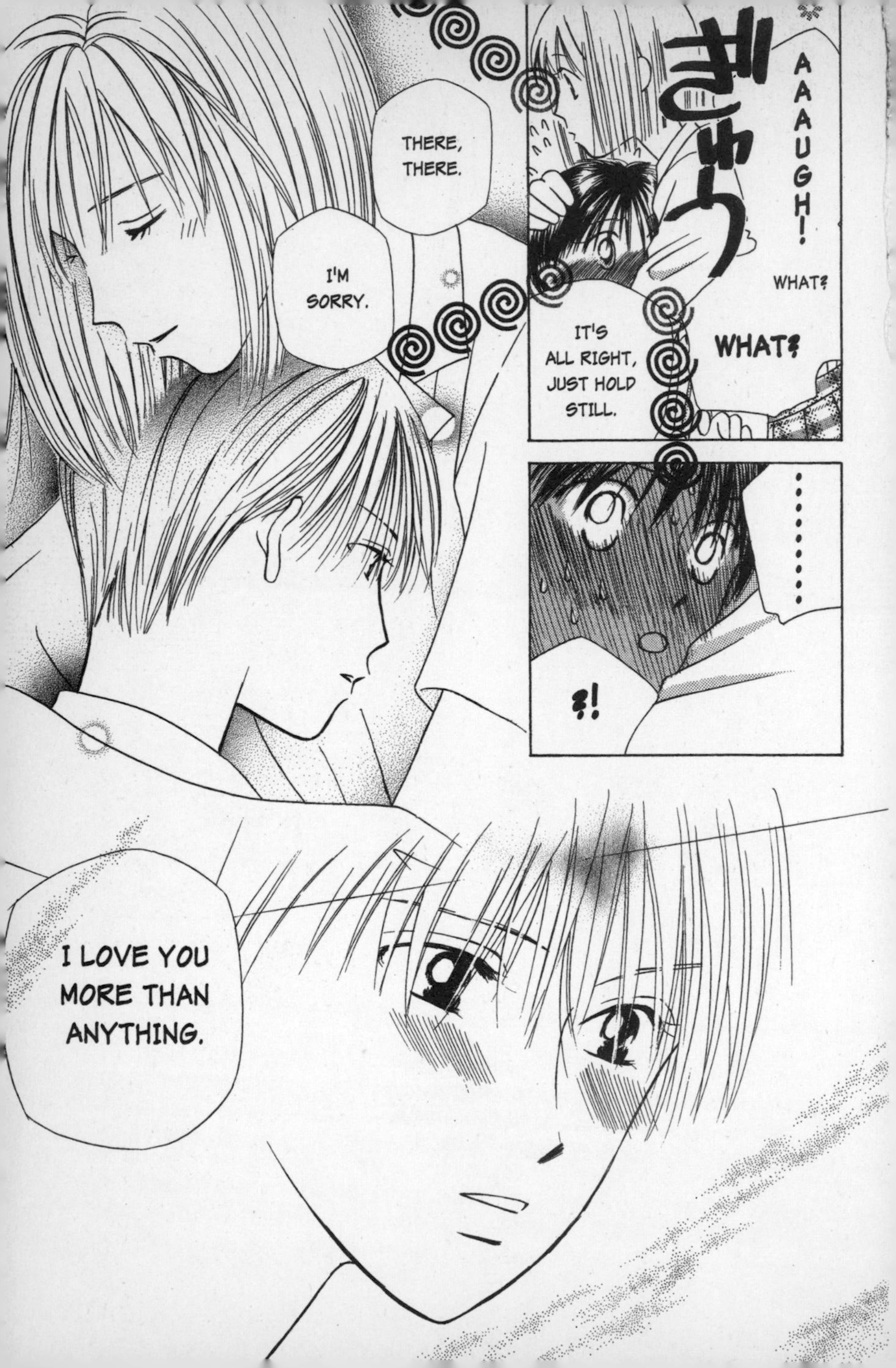

AAAUGH!
ぎゅう
WHAT?
WHAT?
IT'S ALL RIGHT, JUST HOLD STILL.
......
?!
THERE, THERE.
I'M SORRY.
I LOVE YOU MORE THAN ANYTHING.

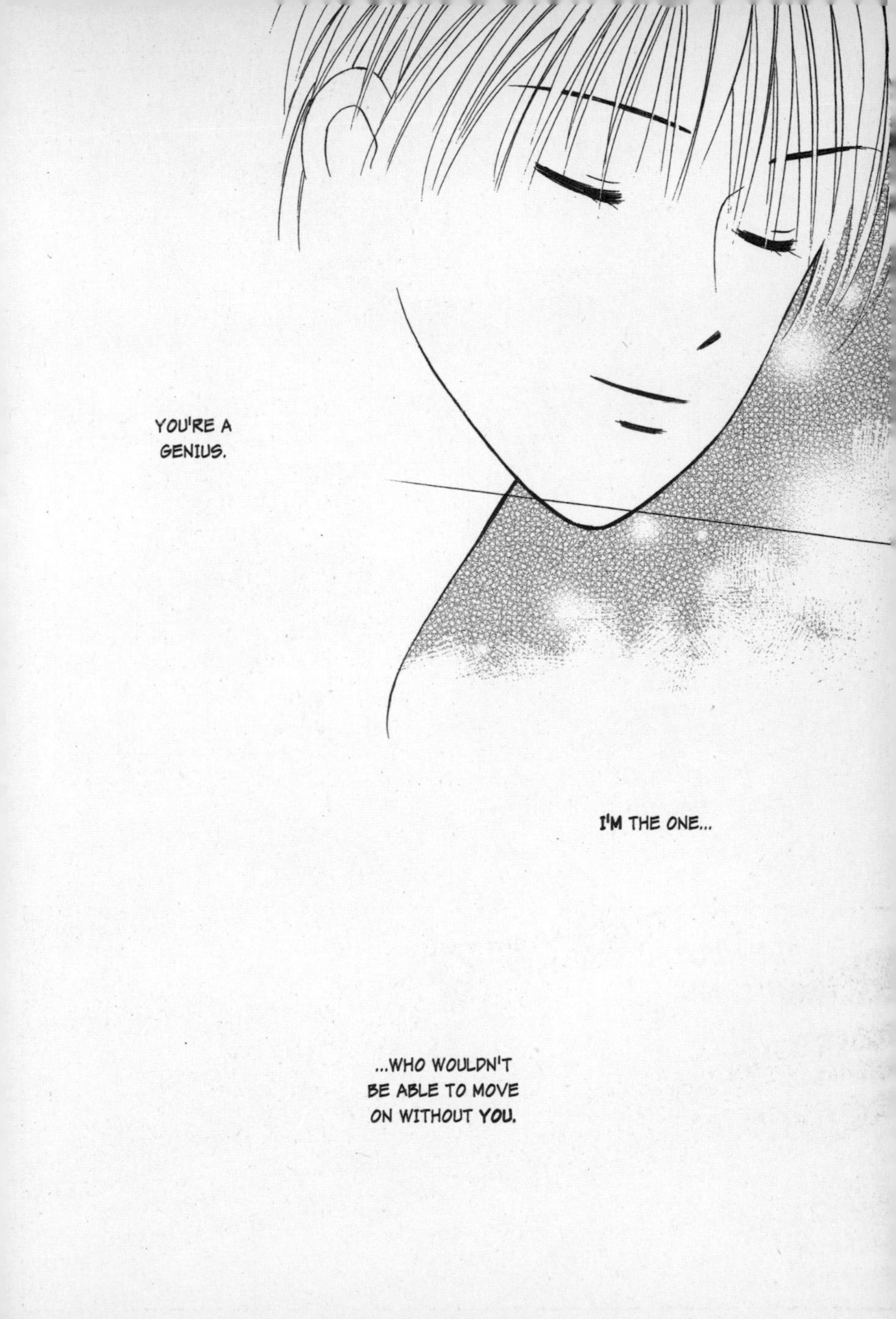
YOU'RE A GENIUS.
I'M THE ONE...
...WHO WOULDN'T BE ABLE TO MOVE ON WITHOUT YOU.

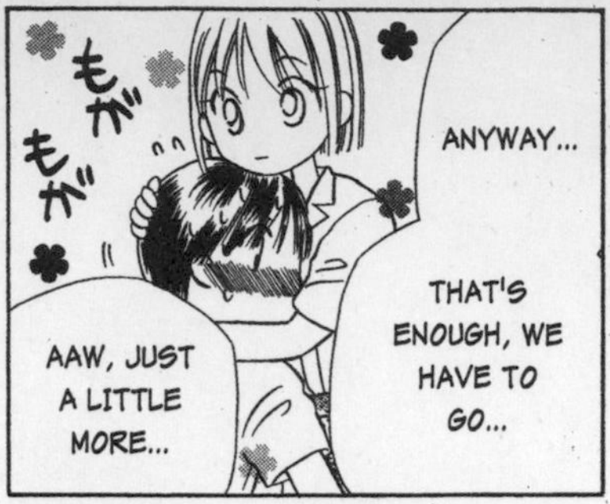
ANYWAY...
THAT'S ENOUGH, WE HAVE TO GO...
もがもが
AAW, JUST A LITTLE MORE...

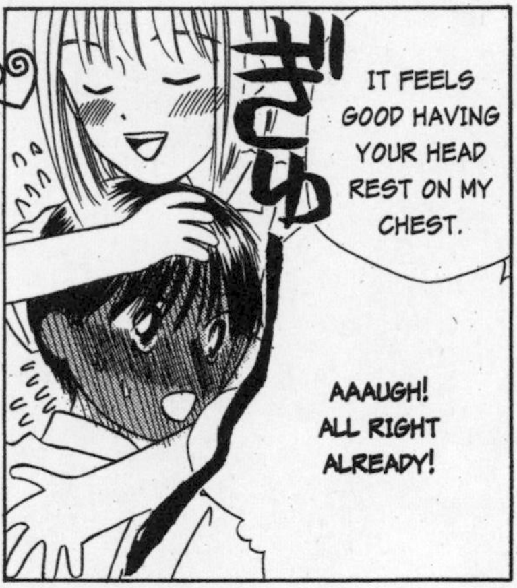
ぎゅ
IT FEELS GOOD HAVING YOUR HEAD REST ON MY CHEST.
AAAUGH! ALL RIGHT ALREADY!

I'M THE ONE WHO CAN'T LEAVE YOU.

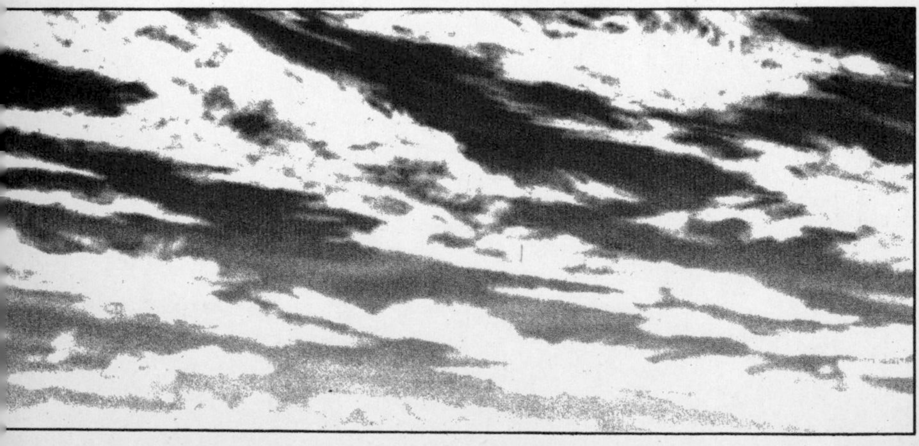

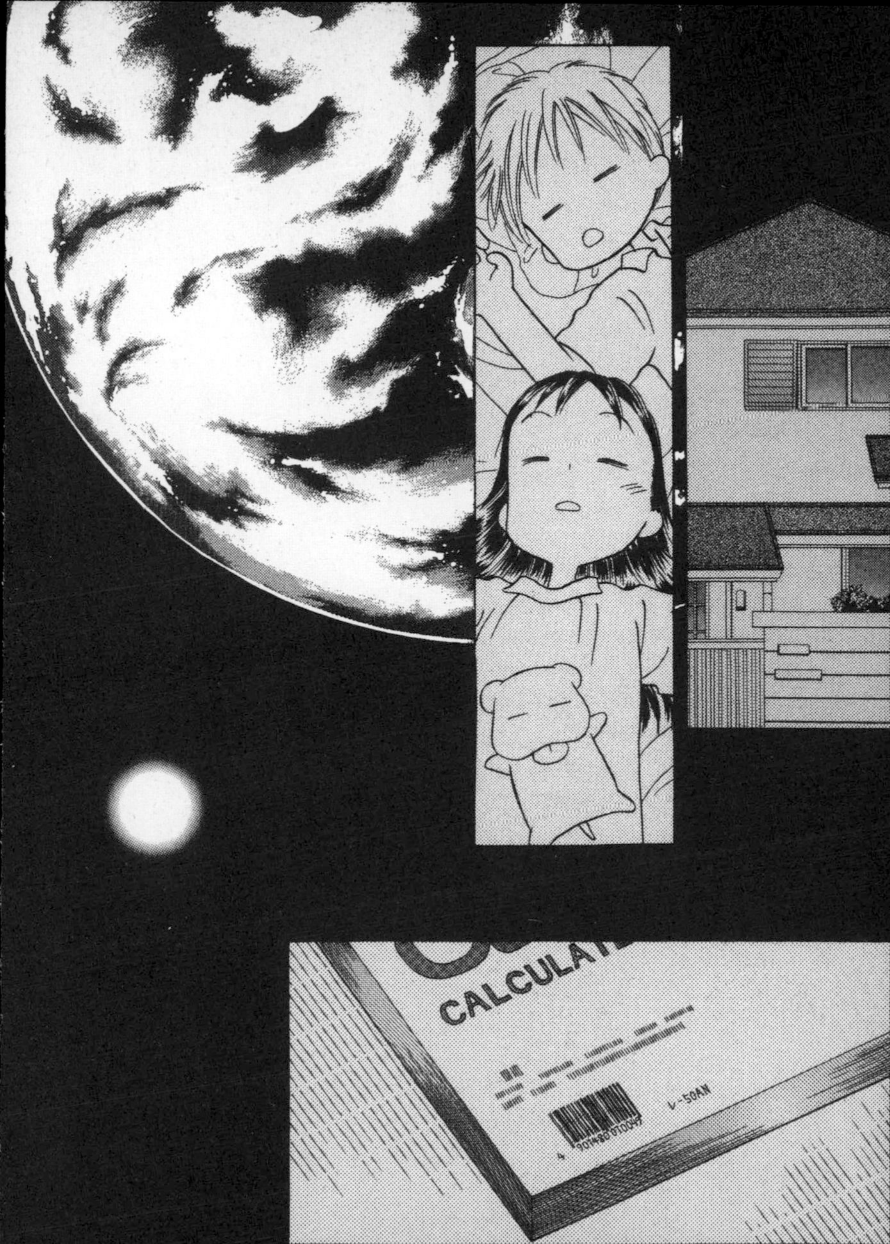
CALCULA
V-50AN

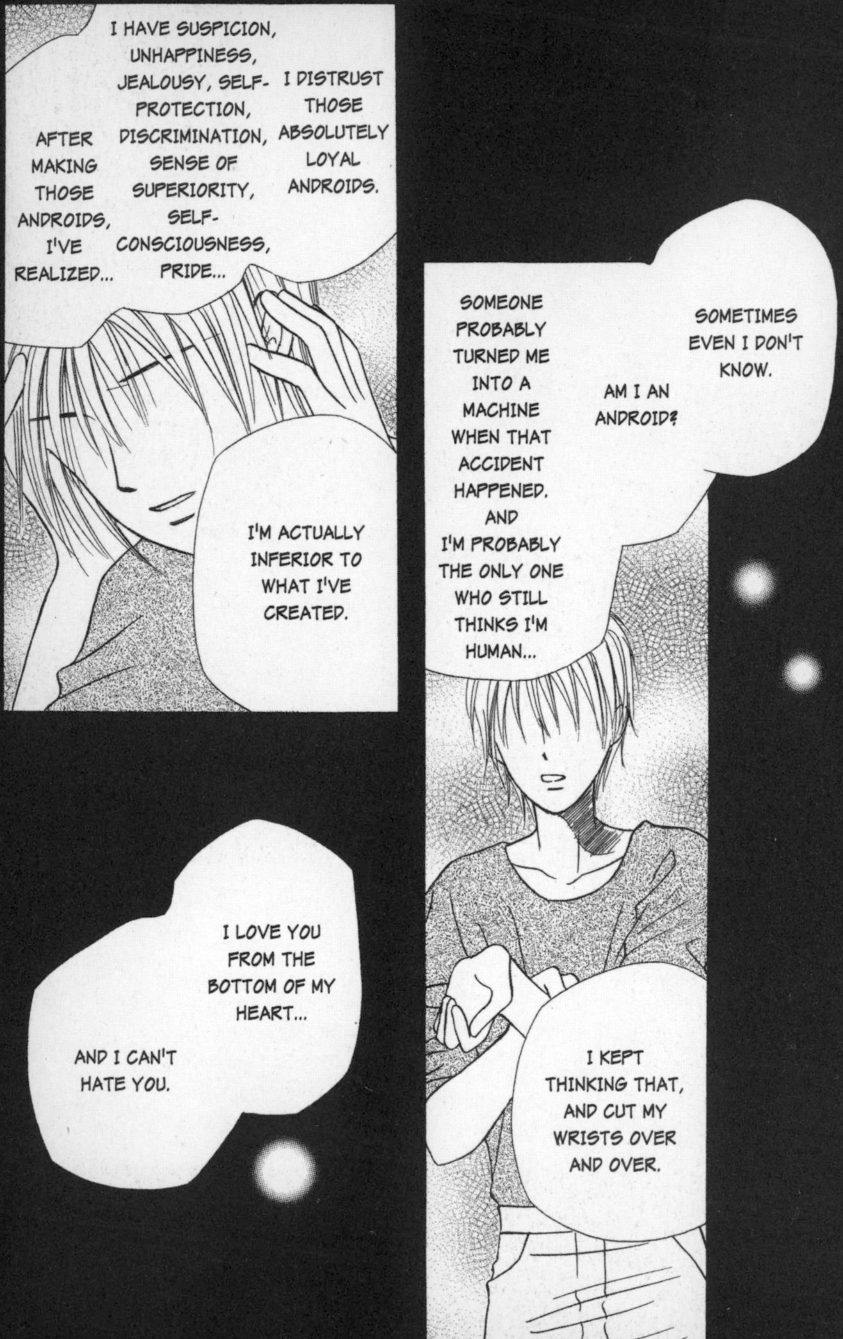

I HAVE SUSPICION, UNHAPPINESS, JEALOUSY, SELF-PROTECTION, DISCRIMINATION, SENSE OF SUPERIORITY, SELF-CONSCIOUSNESS, PRIDE...
I DISTRUST THOSE ABSOLUTELY LOYAL ANDROIDS.
AFTER MAKING THOSE ANDROIDS, I'VE REALIZED...
I'M ACTUALLY INFERIOR TO WHAT I'VE CREATED.
SOMETIMES EVEN I DON'T KNOW.
AM I AN ANDROID?
SOMEONE PROBABLY TURNED ME INTO A MACHINE WHEN THAT ACCIDENT HAPPENED. AND I'M PROBABLY THE ONLY ONE WHO STILL THINKS I'M HUMAN...
I KEPT THINKING THAT, AND CUT MY WRISTS OVER AND OVER.
I LOVE YOU FROM THE BOTTOM OF MY HEART...
AND I CAN'T HATE YOU.

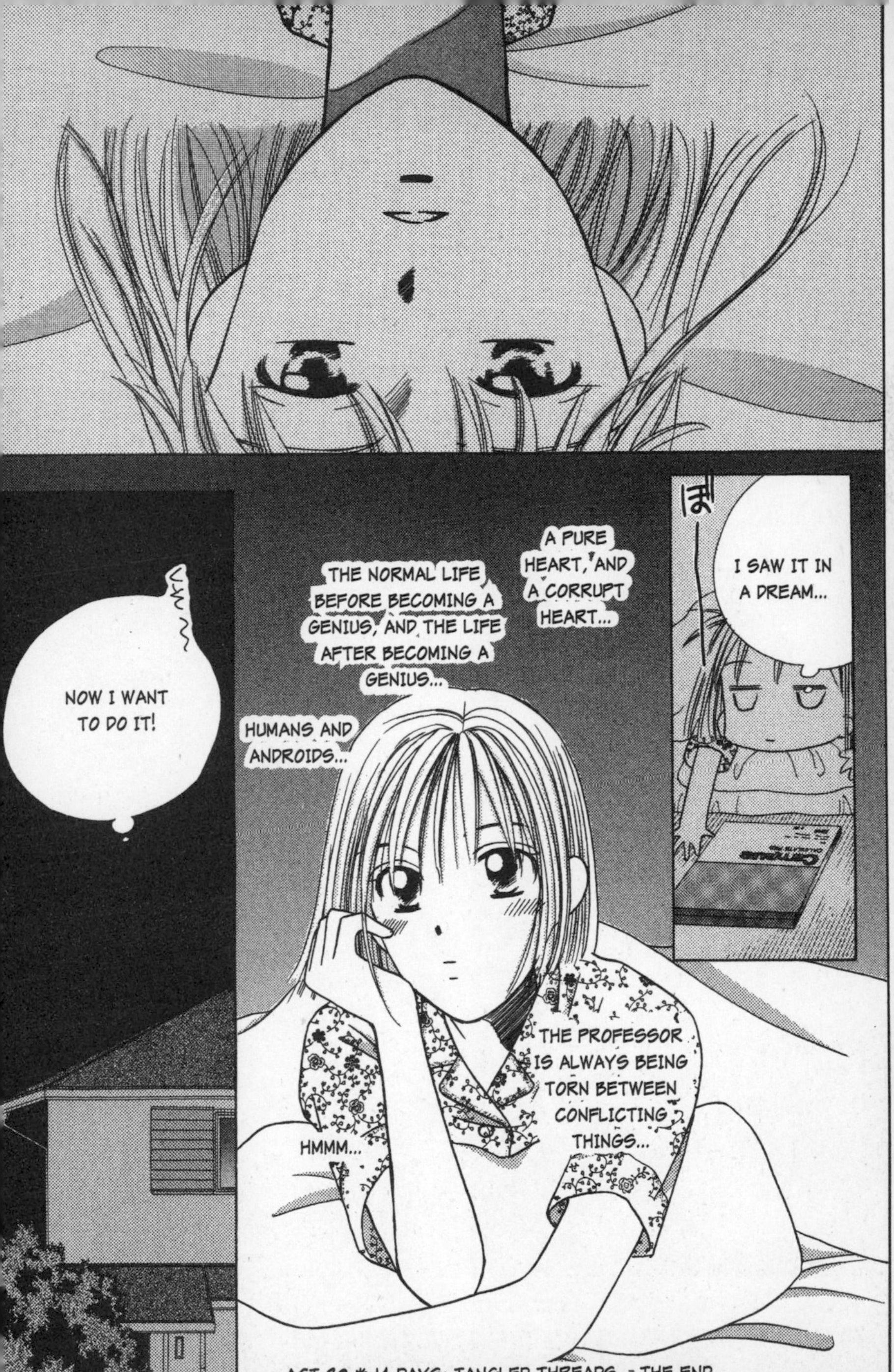
ぼー
I SAW IT IN A DREAM...
A PURE HEART, AND A CORRUPT HEART...
THE NORMAL LIFE BEFORE BECOMING A GENIUS, AND THE LIFE AFTER BECOMING A GENIUS...
HUMANS AND ANDROIDS...
THE PROFESSOR IS ALWAYS BEING TORN BETWEEN CONFLICTING THINGS...
HMMM...
NOW I WANT TO DO IT!

ACT 29 * 14 DAYS: TANGLED THREADS - THE END

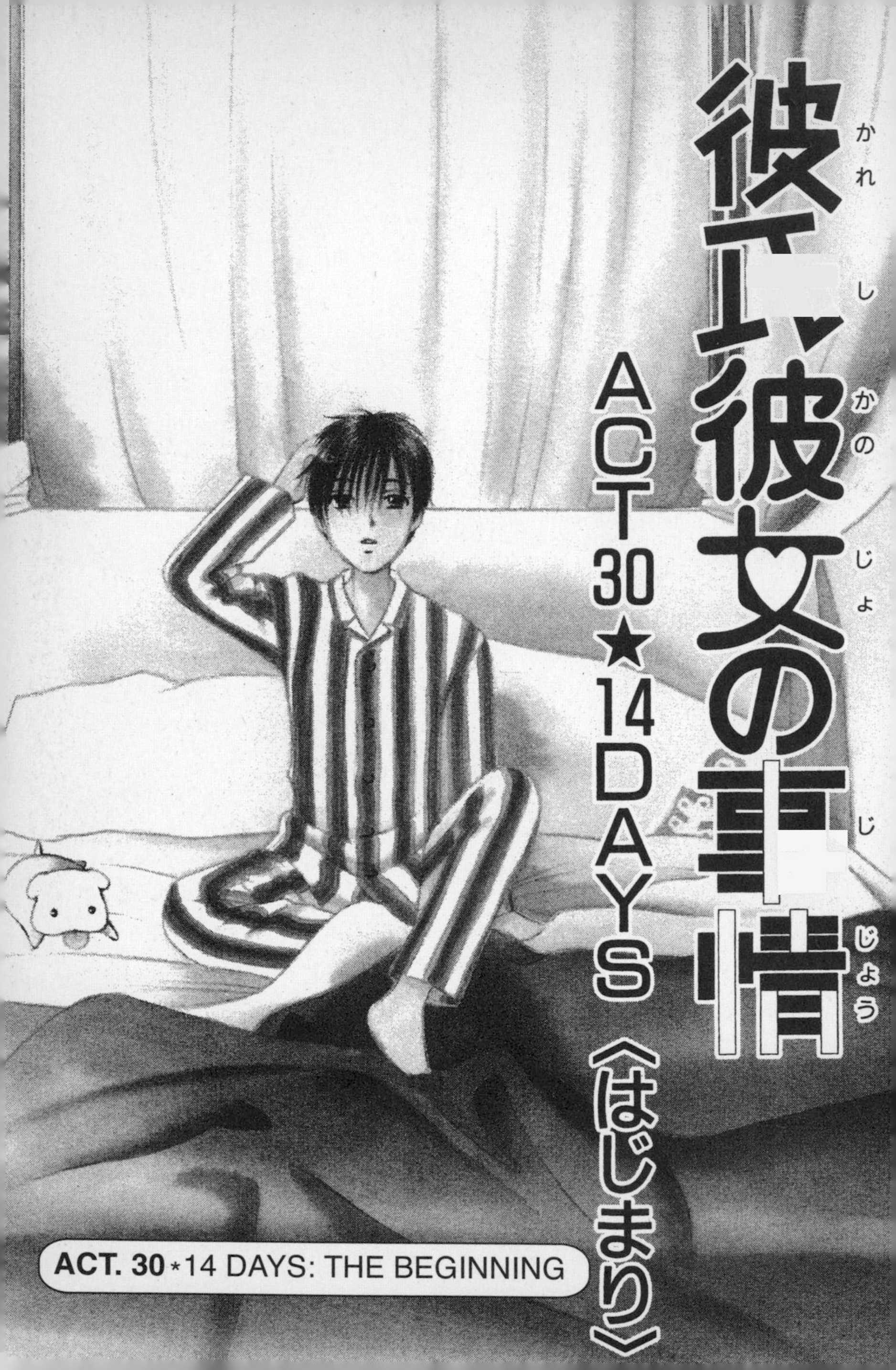
彼氏彼女の事情
かれしかのじょのじじょう
ACT 30★14DAYS〈はじまり〉
ACT. 30 * 14 DAYS: THE BEGINNING

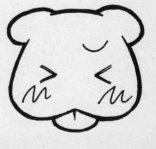

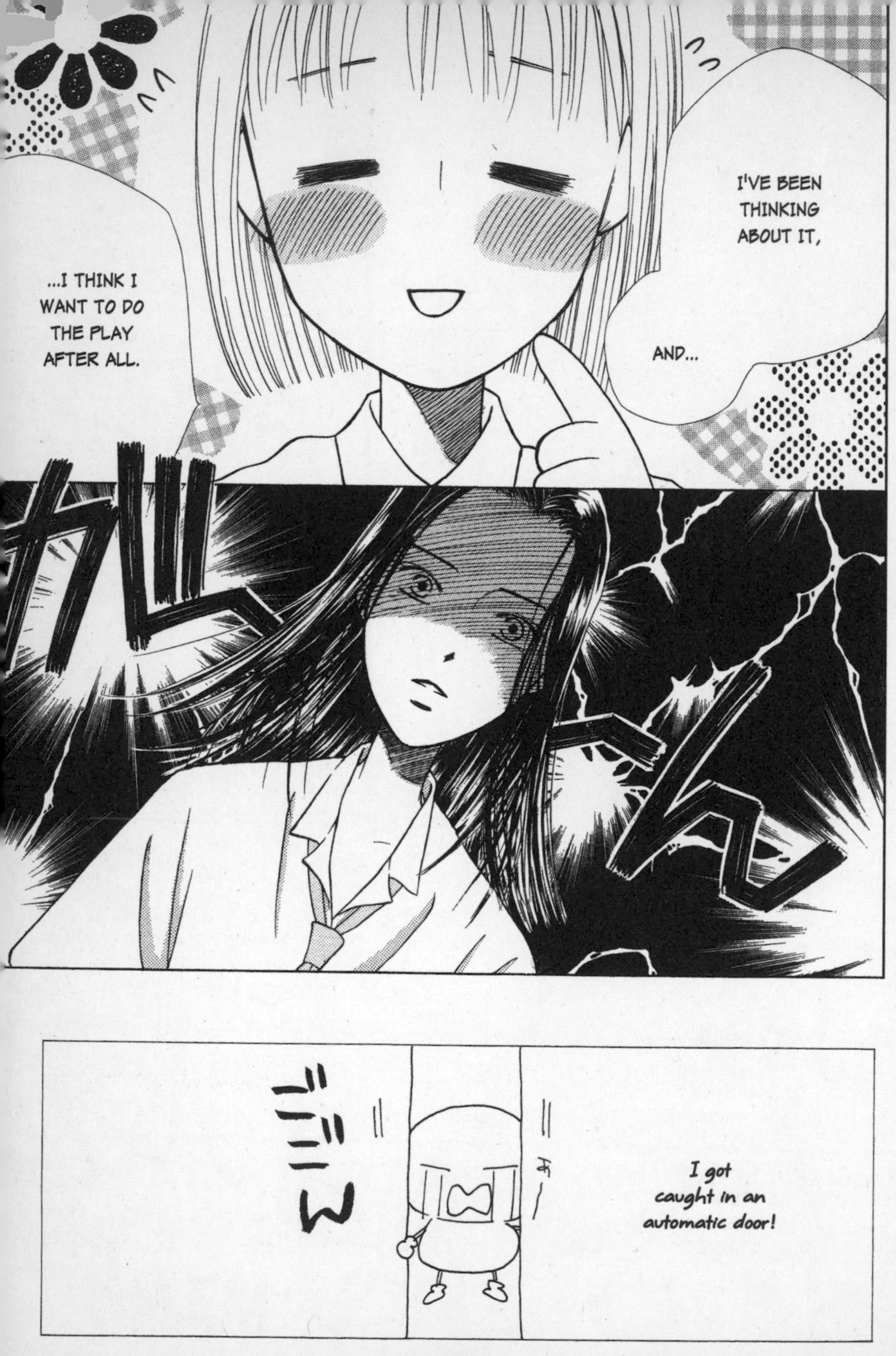
I'VE BEEN THINKING ABOUT IT,
AND...
...I THINK I WANT TO DO THE PLAY AFTER ALL.
I got caught in an automatic door!

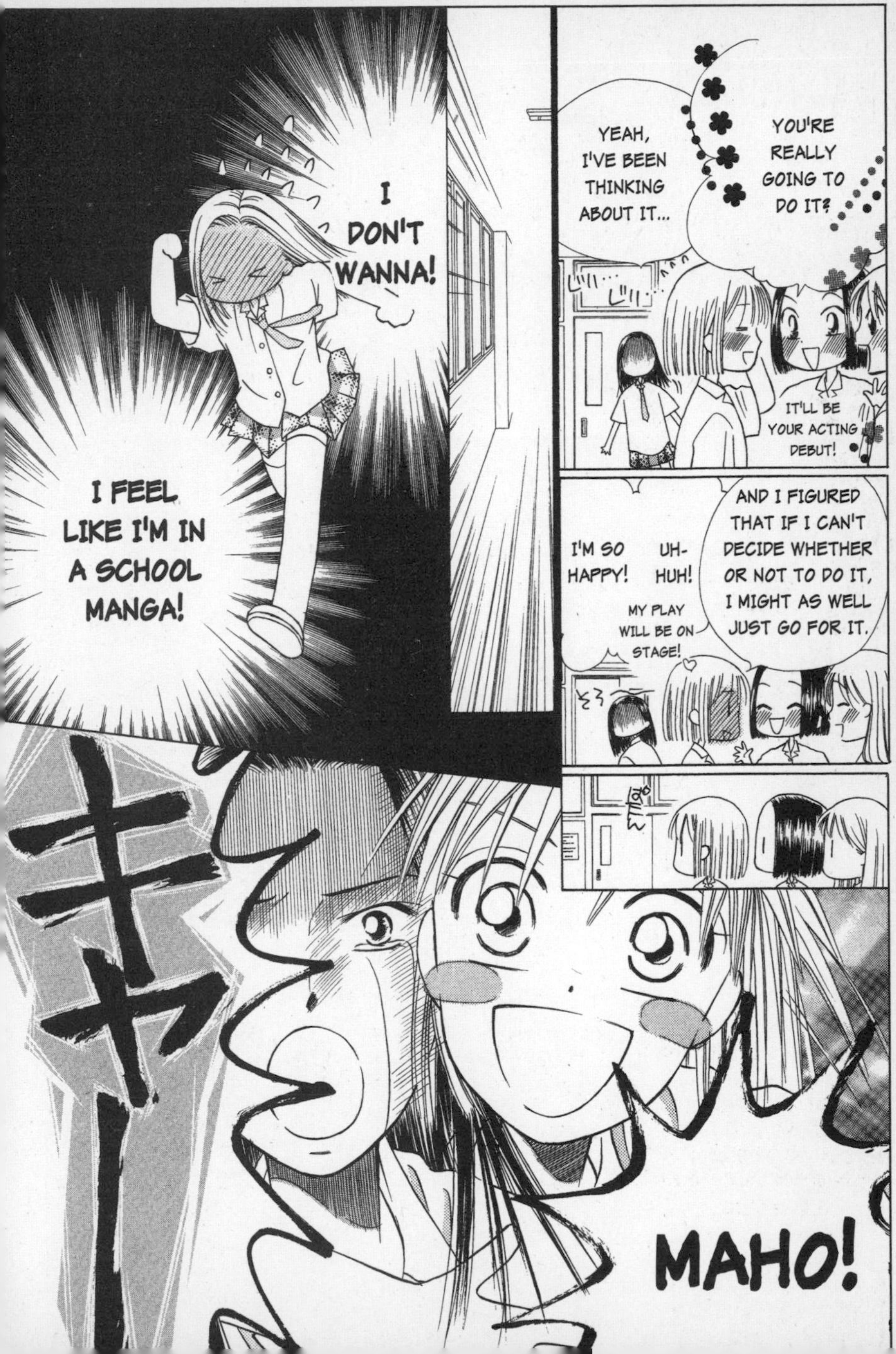
YOU'RE REALLY GOING TO DO IT?
YEAH, I'VE BEEN THINKING ABOUT IT...
IT'LL BE YOUR ACTING DEBUT!
AND I FIGURED THAT IF I CAN'T DECIDE WHETHER OR NOT TO DO IT, I MIGHT AS WELL JUST GO FOR IT.
UH-HUH!
I'M SO HAPPY!
MY PLAY WILL BE ON STAGE!
I DON'T WANNA!
I FEEL LIKE I'M IN A SCHOOL MANGA!
MAHO!

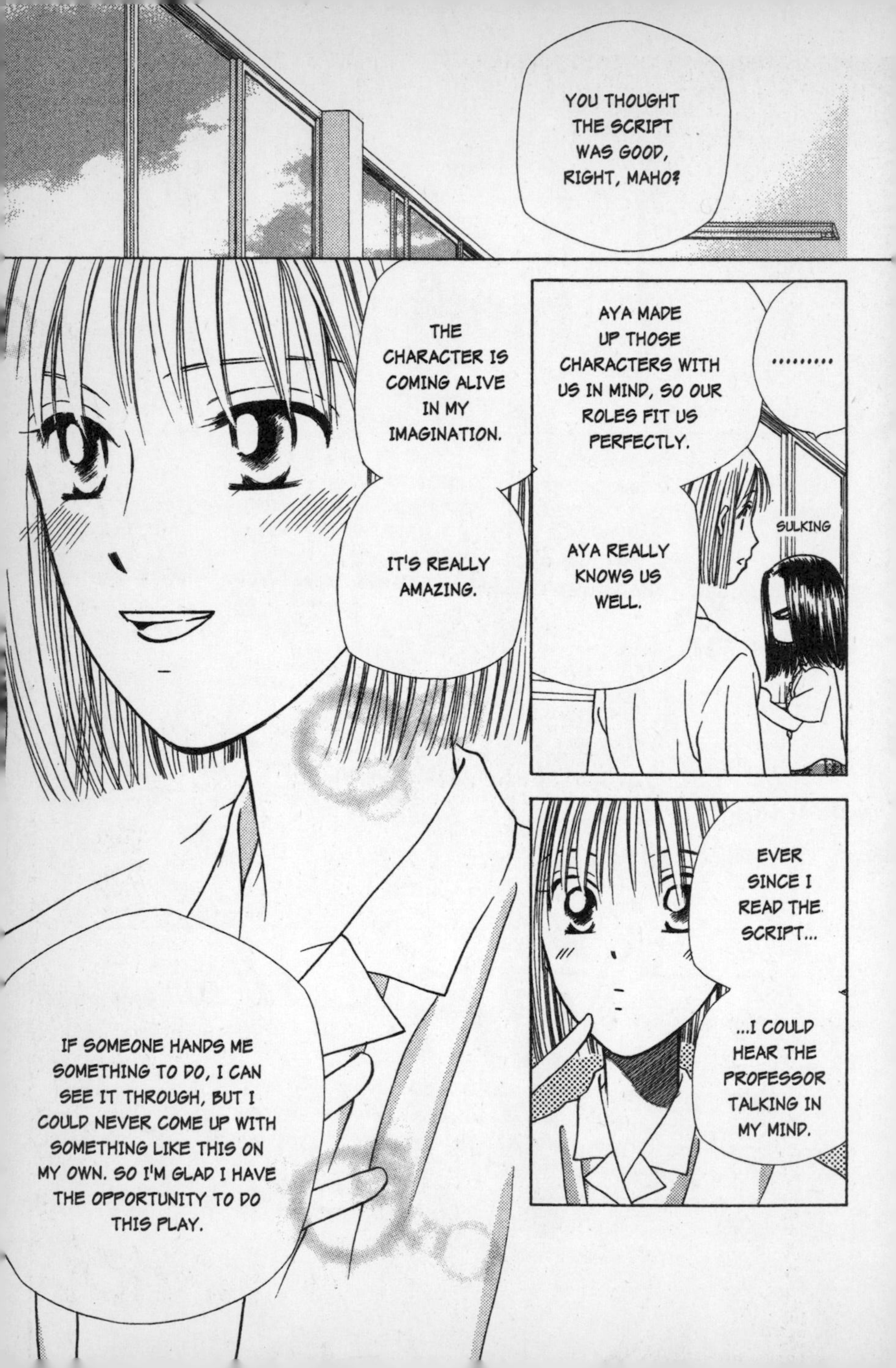
YOU THOUGHT THE SCRIPT WAS GOOD, RIGHT, MAHO?
....
AYA MADE UP THOSE CHARACTERS WITH US IN MIND, SO OUR ROLES FIT US PERFECTLY.
SULKING
AYA REALLY KNOWS US WELL.
EVER SINCE I READ THE SCRIPT...
...I COULD HEAR THE PROFESSOR TALKING IN MY MIND.
THE CHARACTER IS COMING ALIVE IN MY IMAGINATION.
IT'S REALLY AMAZING.
IF SOMEONE HANDS ME SOMETHING TO DO, I CAN SEE IT THROUGH, BUT I COULD NEVER COME UP WITH SOMETHING LIKE THIS ON MY OWN. SO I'M GLAD I HAVE THE OPPORTUNITY TO DO THIS PLAY.

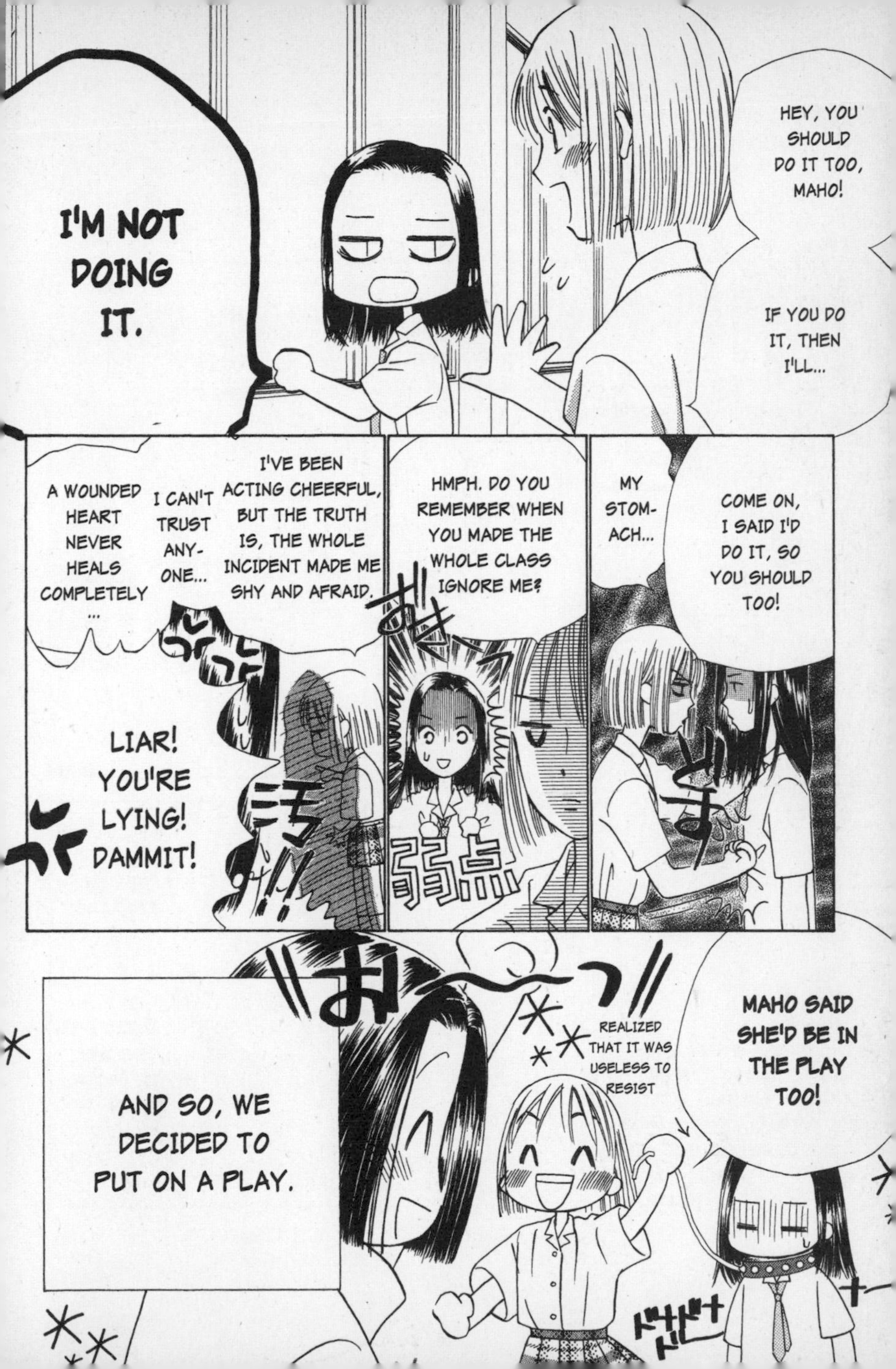
HEY, YOU SHOULD DO IT TOO, MAHO!
IF YOU DO IT, THEN I'LL...
I'M NOT DOING IT.
COME ON, I SAID I'D DO IT, SO YOU SHOULD TOO!
MY STOM-ACH...
HMPH. DO YOU REMEMBER WHEN YOU MADE THE WHOLE CLASS IGNORE ME?
弱点
I'VE BEEN ACTING CHEERFUL, BUT THE TRUTH IS, THE WHOLE INCIDENT MADE ME SHY AND AFRAID.
I CAN'T TRUST ANY-ONE...
A WOUNDED HEART NEVER HEALS COMPLETELY ...
LIAR! YOU'RE LYING! DAMMIT!
MAHO SAID SHE'D BE IN THE PLAY TOO!
REALIZED THAT IT WAS USELESS TO RESIST
AND SO, WE DECIDED TO PUT ON A PLAY.

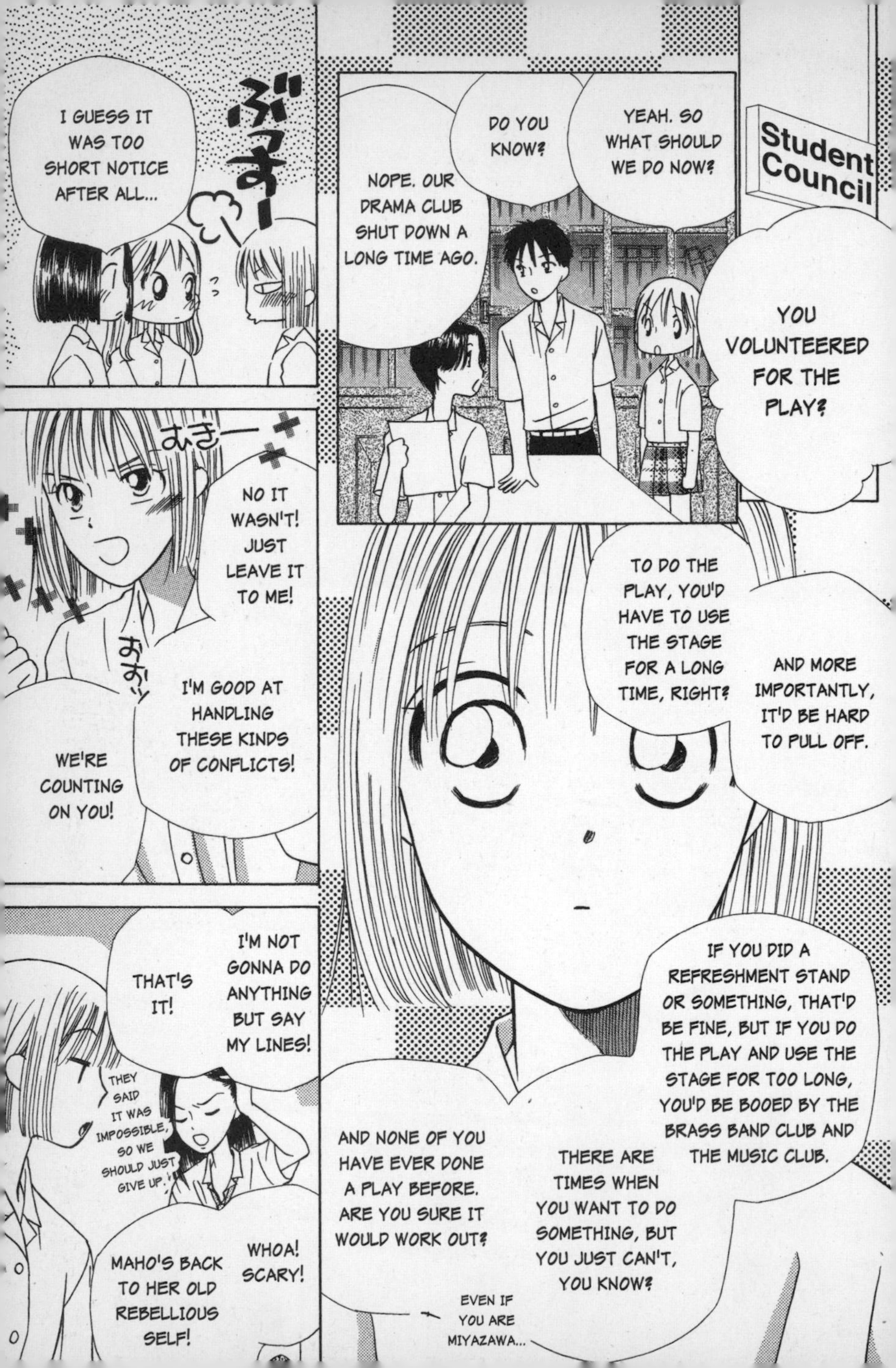

Student Council
YOU VOLUNTEERED FOR THE PLAY?
YEAH. SO WHAT SHOULD WE DO NOW?
DO YOU KNOW?
NOPE. OUR DRAMA CLUB SHUT DOWN A LONG TIME AGO.
TO DO THE PLAY, YOU'D HAVE TO USE THE STAGE FOR A LONG TIME, RIGHT?
AND MORE IMPORTANTLY, IT'D BE HARD TO PULL OFF.
IF YOU DID A REFRESHMENT STAND OR SOMETHING, THAT'D BE FINE, BUT IF YOU DO THE PLAY AND USE THE STAGE FOR TOO LONG, YOU'D BE BOOED BY THE BRASS BAND CLUB AND THE MUSIC CLUB.
AND NONE OF YOU HAVE EVER DONE A PLAY BEFORE. ARE YOU SURE IT WOULD WORK OUT?
THERE ARE TIMES WHEN YOU WANT TO DO SOMETHING, BUT YOU JUST CAN'T, YOU KNOW?
EVEN IF YOU ARE MIYAZAWA...
ぶすー
I GUESS IT WAS TOO SHORT NOTICE AFTER ALL...
むきー
NO IT WASN'T! JUST LEAVE IT TO ME!
I'M GOOD AT HANDLING THESE KINDS OF CONFLICTS!
おおッ
WE'RE COUNTING ON YOU!
I'M NOT GONNA DO ANYTHING BUT SAY MY LINES!
THAT'S IT!
THEY SAID IT WAS IMPOSSIBLE, SO WE SHOULD JUST GIVE UP.
WHOA! SCARY!
MAHO'S BACK TO HER OLD REBELLIOUS SELF!

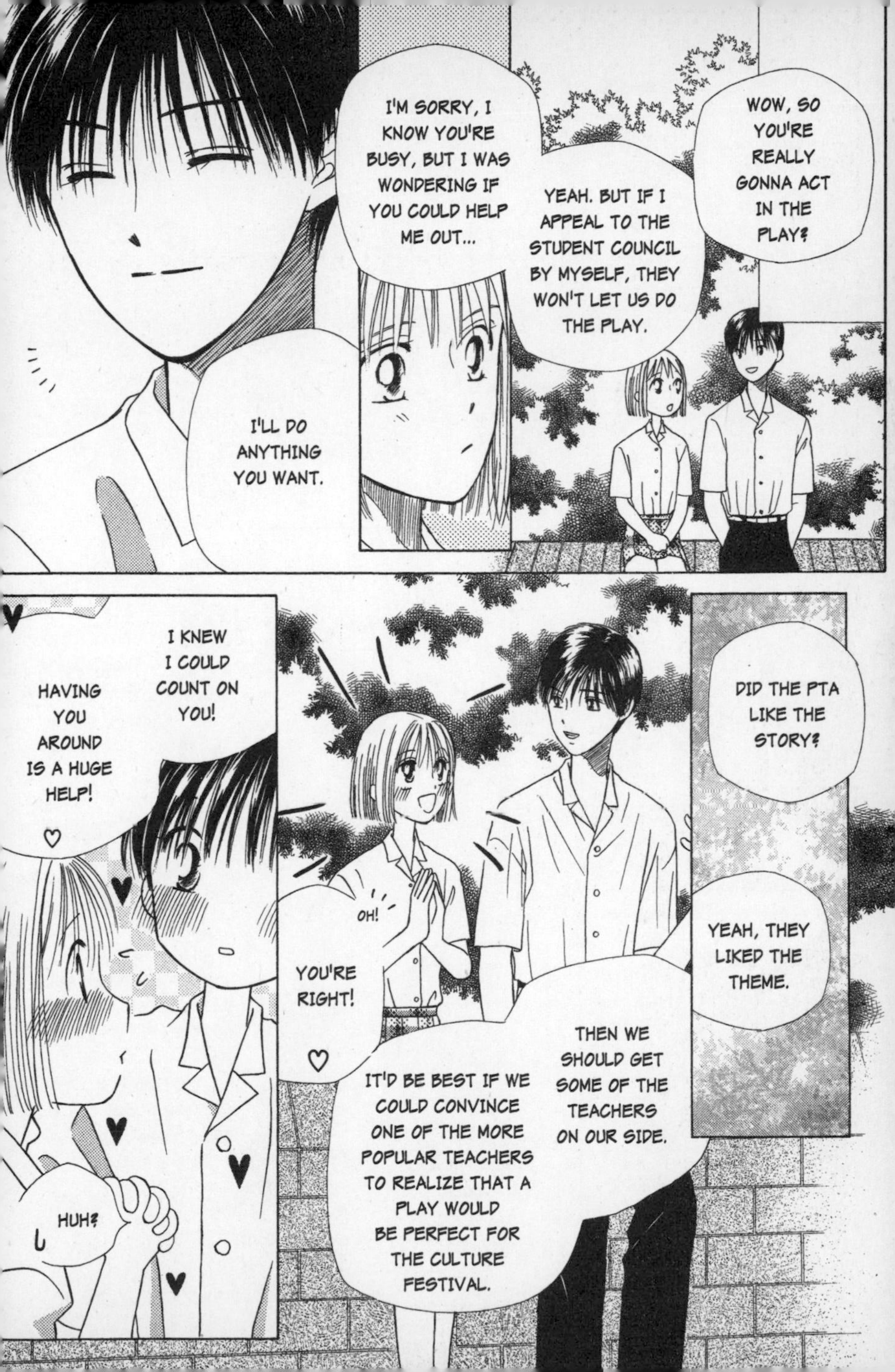
WOW, SO YOU'RE REALLY GONNA ACT IN THE PLAY?
YEAH. BUT IF I APPEAL TO THE STUDENT COUNCIL BY MYSELF, THEY WON'T LET US DO THE PLAY.
I'M SORRY, I KNOW YOU'RE BUSY, BUT I WAS WONDERING IF YOU COULD HELP ME OUT...
I'LL DO ANYTHING YOU WANT.
DID THE PTA LIKE THE STORY?
YEAH, THEY LIKED THE THEME.
THEN WE SHOULD GET SOME OF THE TEACHERS ON OUR SIDE.
IT'D BE BEST IF WE COULD CONVINCE ONE OF THE MORE POPULAR TEACHERS TO REALIZE THAT A PLAY WOULD BE PERFECT FOR THE CULTURE FESTIVAL.
OH!
YOU'RE RIGHT!
I KNEW I COULD COUNT ON YOU!
HAVING YOU AROUND IS A HUGE HELP!
HUH?

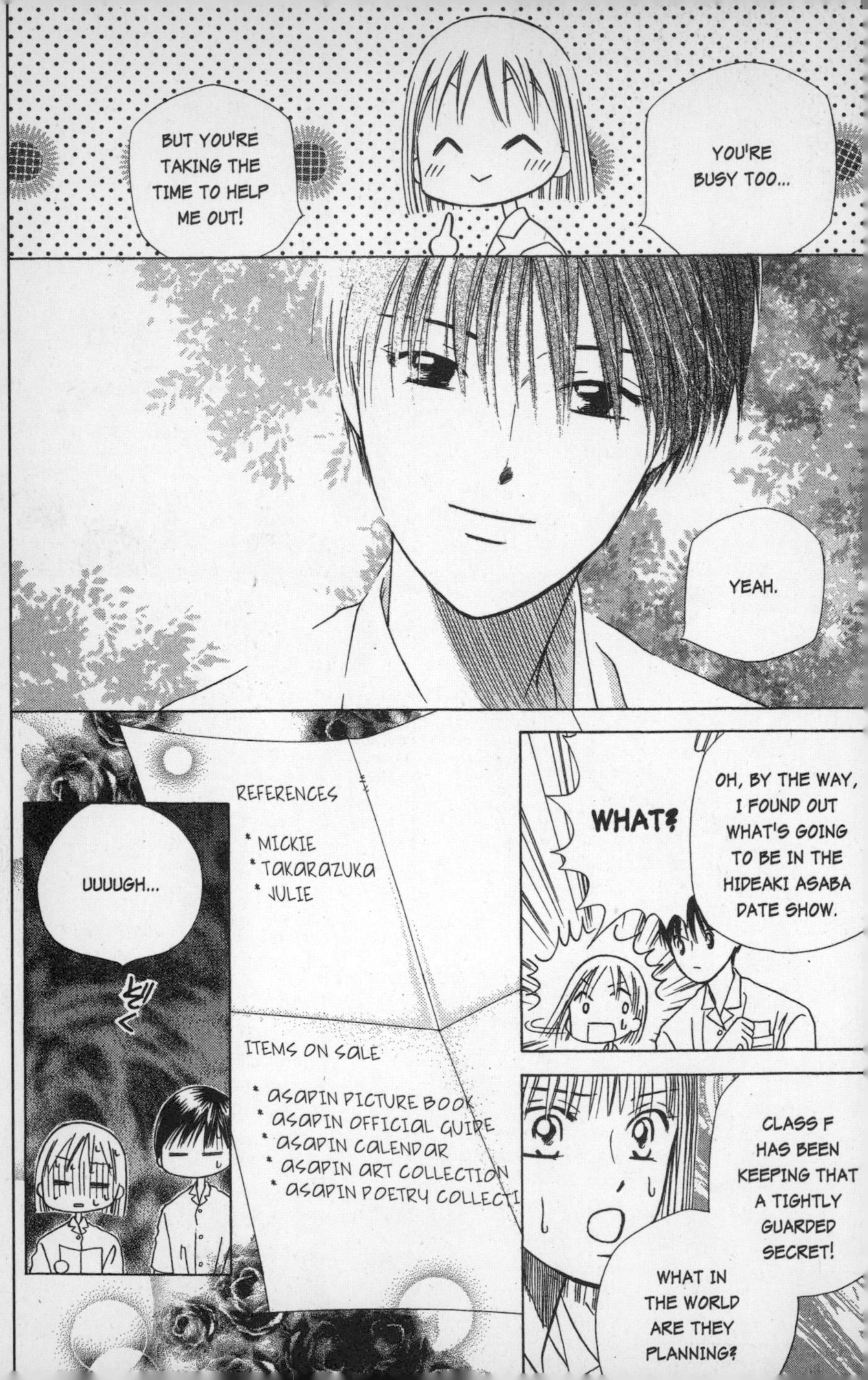

YOU'RE BUSY TOO...
BUT YOU'RE TAKING THE TIME TO HELP ME OUT!
YEAH.
OH, BY THE WAY, I FOUND OUT WHAT'S GOING TO BE IN THE HIDEAKI ASABA DATE SHOW.
WHAT?
CLASS F HAS BEEN KEEPING THAT A TIGHTLY GUARDED SECRET!
WHAT IN THE WORLD ARE THEY PLANNING?
REFERENCES
* MICKIE
* TAKARAZUKA
* JULIE
ITEMS ON SALE
* ASAPIN PICTURE BOOK
* ASAPIN OFFICIAL GUIDE
* ASAPIN CALENDAR
* ASAPIN ART COLLECTION
* ASAPIN POETRY COLLECTI
UUUUGH...

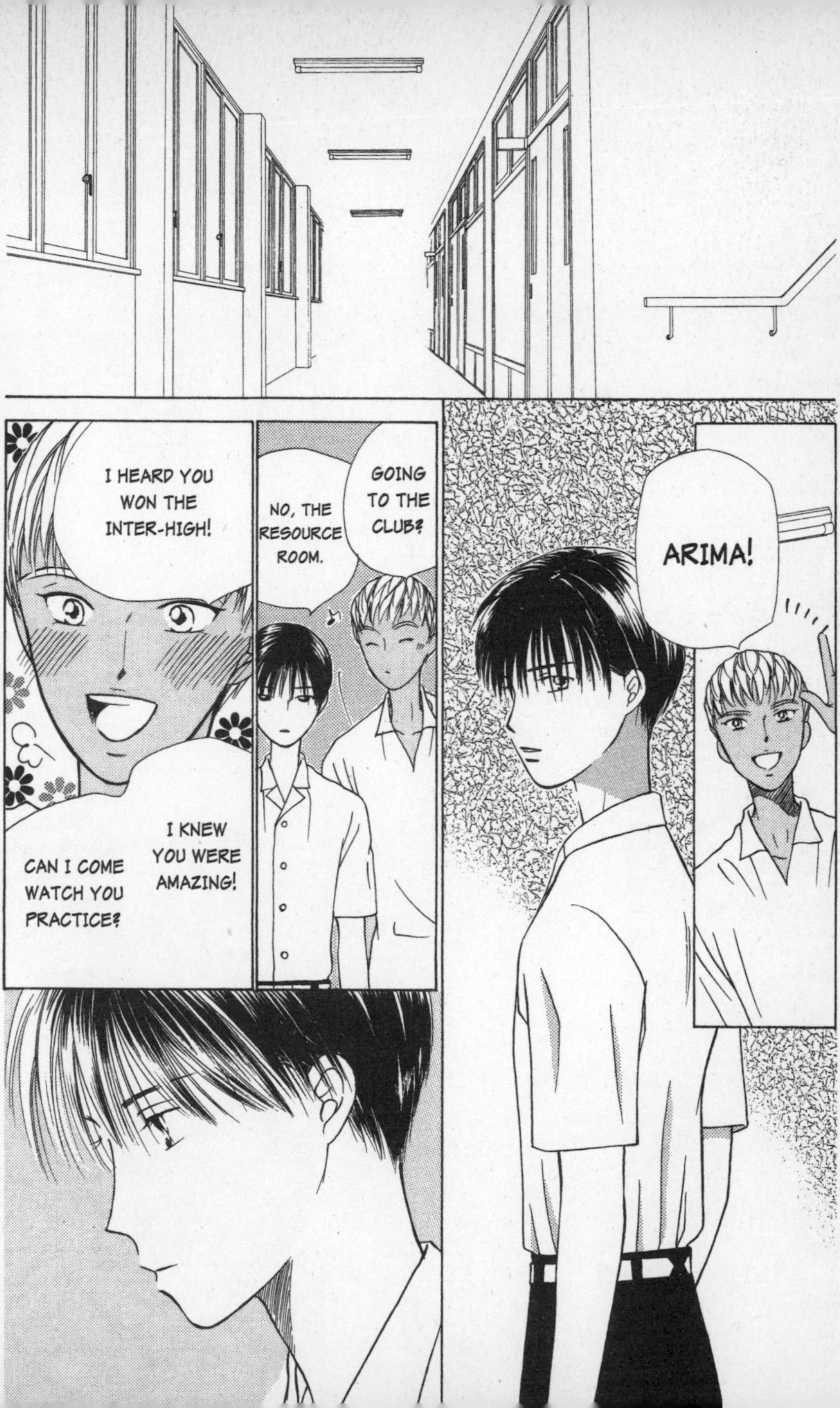
ARIMA!
GOING TO THE CLUB?
NO, THE RESOURCE ROOM.
I HEARD YOU WON THE INTER-HIGH!
I KNEW YOU WERE AMAZING!
CAN I COME WATCH YOU PRACTICE?

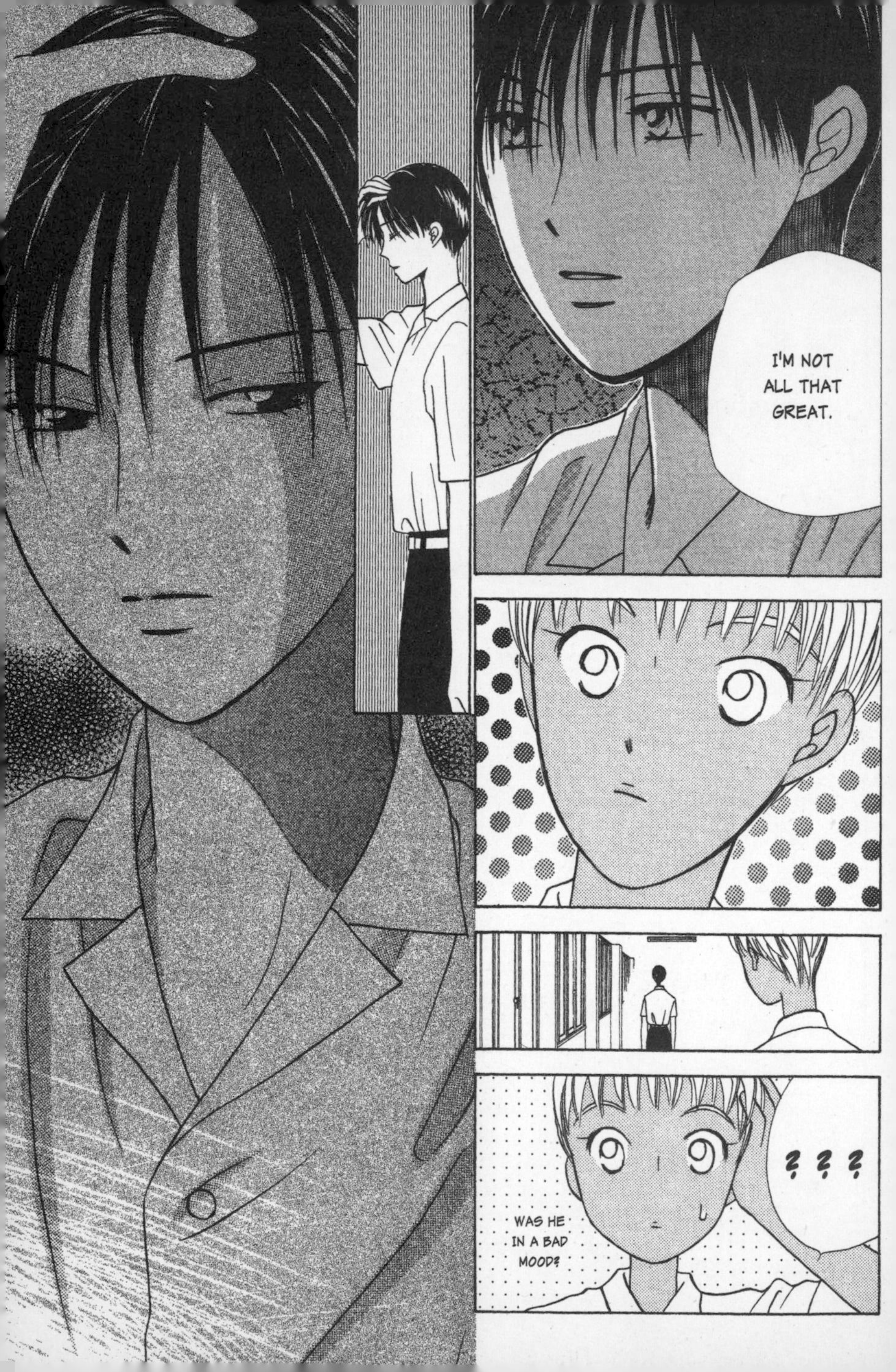
I'M NOT ALL THAT GREAT.
???
WAS HE IN A BAD MOOD?

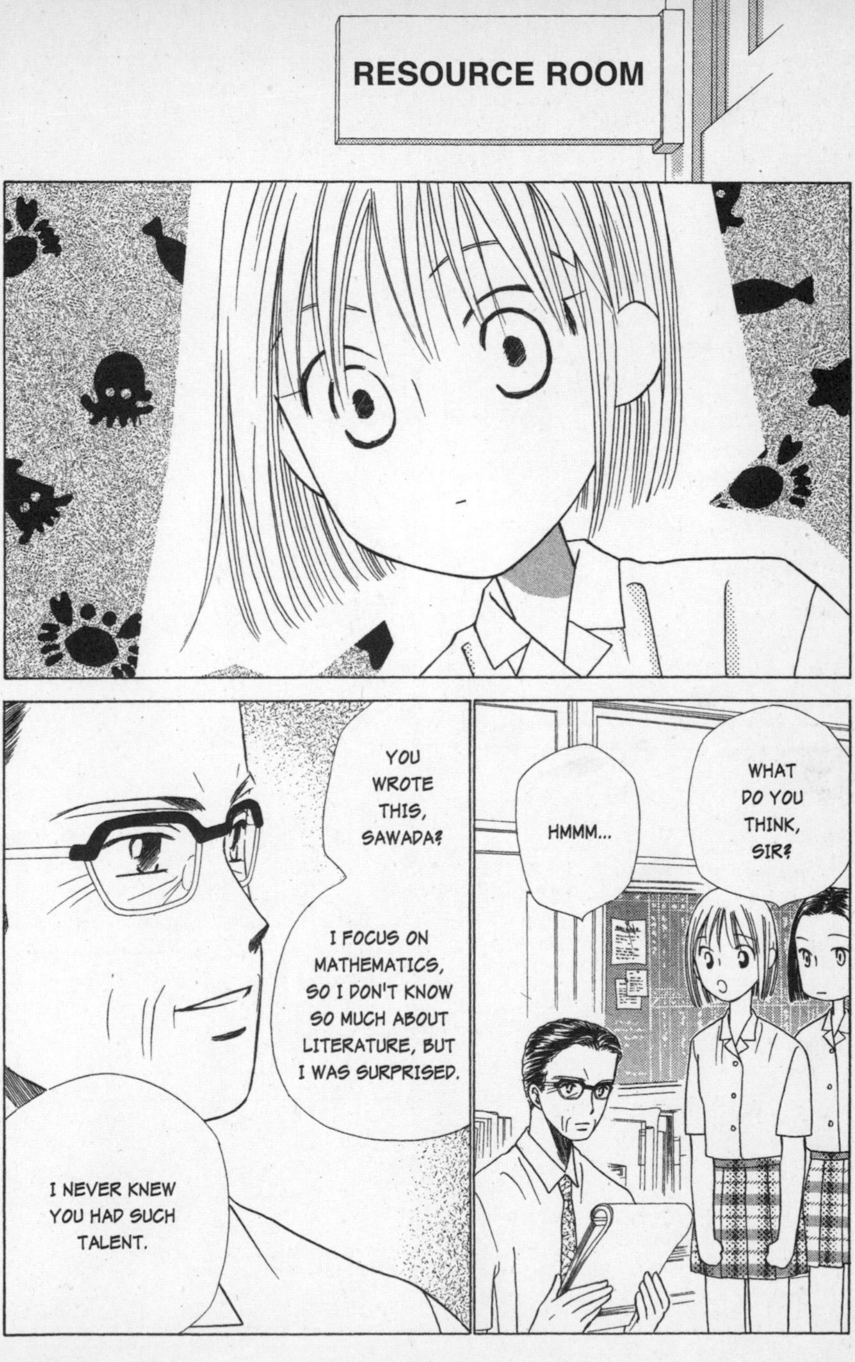
RESOURCE ROOM
WHAT DO YOU THINK, SIR?
HMMM...
YOU WROTE THIS, SAWADA?
I FOCUS ON MATHEMATICS, SO I DON'T KNOW SO MUCH ABOUT LITERATURE, BUT I WAS SURPRISED.
I NEVER KNEW YOU HAD SUCH TALENT.

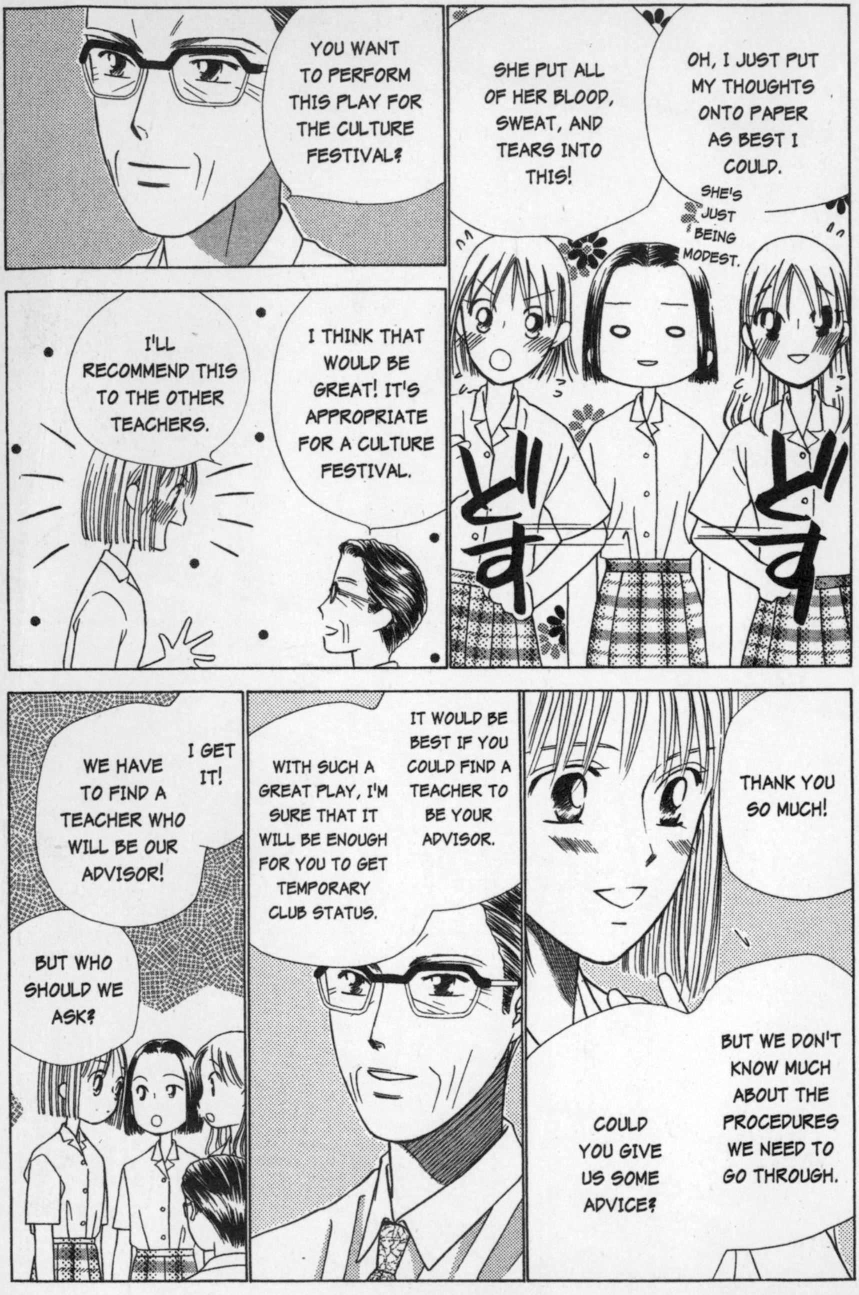

OH, I JUST PUT MY THOUGHTS ONTO PAPER AS BEST I COULD.
SHE PUT ALL OF HER BLOOD, SWEAT, AND TEARS INTO THIS!
SHE'S JUST BEING MODEST.
どす
どす
YOU WANT TO PERFORM THIS PLAY FOR THE CULTURE FESTIVAL?
I THINK THAT WOULD BE GREAT! IT'S APPROPRIATE FOR A CULTURE FESTIVAL.
I'LL RECOMMEND THIS TO THE OTHER TEACHERS.
THANK YOU SO MUCH!
BUT WE DON'T KNOW MUCH ABOUT THE PROCEDURES WE NEED TO GO THROUGH.
COULD YOU GIVE US SOME ADVICE?
WITH SUCH A GREAT PLAY, I'M SURE THAT IT WILL BE ENOUGH FOR YOU TO GET TEMPORARY CLUB STATUS.
IT WOULD BE BEST IF YOU COULD FIND A TEACHER TO BE YOUR ADVISOR.
I GET IT!
WE HAVE TO FIND A TEACHER WHO WILL BE OUR ADVISOR!
BUT WHO SHOULD WE ASK?

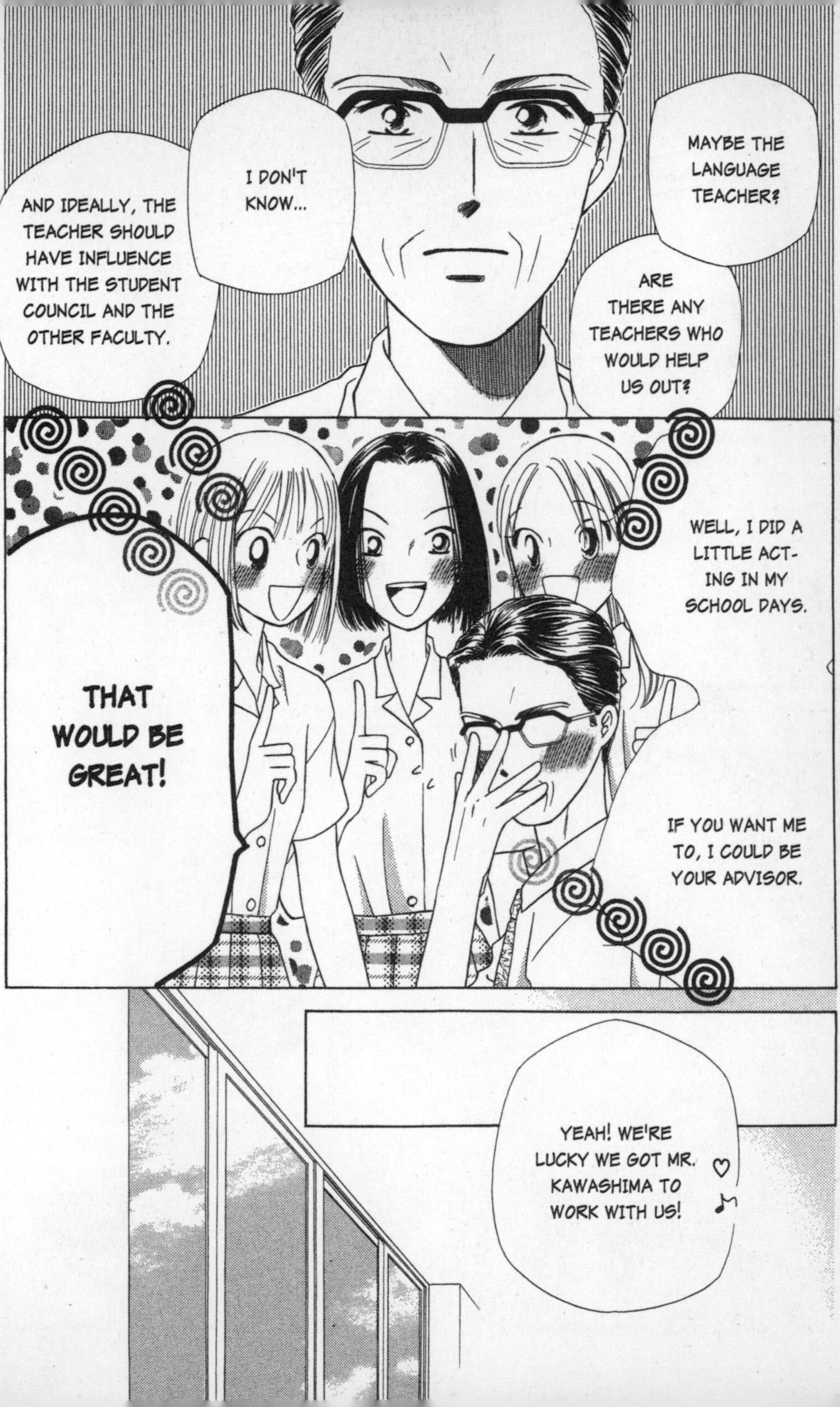
MAYBE THE LANGUAGE TEACHER?
ARE THERE ANY TEACHERS WHO WOULD HELP US OUT?
I DON'T KNOW...
AND IDEALLY, THE TEACHER SHOULD HAVE INFLUENCE WITH THE STUDENT COUNCIL AND THE OTHER FACULTY.
WELL, I DID A LITTLE ACTING IN MY SCHOOL DAYS.
IF YOU WANT ME TO, I COULD BE YOUR ADVISOR.
THAT WOULD BE GREAT!
YEAH! WE'RE LUCKY WE GOT MR. KAWASHIMA TO WORK WITH US! ♡ ♪

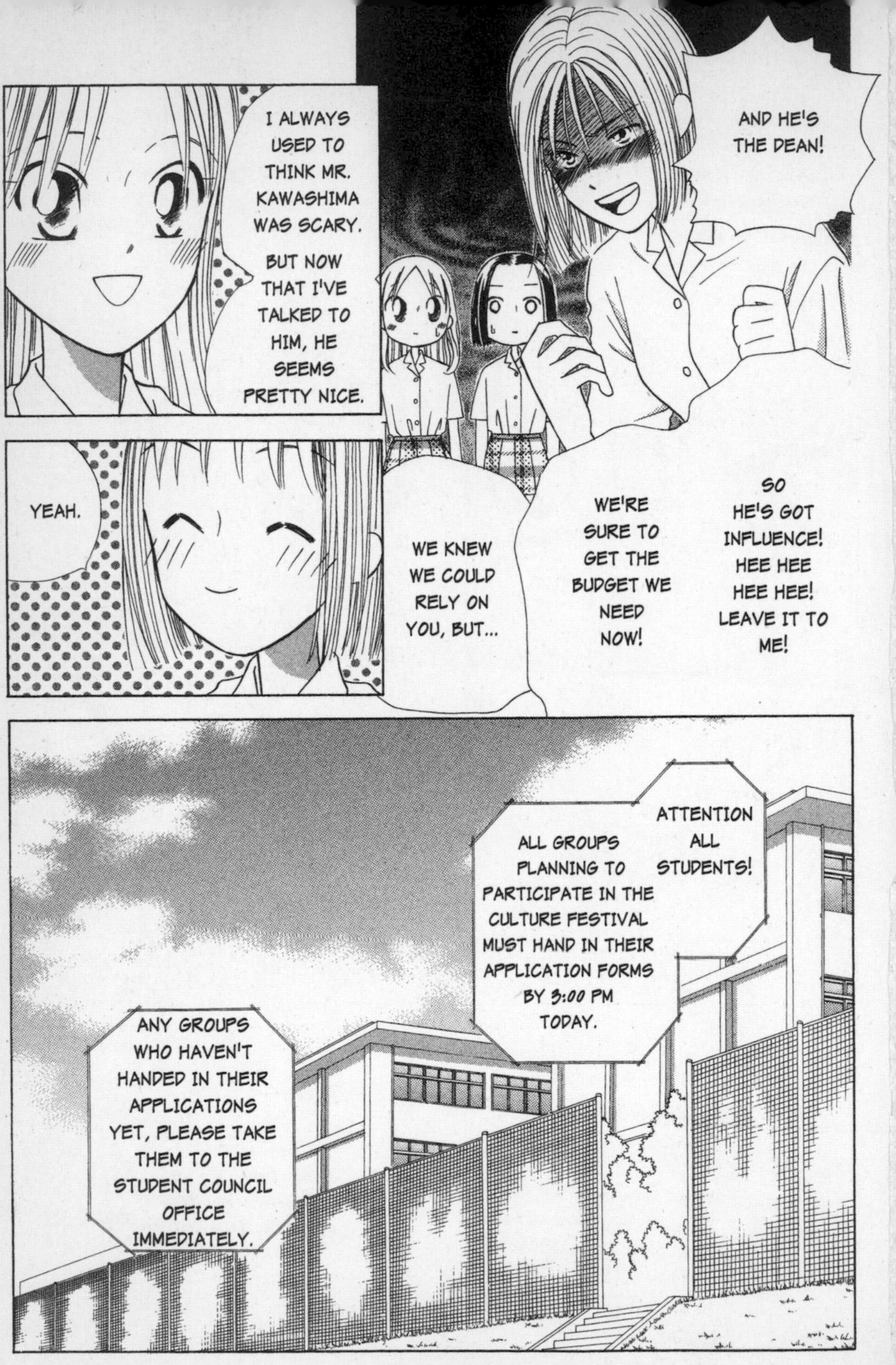
AND HE'S THE DEAN!
SO HE'S GOT INFLUENCE! HEE HEE HEE HEE! LEAVE IT TO ME!
WE'RE SURE TO GET THE BUDGET WE NEED NOW!
WE KNEW WE COULD RELY ON YOU, BUT...
I ALWAYS USED TO THINK MR. KAWASHIMA WAS SCARY.
BUT NOW THAT I'VE TALKED TO HIM, HE SEEMS PRETTY NICE.
YEAH.
ATTENTION ALL STUDENTS!
ALL GROUPS PLANNING TO PARTICIPATE IN THE CULTURE FESTIVAL MUST HAND IN THEIR APPLICATION FORMS BY 3:00 PM TODAY.
ANY GROUPS WHO HAVEN'T HANDED IN THEIR APPLICATIONS YET, PLEASE TAKE THEM TO THE STUDENT COUNCIL OFFICE IMMEDIATELY.

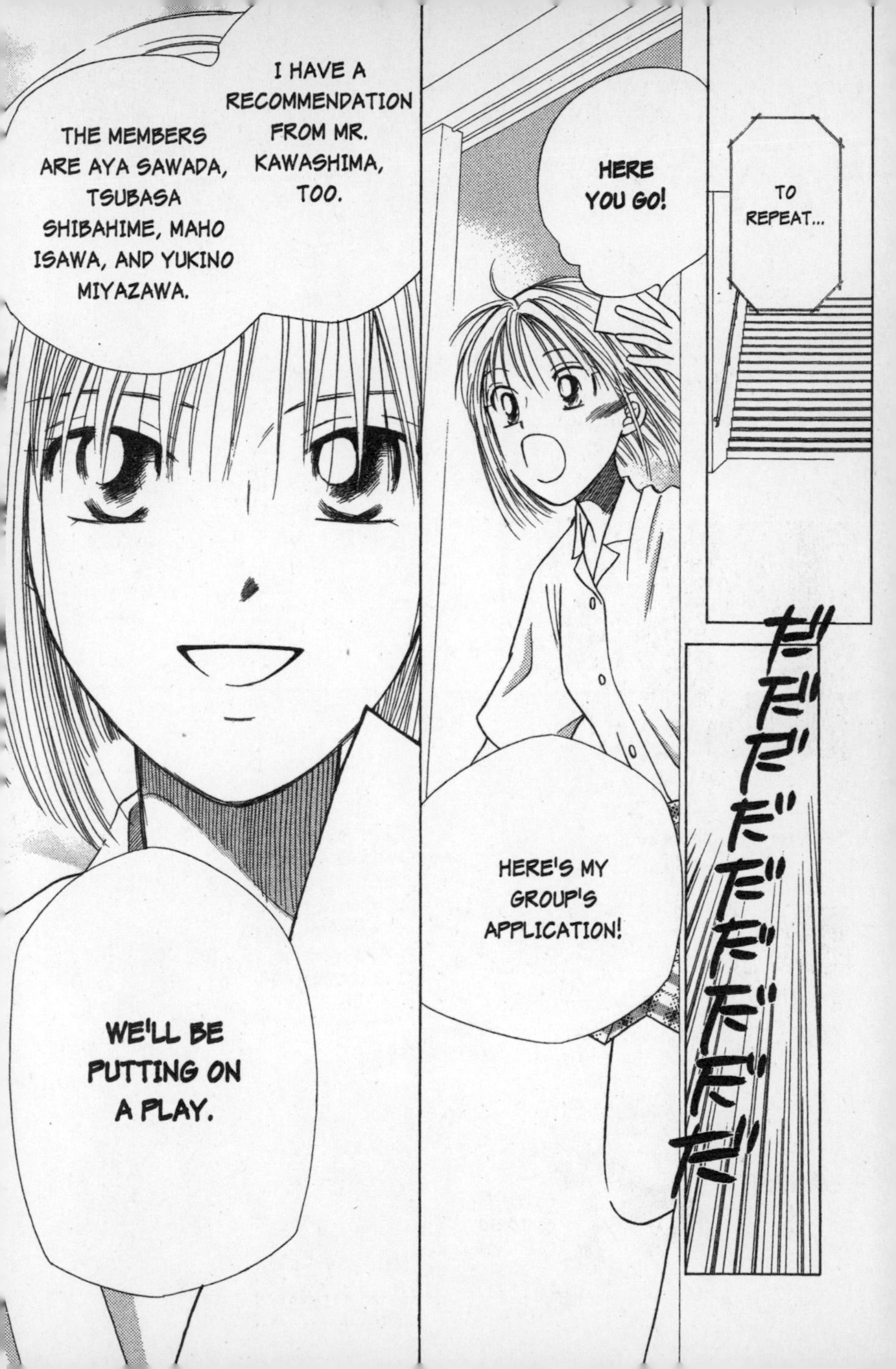
TO REPEAT...
HERE YOU GO!
HERE'S MY GROUP'S APPLICATION!
I HAVE A RECOMMENDATION FROM MR. KAWASHIMA, TOO.
THE MEMBERS ARE AYA SAWADA, TSUBASA SHIBAHIME, MAHO ISAWA, AND YUKINO MIYAZAWA.
WE'LL BE PUTTING ON A PLAY.

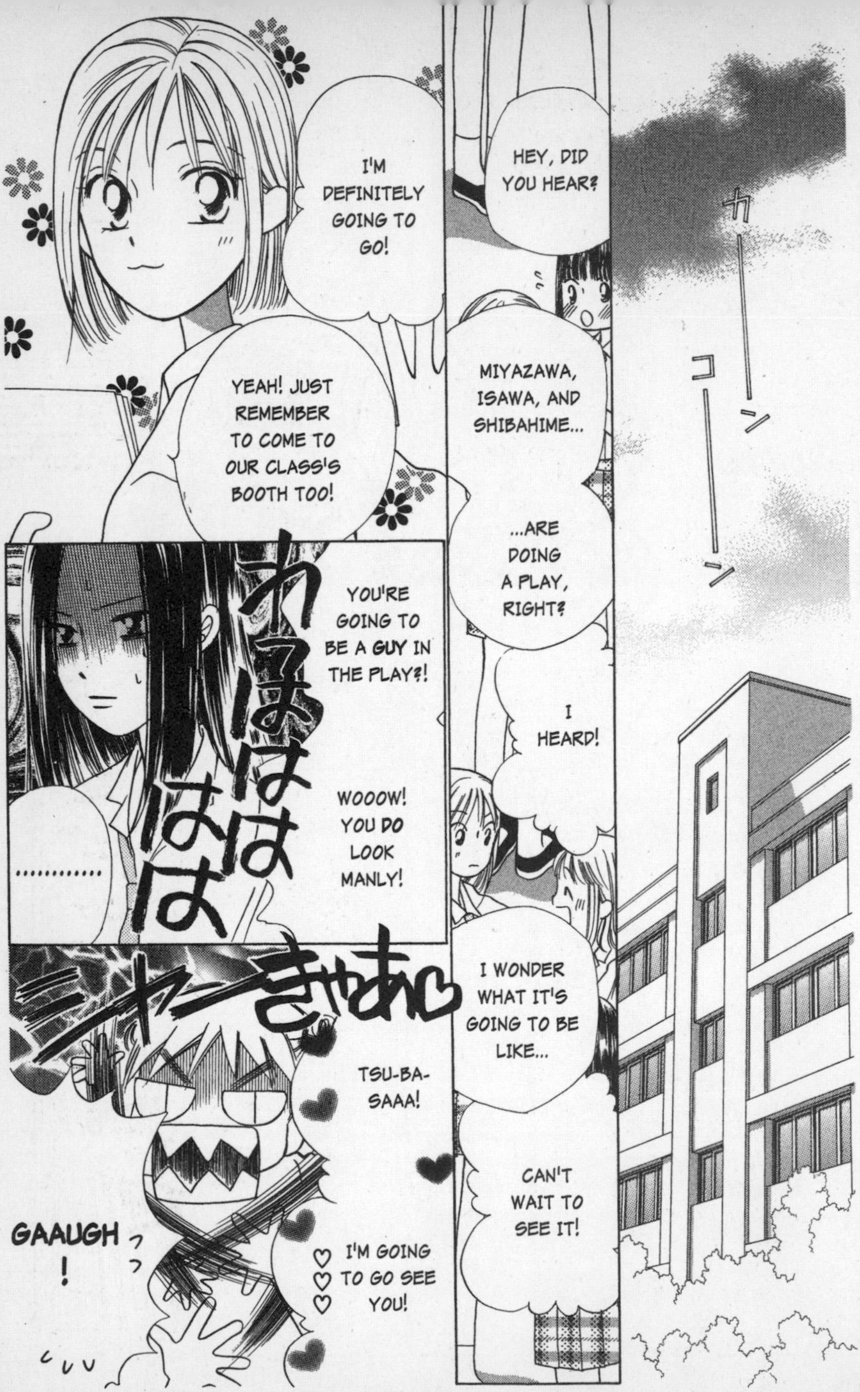
カーン
コーン
HEY, DID YOU HEAR?
MIYAZAWA, ISAWA, AND SHIBAHIME...
...ARE DOING A PLAY, RIGHT?
I HEARD!
I WONDER WHAT IT'S GOING TO BE LIKE...
CAN'T WAIT TO SEE IT!
I'M DEFINITELY GOING TO GO!
YEAH! JUST REMEMBER TO COME TO OUR CLASS'S BOOTH TOO!
わははははは
YOU'RE GOING TO BE A **GUY** IN THE PLAY?!
WOOOW! YOU **DO** LOOK MANLY!
....
きゃあ♡
シャー
TSU-BA-SAAA!
♡ I'M GOING ♡ TO GO SEE ♡ YOU!
GAAUGH!

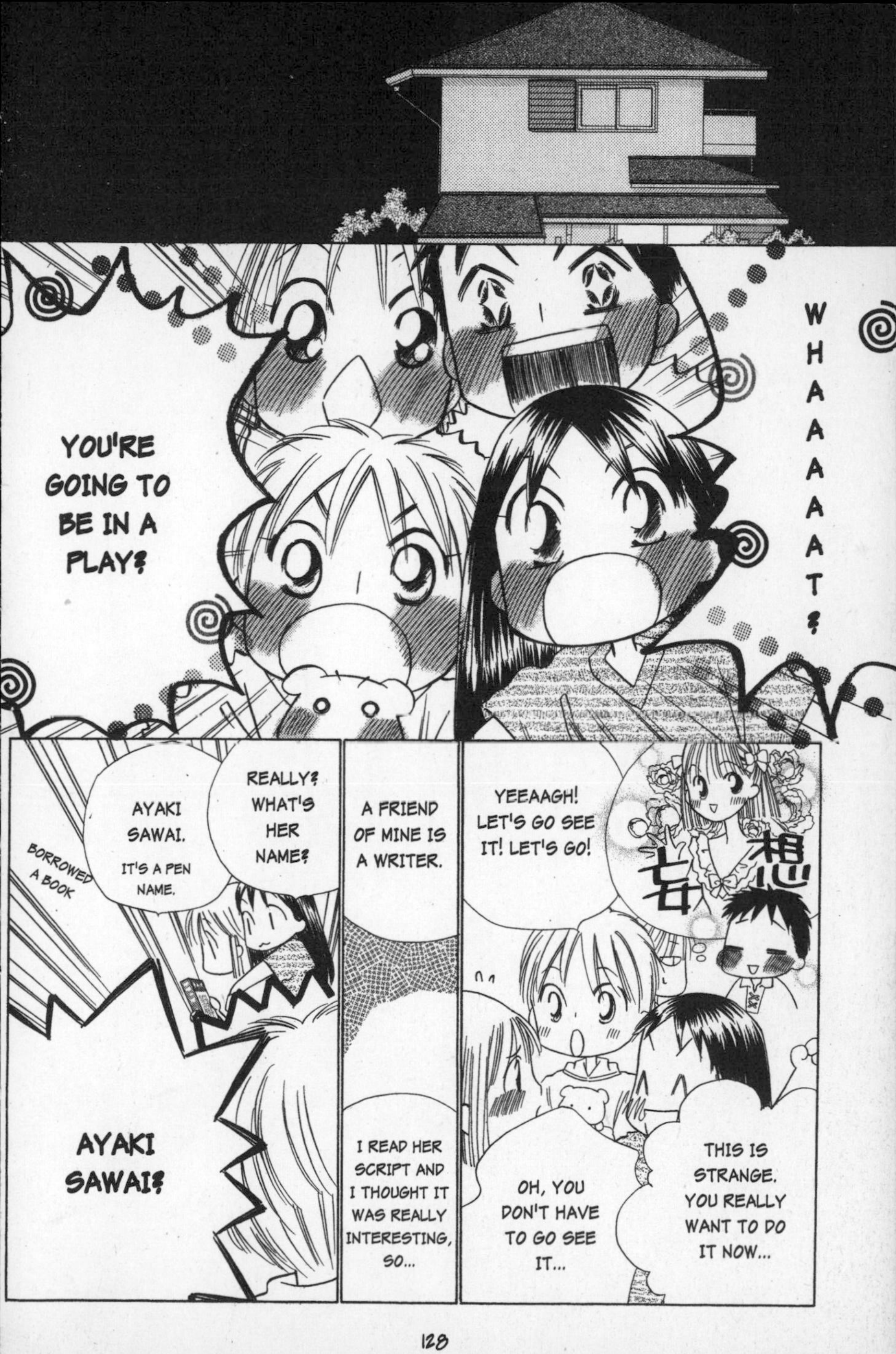

WHAAAAAAT?
YOU'RE GOING TO BE IN A PLAY?
YEEAAGH! LET'S GO SEE IT! LET'S GO!
妄想
THIS IS STRANGE. YOU REALLY WANT TO DO IT NOW...
OH, YOU DON'T HAVE TO GO SEE IT...
A FRIEND OF MINE IS A WRITER.
I READ HER SCRIPT AND I THOUGHT IT WAS REALLY INTERESTING, SO...
REALLY? WHAT'S HER NAME?
AYAKI SAWAI. IT'S A PEN NAME.
BORROWED A BOOK
AYAKI SAWAI?

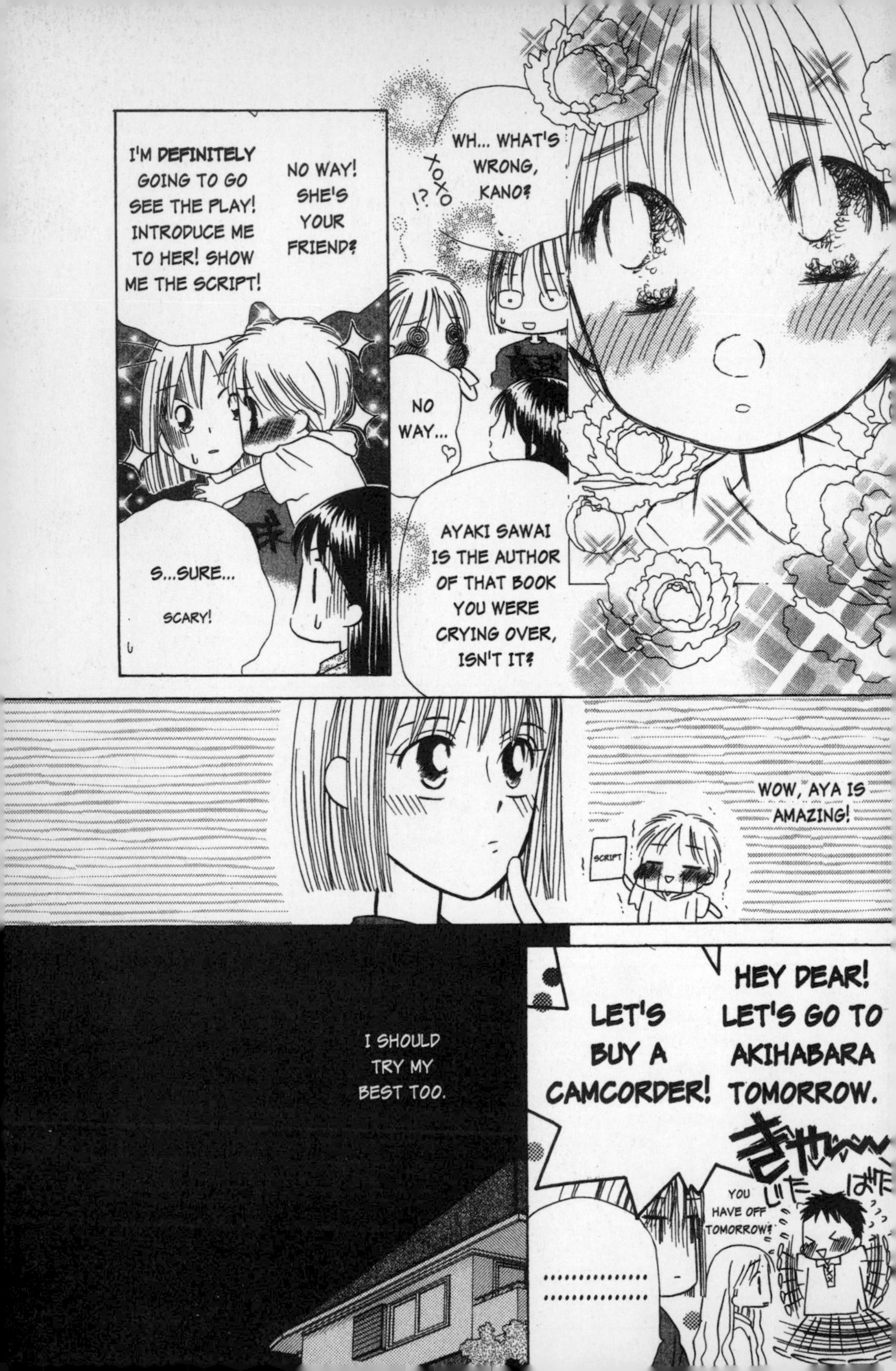
WH... WHAT'S WRONG, KANO?
XOXO
!?
NO WAY...
AYAKI SAWAI IS THE AUTHOR OF THAT BOOK YOU WERE CRYING OVER, ISN'T IT?
NO WAY! SHE'S YOUR FRIEND?
I'M DEFINITELY GOING TO GO SEE THE PLAY! INTRODUCE ME TO HER! SHOW ME THE SCRIPT!
S...SURE...
SCARY!
WOW, AYA IS AMAZING!
SCRIPT
HEY DEAR! LET'S GO TO AKIHABARA TOMORROW.
LET'S BUY A CAMCORDER!
YOU HAVE OFF TOMORROW?
....
....
I SHOULD TRY MY BEST TOO.

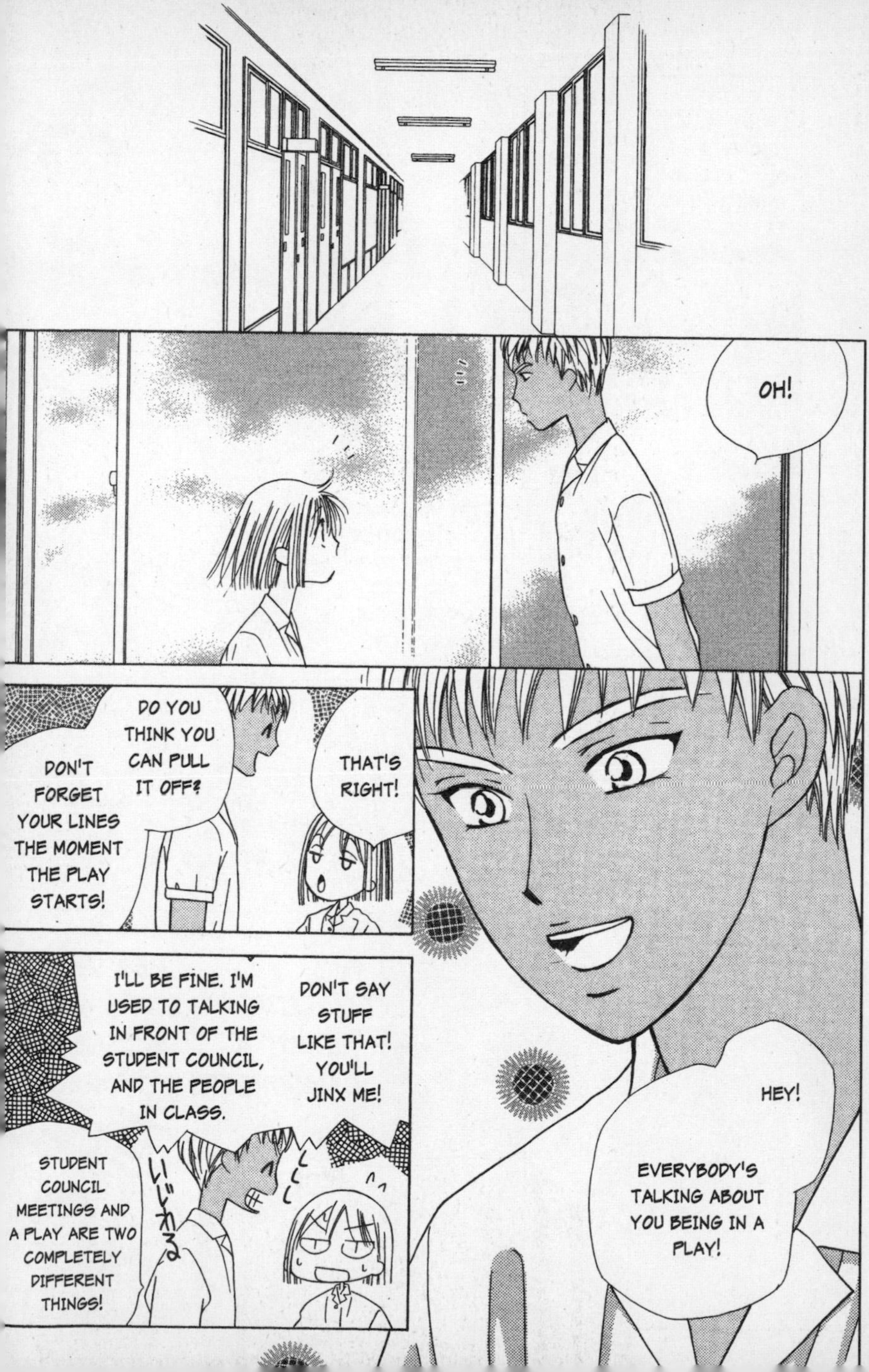
OH!
HEY!
EVERYBODY'S TALKING ABOUT YOU BEING IN A PLAY!
THAT'S RIGHT!
DO YOU THINK YOU CAN PULL IT OFF?
DON'T FORGET YOUR LINES THE MOMENT THE PLAY STARTS!
DON'T SAY STUFF LIKE THAT! YOU'LL JINX ME!
I'LL BE FINE. I'M USED TO TALKING IN FRONT OF THE STUDENT COUNCIL, AND THE PEOPLE IN CLASS.
STUDENT COUNCIL MEETINGS AND A PLAY ARE TWO COMPLETELY DIFFERENT THINGS!

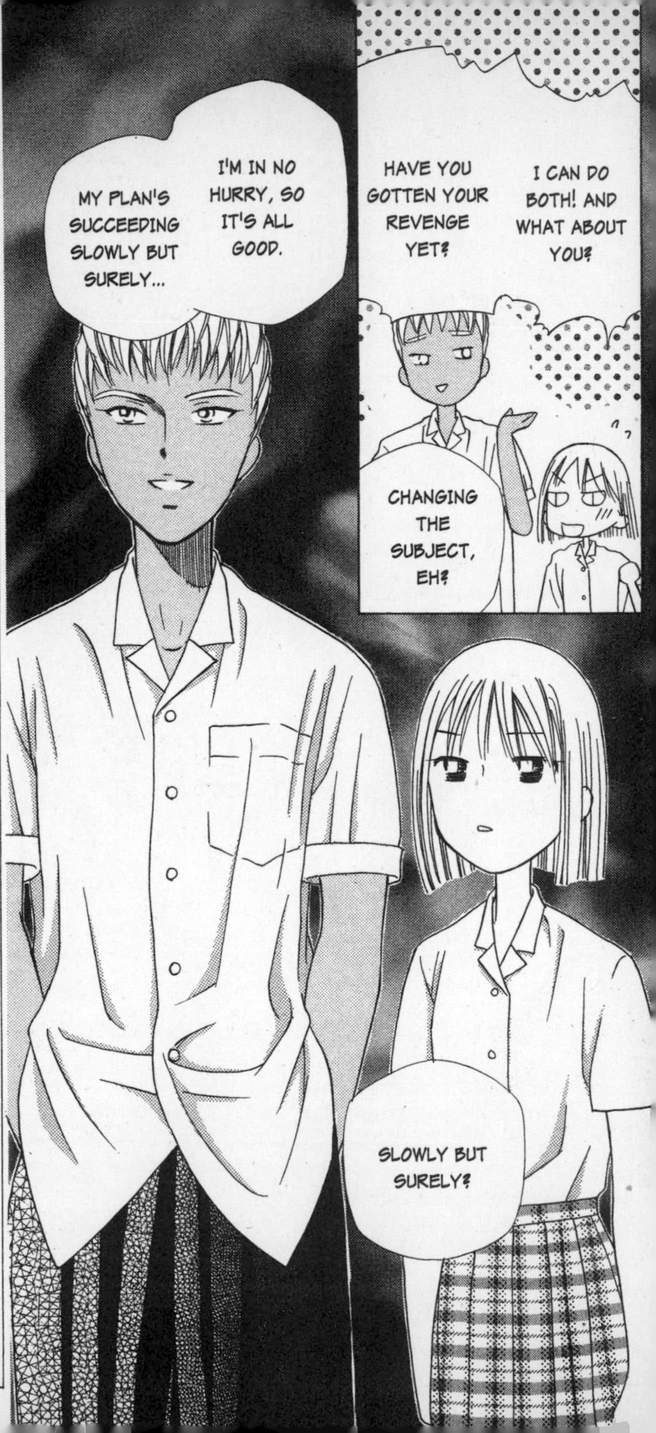
I CAN DO BOTH! AND WHAT ABOUT YOU?
HAVE YOU GOTTEN YOUR REVENGE YET?
CHANGING THE SUBJECT, EH?
I'M IN NO HURRY, SO IT'S ALL GOOD.
MY PLAN'S SUCCEEDING SLOWLY BUT SURELY...
SLOWLY BUT SURELY?

4

I like Japanese tea better than black tea.

I just noticed this recently.

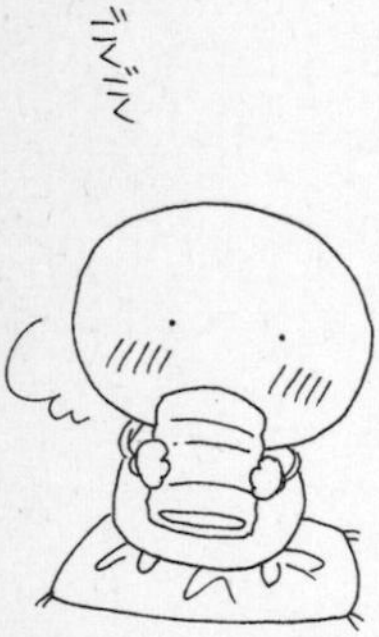

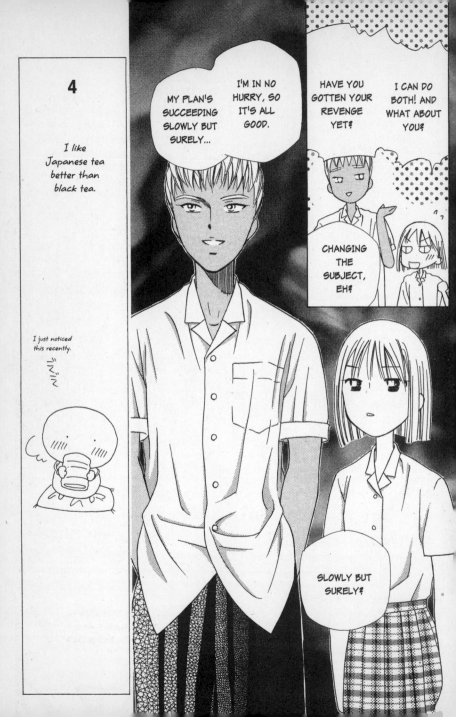

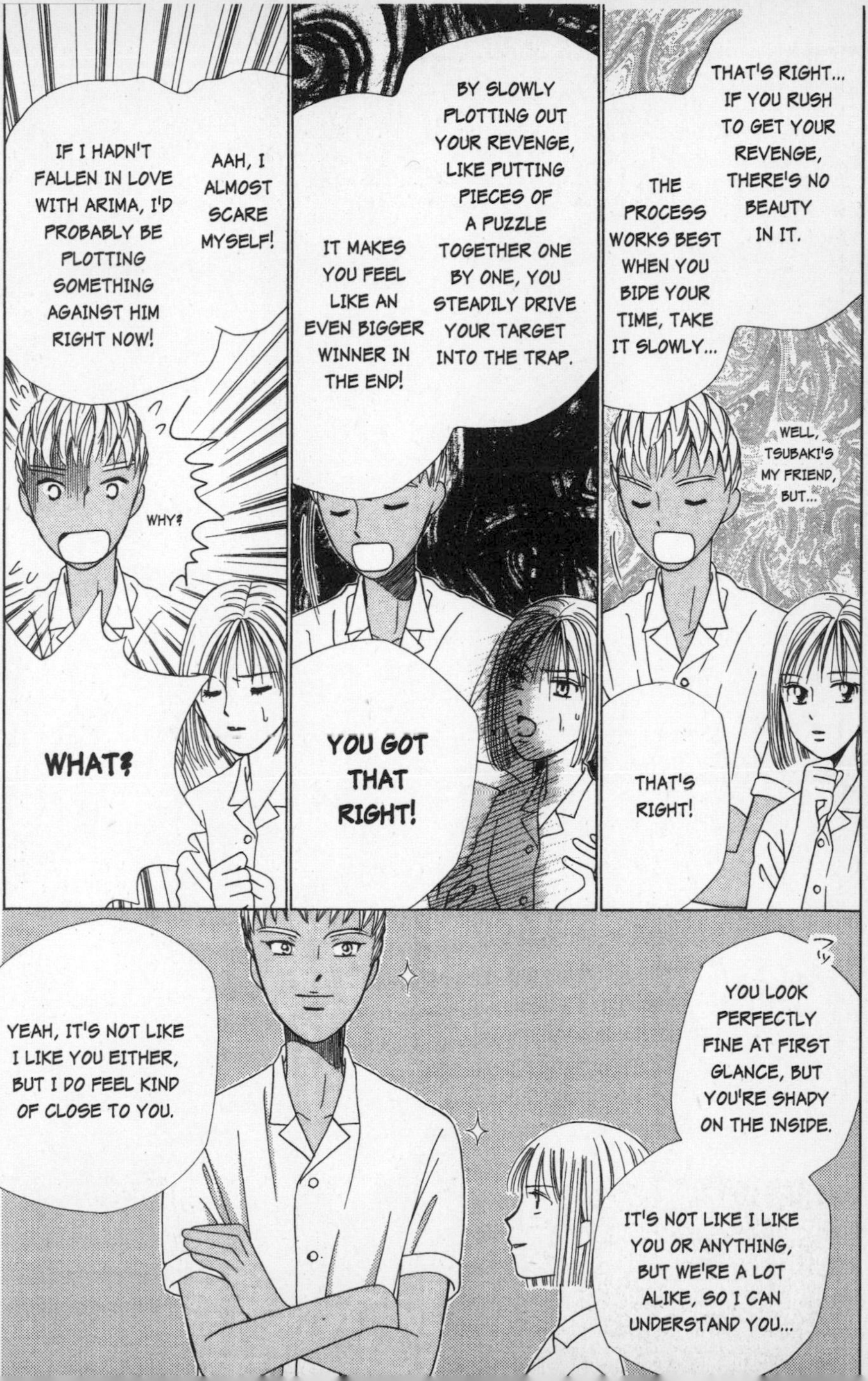
THAT'S RIGHT... IF YOU RUSH TO GET YOUR REVENGE, THERE'S NO BEAUTY IN IT.
THE PROCESS WORKS BEST WHEN YOU BIDE YOUR TIME, TAKE IT SLOWLY...
WELL, TSUBAKI'S MY FRIEND, BUT...
THAT'S RIGHT!
BY SLOWLY PLOTTING OUT YOUR REVENGE, LIKE PUTTING PIECES OF A PUZZLE TOGETHER ONE BY ONE, YOU STEADILY DRIVE YOUR TARGET INTO THE TRAP.
IT MAKES YOU FEEL LIKE AN EVEN BIGGER WINNER IN THE END!
YOU GOT THAT RIGHT!
AAH, I ALMOST SCARE MYSELF!
IF I HADN'T FALLEN IN LOVE WITH ARIMA, I'D PROBABLY BE PLOTTING SOMETHING AGAINST HIM RIGHT NOW!
WHY?
WHAT?
YOU LOOK PERFECTLY FINE AT FIRST GLANCE, BUT YOU'RE SHADY ON THE INSIDE.
IT'S NOT LIKE I LIKE YOU OR ANYTHING, BUT WE'RE A LOT ALIKE, SO I CAN UNDERSTAND YOU...
YEAH, IT'S NOT LIKE I LIKE YOU EITHER, BUT I DO FEEL KIND OF CLOSE TO YOU.

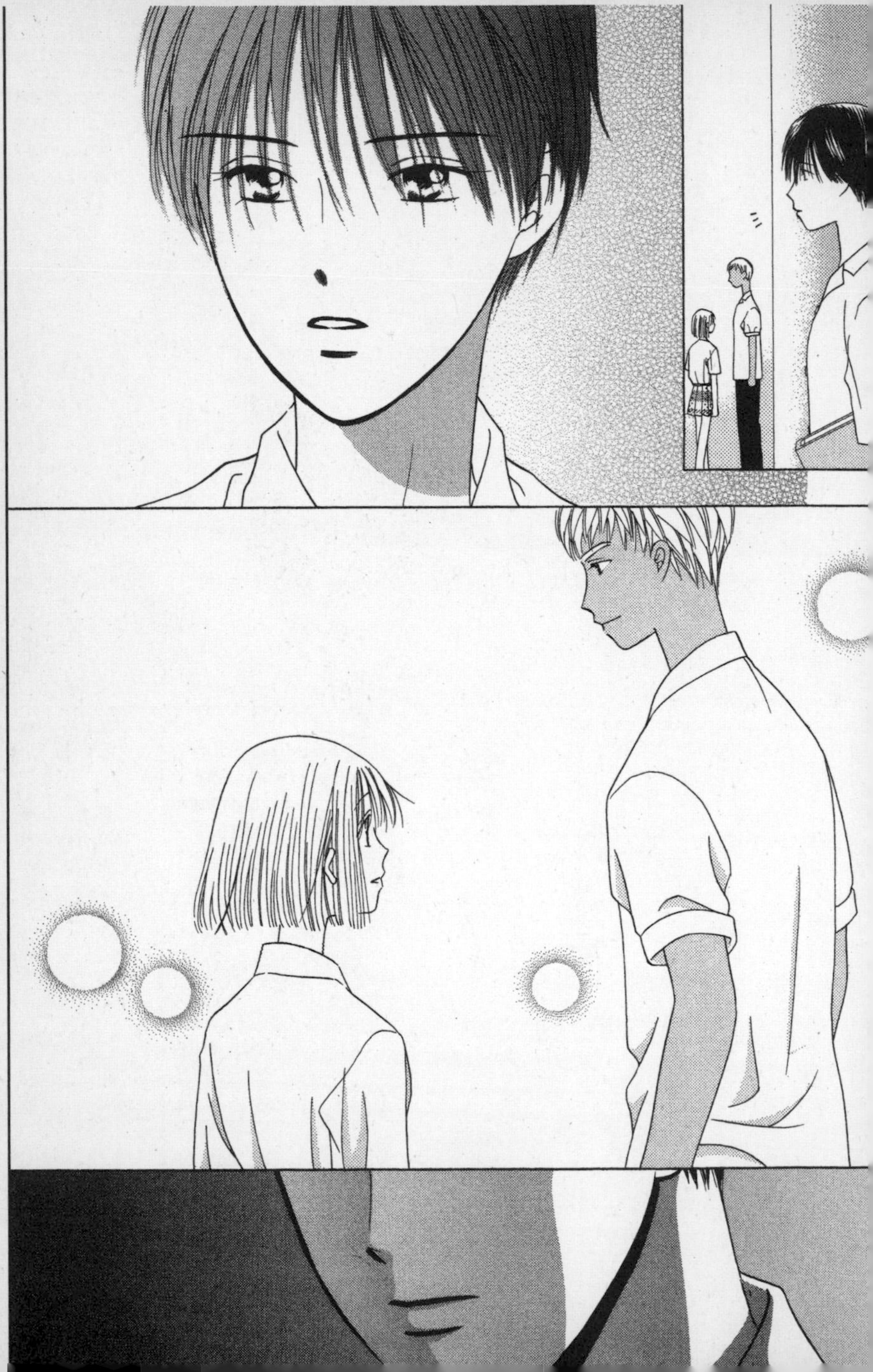

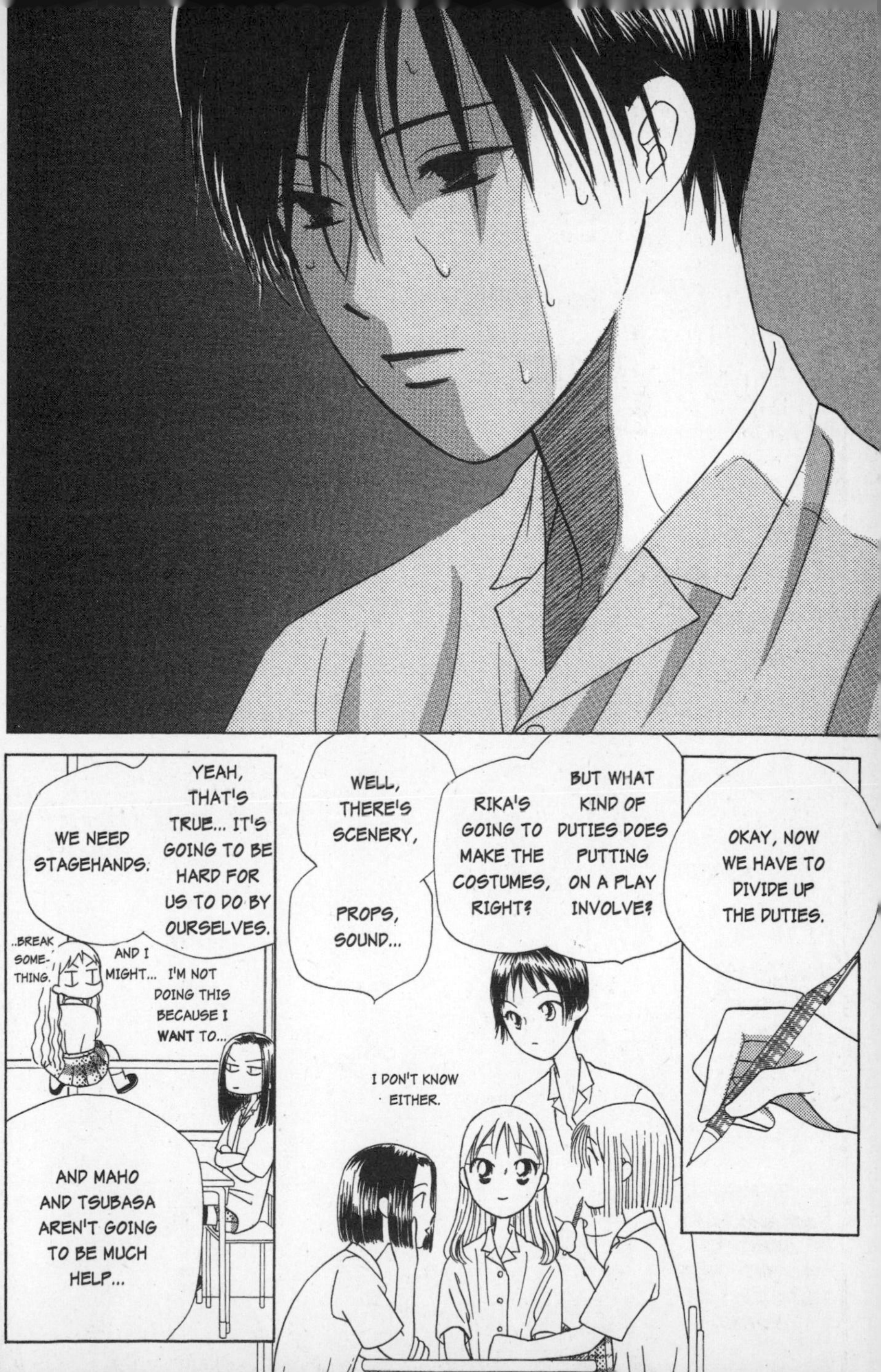
OKAY, NOW WE HAVE TO DIVIDE UP THE DUTIES.
BUT WHAT KIND OF DUTIES DOES PUTTING ON A PLAY INVOLVE?
RIKA'S GOING TO MAKE THE COSTUMES, RIGHT?
WELL, THERE'S SCENERY, PROPS, SOUND...
I DON'T KNOW EITHER.
YEAH, THAT'S TRUE... IT'S GOING TO BE HARD FOR US TO DO BY OURSELVES.
WE NEED STAGEHANDS.
I'M NOT DOING THIS BECAUSE I WANT TO...
AND I MIGHT...
..BREAK SOME-THING.
AND MAHO AND TSUBASA AREN'T GOING TO BE MUCH HELP...

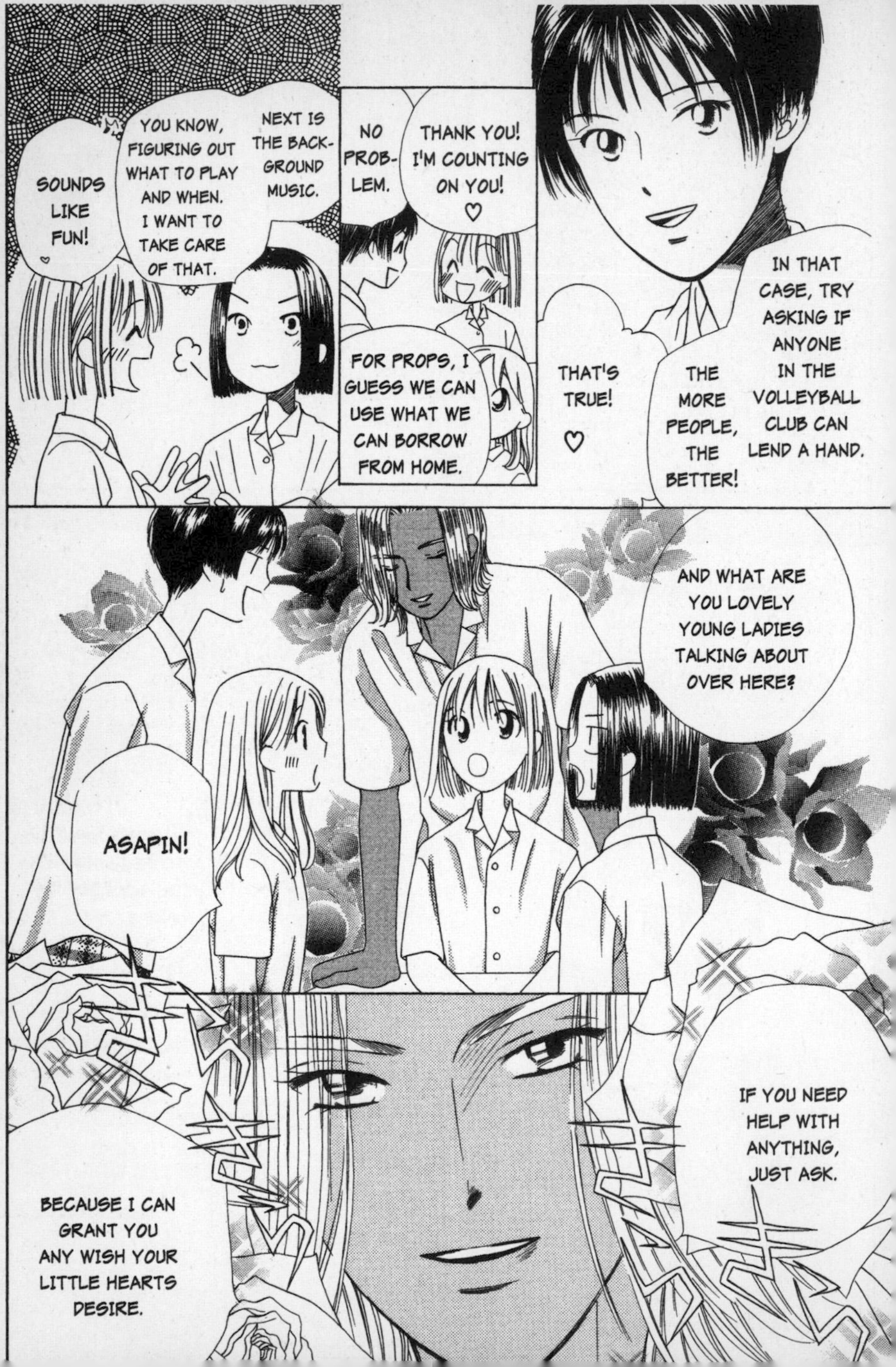
IN THAT CASE, TRY ASKING IF ANYONE IN THE VOLLEYBALL CLUB CAN LEND A HAND.
THE MORE PEOPLE, THE BETTER!
THAT'S TRUE! ♡
THANK YOU! I'M COUNTING ON YOU! ♡
NO PROB-LEM.
FOR PROPS, I GUESS WE CAN USE WHAT WE CAN BORROW FROM HOME.
NEXT IS THE BACK-GROUND MUSIC.
YOU KNOW, FIGURING OUT WHAT TO PLAY AND WHEN. I WANT TO TAKE CARE OF THAT.
SOUNDS LIKE FUN! ♡
AND WHAT ARE YOU LOVELY YOUNG LADIES TALKING ABOUT OVER HERE?
ASAPIN!
IF YOU NEED HELP WITH ANYTHING, JUST ASK.
BECAUSE I CAN GRANT YOU ANY WISH YOUR LITTLE HEARTS DESIRE.

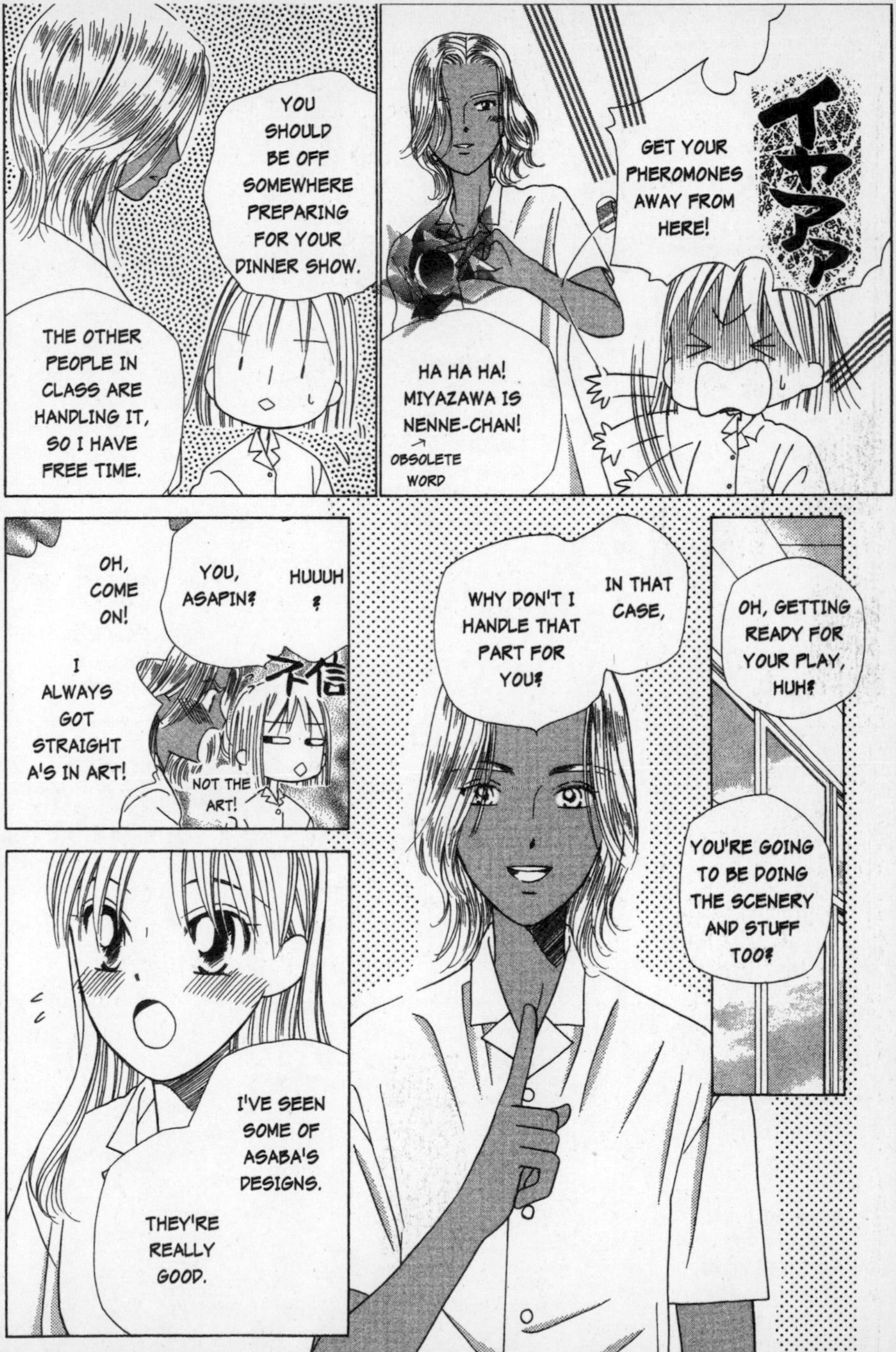

イヤァ
GET YOUR PHEROMONES AWAY FROM HERE!
HA HA HA! MIYAZAWA IS NENNE-CHAN!
OBSOLETE WORD
YOU SHOULD BE OFF SOMEWHERE PREPARING FOR YOUR DINNER SHOW.
THE OTHER PEOPLE IN CLASS ARE HANDLING IT, SO I HAVE FREE TIME.
OH, GETTING READY FOR YOUR PLAY, HUH?
YOU'RE GOING TO BE DOING THE SCENERY AND STUFF TOO?
IN THAT CASE,
WHY DON'T I HANDLE THAT PART FOR YOU?
HUUUH?
YOU, ASAPIN?
OH, COME ON!
I ALWAYS GOT STRAIGHT A'S IN ART!
不信
NOT THE ART!
I'VE SEEN SOME OF ASABA'S DESIGNS.
THEY'RE REALLY GOOD.

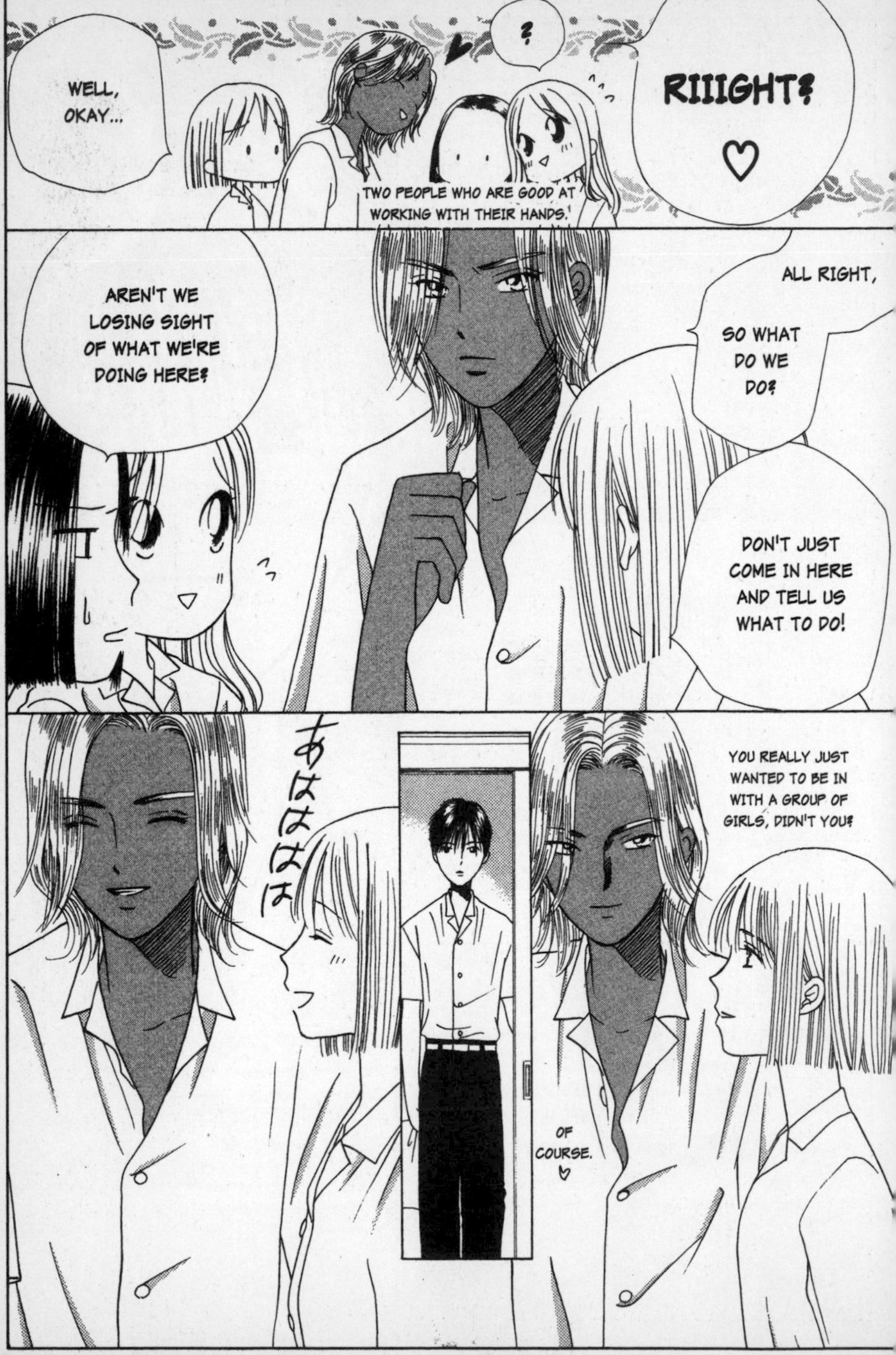
RIIIGHT? ♡
?
TWO PEOPLE WHO ARE GOOD AT WORKING WITH THEIR HANDS.
WELL, OKAY...
ALL RIGHT,
SO WHAT DO WE DO?
DON'T JUST COME IN HERE AND TELL US WHAT TO DO!
AREN'T WE LOSING SIGHT OF WHAT WE'RE DOING HERE?
YOU REALLY JUST WANTED TO BE IN WITH A GROUP OF GIRLS, DIDN'T YOU?
OF COURSE. ♡
あははは

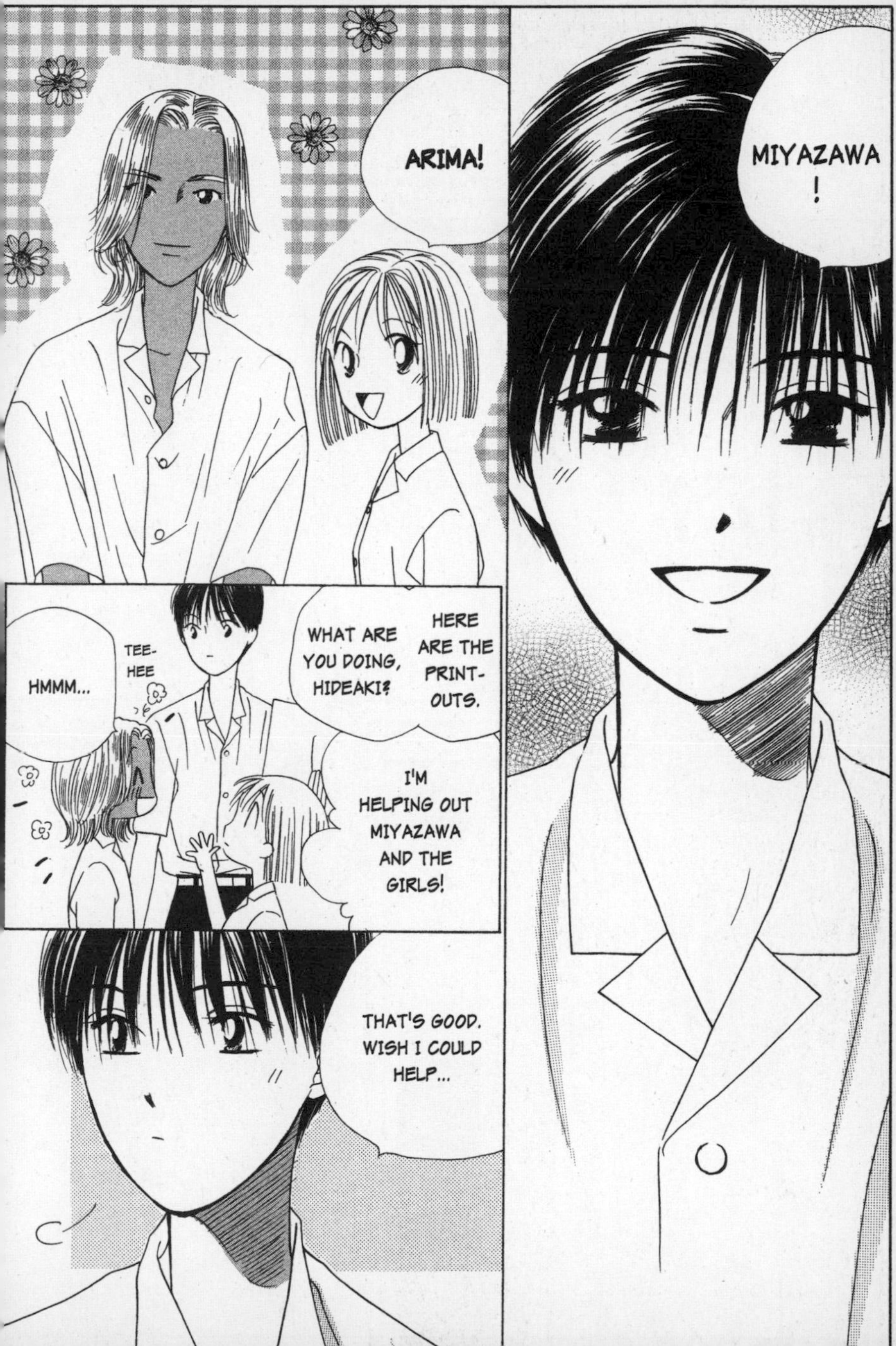
MIYAZAWA!
ARIMA!
HERE ARE THE PRINT-OUTS.
WHAT ARE YOU DOING, HIDEAKI?
TEE-HEE
HMMM...
I'M HELPING OUT MIYAZAWA AND THE GIRLS!
THAT'S GOOD. WISH I COULD HELP...

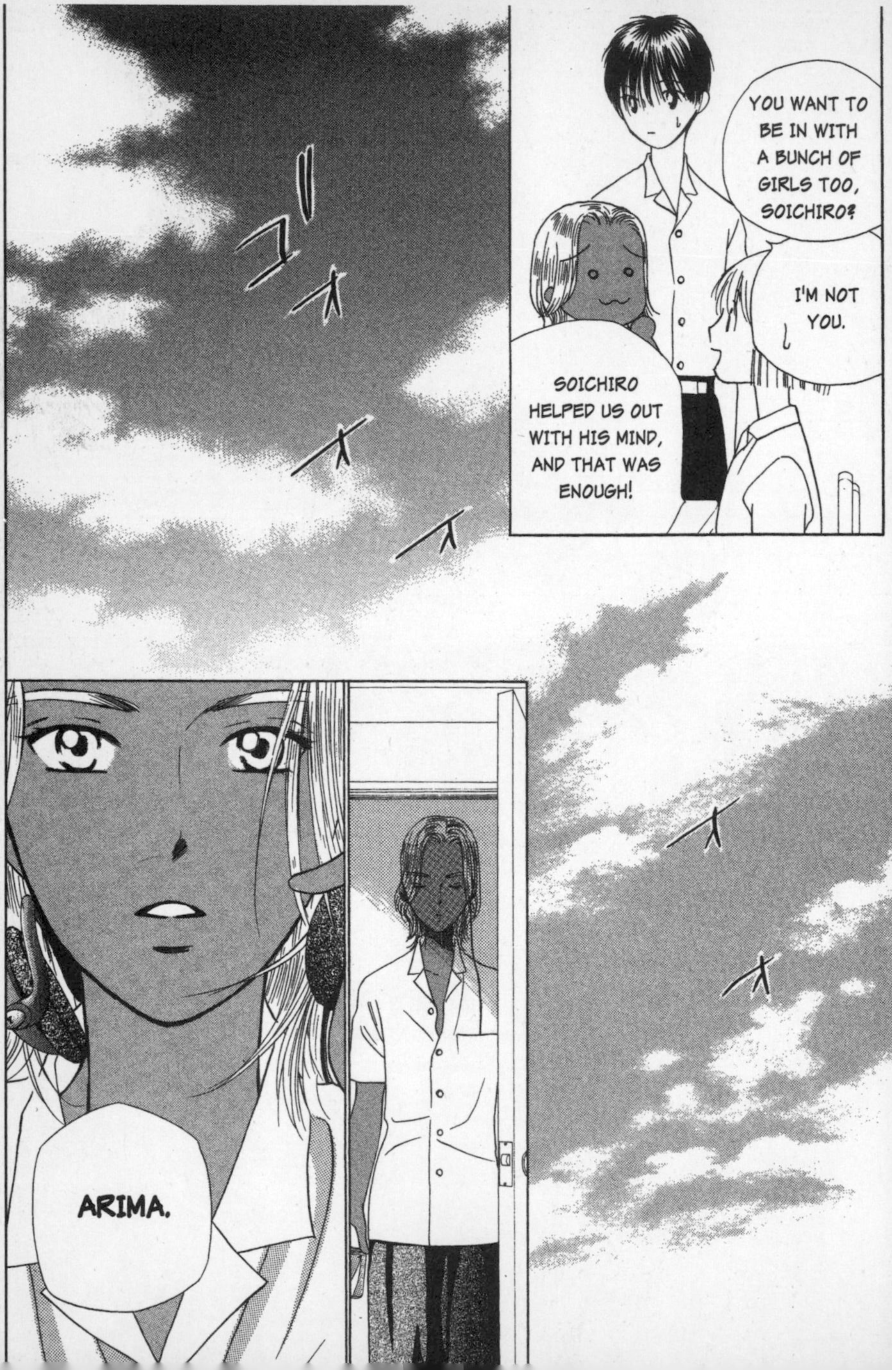
YOU WANT TO BE IN WITH A BUNCH OF GIRLS TOO, SOICHIRO?
I'M NOT YOU.
SOICHIRO HELPED US OUT WITH HIS MIND, AND THAT WAS ENOUGH!
ゴォォォ
ARIMA.

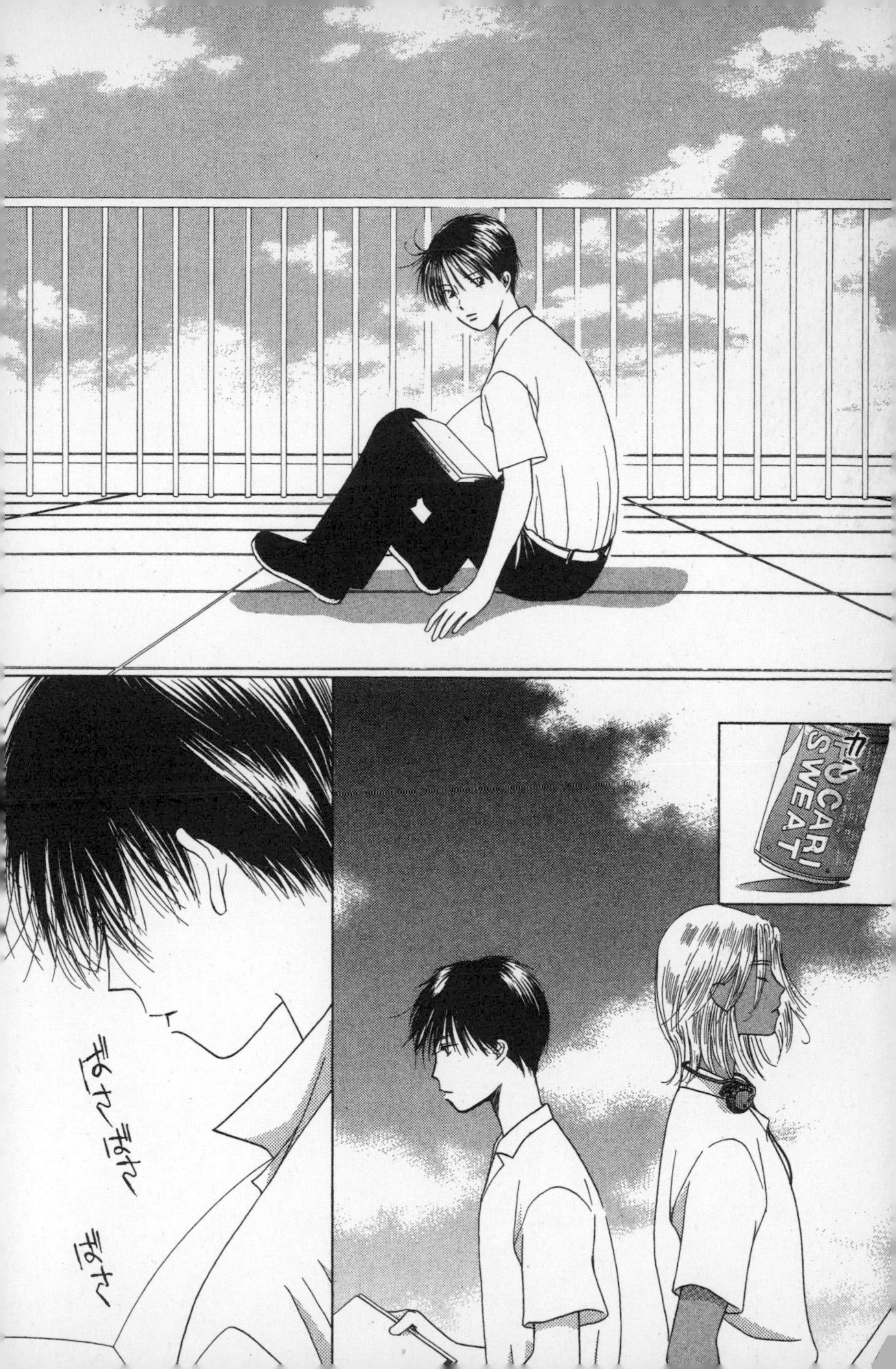
POCARI SWEAT

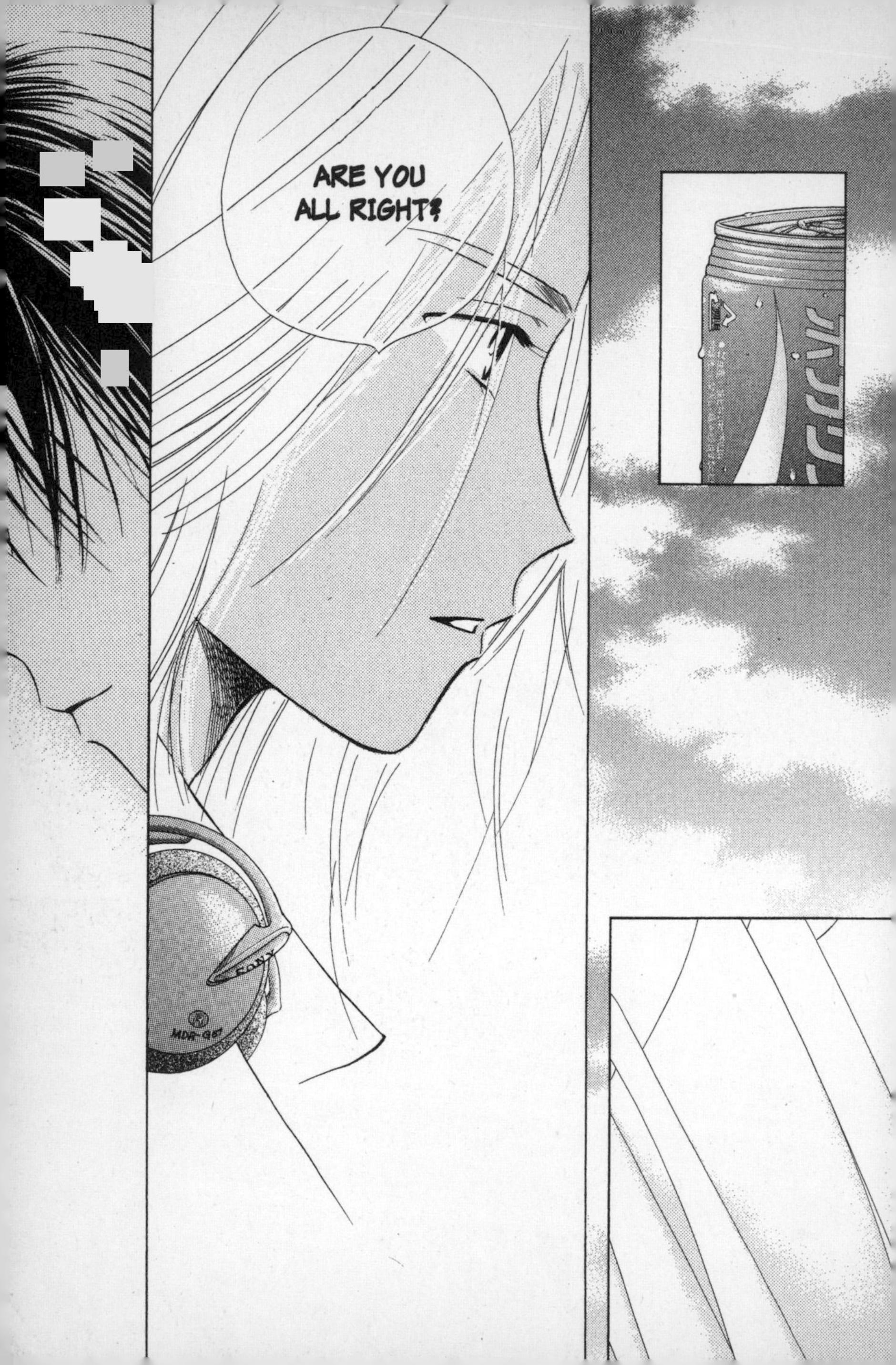
ARE YOU ALL RIGHT?

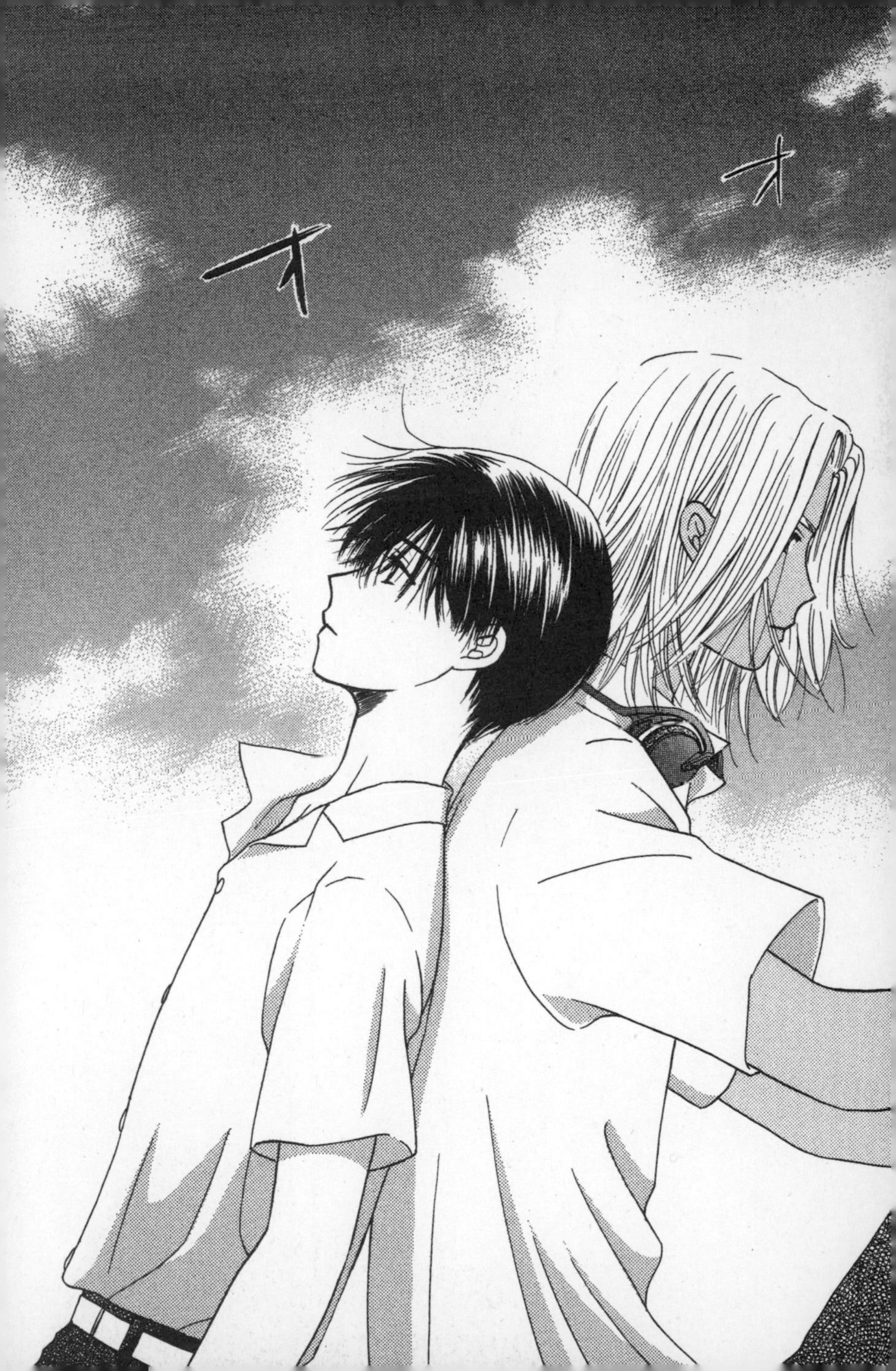
オ
オ

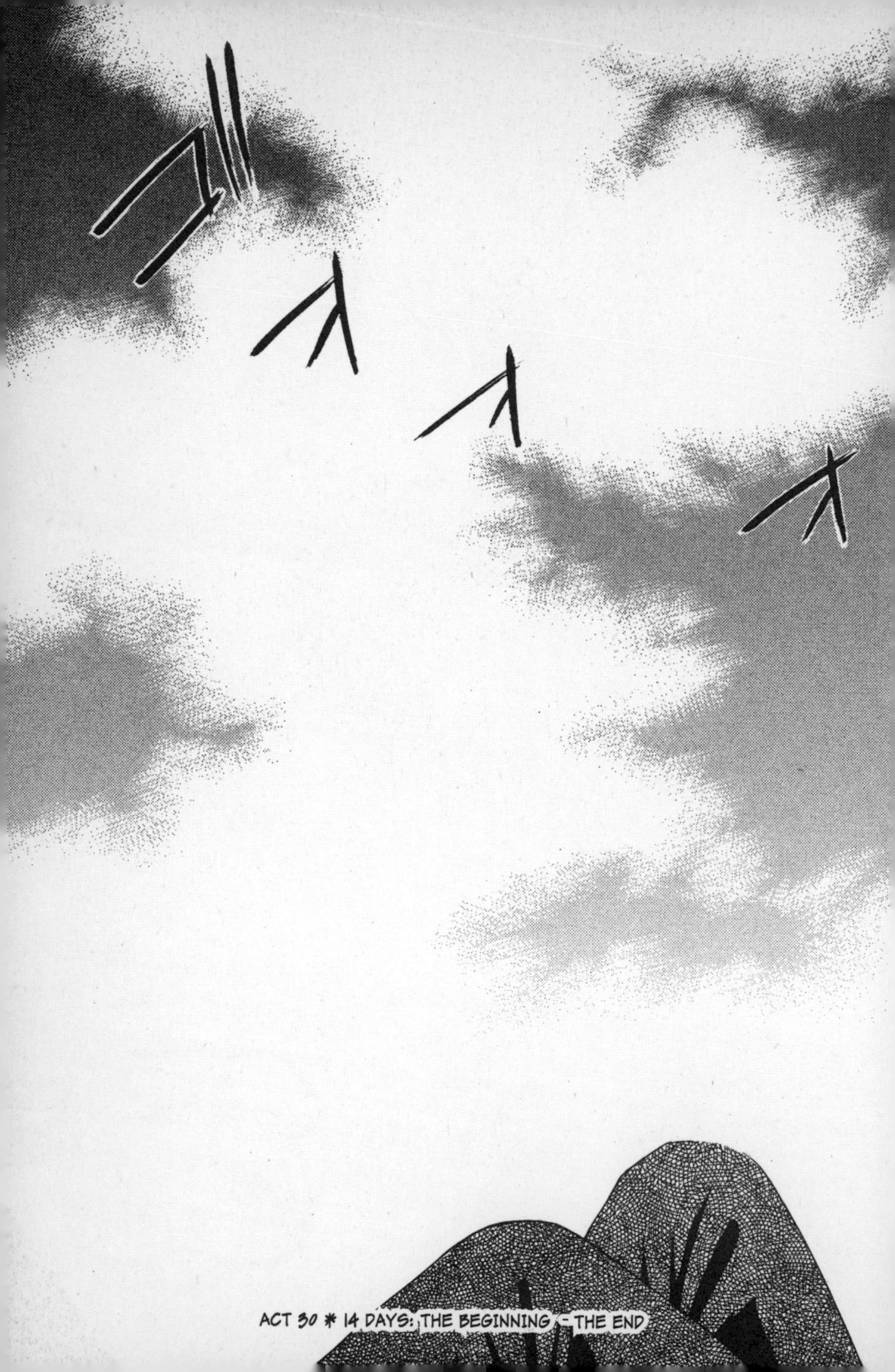
ゴォォオ

ACT 30 * 14 DAYS: THE BEGINNING - THE END

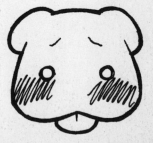

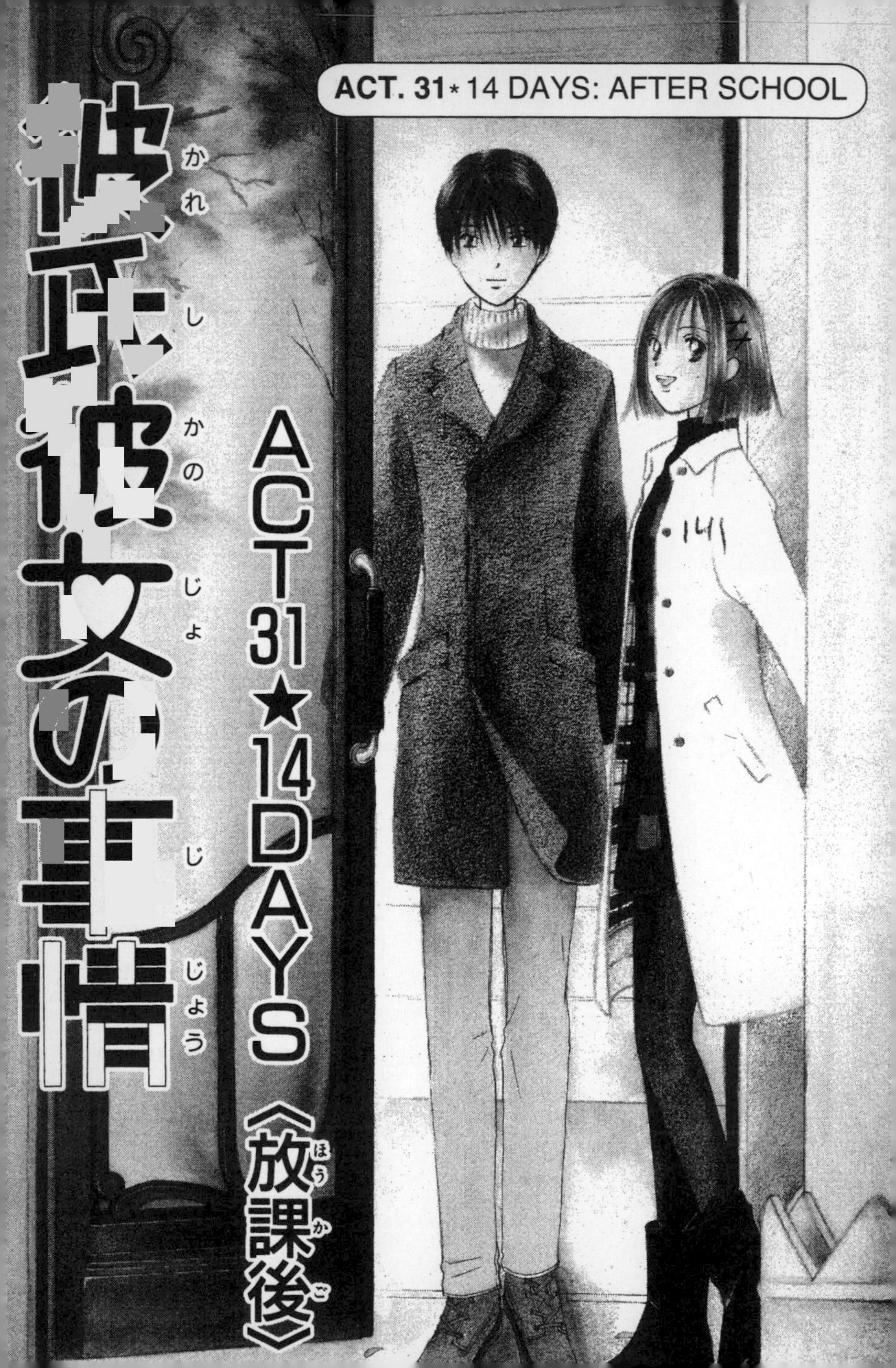
ACT. 31 * 14 DAYS: AFTER SCHOOL
彼氏彼女の事情
かれしかのじょのじじょう
ACT 31★14DAYS
〈放課後〉
ほうかご

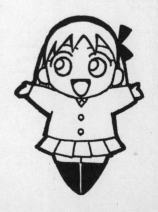

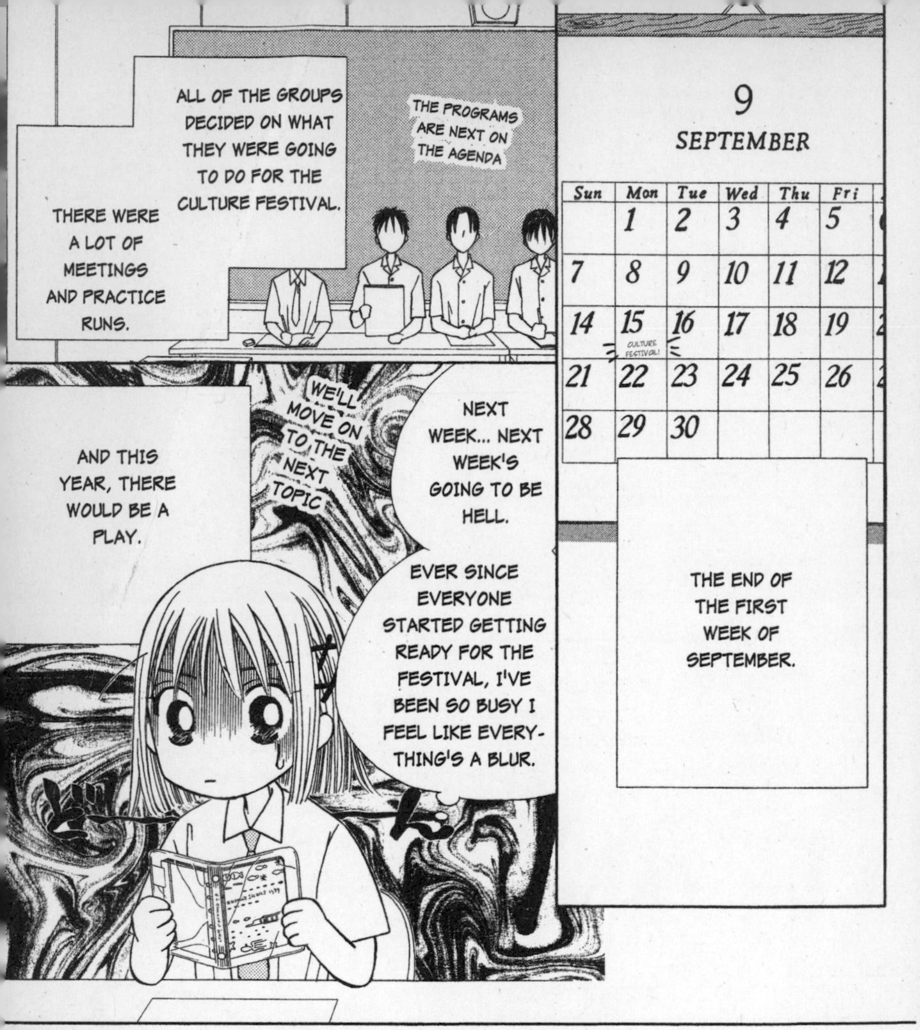
9
SEPTEMBER
Sun Mon Tue Wed Thu Fri
1 2 3 4 5
7 8 9 10 11 12
14 15 16 17 18 19
CULTURE FESTIVAL!
21 22 23 24 25 26
28 29 30
THE END OF THE FIRST WEEK OF SEPTEMBER.
THE PROGRAMS ARE NEXT ON THE AGENDA
ALL OF THE GROUPS DECIDED ON WHAT THEY WERE GOING TO DO FOR THE CULTURE FESTIVAL.
THERE WERE A LOT OF MEETINGS AND PRACTICE RUNS.
NEXT WEEK... NEXT WEEK'S GOING TO BE HELL.
EVER SINCE EVERYONE STARTED GETTING READY FOR THE FESTIVAL, I'VE BEEN SO BUSY I FEEL LIKE EVERYTHING'S A BLUR.
WE'LL MOVE ON TO THE NEXT TOPIC
AND THIS YEAR, THERE WOULD BE A PLAY.

About the foods I hate...

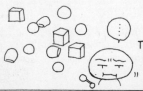

THERE AREN'T ANY FOODS THAT I PARTICULARLY LOVE OR HATE. BUT THERE ARE SOME FOODS THAT I DON'T PARTICULARLY LIKE. I'LL EAT THEM ALMOST ROBOTICALLY, THINKING ALL THE TIME, "I REALLY DON'T UNDERSTAND WHAT SOME PEOPLE LIKE ABOUT THIS..."

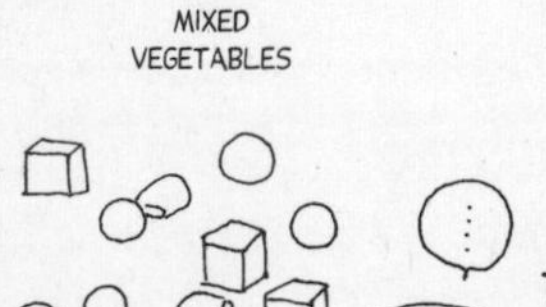
MIXED VEGETABLES

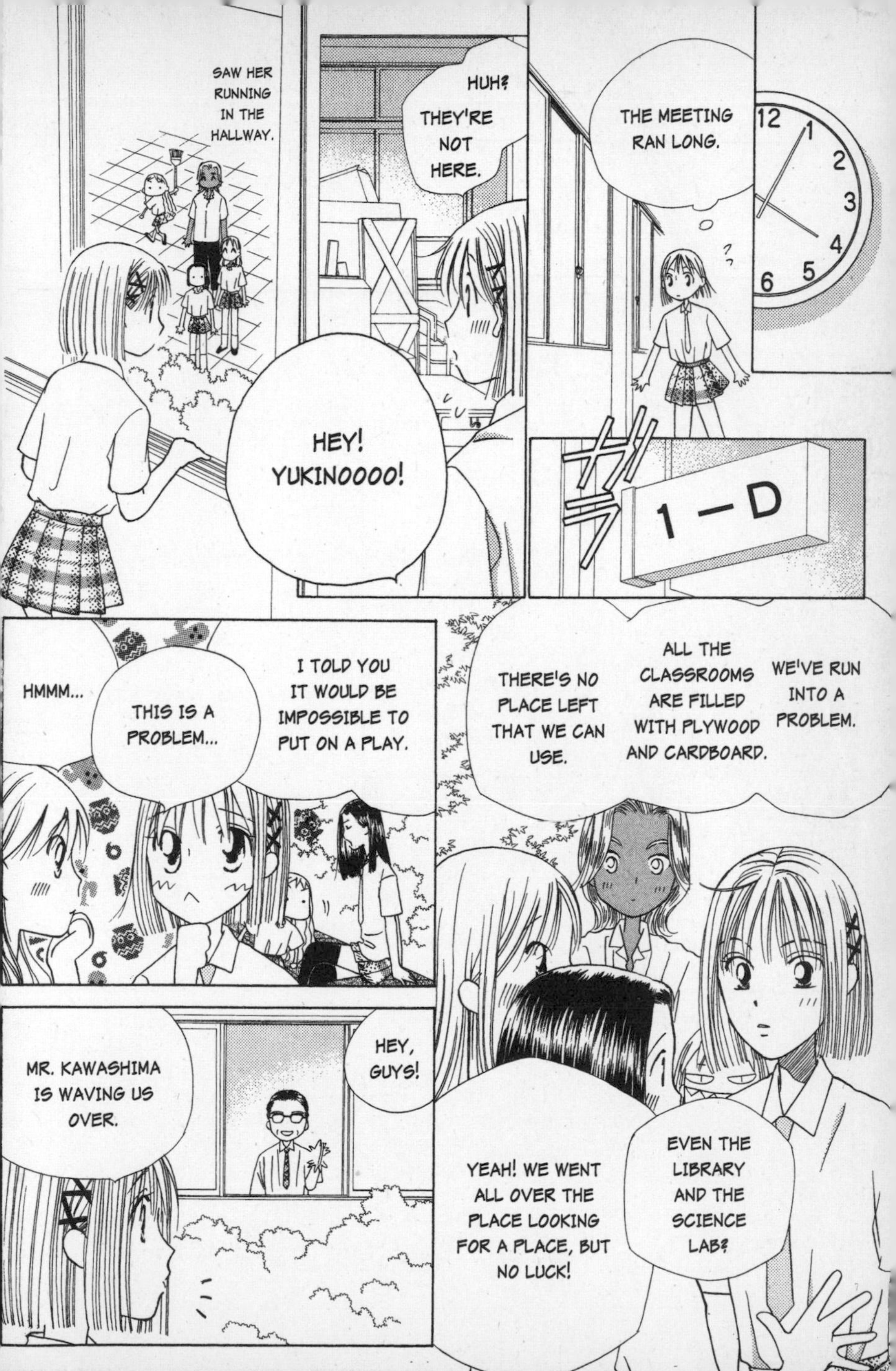
THE MEETING RAN LONG.
1 – D
HUH? THEY'RE NOT HERE.
HEY! YUKINOOOO!
SAW HER RUNNING IN THE HALLWAY.
WE'VE RUN INTO A PROBLEM.
ALL THE CLASSROOMS ARE FILLED WITH PLYWOOD AND CARDBOARD.
THERE'S NO PLACE LEFT THAT WE CAN USE.
EVEN THE LIBRARY AND THE SCIENCE LAB?
YEAH! WE WENT ALL OVER THE PLACE LOOKING FOR A PLACE, BUT NO LUCK!
I TOLD YOU IT WOULD BE IMPOSSIBLE TO PUT ON A PLAY.
THIS IS A PROBLEM...
HMMM...
HEY, GUYS!
MR. KAWASHIMA IS WAVING US OVER.

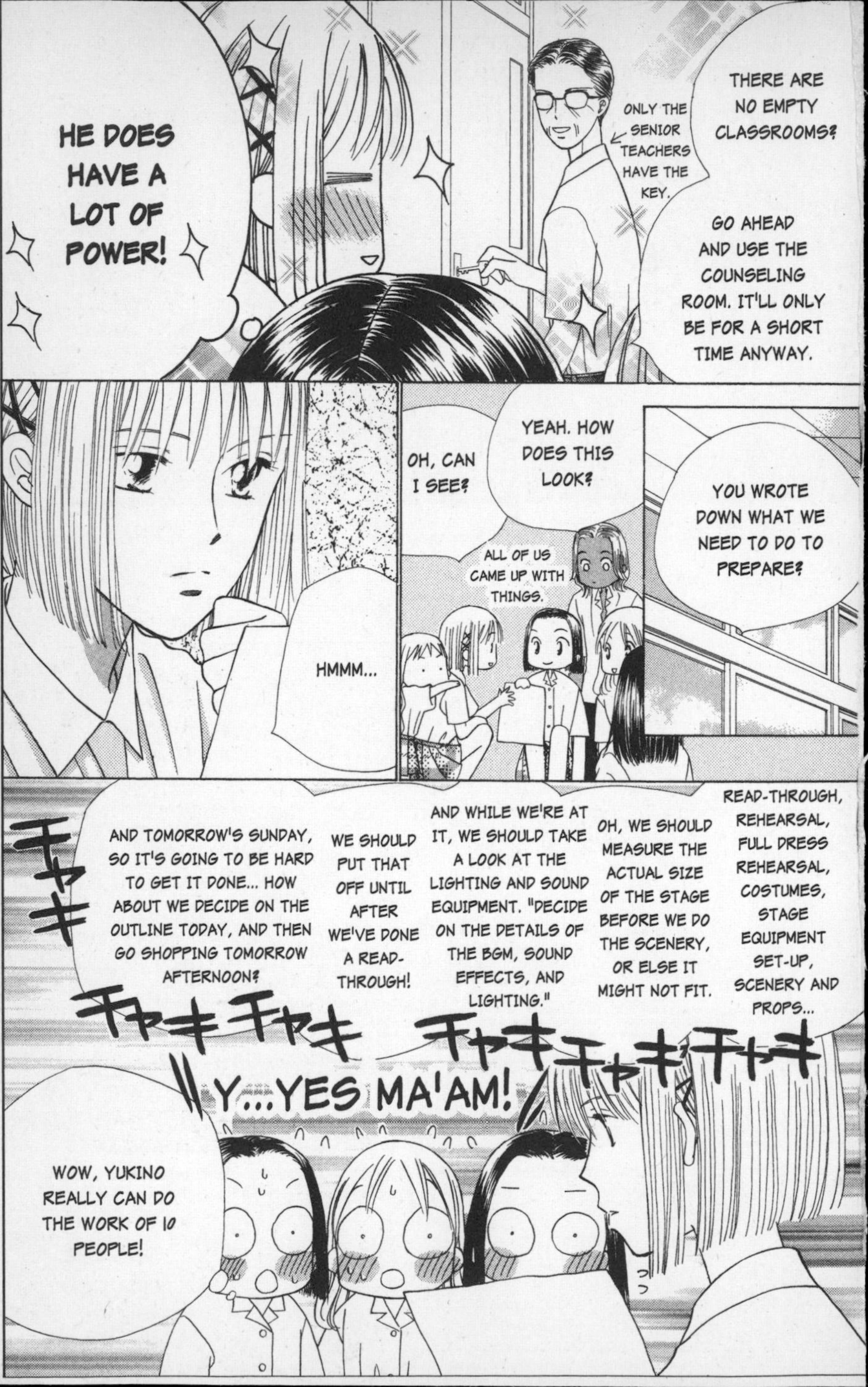
THERE ARE NO EMPTY CLASSROOMS?
ONLY THE SENIOR TEACHERS HAVE THE KEY.
GO AHEAD AND USE THE COUNSELING ROOM. IT'LL ONLY BE FOR A SHORT TIME ANYWAY.
HE DOES HAVE A LOT OF POWER!
YOU WROTE DOWN WHAT WE NEED TO DO TO PREPARE?
YEAH. HOW DOES THIS LOOK?
OH, CAN I SEE?
ALL OF US CAME UP WITH THINGS.
HMMM...
READ-THROUGH, REHEARSAL, FULL DRESS REHEARSAL, COSTUMES, STAGE EQUIPMENT SET-UP, SCENERY AND PROPS...
OH, WE SHOULD MEASURE THE ACTUAL SIZE OF THE STAGE BEFORE WE DO THE SCENERY, OR ELSE IT MIGHT NOT FIT.
AND WHILE WE'RE AT IT, WE SHOULD TAKE A LOOK AT THE LIGHTING AND SOUND EQUIPMENT. "DECIDE ON THE DETAILS OF THE BGM, SOUND EFFECTS, AND LIGHTING."
WE SHOULD PUT THAT OFF UNTIL AFTER WE'VE DONE A READ-THROUGH!
AND TOMORROW'S SUNDAY, SO IT'S GOING TO BE HARD TO GET IT DONE... HOW ABOUT WE DECIDE ON THE OUTLINE TODAY, AND THEN GO SHOPPING TOMORROW AFTERNOON?
チャキ
チャキチャキ
チャキチャキチャキ
Y...YES MA'AM!
WOW, YUKINO REALLY CAN DO THE WORK OF 10 PEOPLE!

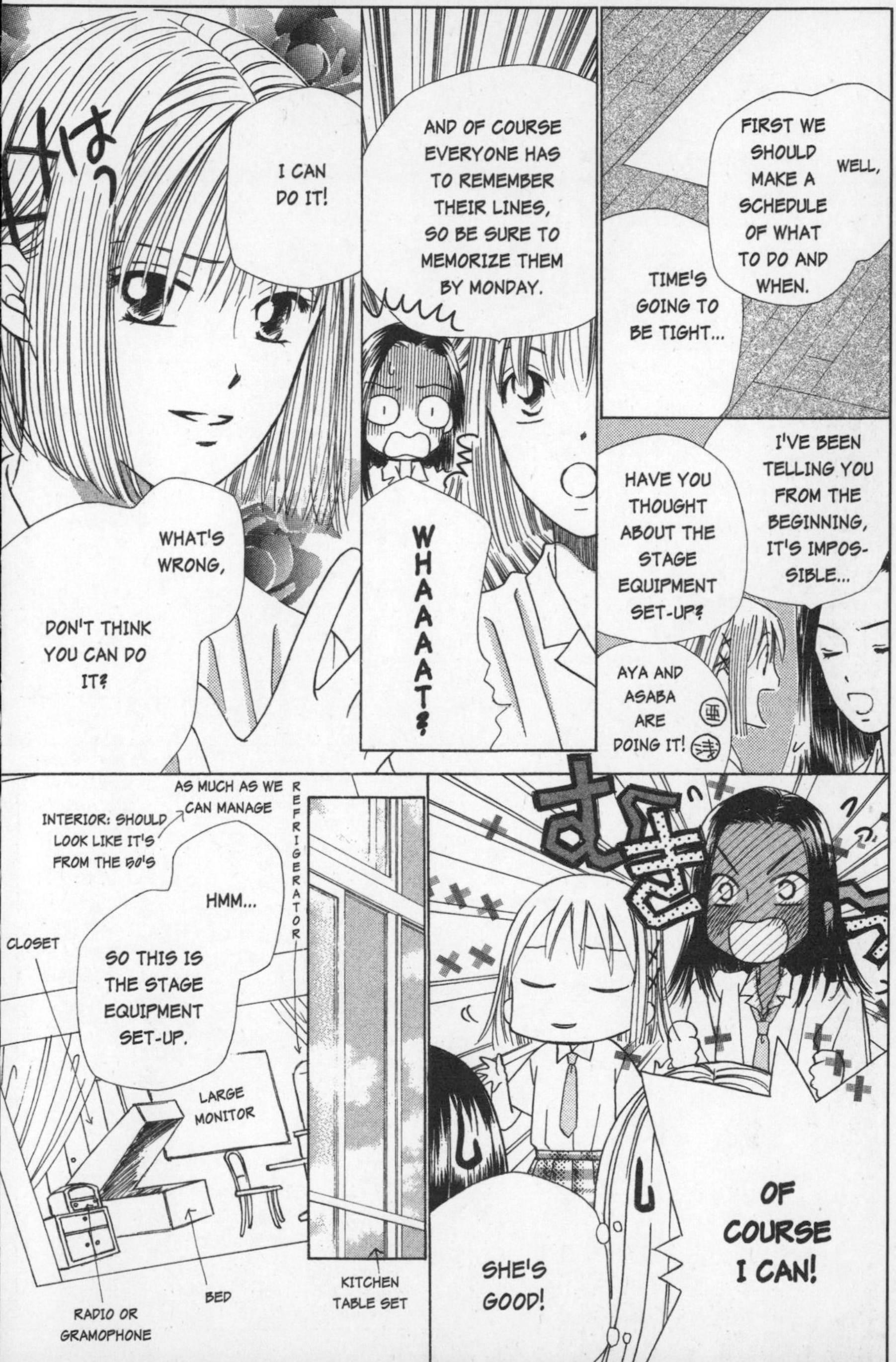
WELL,
FIRST WE SHOULD MAKE A SCHEDULE OF WHAT TO DO AND WHEN.
TIME'S GOING TO BE TIGHT...
I'VE BEEN TELLING YOU FROM THE BEGINNING, IT'S IMPOSSIBLE...
HAVE YOU THOUGHT ABOUT THE STAGE EQUIPMENT SET-UP?
AYA AND ASABA ARE DOING IT!
亜
浅
AND OF COURSE EVERYONE HAS TO REMEMBER THEIR LINES, SO BE SURE TO MEMORIZE THEM BY MONDAY.
WHAAAAAT?
はっ
I CAN DO IT!
WHAT'S WRONG,
DON'T THINK YOU CAN DO IT?
OF COURSE I CAN!
SHE'S GOOD!
HMM...
SO THIS IS THE STAGE EQUIPMENT SET-UP.
AS MUCH AS WE CAN MANAGE
INTERIOR: SHOULD LOOK LIKE IT'S FROM THE 50'S
REFRIGERATOR
CLOSET
LARGE MONITOR
KITCHEN TABLE SET
BED
RADIO OR GRAMOPHONE

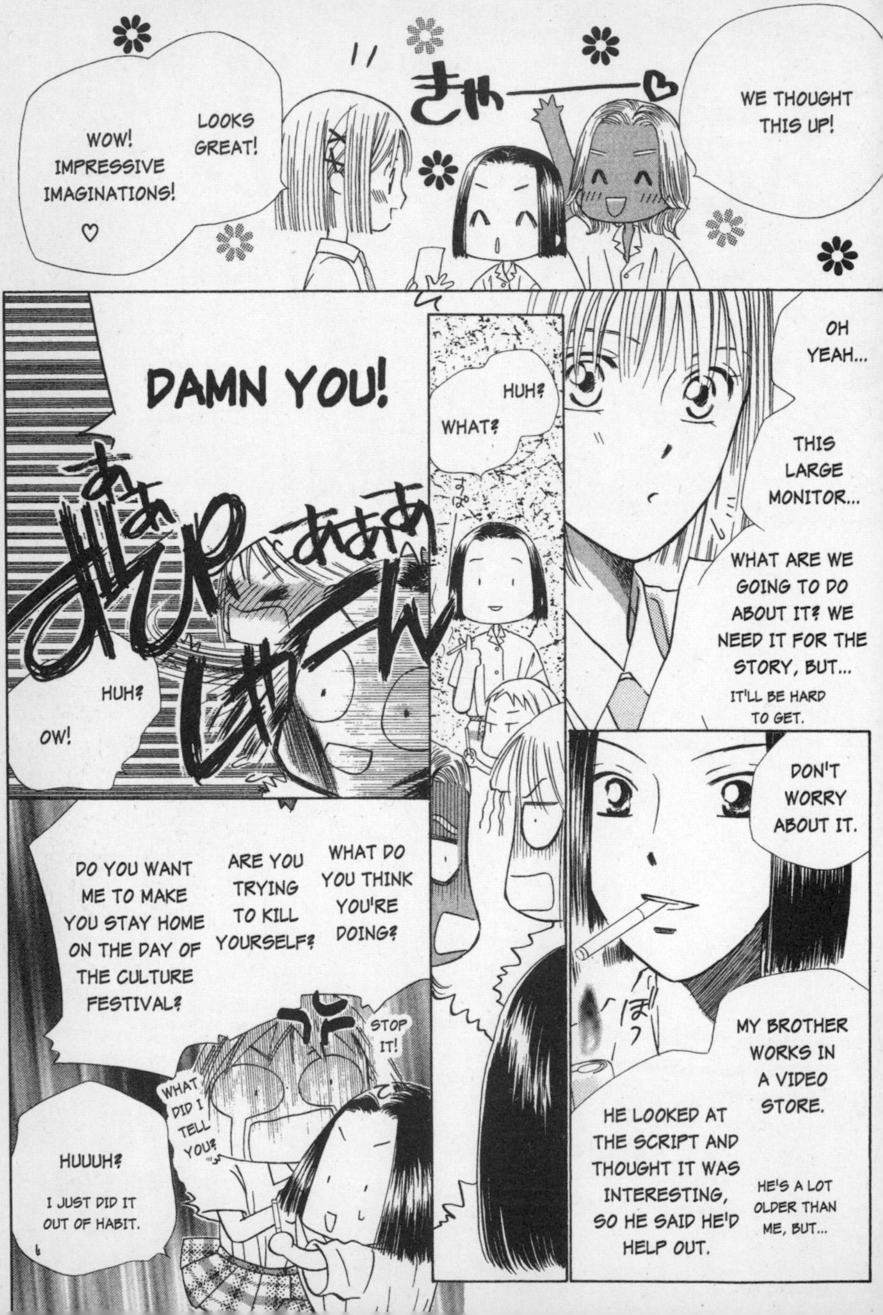
WE THOUGHT THIS UP!
きゃー
LOOKS GREAT!
WOW! IMPRESSIVE IMAGINATIONS! ♡
OH YEAH...
THIS LARGE MONITOR...
WHAT ARE WE GOING TO DO ABOUT IT? WE NEED IT FOR THE STORY, BUT...
IT'LL BE HARD TO GET.
DON'T WORRY ABOUT IT.
MY BROTHER WORKS IN A VIDEO STORE.
HE'S A LOT OLDER THAN ME, BUT...
HE LOOKED AT THE SCRIPT AND THOUGHT IT WAS INTERESTING, SO HE SAID HE'D HELP OUT.
HUH? WHAT?
DAMN YOU!
HUH? OW!
WHAT DO YOU THINK YOU'RE DOING?
ARE YOU TRYING TO KILL YOURSELF?
DO YOU WANT ME TO MAKE YOU STAY HOME ON THE DAY OF THE CULTURE FESTIVAL?
STOP IT!
WHAT DID I TELL YOU?
HUUUH?
I JUST DID IT OUT OF HABIT.

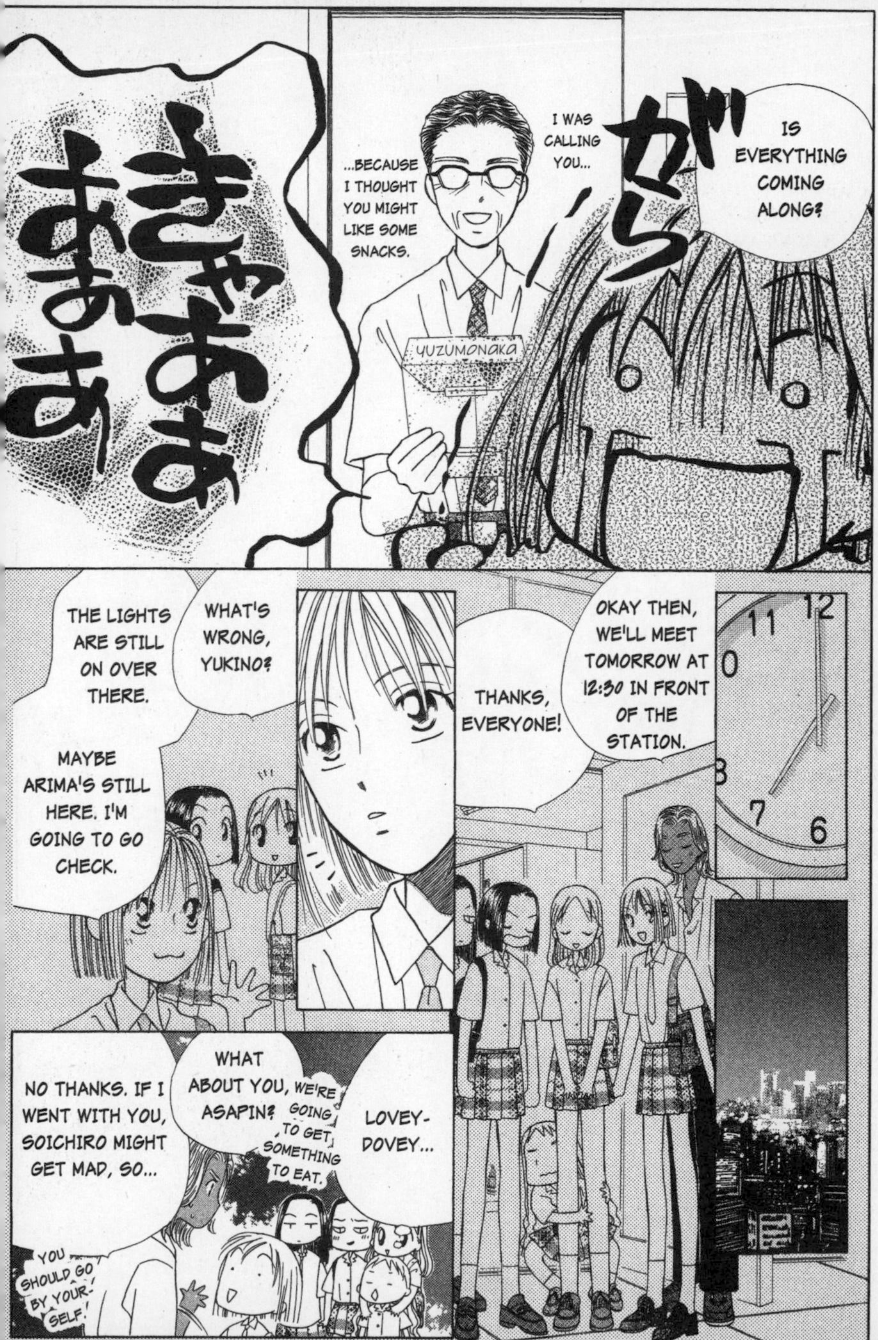
がら
IS EVERYTHING COMING ALONG?
I WAS CALLING YOU...
...BECAUSE I THOUGHT YOU MIGHT LIKE SOME SNACKS.
YUZUMONAKA
きゃああああああ
OKAY THEN, WE'LL MEET TOMORROW AT 12:30 IN FRONT OF THE STATION.
THANKS, EVERYONE!
WHAT'S WRONG, YUKINO?
THE LIGHTS ARE STILL ON OVER THERE.
MAYBE ARIMA'S STILL HERE. I'M GOING TO GO CHECK.
LOVEY-DOVEY...
WHAT ABOUT YOU, ASAPIN?
WE'RE GOING TO GET SOMETHING TO EAT.
NO THANKS. IF I WENT WITH YOU, SOICHIRO MIGHT GET MAD, SO...
YOU SHOULD GO BY YOUR-SELF!

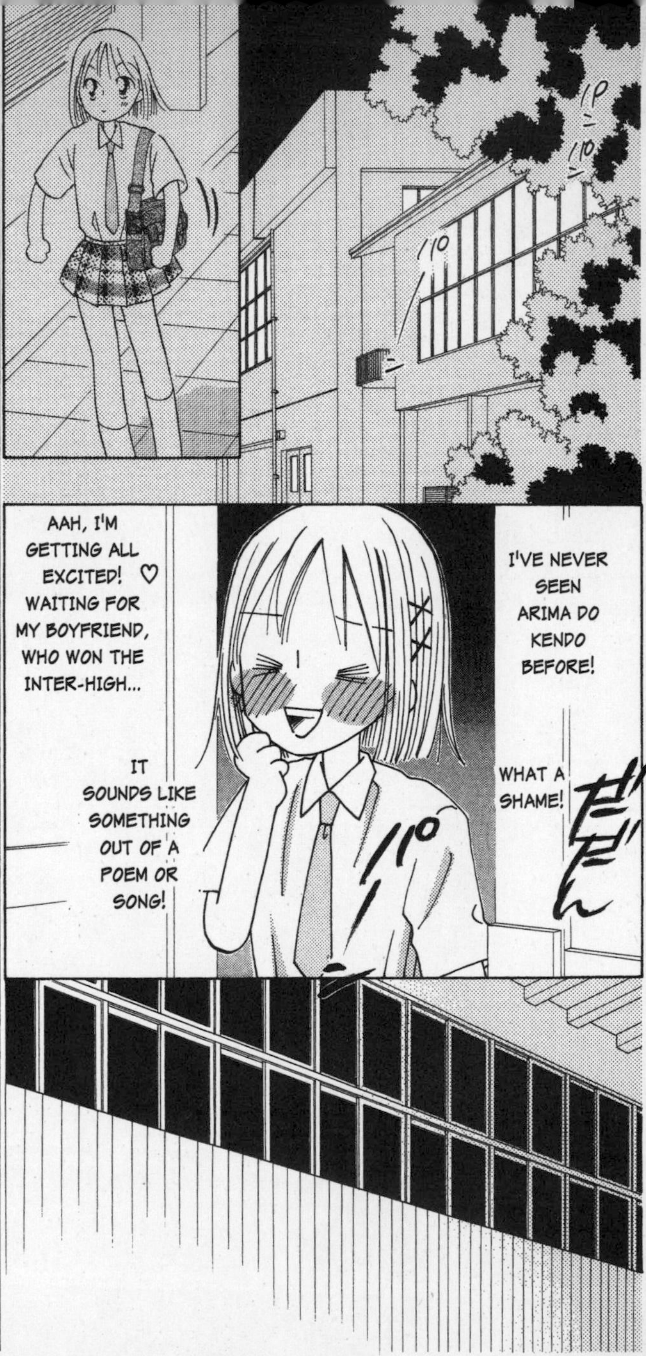
I'VE NEVER SEEN ARIMA DO KENDO BEFORE!
WHAT A SHAME!
AAH, I'M GETTING ALL EXCITED! ♡ WAITING FOR MY BOYFRIEND, WHO WON THE INTER-HIGH...
IT SOUNDS LIKE SOMETHING OUT OF A POEM OR SONG!

5

I've been making myself go for walks as soon as possible to get more physically fit. But I'm afraid of crows. Really! Whenever I notice one close by, I jump!

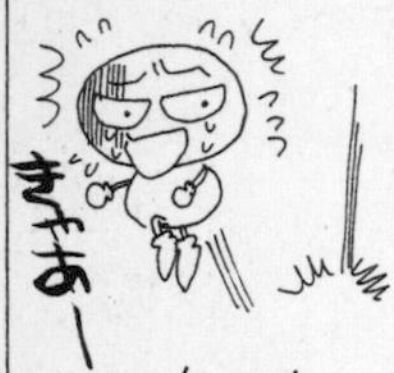

...dammit.

If I notice a crow in front of me, I run away. I don't care how I look when I do it. I never take a walk after 2:00.

↑ Because there's even more of them.

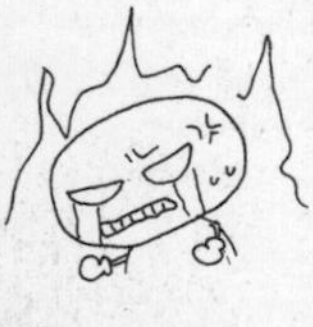

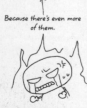

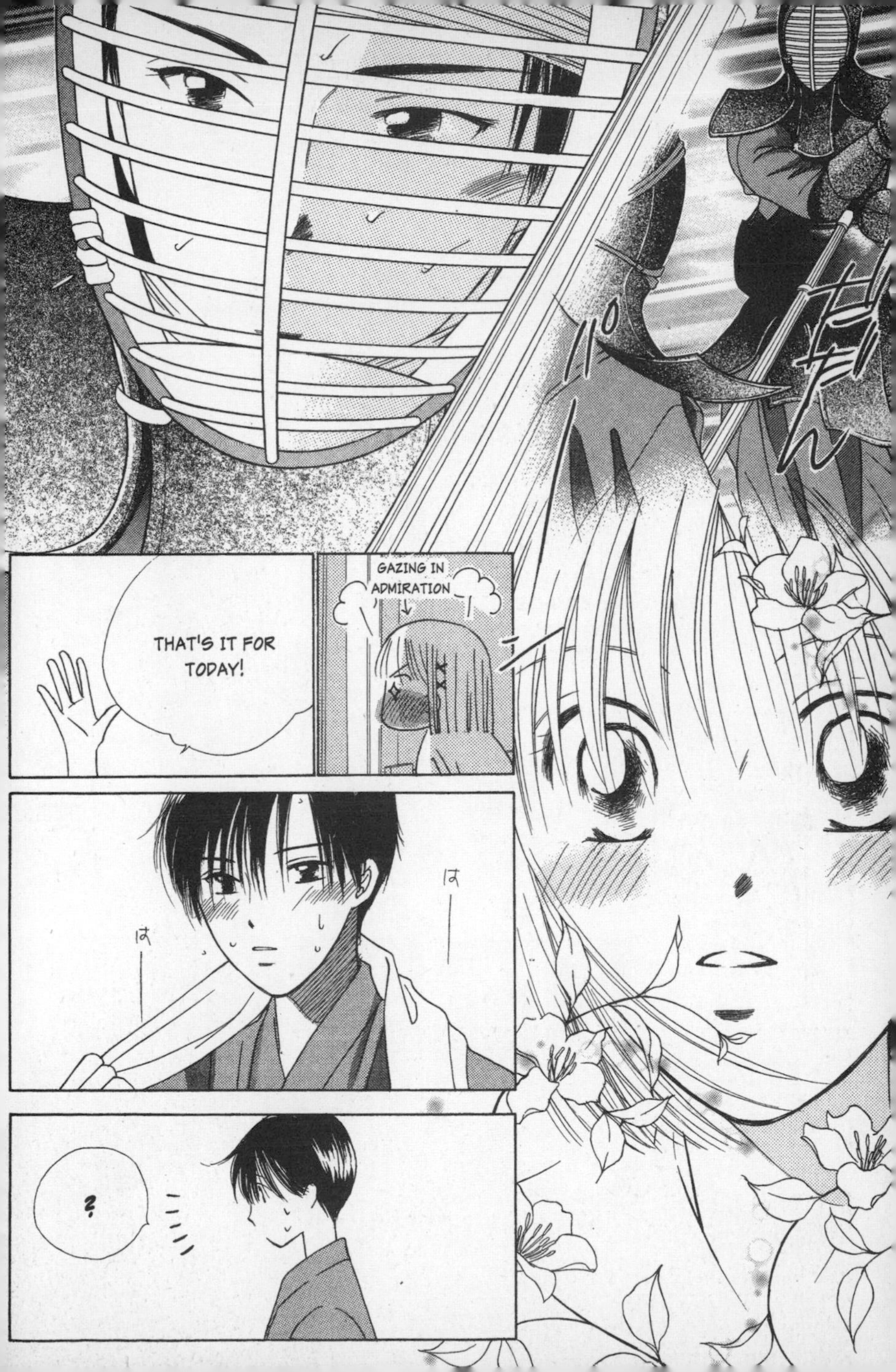
GAZING IN ADMIRATION
THAT'S IT FOR TODAY!
はー
はー
?

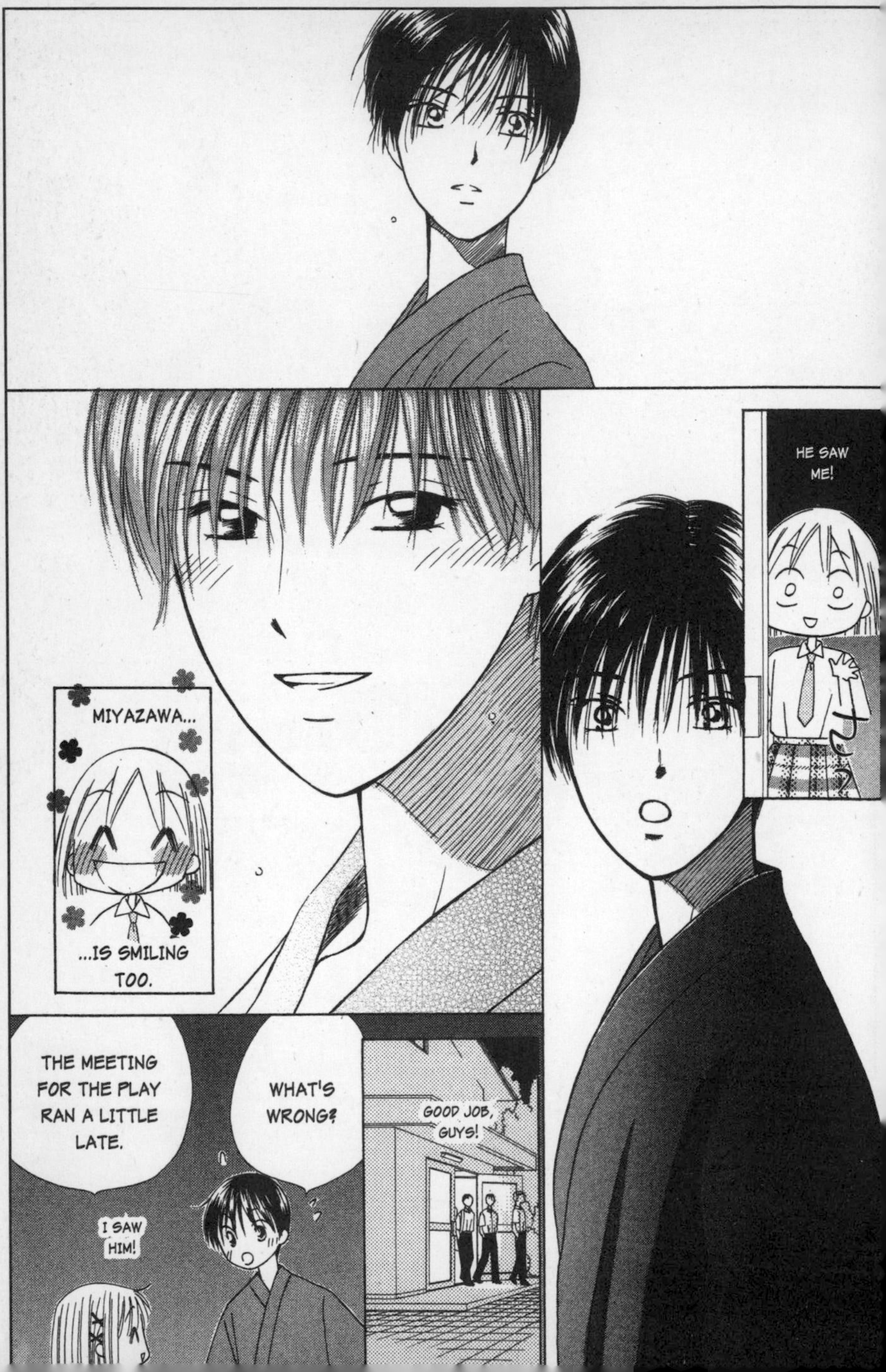
HE SAW ME!
MIYAZAWA...
...IS SMILING TOO.
GOOD JOB, GUYS!
WHAT'S WRONG?
THE MEETING FOR THE PLAY RAN A LITTLE LATE.
I SAW HIM!

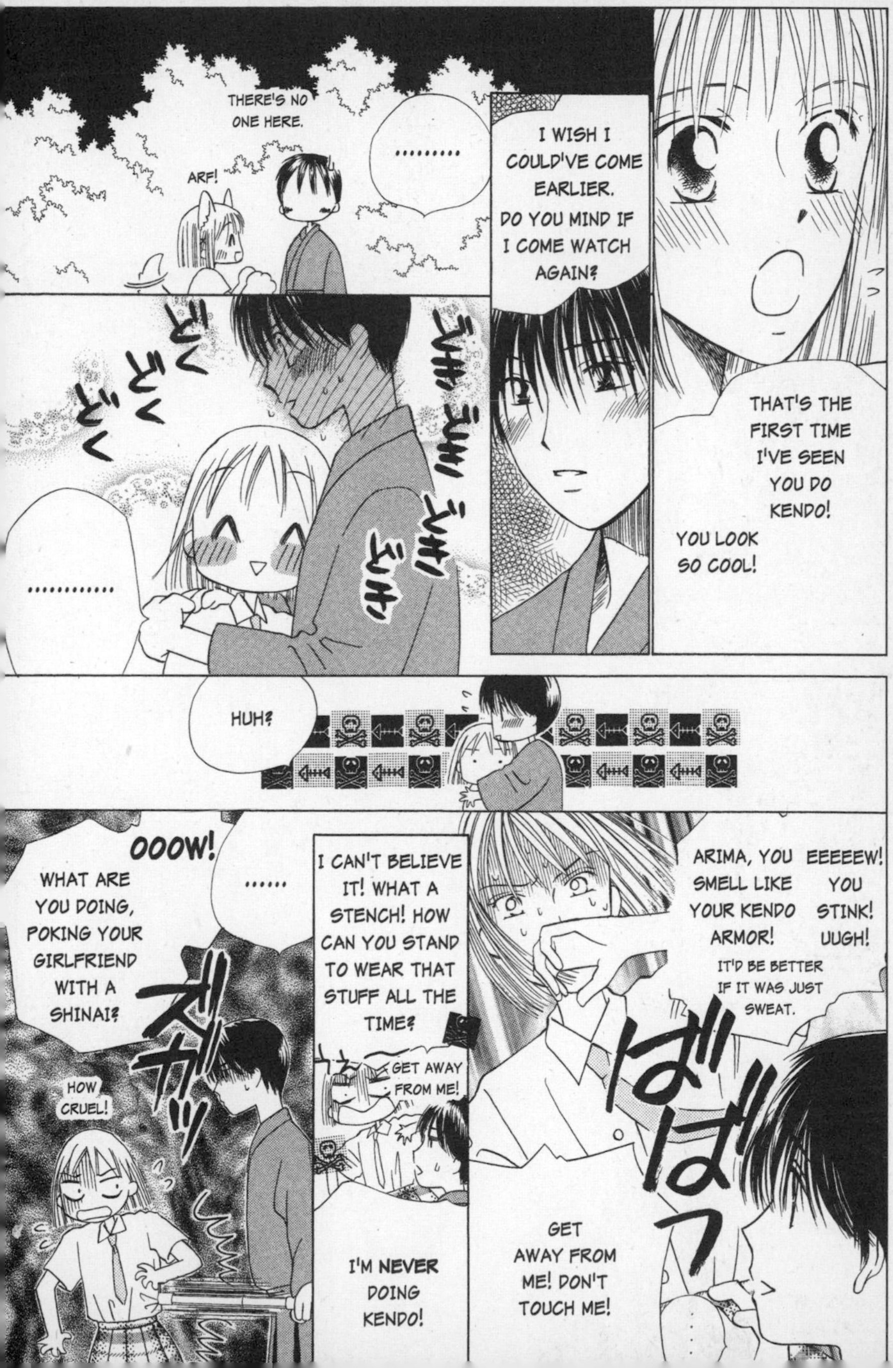
THAT'S THE FIRST TIME I'VE SEEN YOU DO KENDO!
YOU LOOK SO COOL!
I WISH I COULD'VE COME EARLIER.
DO YOU MIND IF I COME WATCH AGAIN?
....
THERE'S NO ONE HERE.
ARF!
どきどきどきどき
どくどくどく
....
HUH?
EEEEEW! YOU STINK! UUGH!
ARIMA, YOU SMELL LIKE YOUR KENDO ARMOR!
IT'D BE BETTER IF IT WAS JUST SWEAT.
ばばっ
GET AWAY FROM ME! DON'T TOUCH ME!
I CAN'T BELIEVE IT! WHAT A STENCH! HOW CAN YOU STAND TO WEAR THAT STUFF ALL THE TIME?
GET AWAY FROM ME!
I'M NEVER DOING KENDO!
......
OOOW!
WHAT ARE YOU DOING, POKING YOUR GIRLFRIEND WITH A SHINAI?
HOW CRUEL!

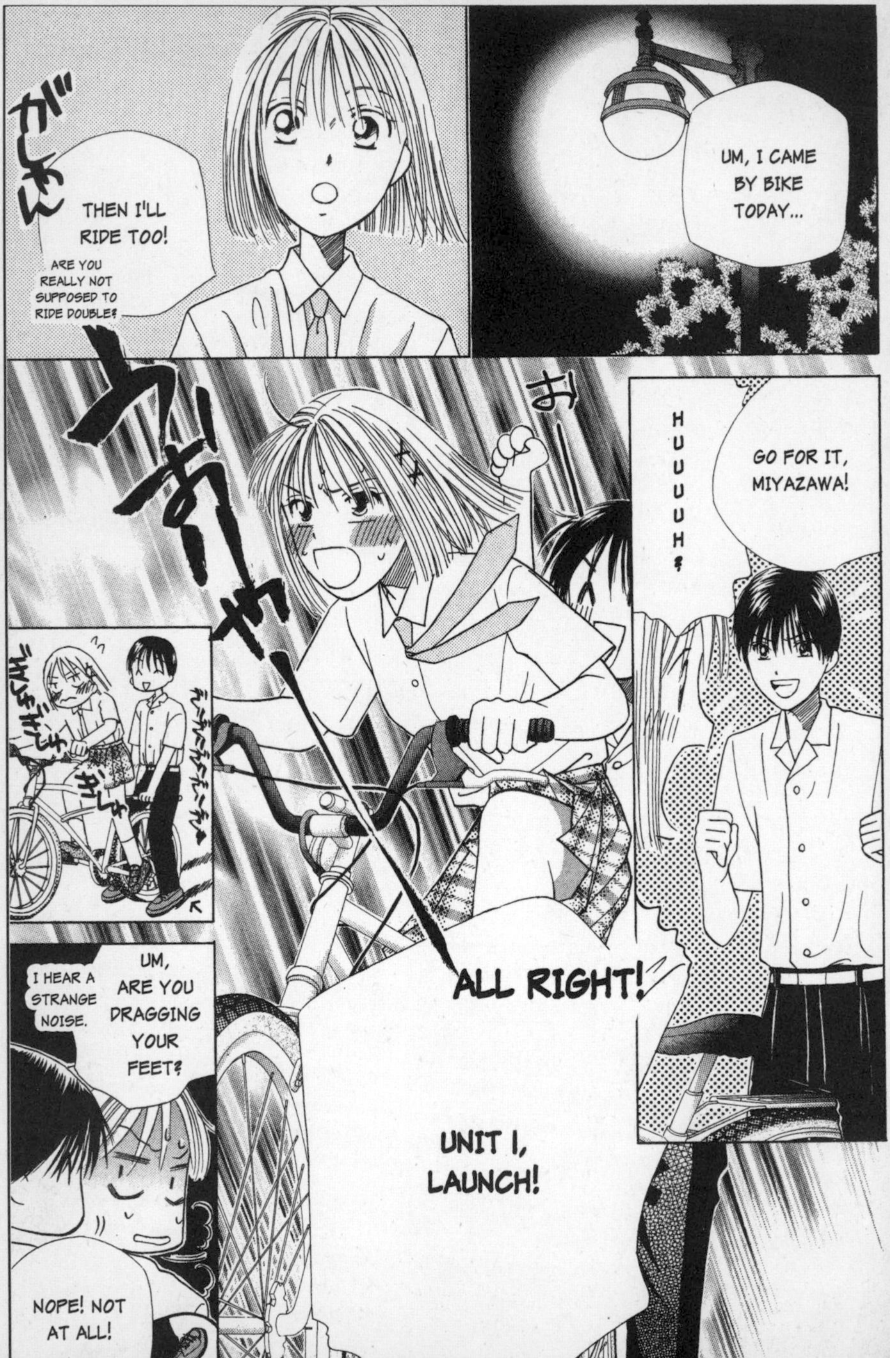
UM, I CAME BY BIKE TODAY...
THEN I'LL RIDE TOO!
ARE YOU REALLY NOT SUPPOSED TO RIDE DOUBLE?
HUUUUUH?
GO FOR IT, MIYAZAWA!
ALL RIGHT!
UNIT 1, LAUNCH!
UM, ARE YOU DRAGGING YOUR FEET?
I HEAR A STRANGE NOISE.
NOPE! NOT AT ALL!

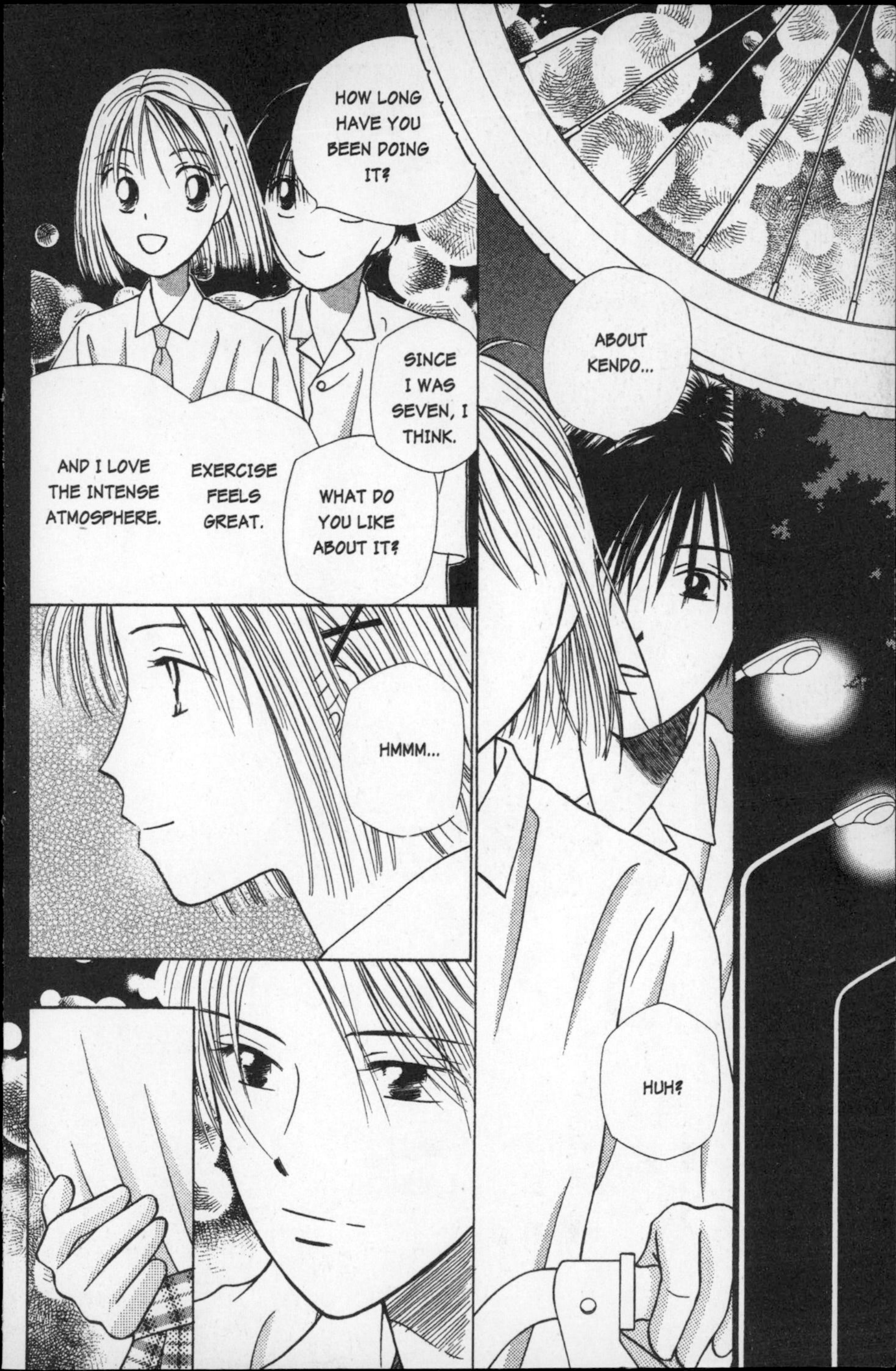
ABOUT KENDO...
HUH?
HOW LONG HAVE YOU BEEN DOING IT?
SINCE I WAS SEVEN, I THINK.
WHAT DO YOU LIKE ABOUT IT?
EXERCISE FEELS GREAT.
AND I LOVE THE INTENSE ATMOSPHERE.
HMMM...

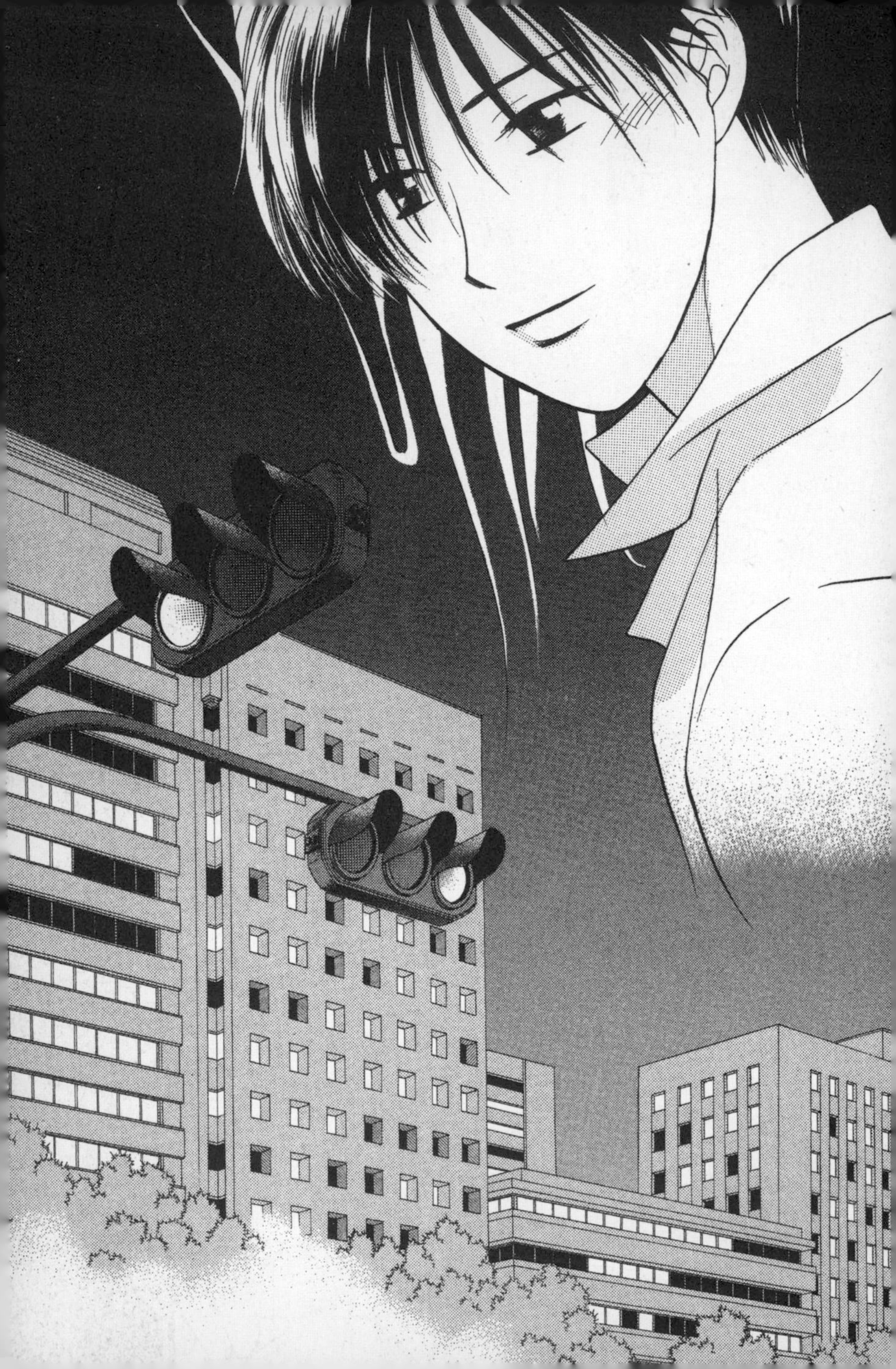

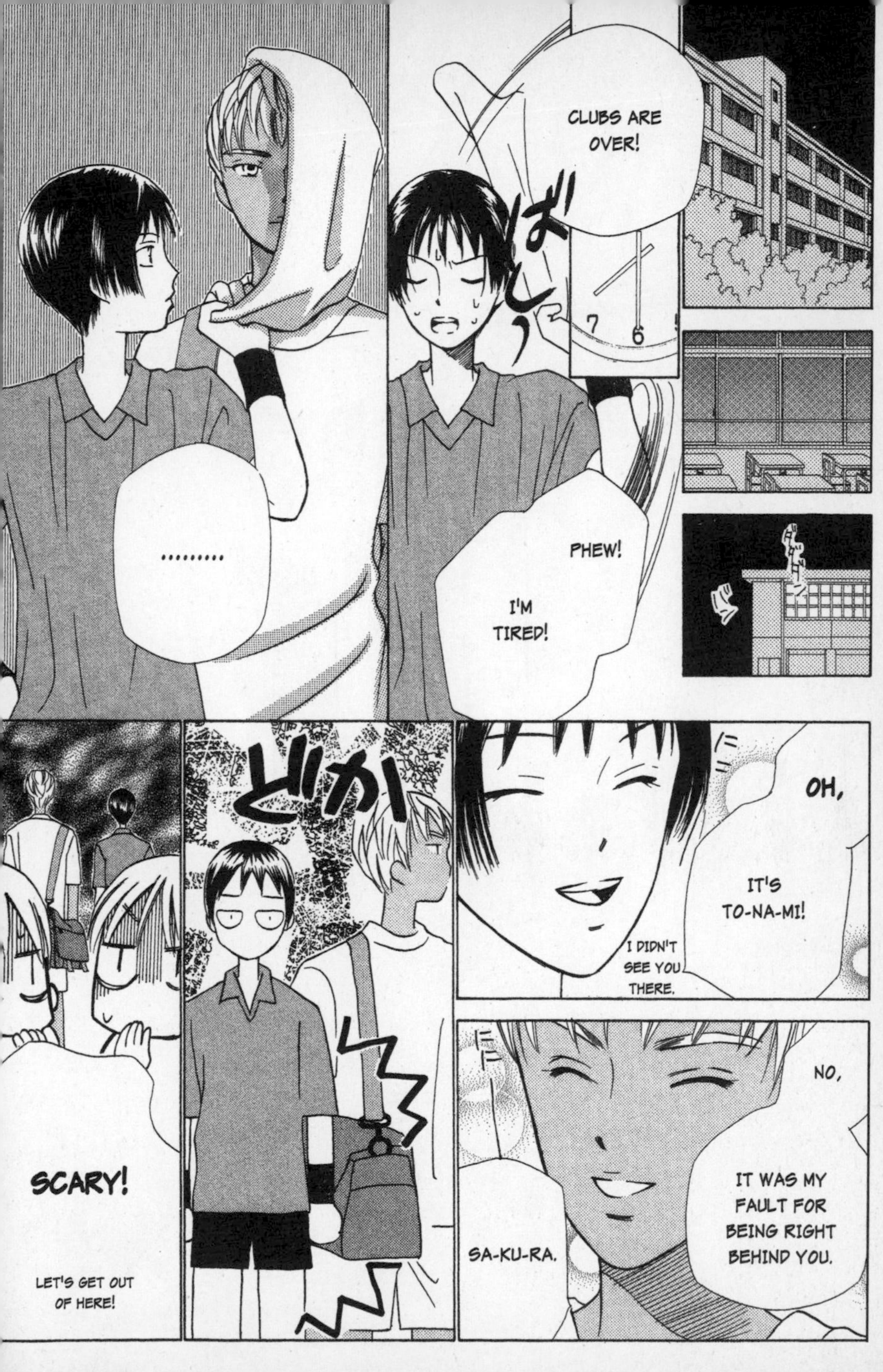
CLUBS ARE OVER!
PHEW!
I'M TIRED!
....
OH,
IT'S TO-NA-MI!
I DIDN'T SEE YOU THERE.
NO,
IT WAS MY FAULT FOR BEING RIGHT BEHIND YOU.
SA-KU-RA.
SCARY!
LET'S GET OUT OF HERE!

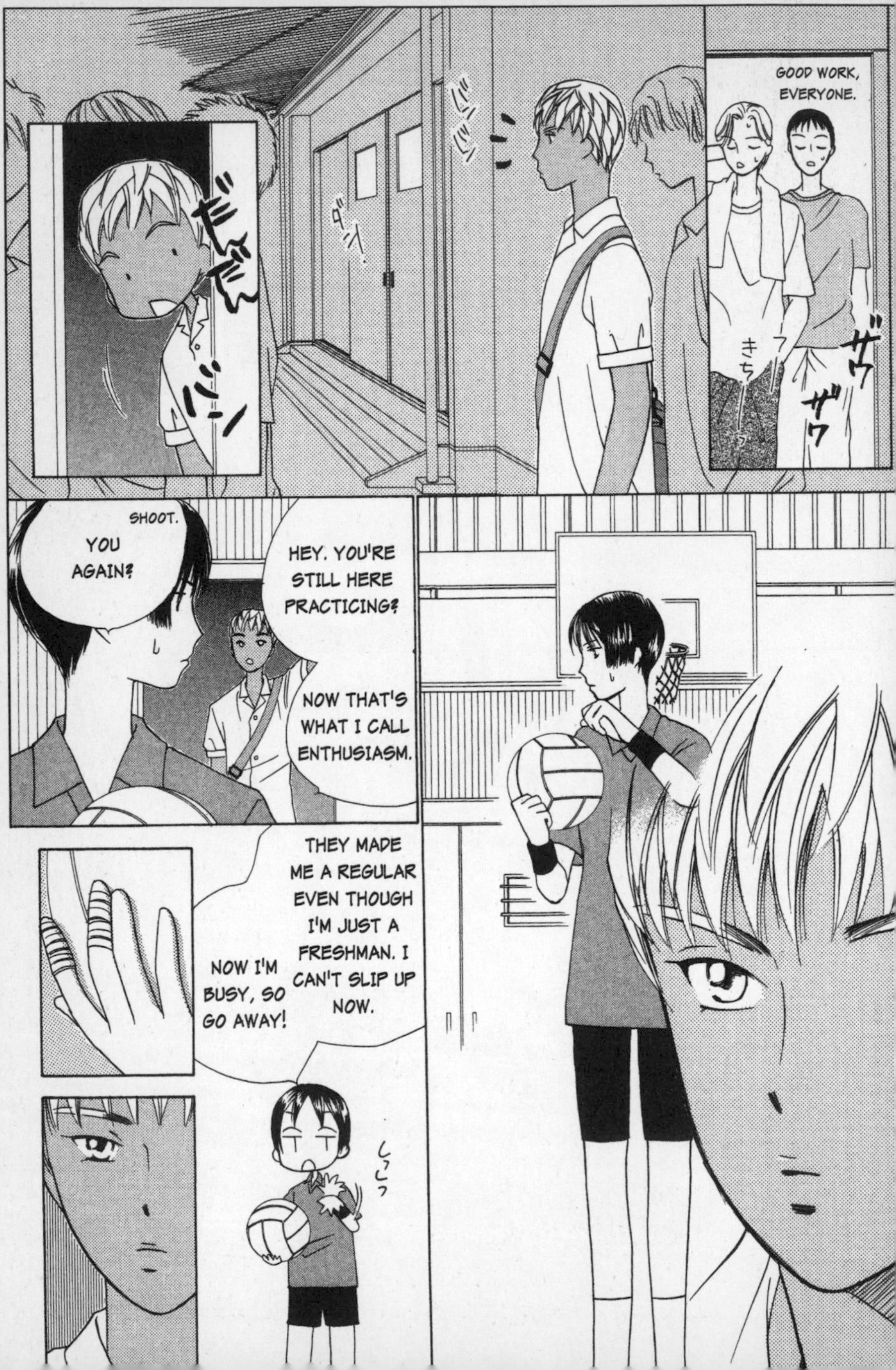
GOOD WORK, EVERYONE.
ザワ ザワ
HEY. YOU'RE STILL HERE PRACTICING?
NOW THAT'S WHAT I CALL ENTHUSIASM.
SHOOT.
YOU AGAIN?
THEY MADE ME A REGULAR EVEN THOUGH I'M JUST A FRESHMAN. I CAN'T SLIP UP NOW.
NOW I'M BUSY, SO GO AWAY!

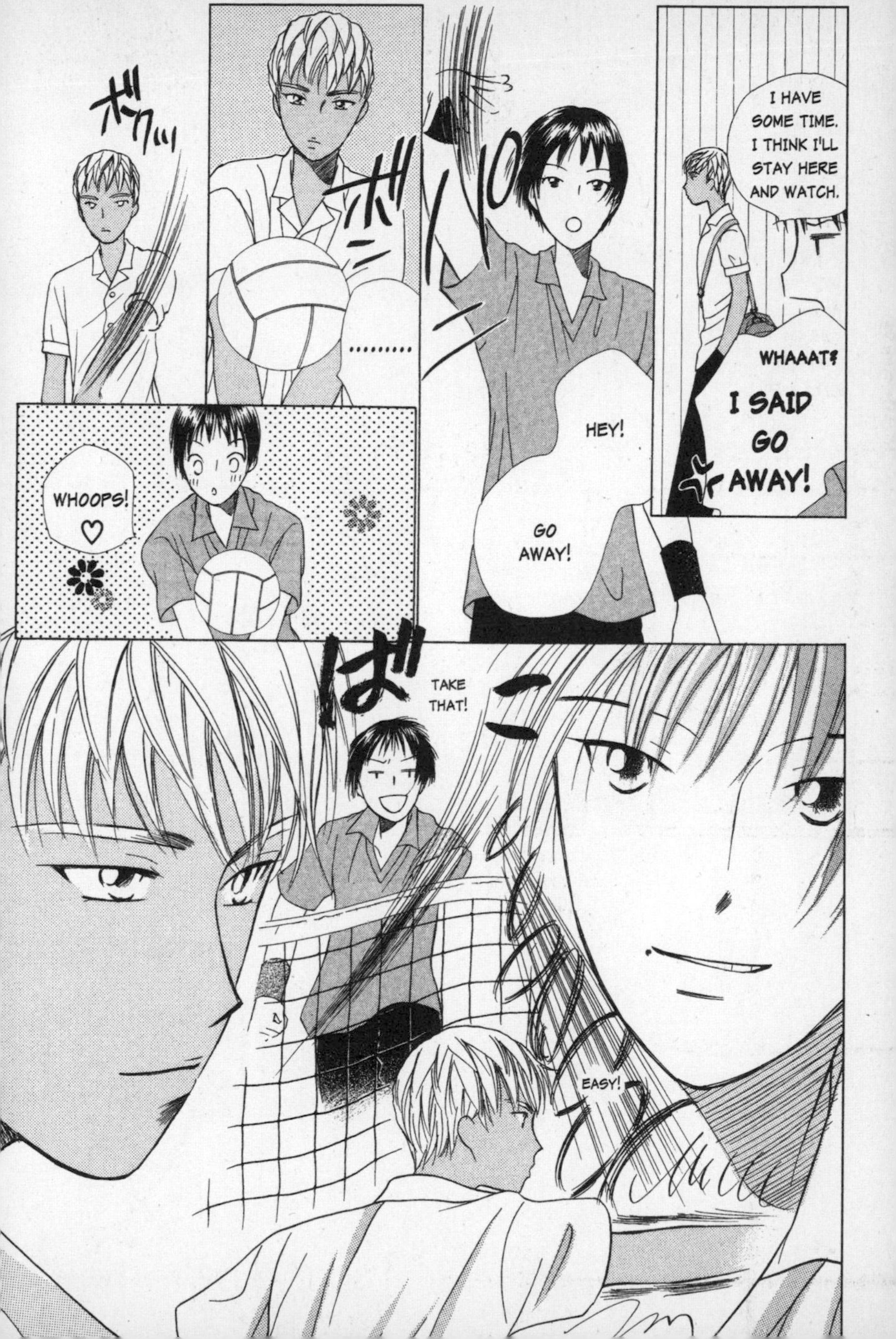

I HAVE SOME TIME. I THINK I'LL STAY HERE AND WATCH.
WHAAAT?
I SAID GO AWAY!
HEY!
GO AWAY!
....
WHOOPS! ♡
TAKE THAT!
EASY!

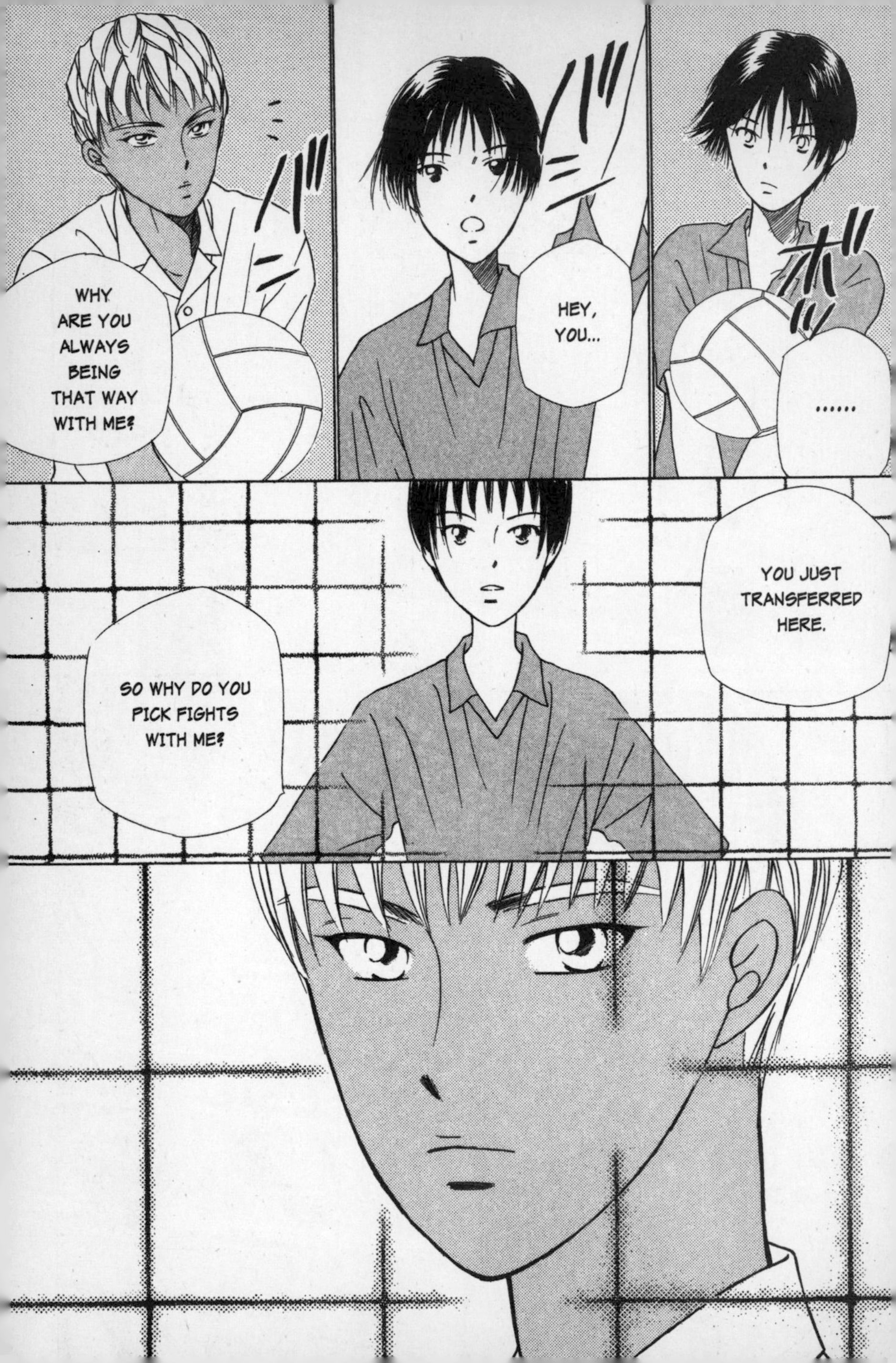
......
HEY, YOU...
WHY ARE YOU ALWAYS BEING THAT WAY WITH ME?
YOU JUST TRANSFERRED HERE.
SO WHY DO YOU PICK FIGHTS WITH ME?

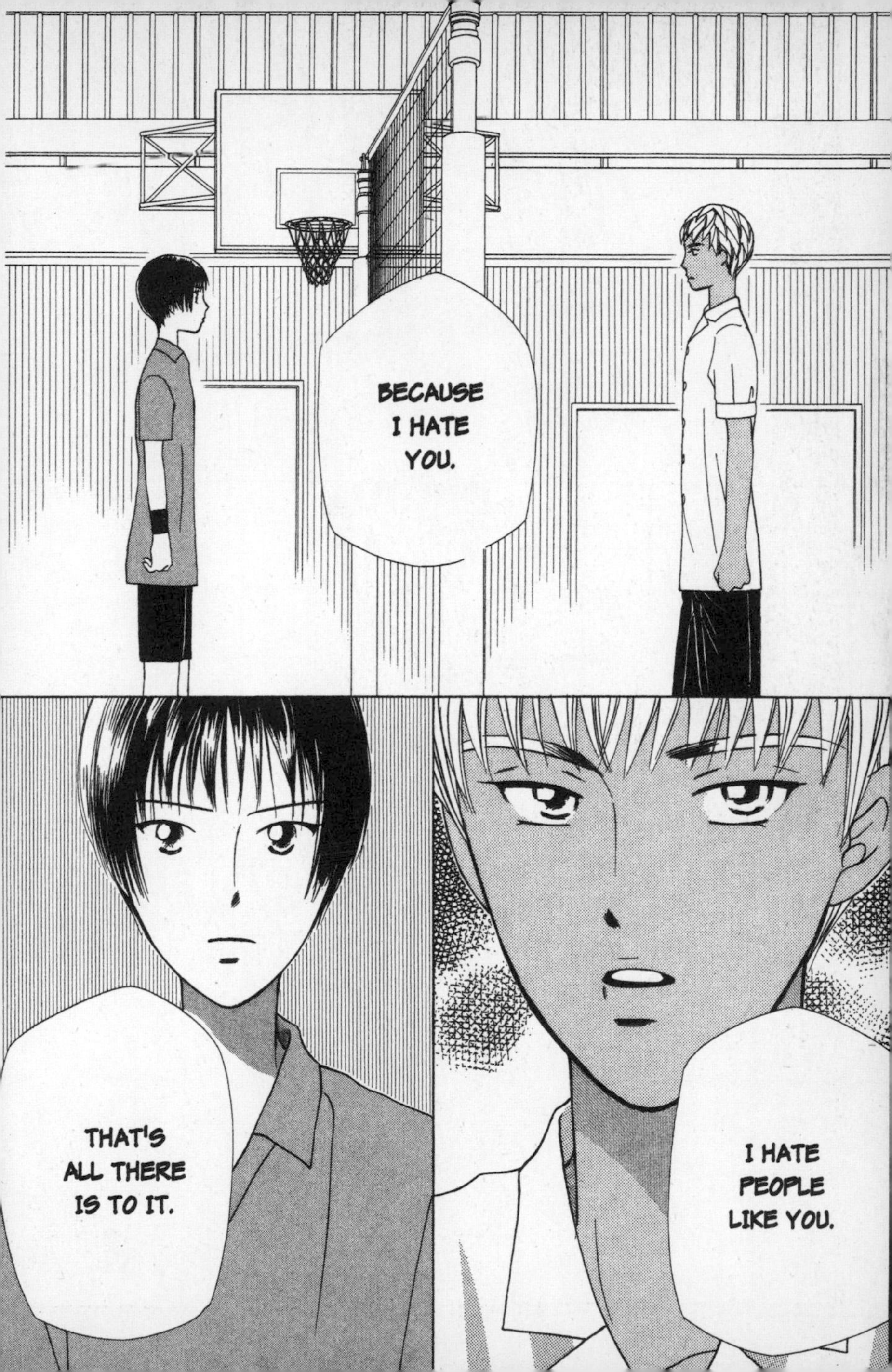
BECAUSE I HATE YOU.
I HATE PEOPLE LIKE YOU.
THAT'S ALL THERE IS TO IT.

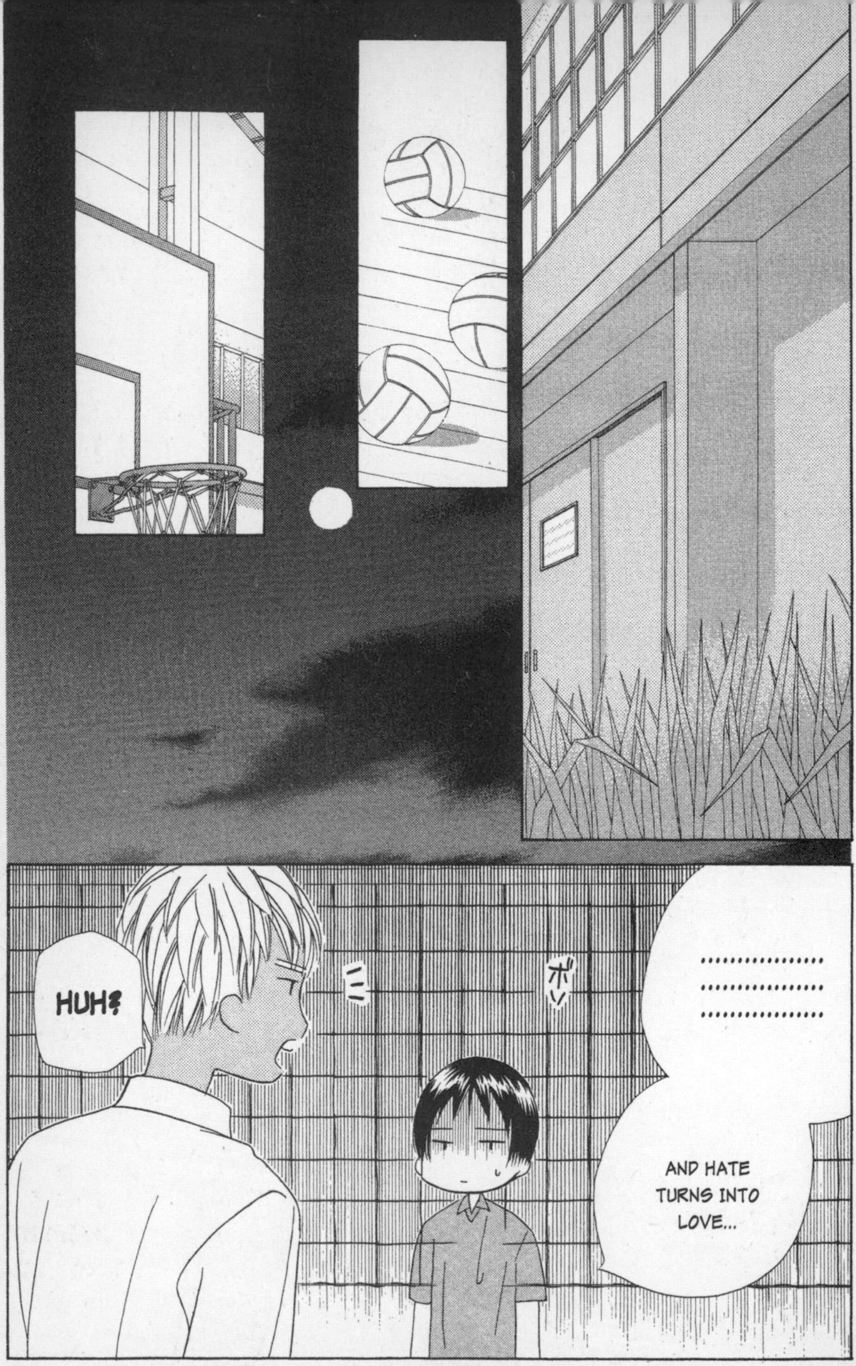
....
....
....
AND HATE TURNS INTO LOVE...
HUH?

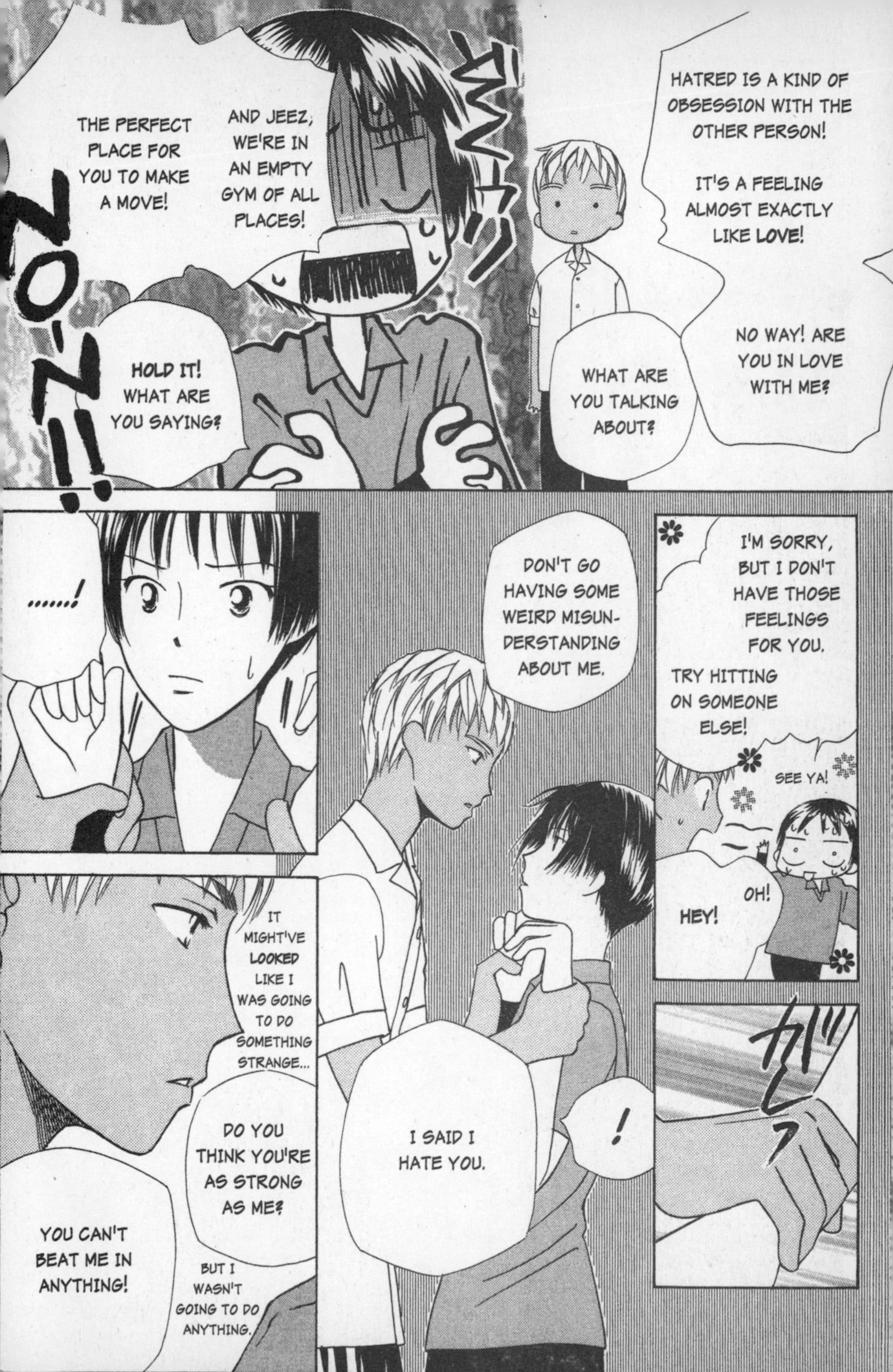
HATRED IS A KIND OF OBSESSION WITH THE OTHER PERSON!
IT'S A FEELING ALMOST EXACTLY LIKE LOVE!
NO WAY! ARE YOU IN LOVE WITH ME?
WHAT ARE YOU TALKING ABOUT?
AND JEEZ, WE'RE IN AN EMPTY GYM OF ALL PLACES!
THE PERFECT PLACE FOR YOU TO MAKE A MOVE!
HOLD IT! WHAT ARE YOU SAYING?
I'M SORRY, BUT I DON'T HAVE THOSE FEELINGS FOR YOU.
TRY HITTING ON SOMEONE ELSE!
SEE YA!
OH!
HEY!
DON'T GO HAVING SOME WEIRD MISUNDERSTANDING ABOUT ME.
!
I SAID I HATE YOU.
......!
IT MIGHT'VE LOOKED LIKE I WAS GOING TO DO SOMETHING STRANGE...
DO YOU THINK YOU'RE AS STRONG AS ME?
YOU CAN'T BEAT ME IN ANYTHING!
BUT I WASN'T GOING TO DO ANYTHING.

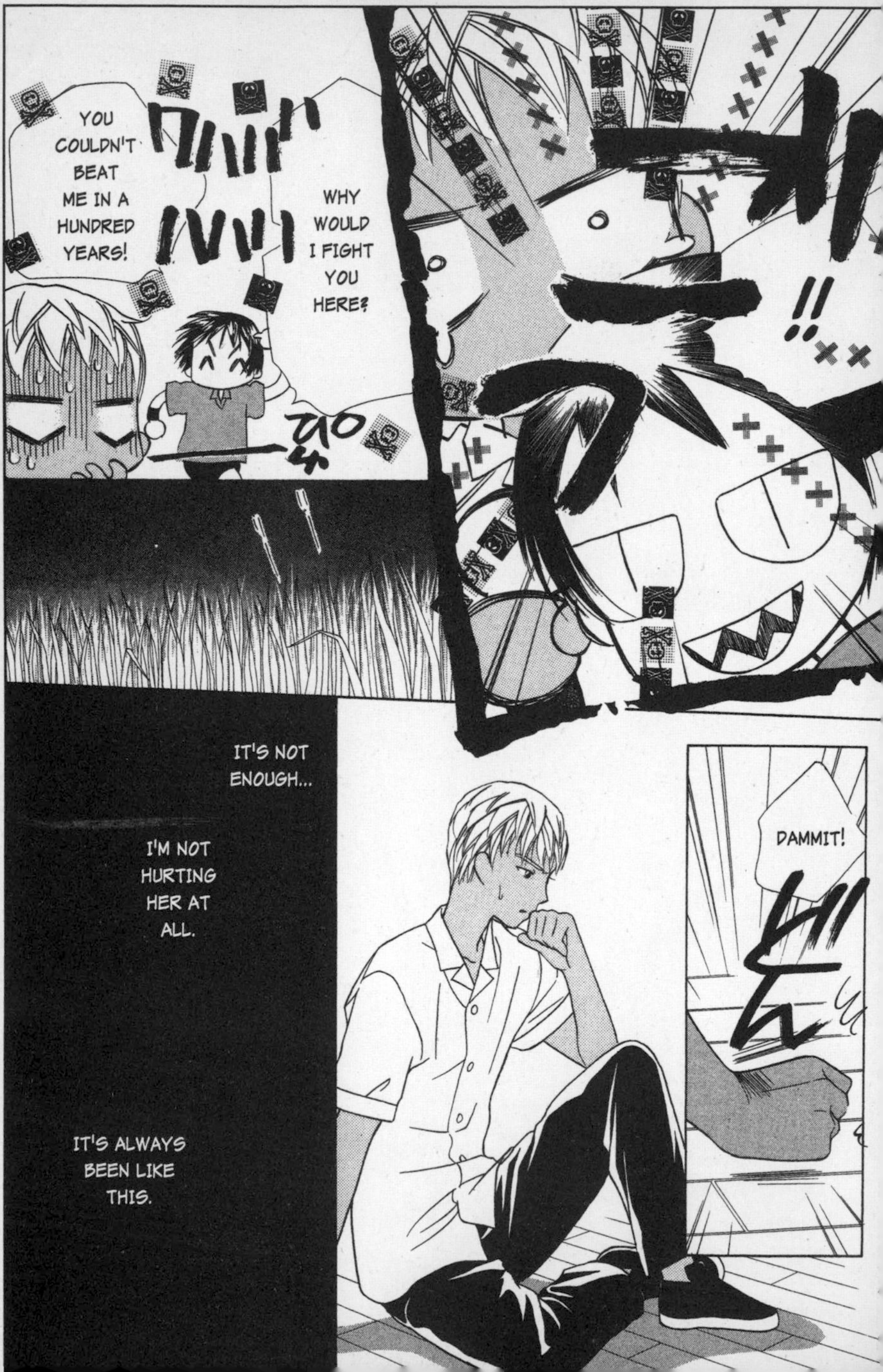
YOU COULDN'T BEAT ME IN A HUNDRED YEARS!
WHY WOULD I FIGHT YOU HERE?
DAMMIT!
IT'S NOT ENOUGH...
I'M NOT HURTING HER AT ALL.
IT'S ALWAYS BEEN LIKE THIS.

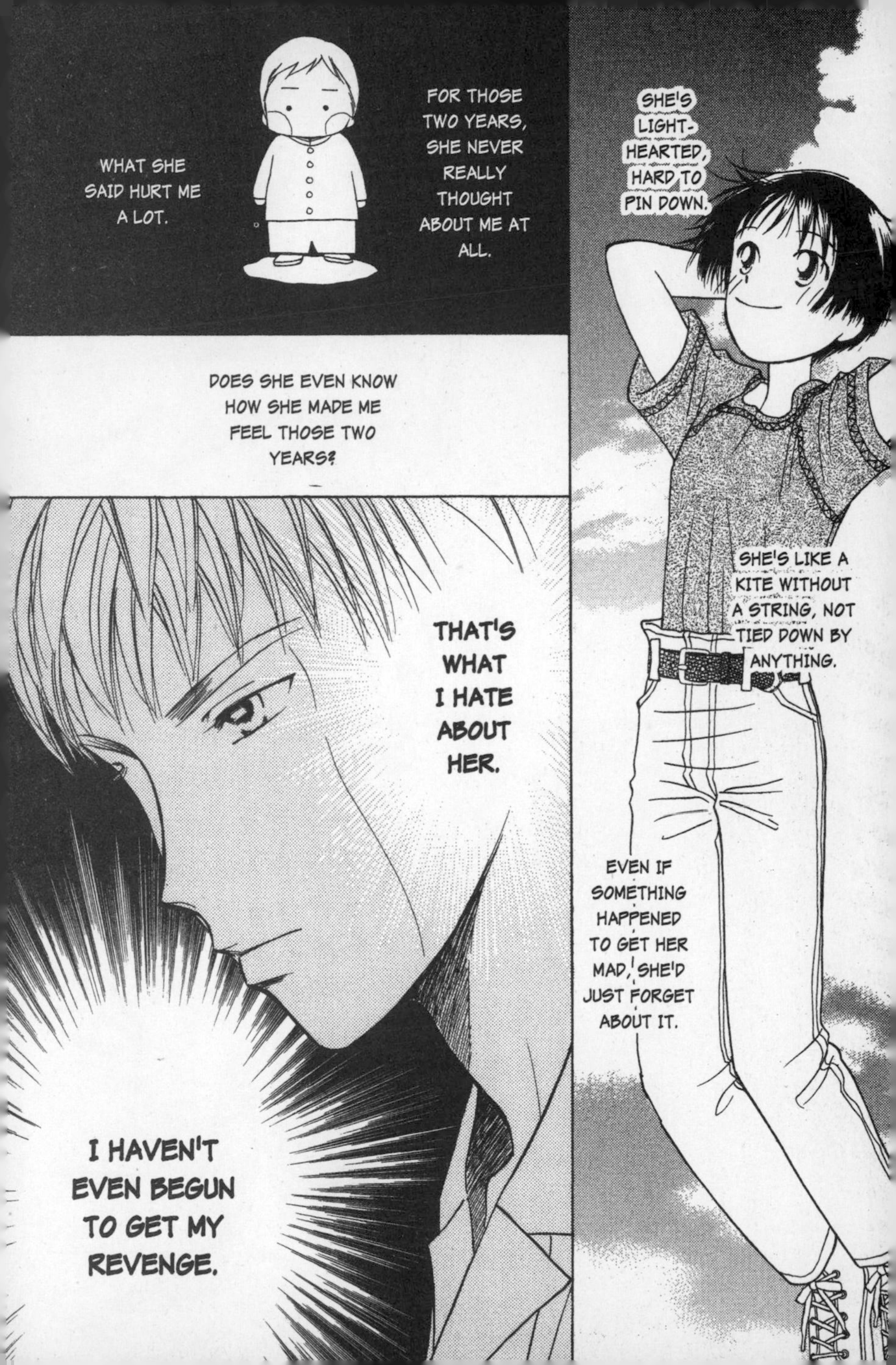
SHE'S LIGHT-HEARTED, HARD TO PIN DOWN.
SHE'S LIKE A KITE WITHOUT A STRING, NOT TIED DOWN BY ANYTHING.
EVEN IF SOMETHING HAPPENED TO GET HER MAD, SHE'D JUST FORGET ABOUT IT.
FOR THOSE TWO YEARS, SHE NEVER REALLY THOUGHT ABOUT ME AT ALL.
WHAT SHE SAID HURT ME A LOT.
DOES SHE EVEN KNOW HOW SHE MADE ME FEEL THOSE TWO YEARS?
THAT'S WHAT I HATE ABOUT HER.
I HAVEN'T EVEN BEGUN TO GET MY REVENGE.

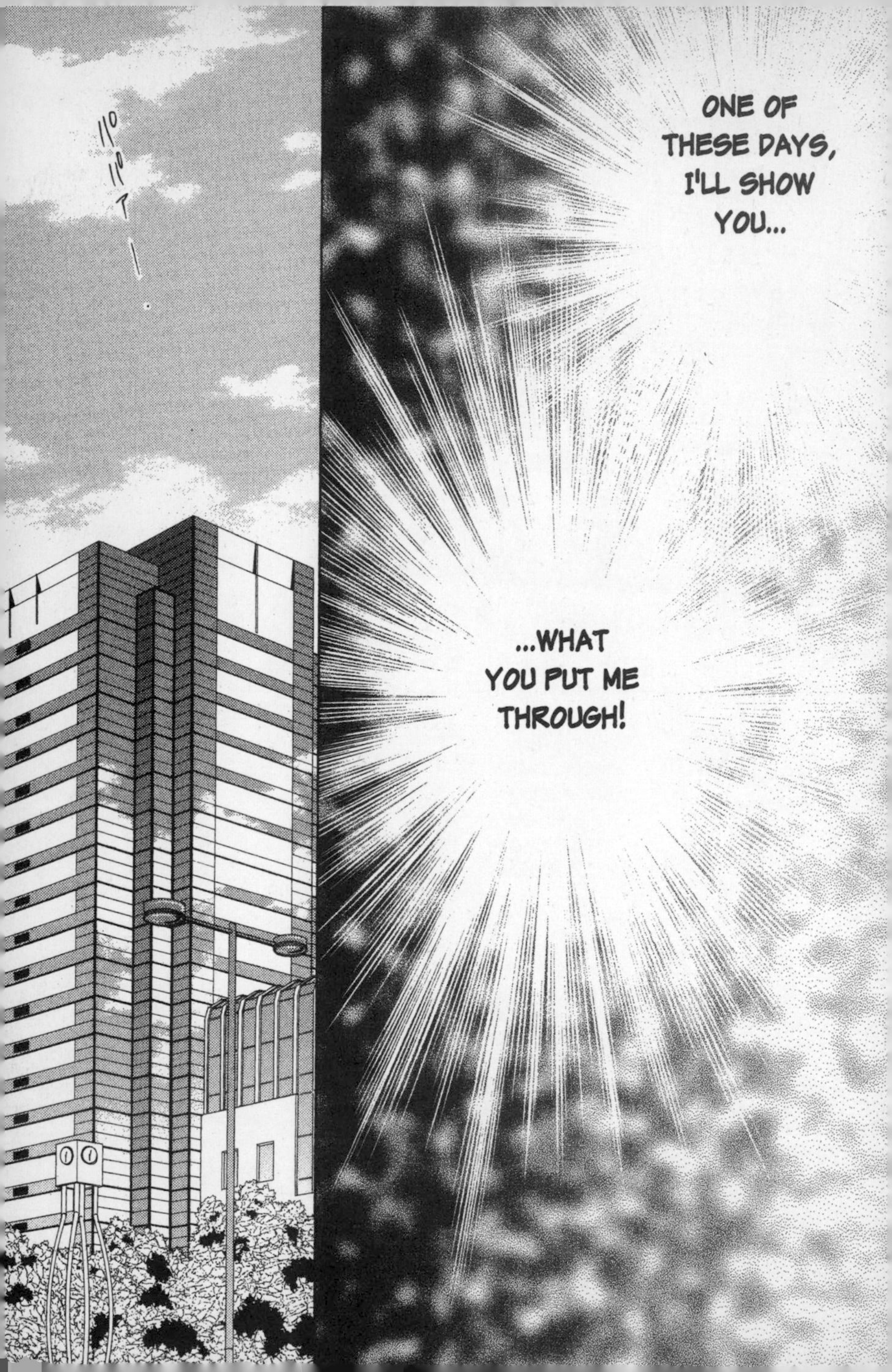
ONE OF THESE DAYS, I'LL SHOW YOU...
...WHAT YOU PUT ME THROUGH!
パパアー

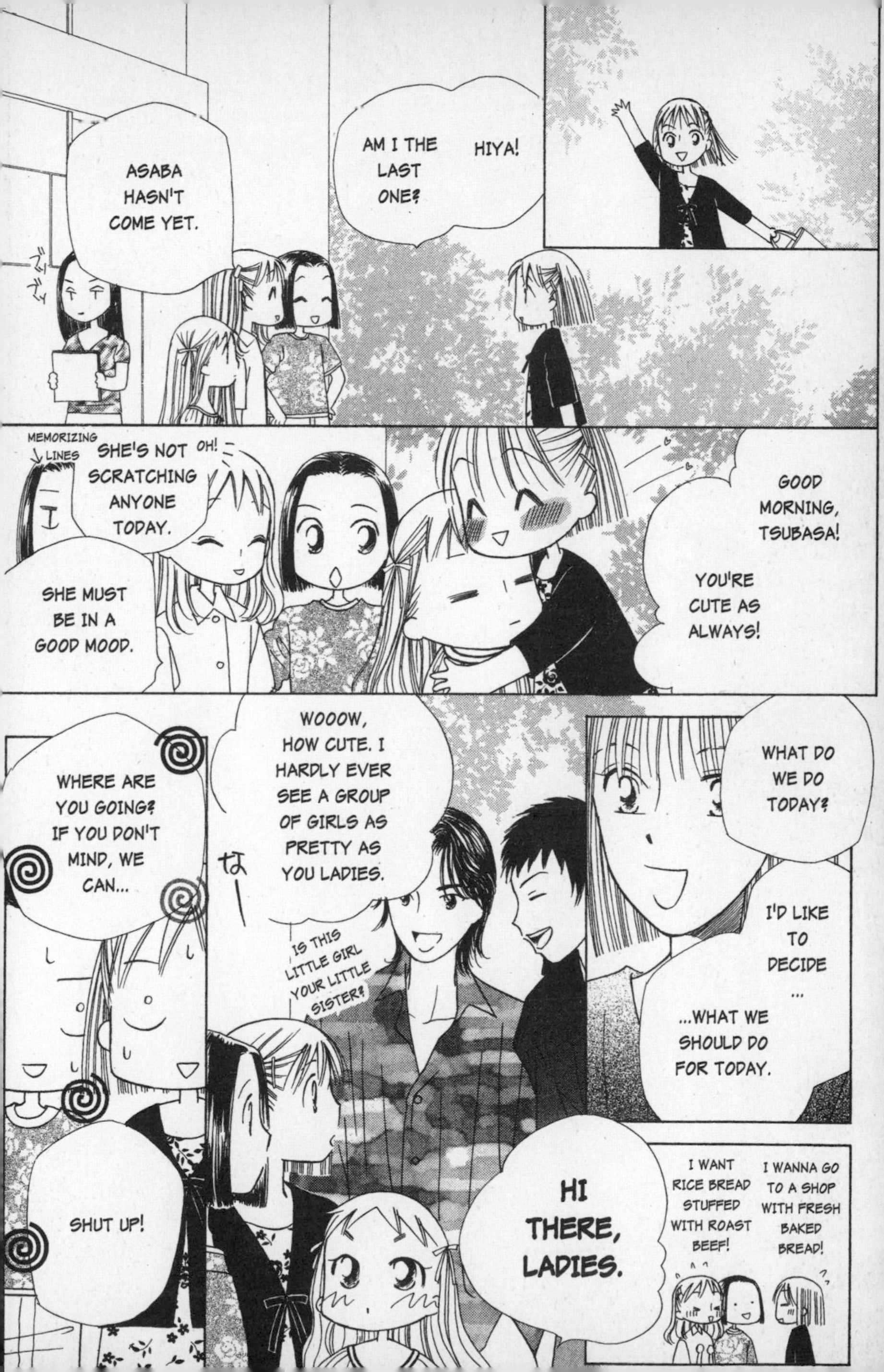

HIYA!
AM I THE LAST ONE?
ASABA HASN'T COME YET.
GOOD MORNING, TSUBASA!
YOU'RE CUTE AS ALWAYS!
OH!
SHE'S NOT SCRATCHING ANYONE TODAY.
MEMORIZING LINES
SHE MUST BE IN A GOOD MOOD.
WHAT DO WE DO TODAY?
I'D LIKE TO DECIDE ...
...WHAT WE SHOULD DO FOR TODAY.
I WANNA GO TO A SHOP WITH FRESH BAKED BREAD!
I WANT RICE BREAD STUFFED WITH ROAST BEEF!
WOOOW, HOW CUTE. I HARDLY EVER SEE A GROUP OF GIRLS AS PRETTY AS YOU LADIES.
なー
IS THIS LITTLE GIRL YOUR LITTLE SISTER?
WHERE ARE YOU GOING? IF YOU DON'T MIND, WE CAN...
HI THERE, LADIES.
SHUT UP!

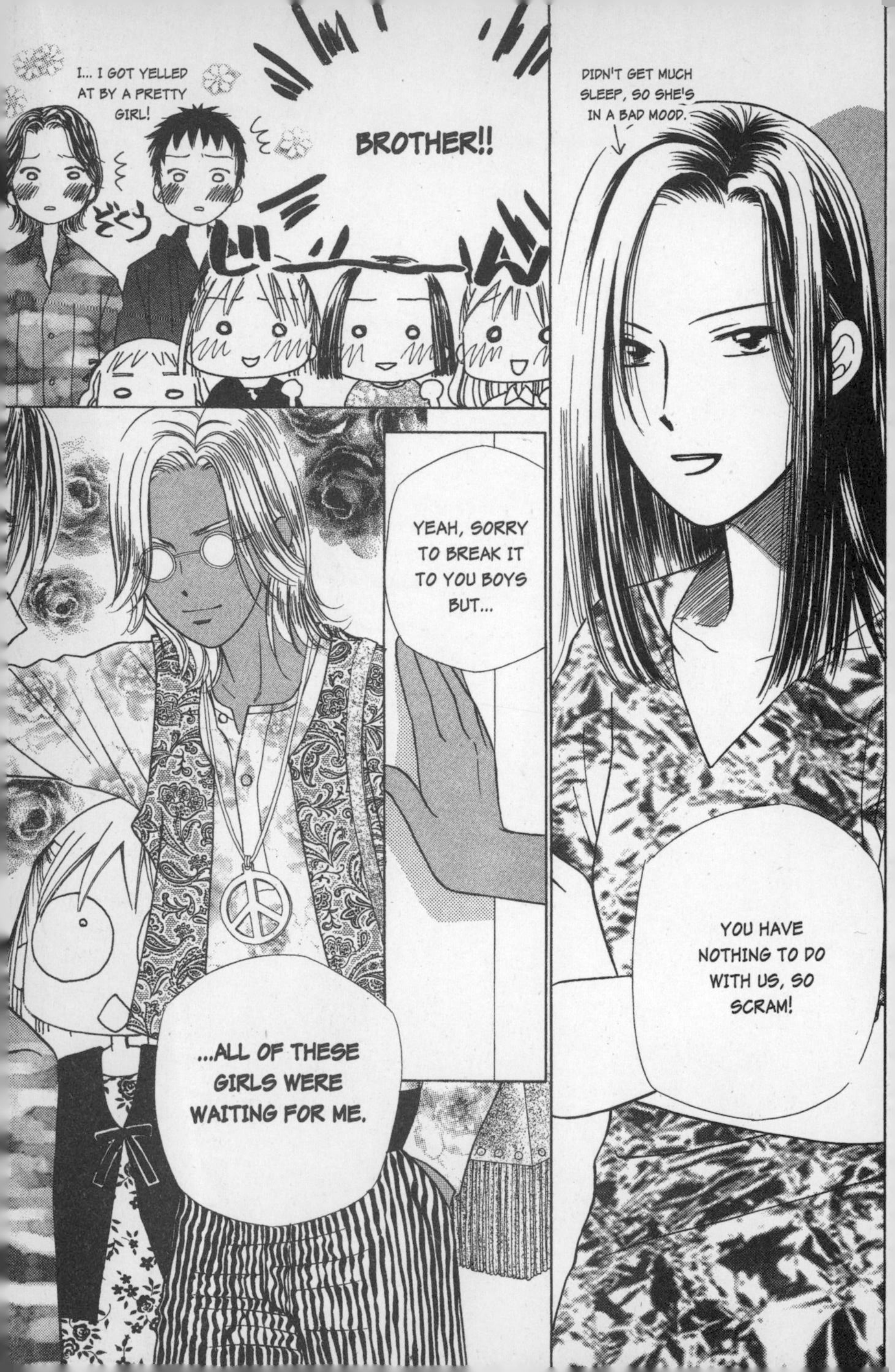
DIDN'T GET MUCH SLEEP, SO SHE'S IN A BAD MOOD.
YOU HAVE NOTHING TO DO WITH US, SO SCRAM!
BROTHER!!
I... I GOT YELLED AT BY A PRETTY GIRL!
YEAH, SORRY TO BREAK IT TO YOU BOYS BUT...
...ALL OF THESE GIRLS WERE WAITING FOR ME.

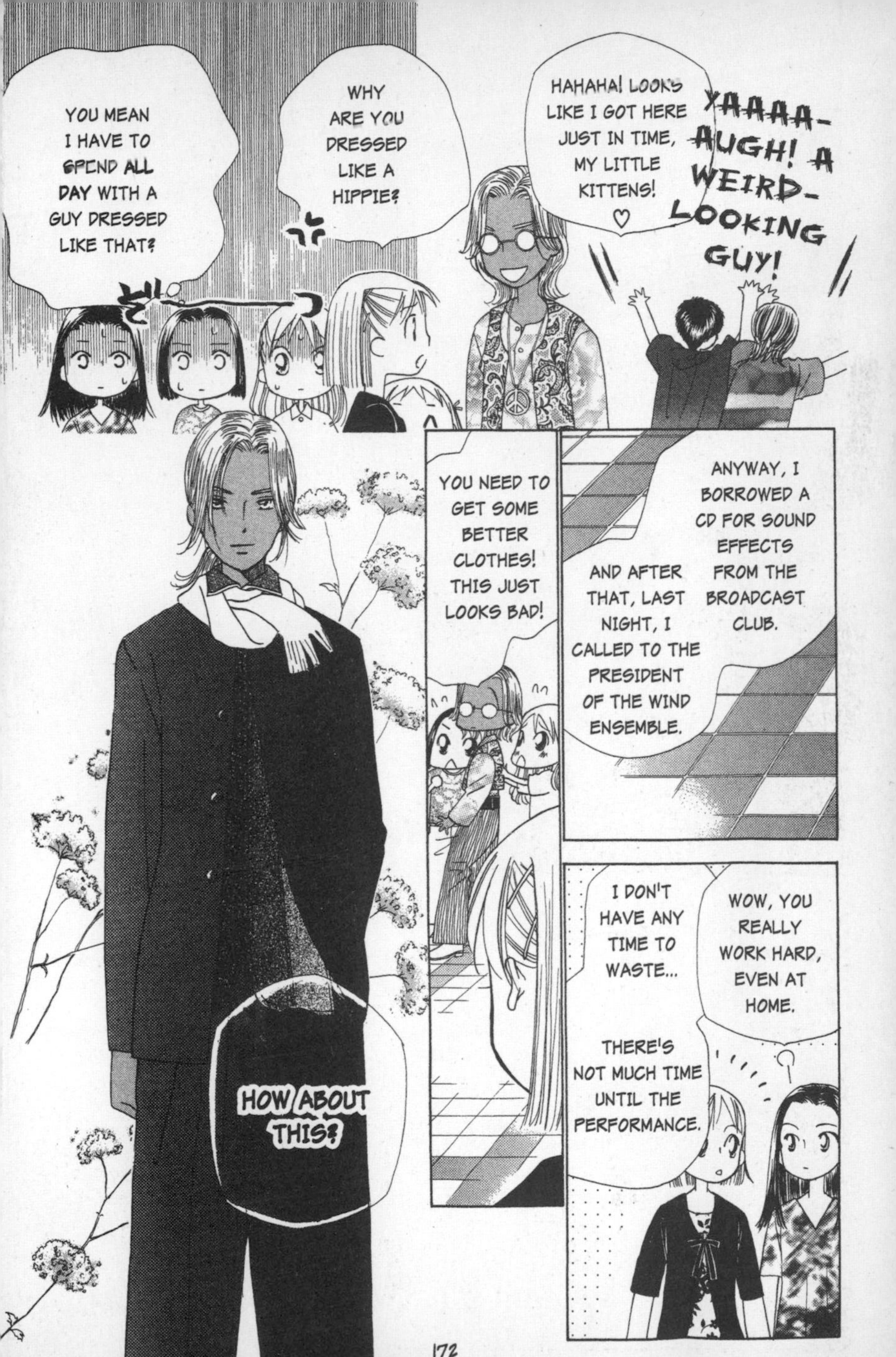

YAAAA-AUGH! A WEIRD-LOOKING GUY!
HAHAHA! LOOKS LIKE I GOT HERE JUST IN TIME, MY LITTLE KITTENS! ♡
WHY ARE YOU DRESSED LIKE A HIPPIE?
YOU MEAN I HAVE TO SPEND ALL DAY WITH A GUY DRESSED LIKE THAT?
ANYWAY, I BORROWED A CD FOR SOUND EFFECTS FROM THE BROADCAST CLUB.
AND AFTER THAT, LAST NIGHT, I CALLED TO THE PRESIDENT OF THE WIND ENSEMBLE.
WOW, YOU REALLY WORK HARD, EVEN AT HOME.
I DON'T HAVE ANY TIME TO WASTE...
THERE'S NOT MUCH TIME UNTIL THE PERFORMANCE.
YOU NEED TO GET SOME BETTER CLOTHES! THIS JUST LOOKS BAD!
HOW ABOUT THIS?

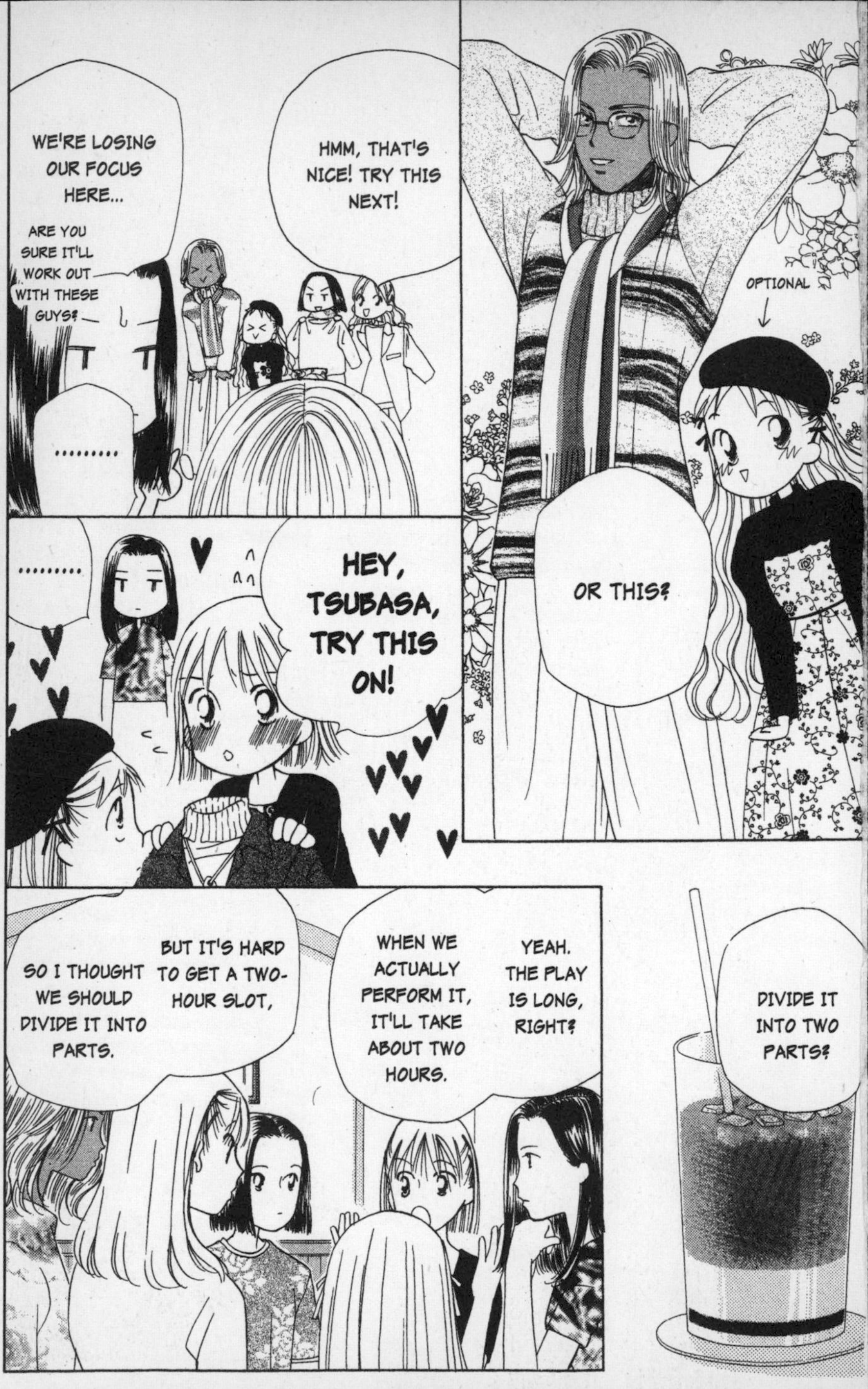
OPTIONAL
OR THIS?
HMM, THAT'S NICE! TRY THIS NEXT!
WE'RE LOSING OUR FOCUS HERE...
ARE YOU SURE IT'LL WORK OUT WITH THESE GUYS?
....
HEY, TSUBASA, TRY THIS ON!
....
DIVIDE IT INTO TWO PARTS?
YEAH. THE PLAY IS LONG, RIGHT?
WHEN WE ACTUALLY PERFORM IT, IT'LL TAKE ABOUT TWO HOURS.
BUT IT'S HARD TO GET A TWO-HOUR SLOT,
SO I THOUGHT WE SHOULD DIVIDE IT INTO PARTS.

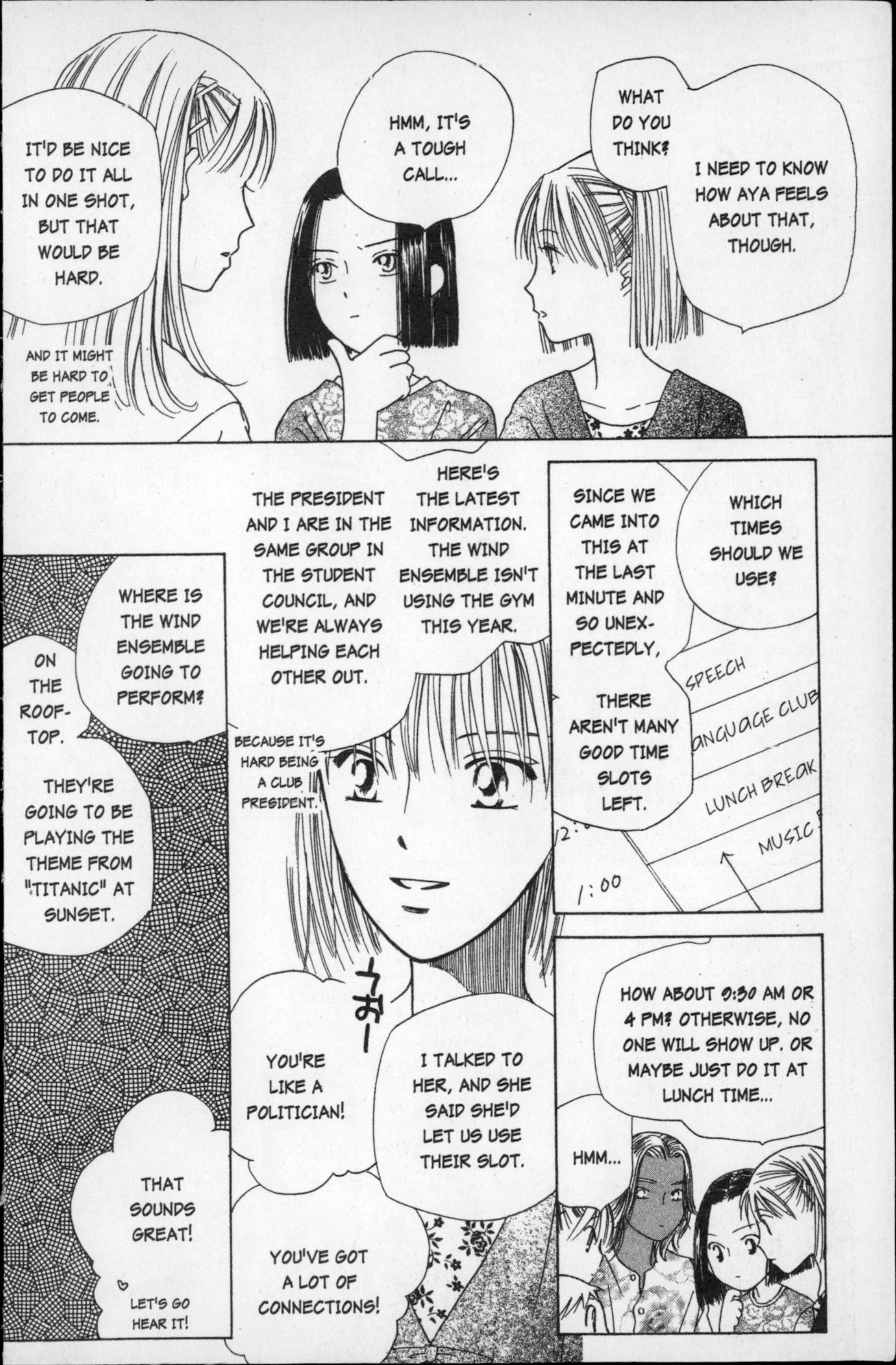
WHAT DO YOU THINK?
I NEED TO KNOW HOW AYA FEELS ABOUT THAT, THOUGH.
HMM, IT'S A TOUGH CALL...
IT'D BE NICE TO DO IT ALL IN ONE SHOT, BUT THAT WOULD BE HARD.
AND IT MIGHT BE HARD TO GET PEOPLE TO COME.
WHICH TIMES SHOULD WE USE?
SINCE WE CAME INTO THIS AT THE LAST MINUTE AND SO UNEX-PECTEDLY,
THERE AREN'T MANY GOOD TIME SLOTS LEFT.
SPEECH
ANGUAGE CLUB
LUNCH BREAK
MUSIC
1:00
HOW ABOUT 9:30 AM OR 4 PM? OTHERWISE, NO ONE WILL SHOW UP. OR MAYBE JUST DO IT AT LUNCH TIME...
HMM...
HERE'S THE LATEST INFORMATION. THE WIND ENSEMBLE ISN'T USING THE GYM THIS YEAR.
THE PRESIDENT AND I ARE IN THE SAME GROUP IN THE STUDENT COUNCIL, AND WE'RE ALWAYS HELPING EACH OTHER OUT.
BECAUSE IT'S HARD BEING A CLUB PRESIDENT.
WHERE IS THE WIND ENSEMBLE GOING TO PERFORM?
ON THE ROOF-TOP.
THEY'RE GOING TO BE PLAYING THE THEME FROM "TITANIC" AT SUNSET.
うおー
I TALKED TO HER, AND SHE SAID SHE'D LET US USE THEIR SLOT.
YOU'RE LIKE A POLITICIAN!
YOU'VE GOT A LOT OF CONNECTIONS!
THAT SOUNDS GREAT!
LET'S GO HEAR IT!

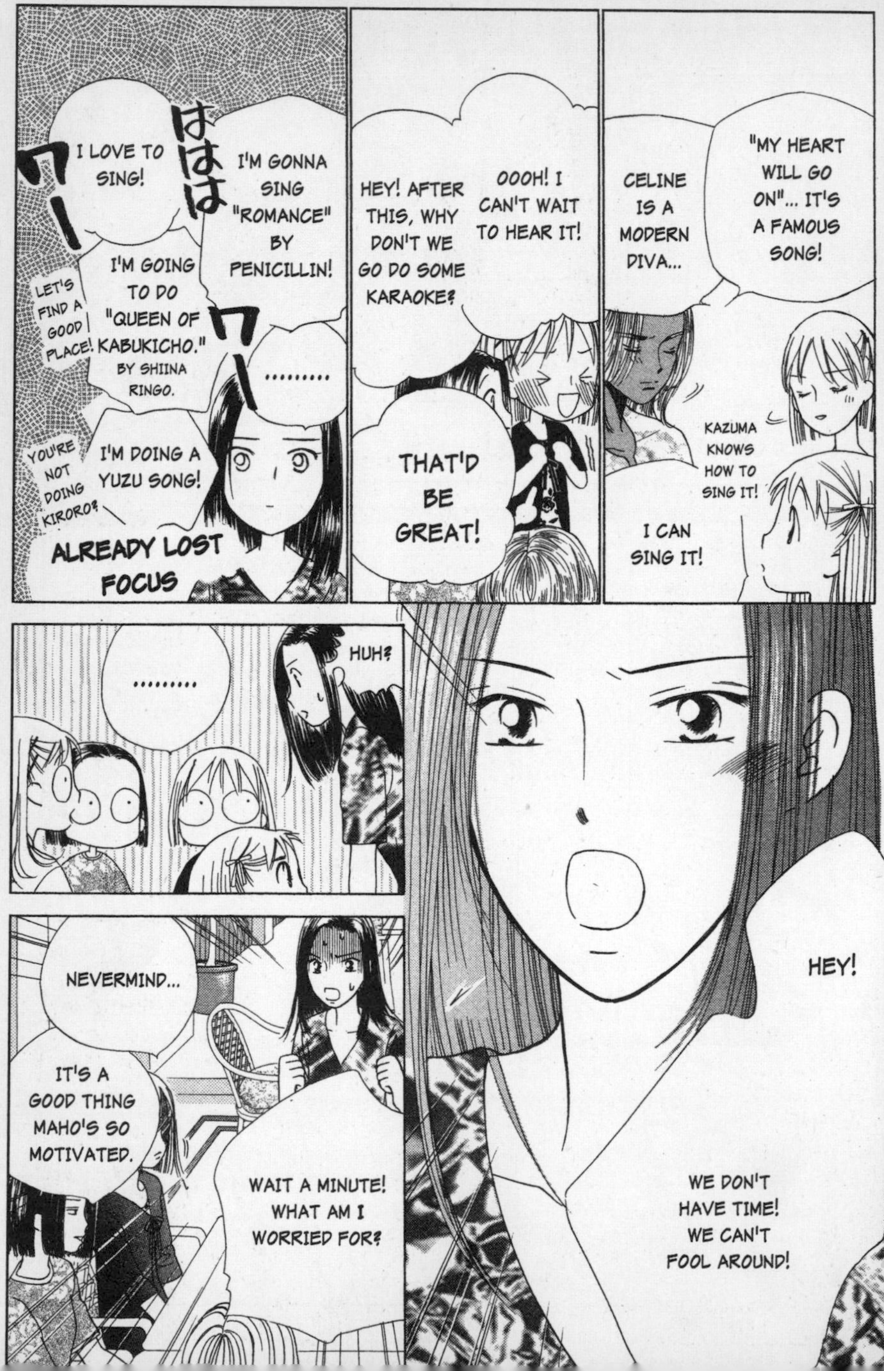
"MY HEART WILL GO ON"... IT'S A FAMOUS SONG!
CELINE IS A MODERN DIVA...
KAZUMA KNOWS HOW TO SING IT!
I CAN SING IT!
OOOH! I CAN'T WAIT TO HEAR IT!
HEY! AFTER THIS, WHY DON'T WE GO DO SOME KARAOKE?
THAT'D BE GREAT!
I'M GONNA SING "ROMANCE" BY PENICILLIN!
ははは
I LOVE TO SING!
ワー
ワー
....
I'M GOING TO DO "QUEEN OF KABUKICHO." BY SHIINA RINGO.
LET'S FIND A GOOD PLACE!
I'M DOING A YUZU SONG!
YOU'RE NOT DOING KIRORO?
ALREADY LOST FOCUS
HEY!
WE DON'T HAVE TIME! WE CAN'T FOOL AROUND!
HUH?
....
NEVERMIND...
IT'S A GOOD THING MAHO'S SO MOTIVATED.
WAIT A MINUTE! WHAT AM I WORRIED FOR?

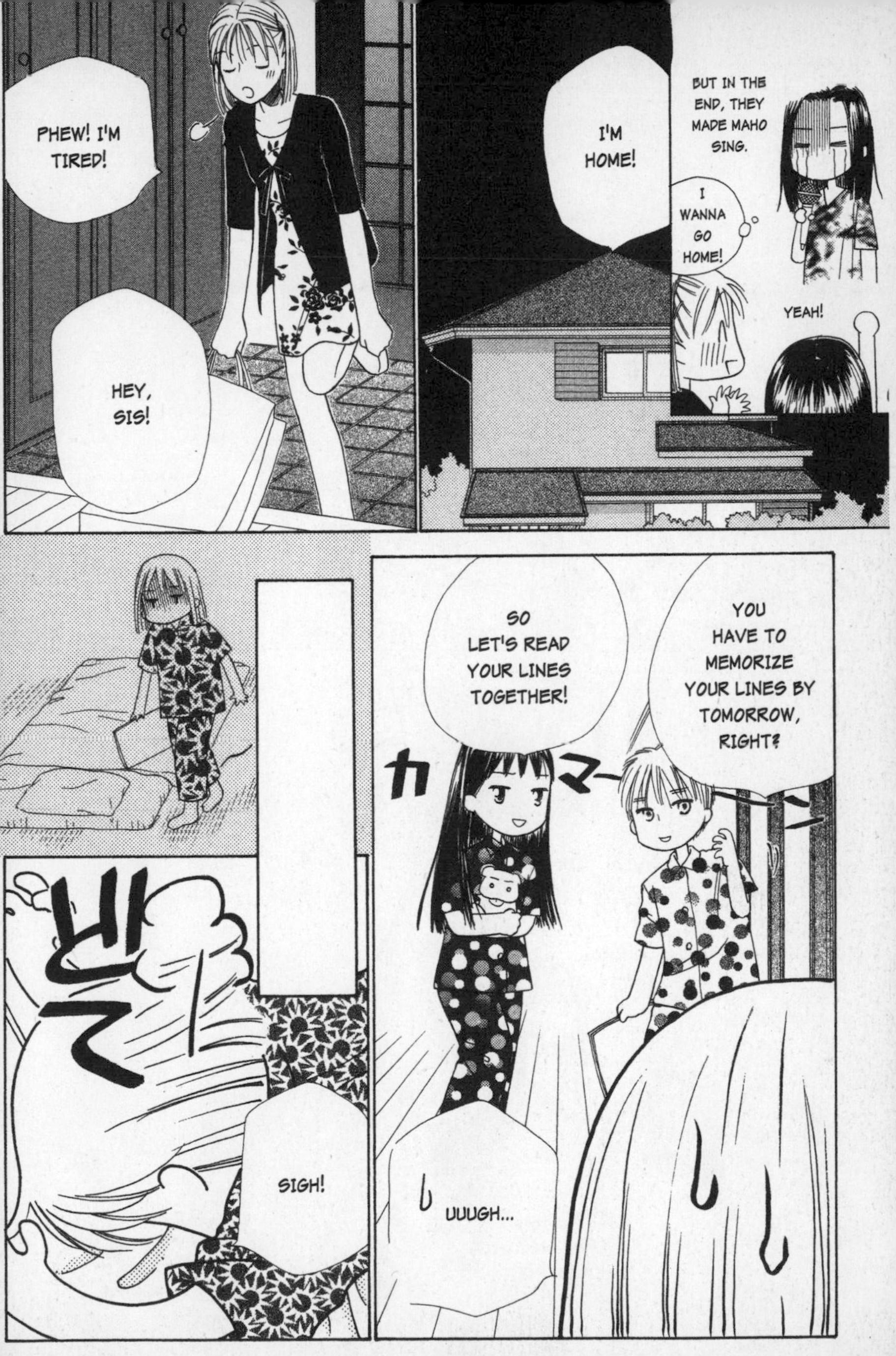
BUT IN THE END, THEY MADE MAHO SING.
I WANNA GO HOME!
YEAH!
I'M HOME!
PHEW! I'M TIRED!
HEY, SIS!
YOU HAVE TO MEMORIZE YOUR LINES BY TOMORROW, RIGHT?
SO LET'S READ YOUR LINES TOGETHER!
UUUGH...
SIGH!

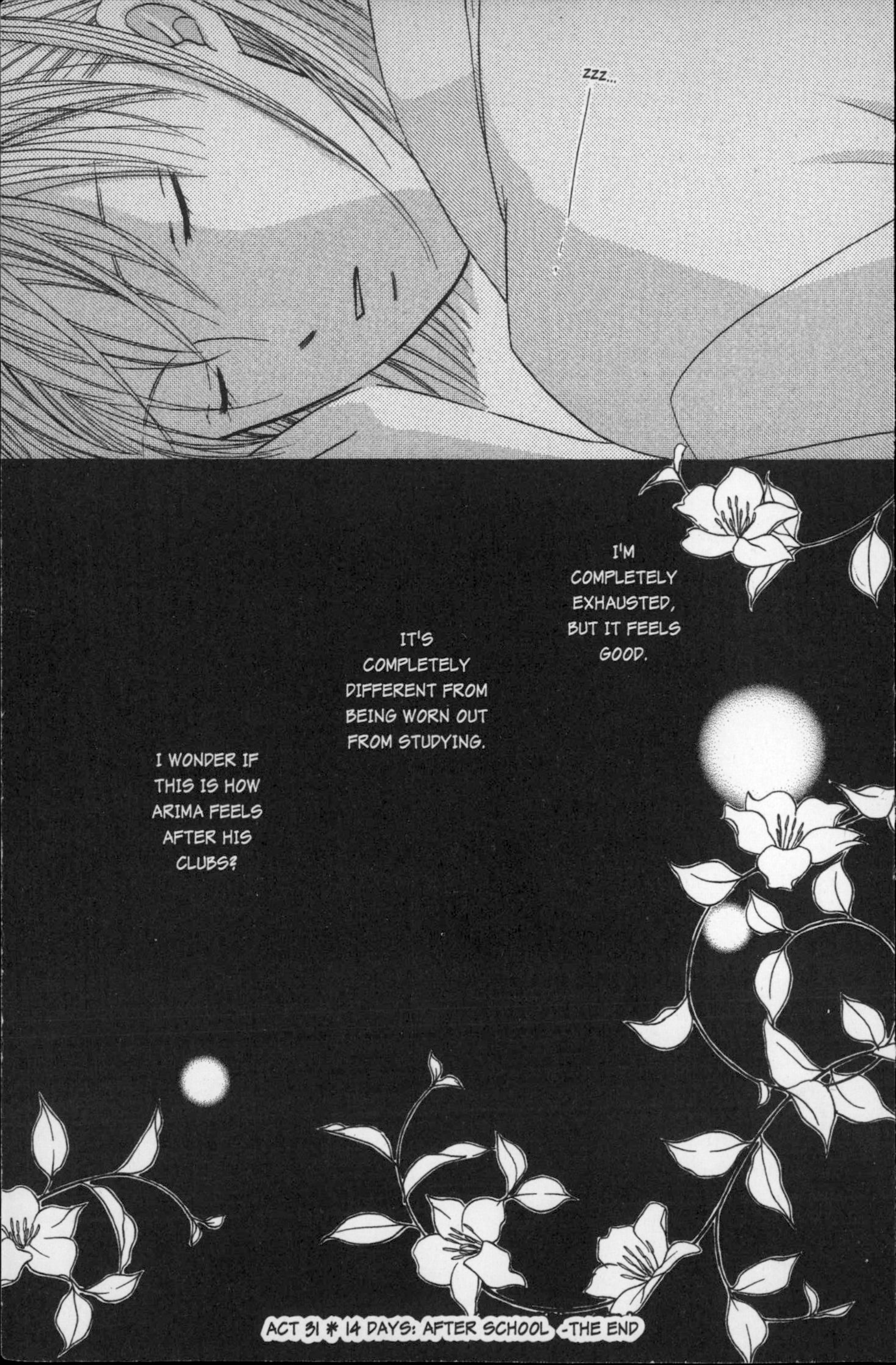

ZZZ...
I'M COMPLETELY EXHAUSTED, BUT IT FEELS GOOD.
IT'S COMPLETELY DIFFERENT FROM BEING WORN OUT FROM STUDYING.
I WONDER IF THIS IS HOW ARIMA FEELS AFTER HIS CLUBS?
ACT 31 * 14 DAYS: AFTER SCHOOL -THE END

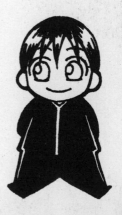

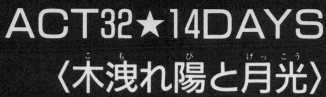

ACT32★14DAYS

〈木洩れ陽と月光〉

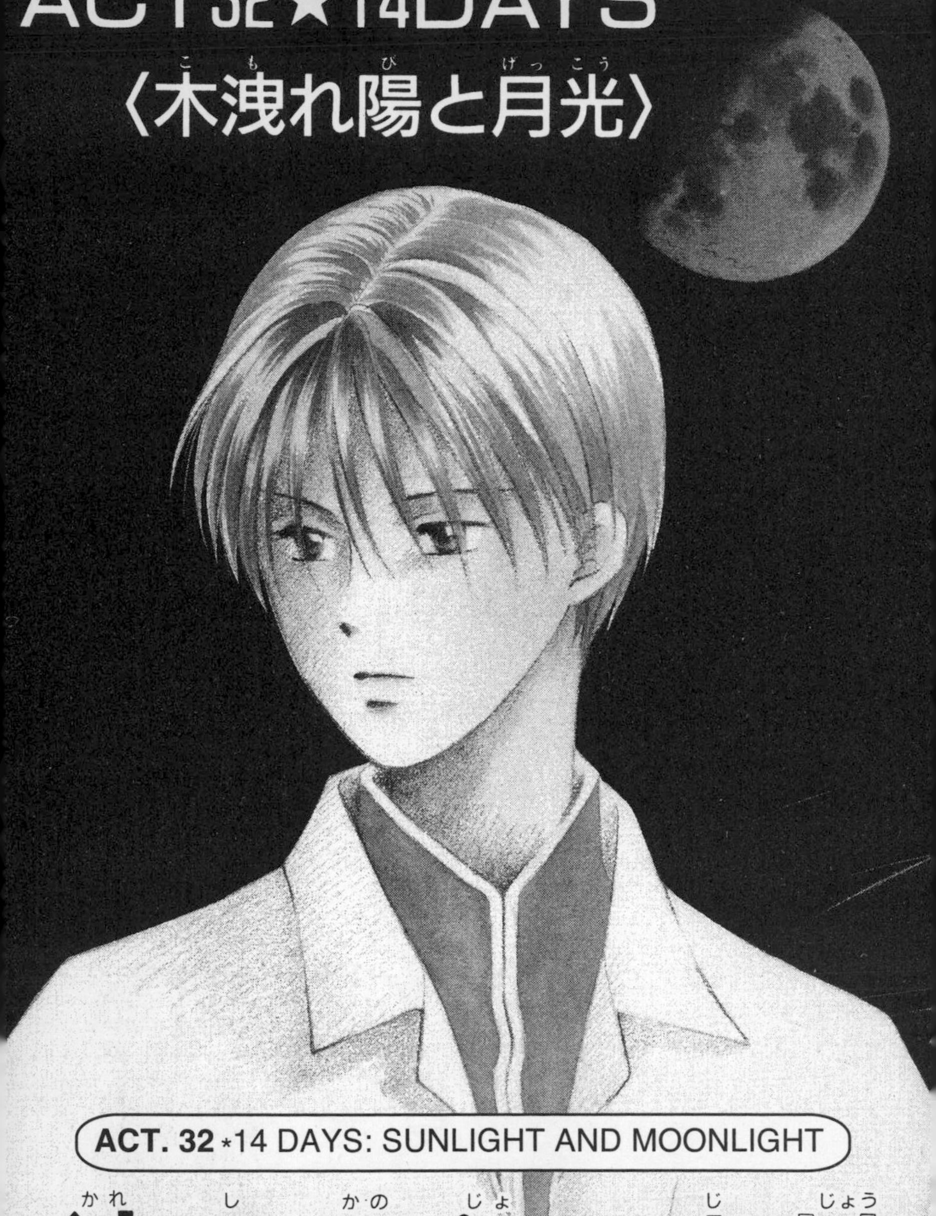

ACT. 32 *14 DAYS: SUNLIGHT AND MOONLIGHT

彼氏彼女の事情

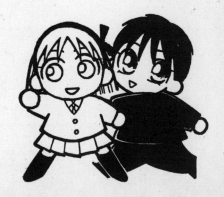

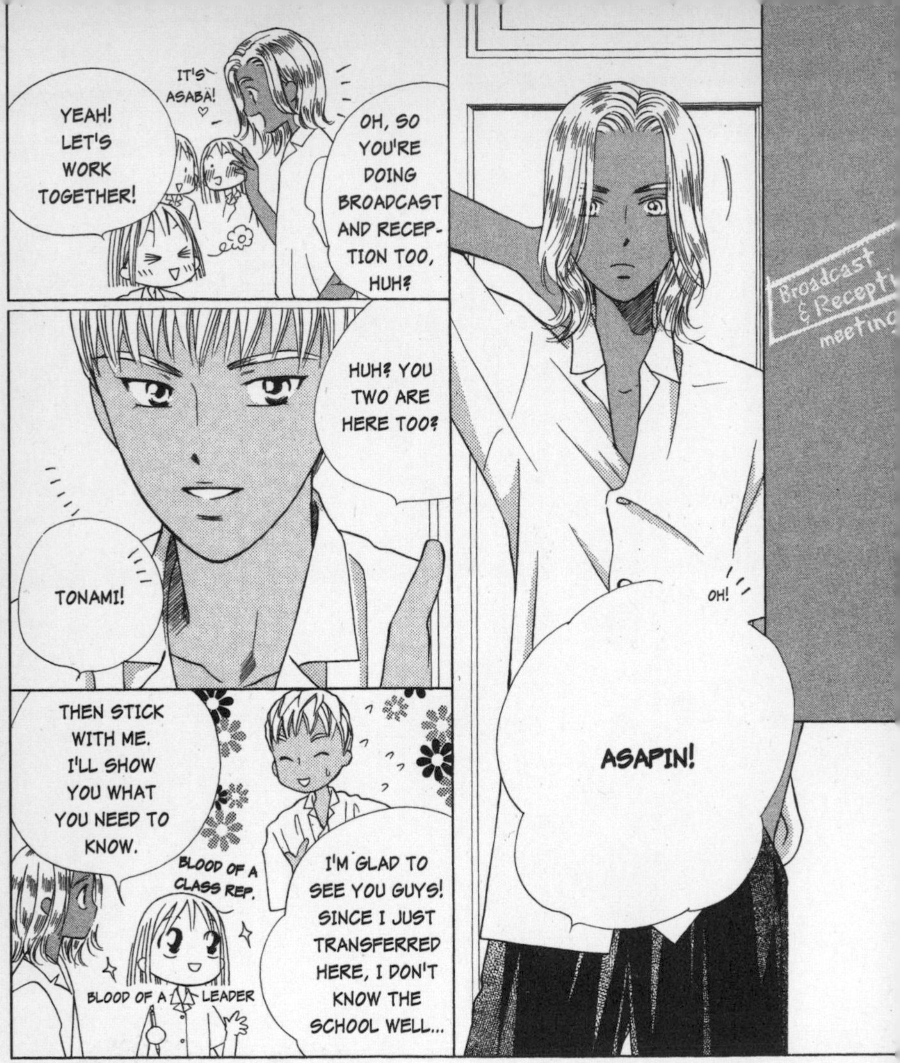
Broadcast & Recepti
meeting
OH!
ASAPIN!
OH, SO YOU'RE DOING BROADCAST AND RECEPTION TOO, HUH?
IT'S ASABA! ♡
YEAH! LET'S WORK TOGETHER!
HUH? YOU TWO ARE HERE TOO?
TONAMI!
I'M GLAD TO SEE YOU GUYS! SINCE I JUST TRANSFERRED HERE, I DON'T KNOW THE SCHOOL WELL...
THEN STICK WITH ME. I'LL SHOW YOU WHAT YOU NEED TO KNOW.
BLOOD OF A CLASS REP.
BLOOD OF A LEADER

December 1998, January 1999

IN MY CASE, BEING CONSTANTLY BUSY HAS BECOME MY WAY OF LIFE, BUT THESE TWO MONTHS HAVE BEEN AMONG THE BUSIEST. TO GIVE YOU AN IDEA, I'LL WRITE DOWN ALL THE WORK I DID.

*LA LA COVER
*2 MONTHS WORTH OF KARE KANO (FROM DRAFT TO FINAL COPY) 62 P., AND 2 COLOR PAGES
*FOR VOLUME 7: FINISHING COVER, EDITING DRAFT, ILLUSTRATIONS FOR OPENING PAGES
*TWO ILLUSTRATIONS FOR CARDS
*FOR THINGS TO BE GIVEN TO LALA READERS: KARE KANO DRAMA CD, 3 COLOR ILLUSTRATIONS, 1 BLACK AND WHITE ILLUSTRATION, 45 PAGE ORIGINAL STORY,

LATER, THINGS WILL GET BACK TO NORMAL...

YEAH! IT'S OVER! ... OR SO I THOUGHT. MORE WORK CAME IN TO DO, TO JUDGE A CONTEST AND MAKE AN ILLUSTRATION FOR A TELEPHONE CARD.

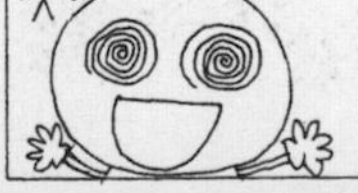
わあ

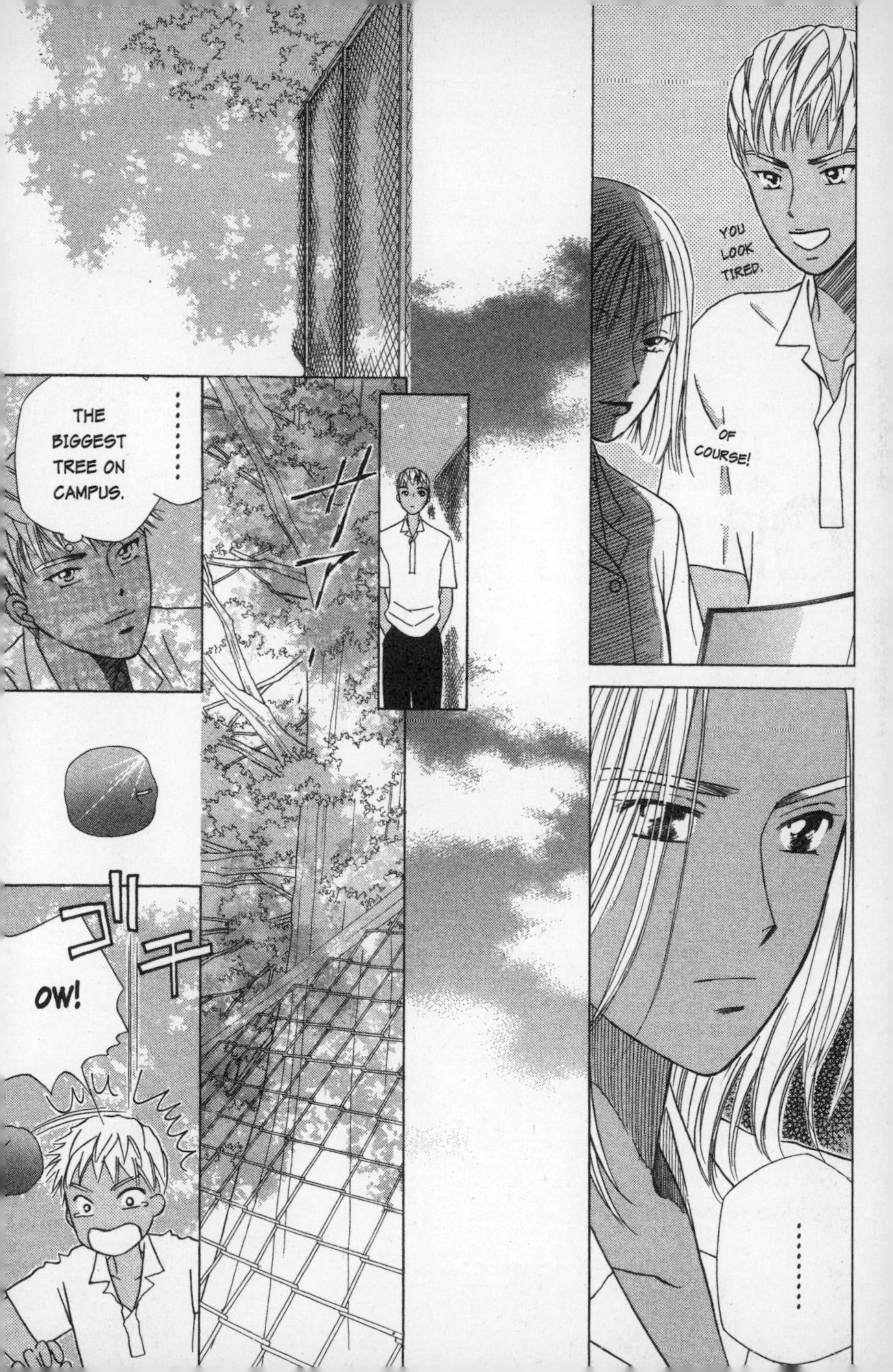

YOU LOOK TIRED.
OF COURSE!
……
……
THE BIGGEST TREE ON CAMPUS.
OW!

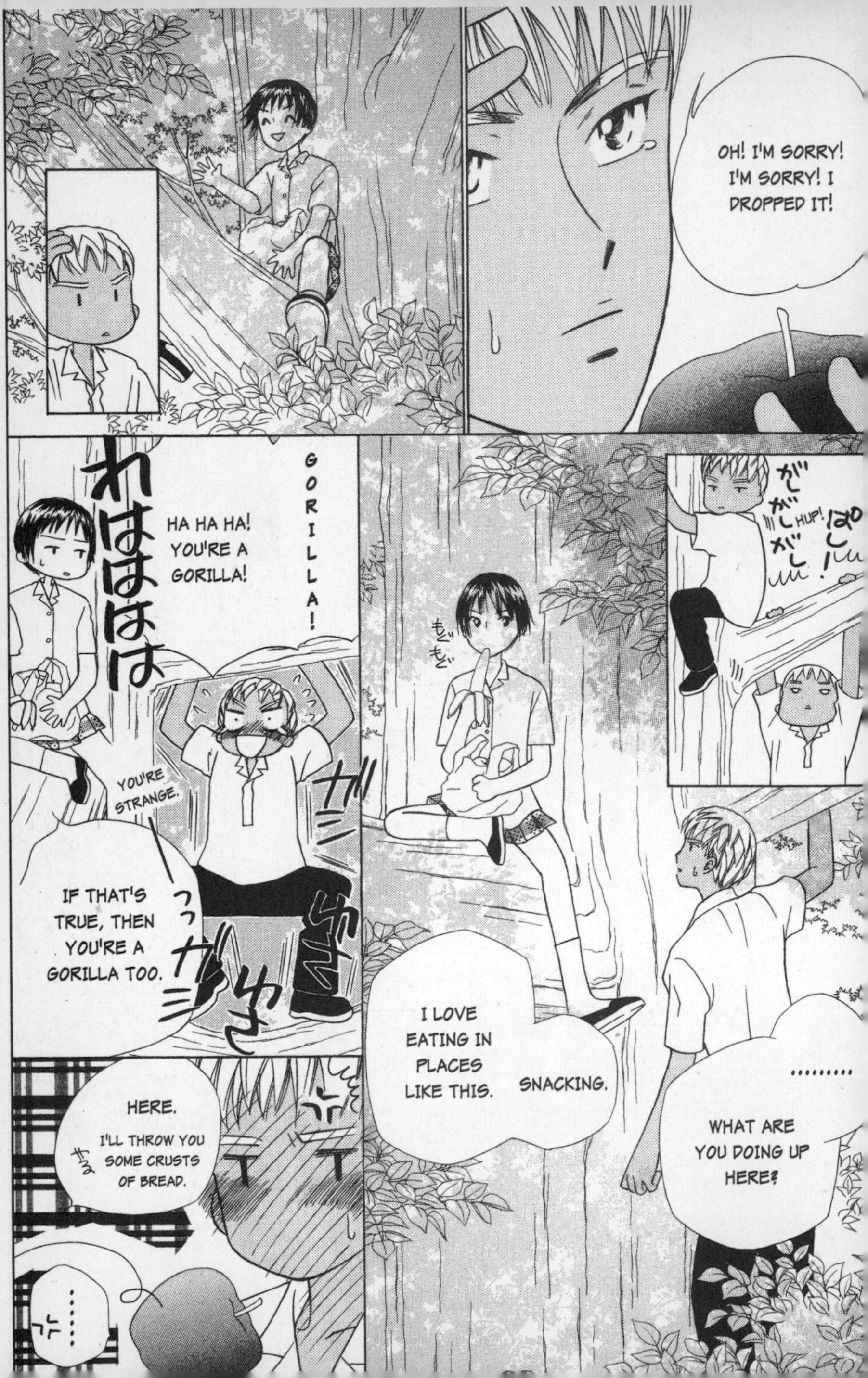
OH! I'M SORRY! I'M SORRY! I DROPPED IT!
がしがしがし
HUP!
ぱしっ
....
WHAT ARE YOU DOING UP HERE?
SNACKING.
I LOVE EATING IN PLACES LIKE THIS.
もぐもぐ
GORILLA!
HA HA HA! YOU'RE A GORILLA!
わはははは
YOU'RE STRANGE.
IF THAT'S TRUE, THEN YOU'RE A GORILLA TOO.
ゆさゆさ
HERE.
I'LL THROW YOU SOME CRUSTS OF BREAD.
......

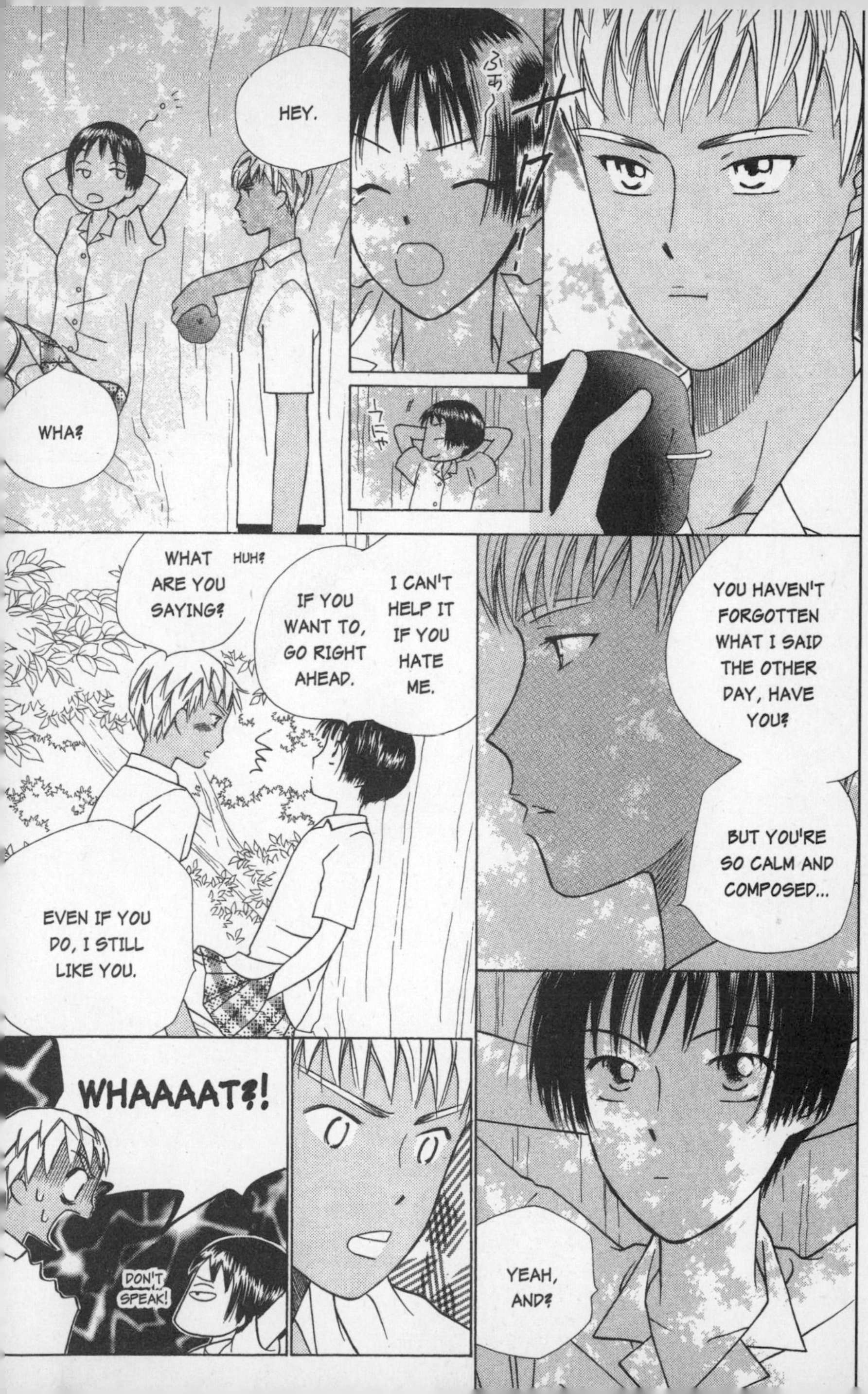
HEY.
WHA?
YOU HAVEN'T FORGOTTEN WHAT I SAID THE OTHER DAY, HAVE YOU?
BUT YOU'RE SO CALM AND COMPOSED...
YEAH, AND?
I CAN'T HELP IT IF YOU HATE ME.
IF YOU WANT TO, GO RIGHT AHEAD.
HUH?
WHAT ARE YOU SAYING?
EVEN IF YOU DO, I STILL LIKE YOU.
WHAAAAT?!
DON'T SPEAK!

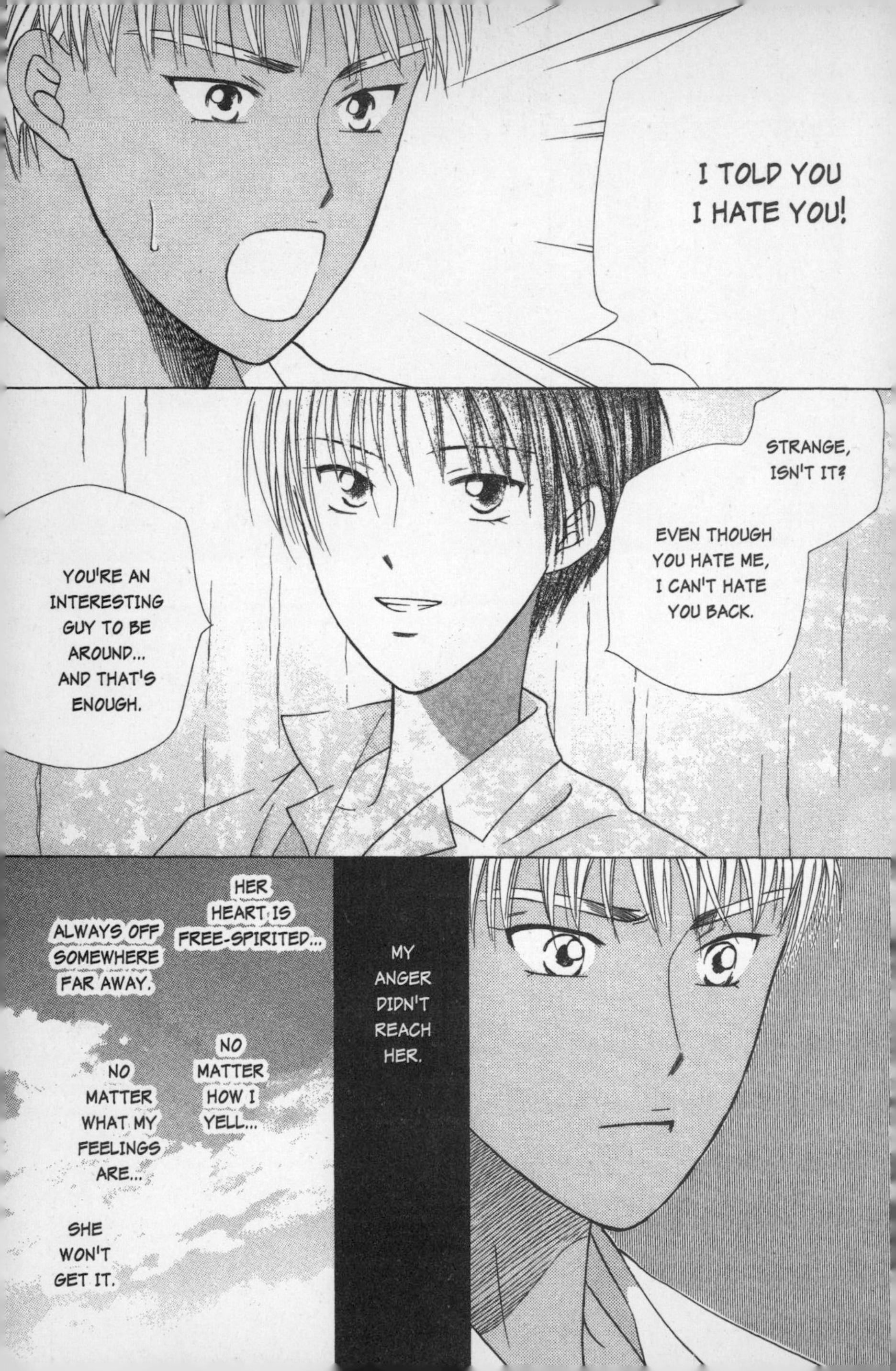
I TOLD YOU I HATE YOU!
STRANGE, ISN'T IT?
EVEN THOUGH YOU HATE ME, I CAN'T HATE YOU BACK.
YOU'RE AN INTERESTING GUY TO BE AROUND... AND THAT'S ENOUGH.
MY ANGER DIDN'T REACH HER.
HER HEART IS FREE-SPIRITED...
ALWAYS OFF SOMEWHERE FAR AWAY.
NO MATTER HOW I YELL...
NO MATTER WHAT MY FEELINGS ARE...
SHE WON'T GET IT.

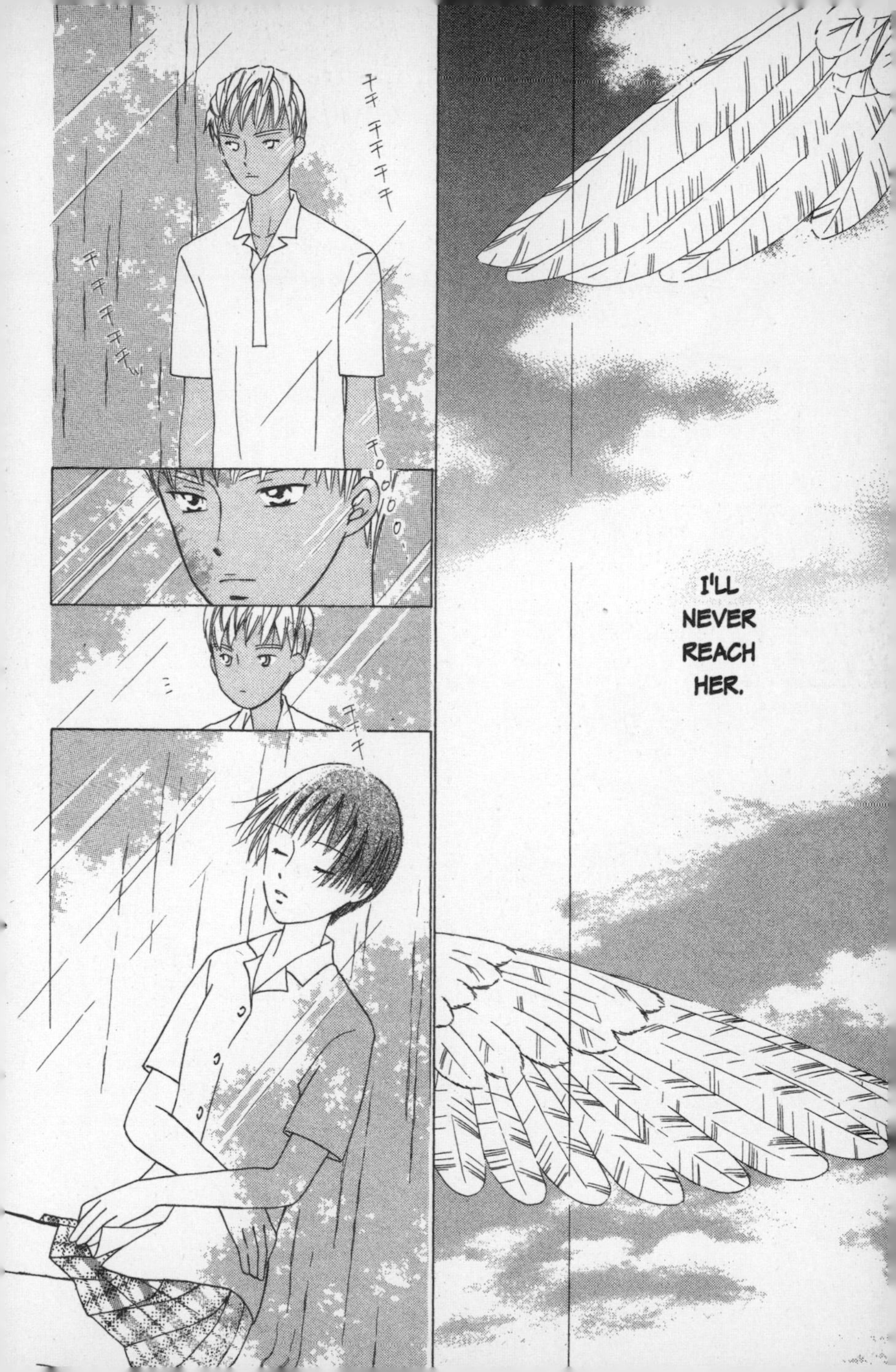
I'LL NEVER REACH HER.

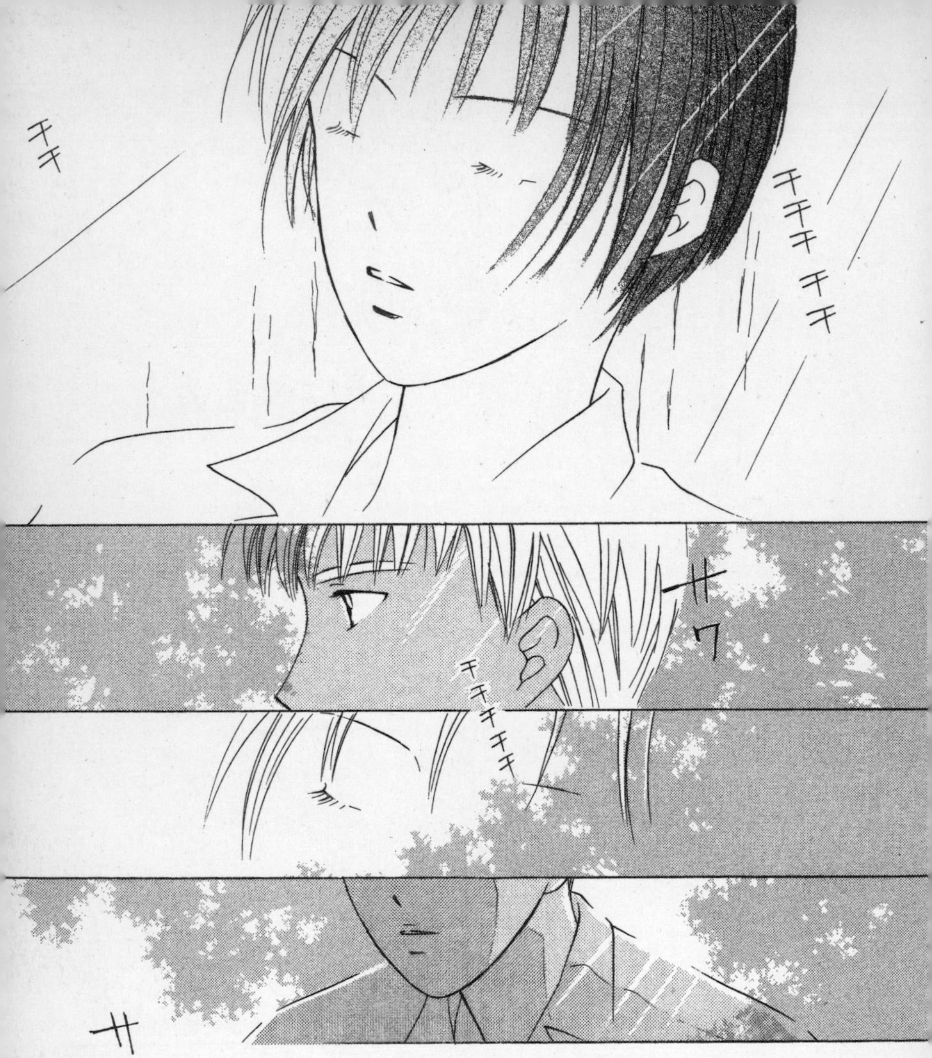
チチチ
チチ
チチ
サク
チチチチチ
サ

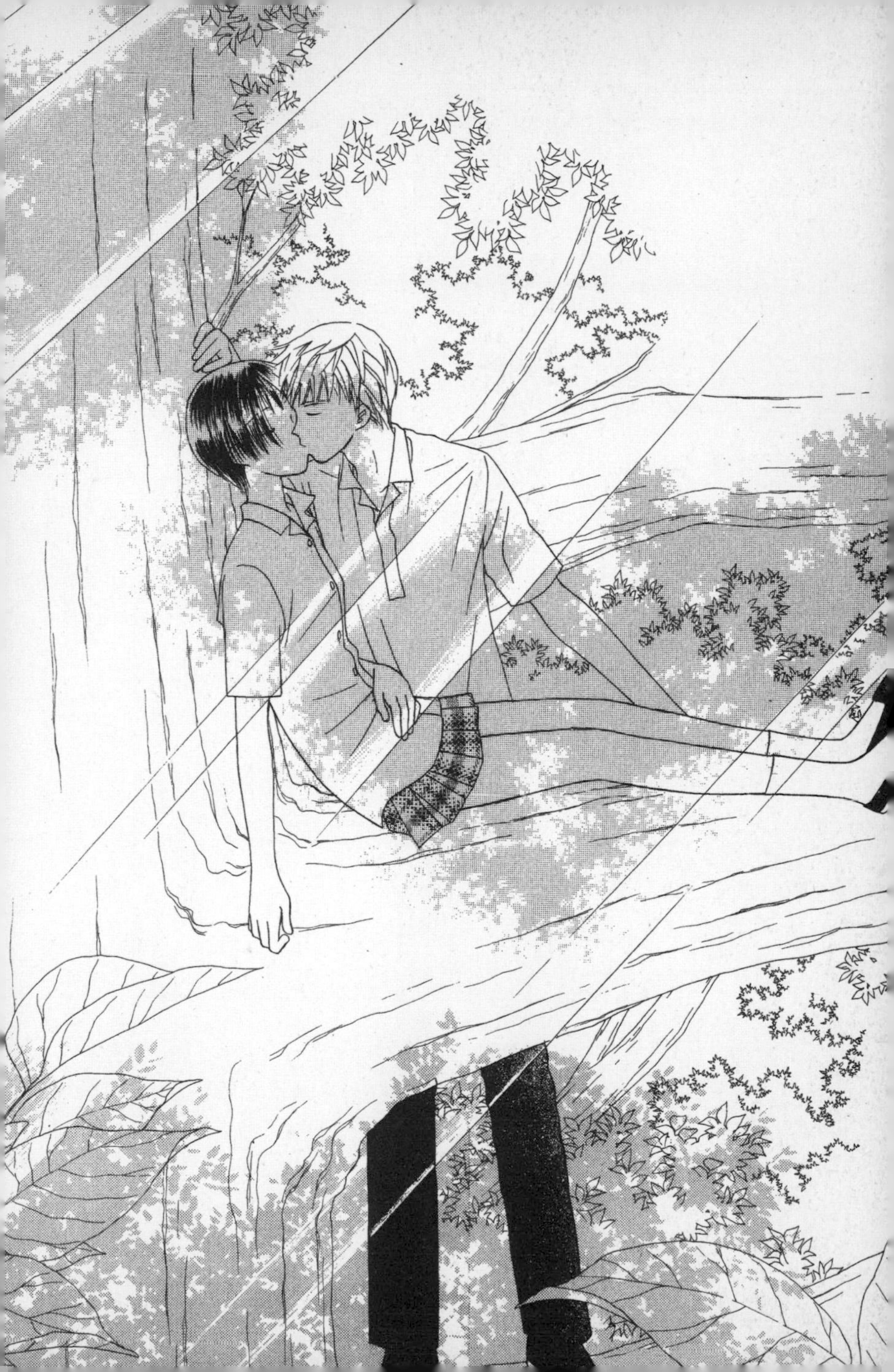

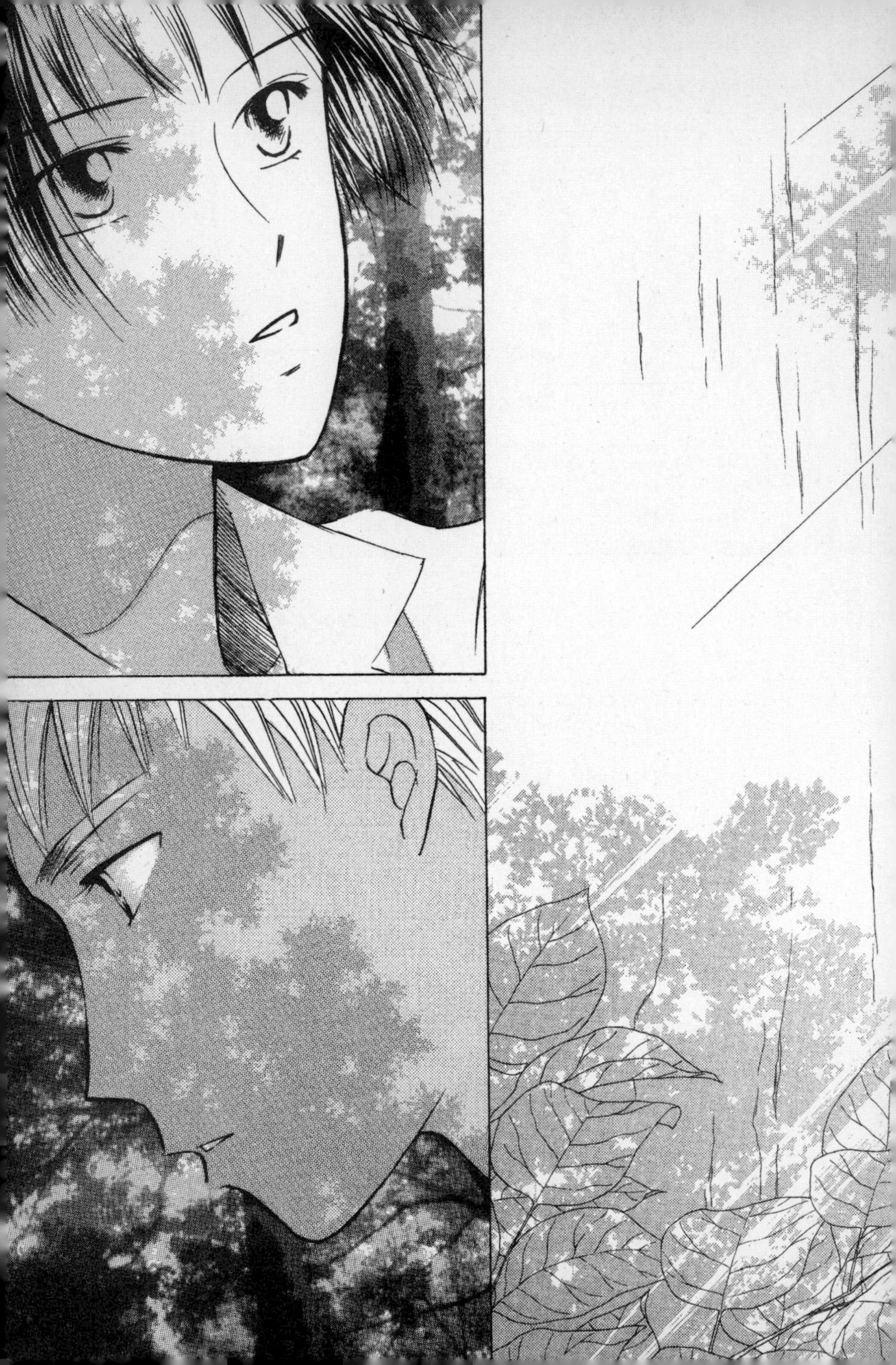

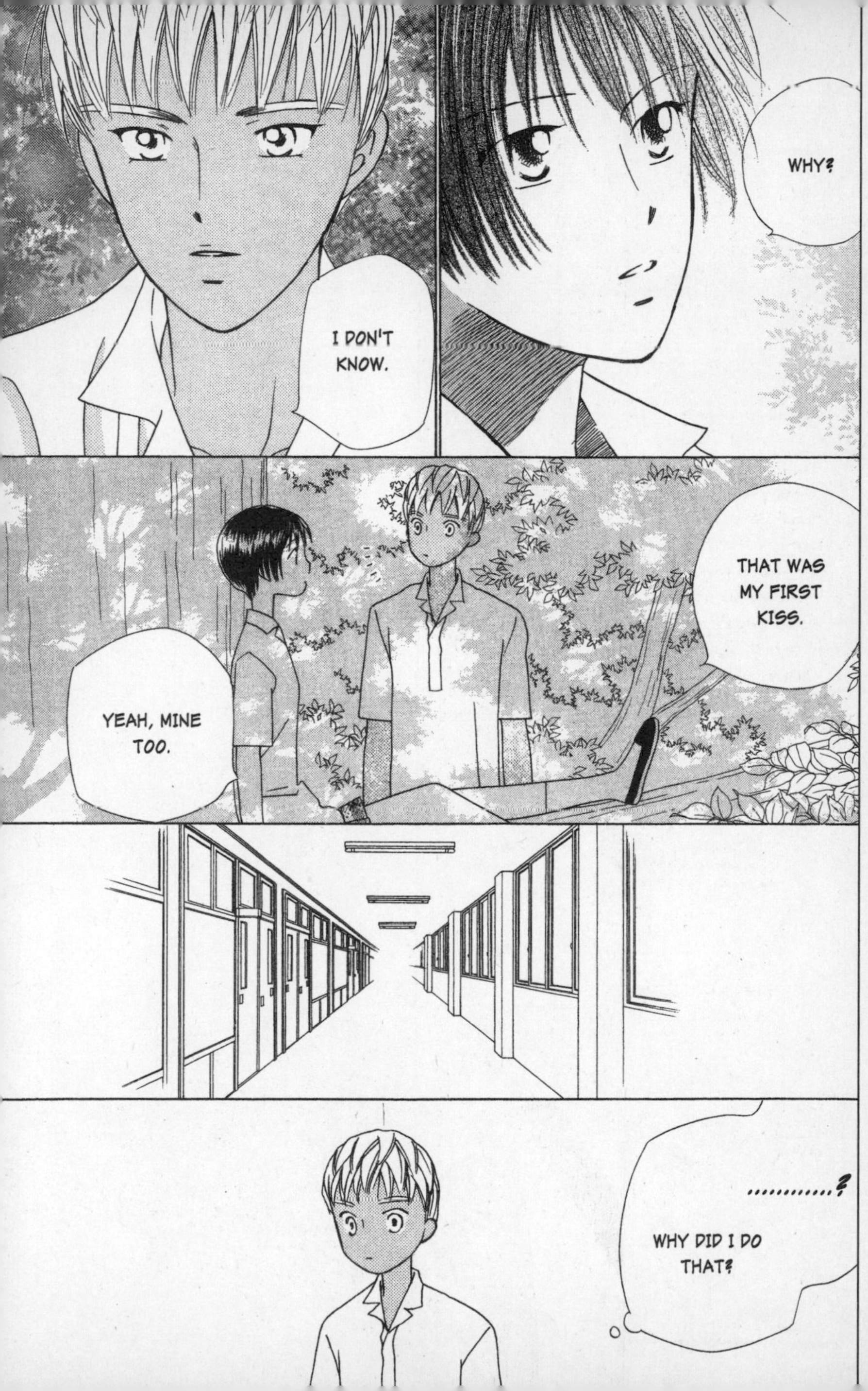
WHY?
I DON'T KNOW.
THAT WAS MY FIRST KISS.
YEAH, MINE TOO.
............?
WHY DID I DO THAT?

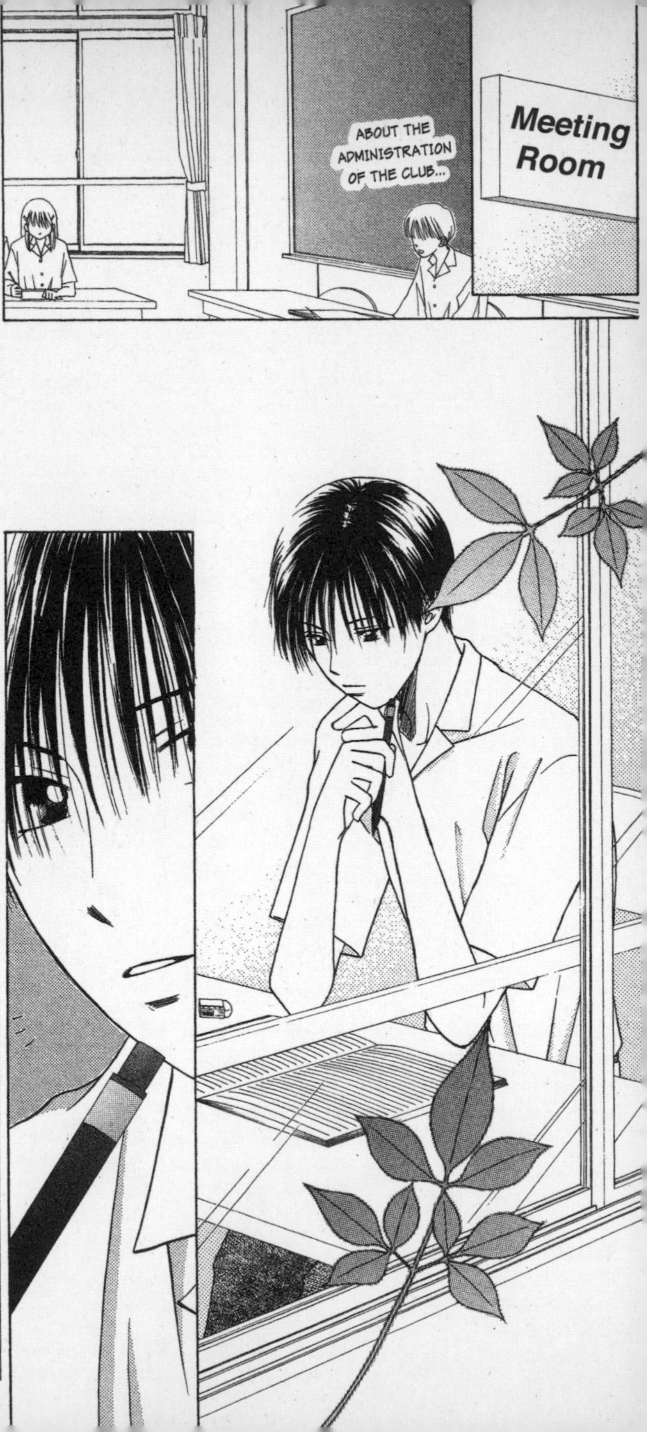
Meeting Room
ABOUT THE ADMINISTRATION OF THE CLUB...

6

So this is the end of Volume 7. I'm sorry that it's such a bad place to stop.

When I'm not so busy, I'd like to take my time and check out some cookware. I want to buy an open range and try making bread. Once people get an interest, their lives seem richer and they're more cheerful at work too.

You have to appreciate the efforts of the housewives who cook every day.

Well then, see you in Volume 8!

Masami Tsuda

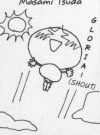

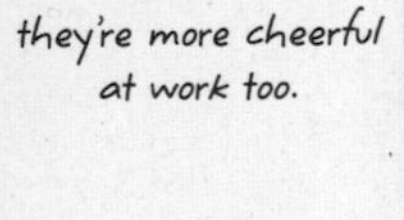
GLORIA!
(SHOUT)

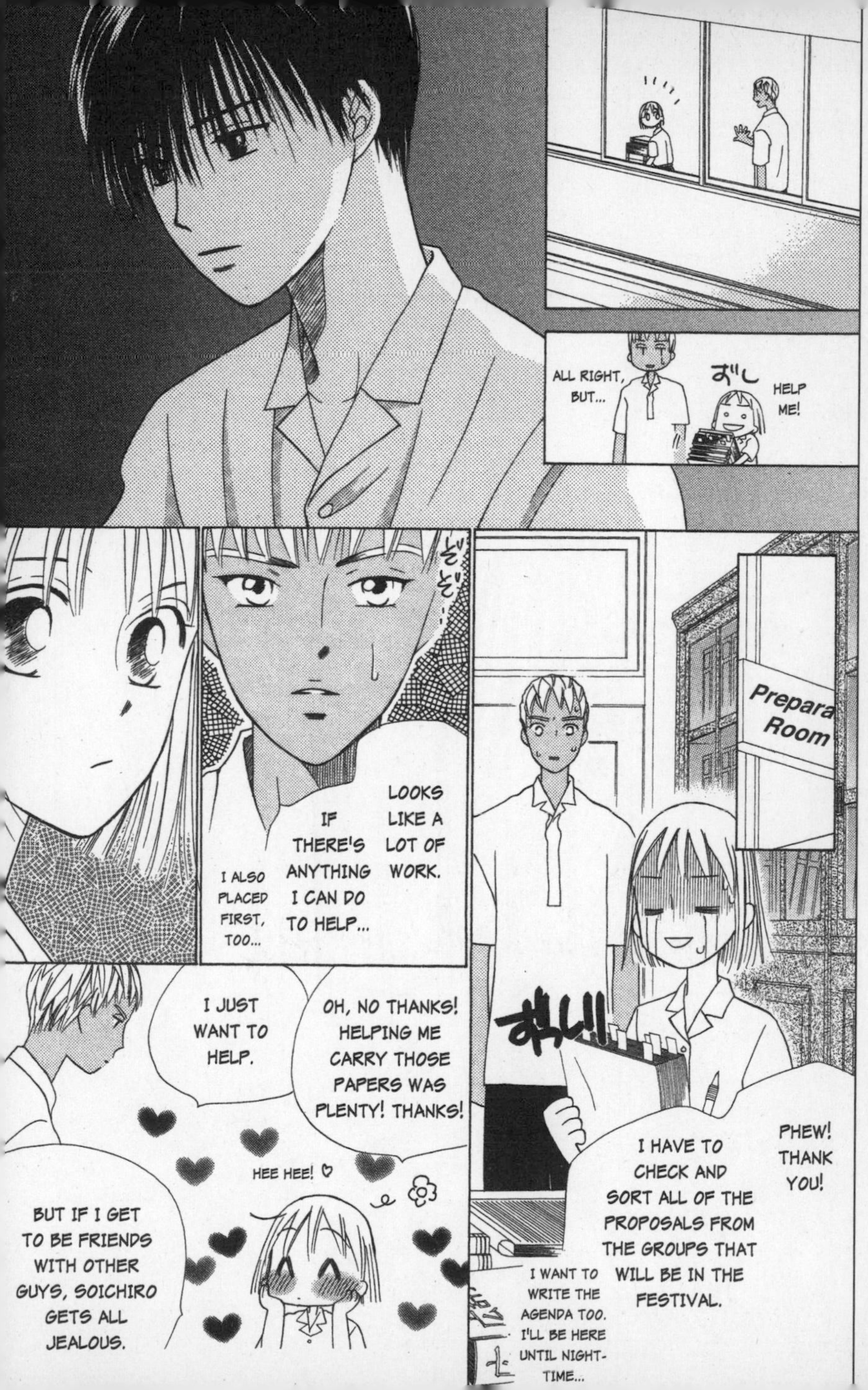
HELP ME!
ずし
ALL RIGHT, BUT...
Prepara Room
PHEW! THANK YOU!
I HAVE TO CHECK AND SORT ALL OF THE PROPOSALS FROM THE GROUPS THAT WILL BE IN THE FESTIVAL.
I WANT TO WRITE THE AGENDA TOO. I'LL BE HERE UNTIL NIGHT-TIME...
LOOKS LIKE A LOT OF WORK.
IF THERE'S ANYTHING I CAN DO TO HELP...
I ALSO PLACED FIRST, TOO...
OH, NO THANKS! HELPING ME CARRY THOSE PAPERS WAS PLENTY! THANKS!
I JUST WANT TO HELP.
HEE HEE! ♡
BUT IF I GET TO BE FRIENDS WITH OTHER GUYS, SOICHIRO GETS ALL JEALOUS.

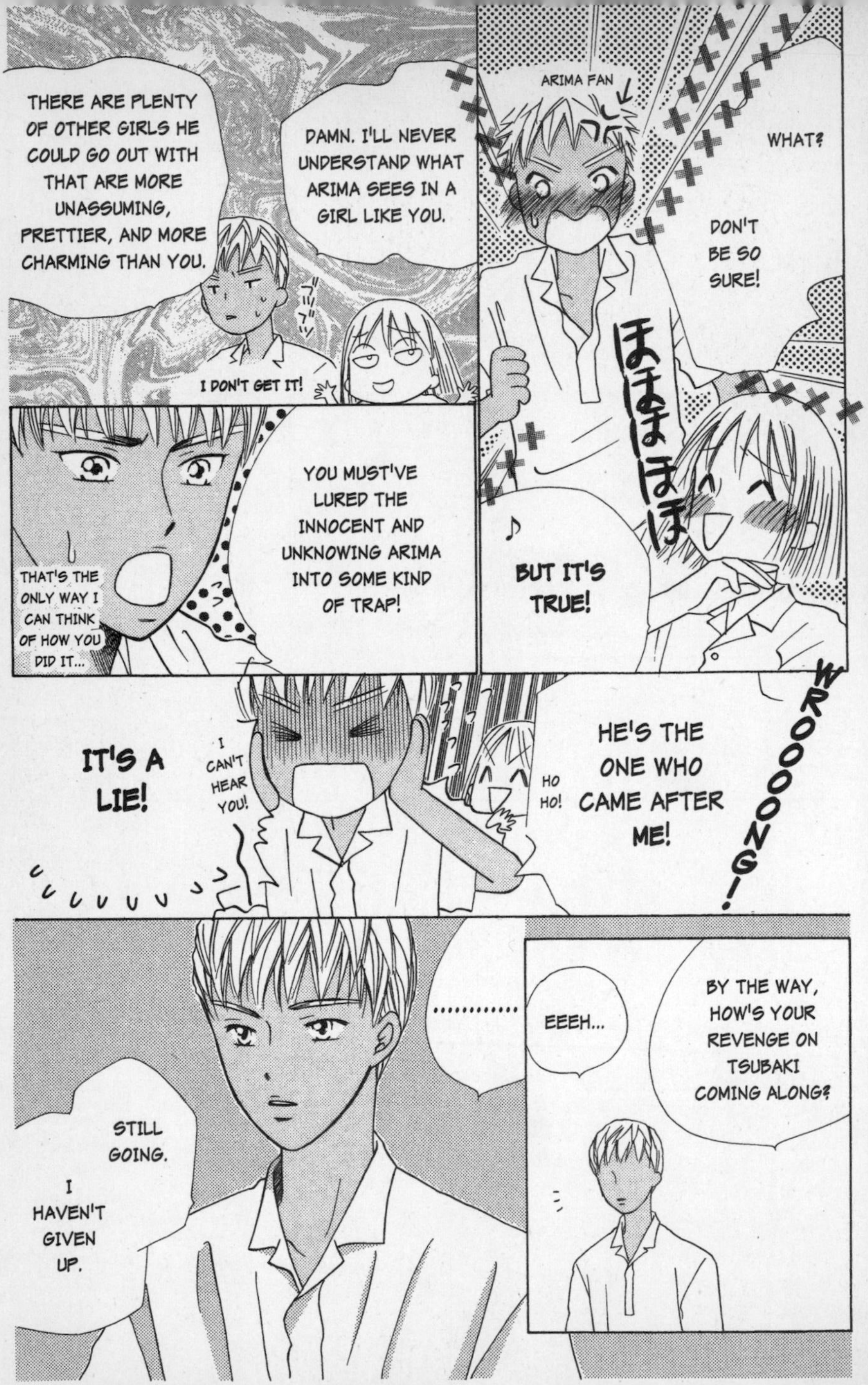
ARIMA FAN
WHAT?
DON'T BE SO SURE!
ほほほほ
BUT IT'S TRUE!
DAMN. I'LL NEVER UNDERSTAND WHAT ARIMA SEES IN A GIRL LIKE YOU.
THERE ARE PLENTY OF OTHER GIRLS HE COULD GO OUT WITH THAT ARE MORE UNASSUMING, PRETTIER, AND MORE CHARMING THAN YOU.
I DON'T GET IT!
YOU MUST'VE LURED THE INNOCENT AND UNKNOWING ARIMA INTO SOME KIND OF TRAP!
THAT'S THE ONLY WAY I CAN THINK OF HOW YOU DID IT...
WROOOOONG!
HE'S THE ONE WHO CAME AFTER ME!
HO HO!
I CAN'T HEAR YOU!
IT'S A LIE!
BY THE WAY, HOW'S YOUR REVENGE ON TSUBAKI COMING ALONG?
EEEH...
....
STILL GOING.
I HAVEN'T GIVEN UP.

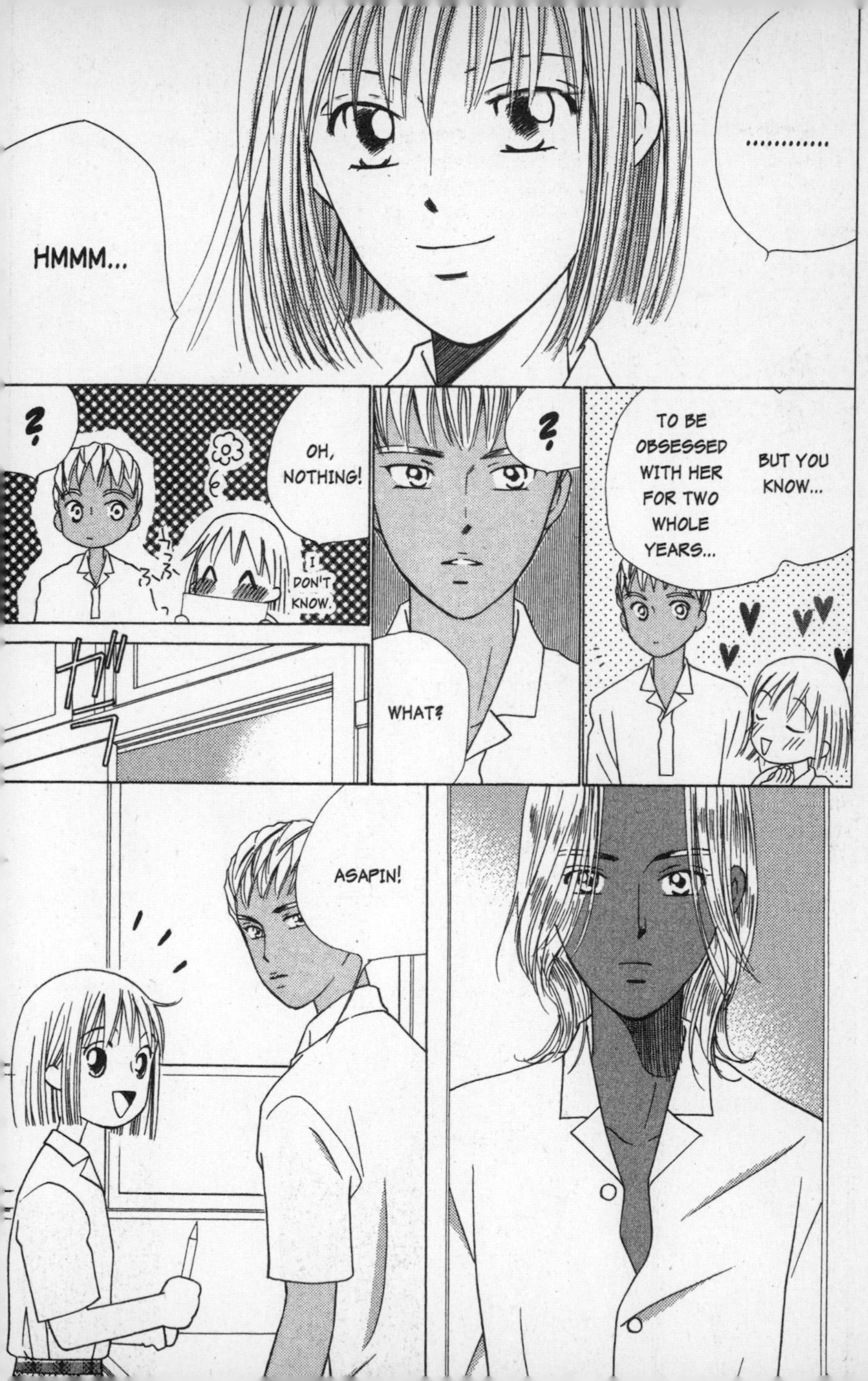
....
HMMM...
BUT YOU KNOW...
TO BE OBSESSED WITH HER FOR TWO WHOLE YEARS...
?
WHAT?
OH, NOTHING!
I DON'T KNOW.
?
ASAPIN!

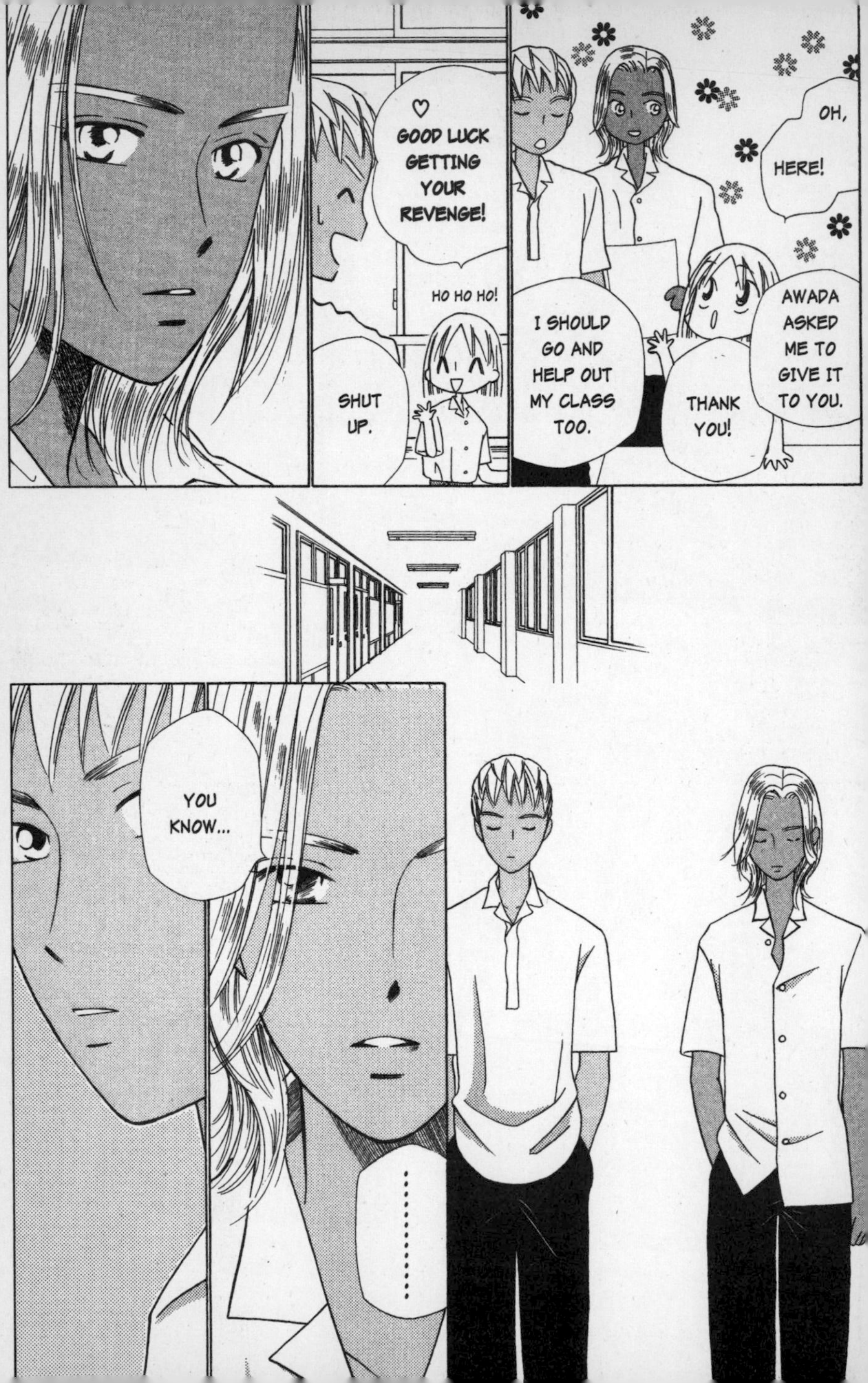
OH,
HERE!
AWADA ASKED ME TO GIVE IT TO YOU.
THANK YOU!
I SHOULD GO AND HELP OUT MY CLASS TOO.
♡ GOOD LUCK GETTING YOUR REVENGE!
HO HO HO!
SHUT UP.
YOU KNOW...
......

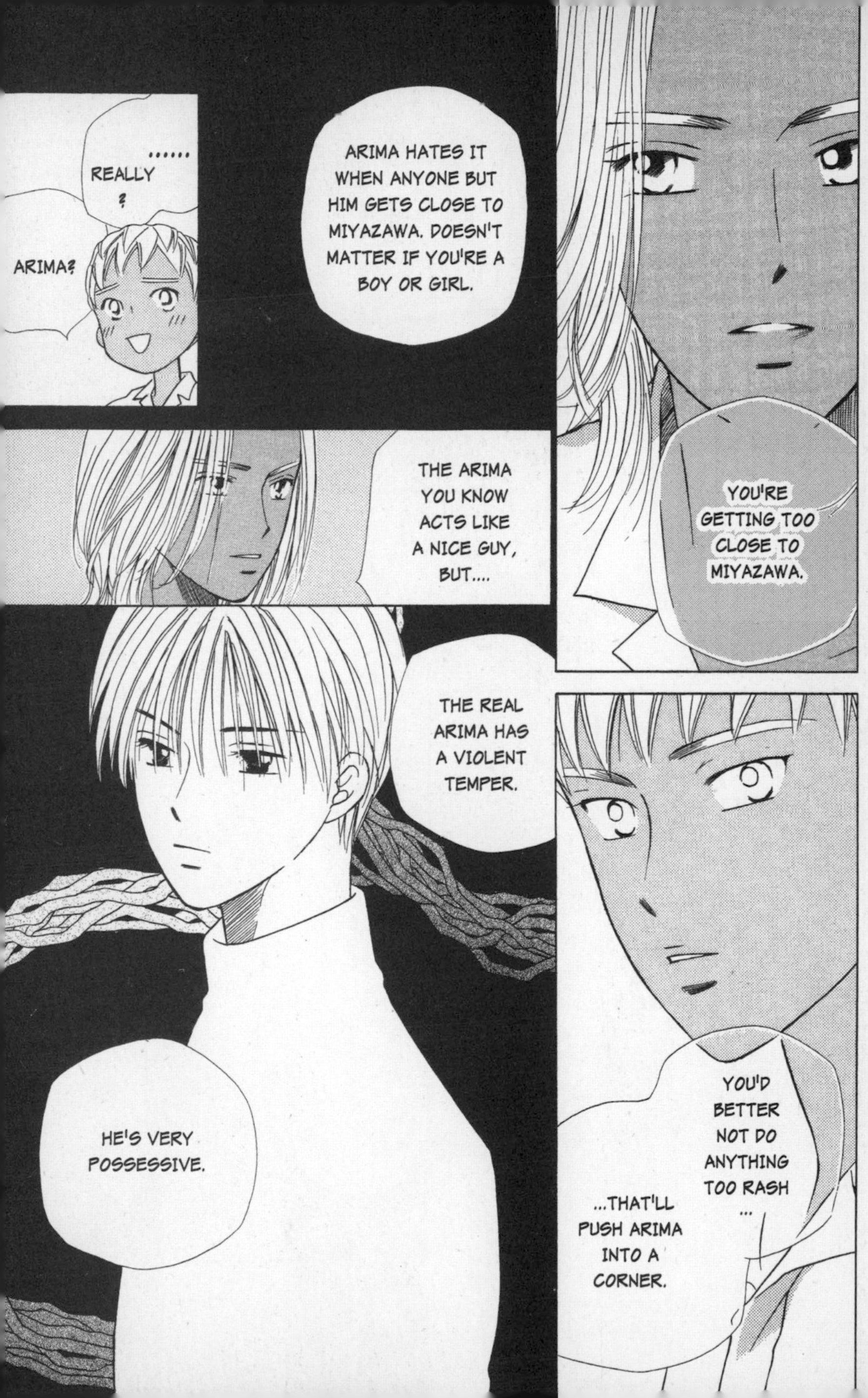
YOU'RE GETTING TOO CLOSE TO MIYAZAWA.
YOU'D BETTER NOT DO ANYTHING TOO RASH ...
...THAT'LL PUSH ARIMA INTO A CORNER.
ARIMA?
......REALLY?
ARIMA HATES IT WHEN ANYONE BUT HIM GETS CLOSE TO MIYAZAWA. DOESN'T MATTER IF YOU'RE A BOY OR GIRL.
THE ARIMA YOU KNOW ACTS LIKE A NICE GUY, BUT....
THE REAL ARIMA HAS A VIOLENT TEMPER.
HE'S VERY POSSESSIVE.

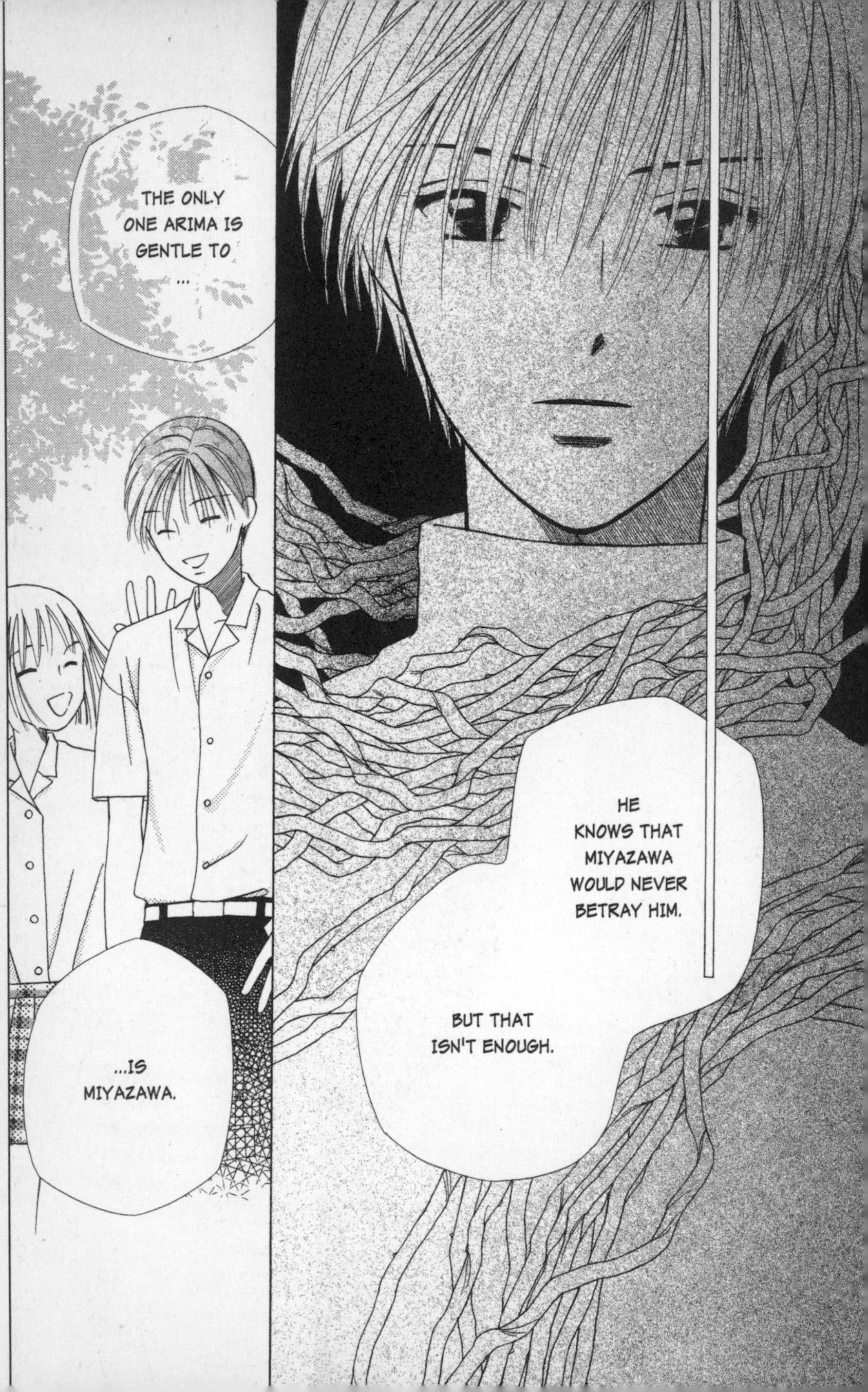
HE KNOWS THAT MIYAZAWA WOULD NEVER BETRAY HIM.
BUT THAT ISN'T ENOUGH.
THE ONLY ONE ARIMA IS GENTLE TO ...
...IS MIYAZAWA.

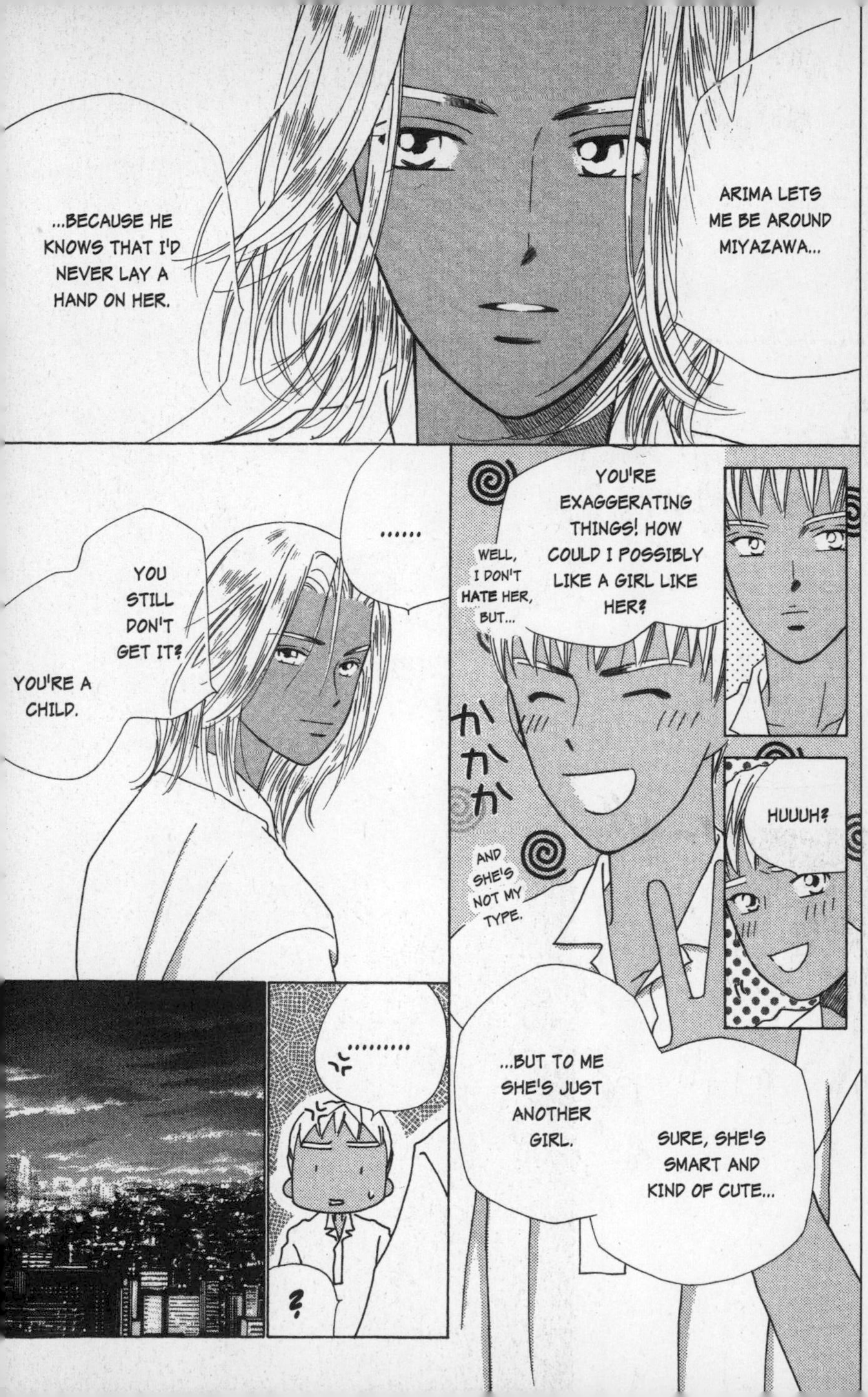
ARIMA LETS ME BE AROUND MIYAZAWA...
...BECAUSE HE KNOWS THAT I'D NEVER LAY A HAND ON HER.
YOU'RE EXAGGERATING THINGS! HOW COULD I POSSIBLY LIKE A GIRL LIKE HER?
WELL, I DON'T HATE HER, BUT...
かかか
HUUUH?
SURE, SHE'S SMART AND KIND OF CUTE...
...BUT TO ME SHE'S JUST ANOTHER GIRL.
AND SHE'S NOT MY TYPE.
......
YOU STILL DON'T GET IT?
YOU'RE A CHILD.
....
?

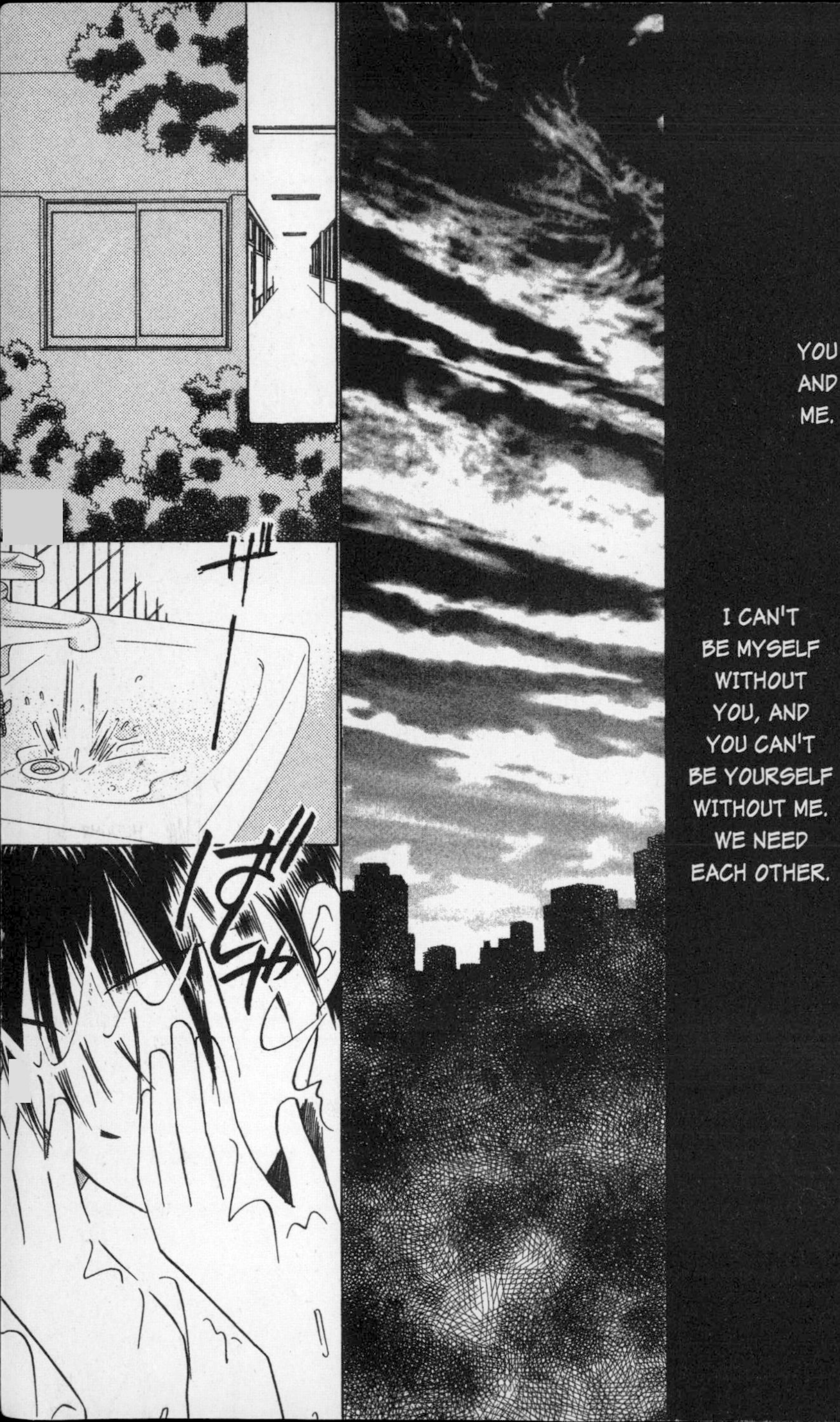
YOU AND ME.
I CAN'T BE MYSELF WITHOUT YOU, AND YOU CAN'T BE YOURSELF WITHOUT ME. WE NEED EACH OTHER.

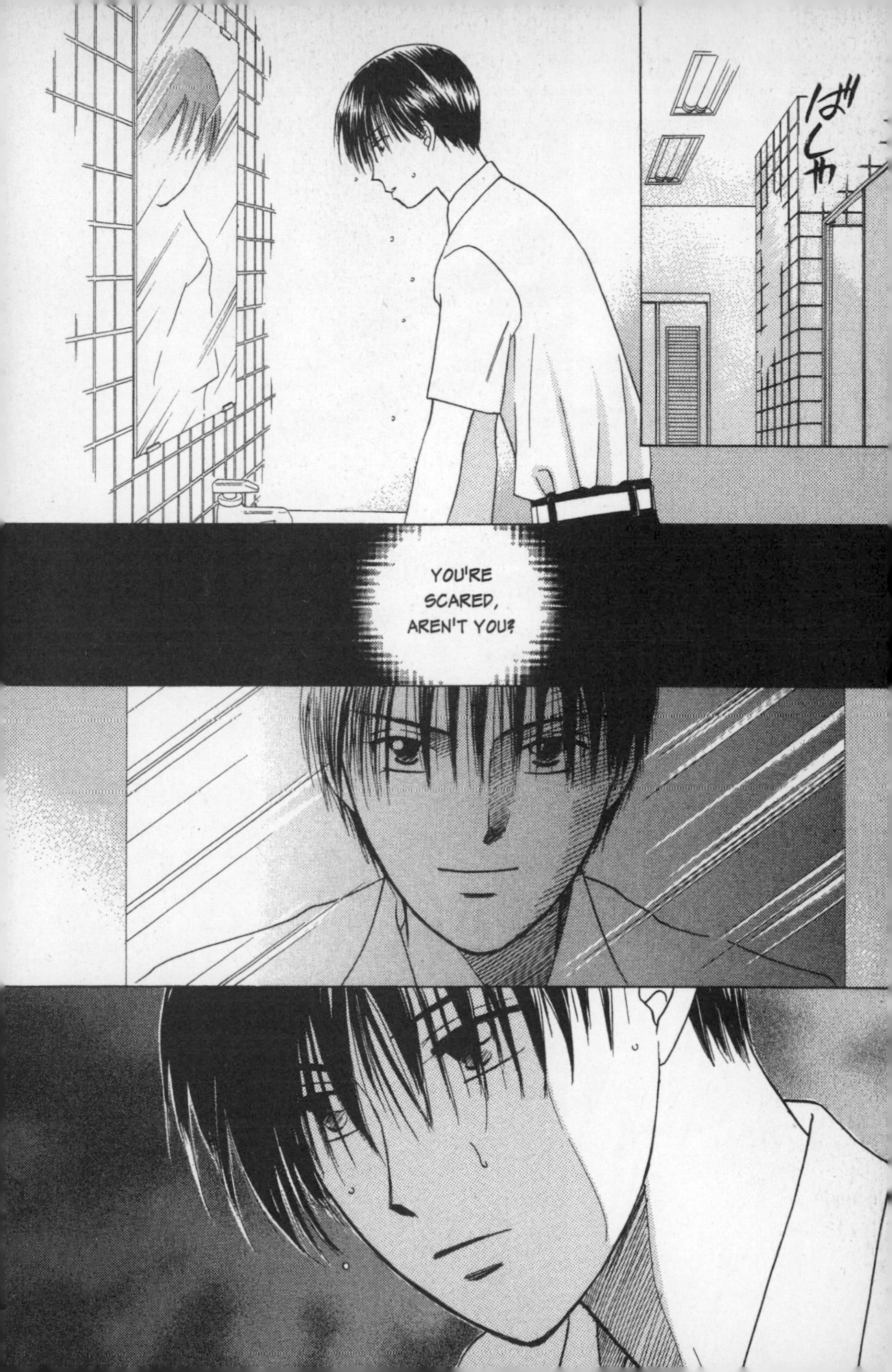
ばしゃ
YOU'RE SCARED, AREN'T YOU?

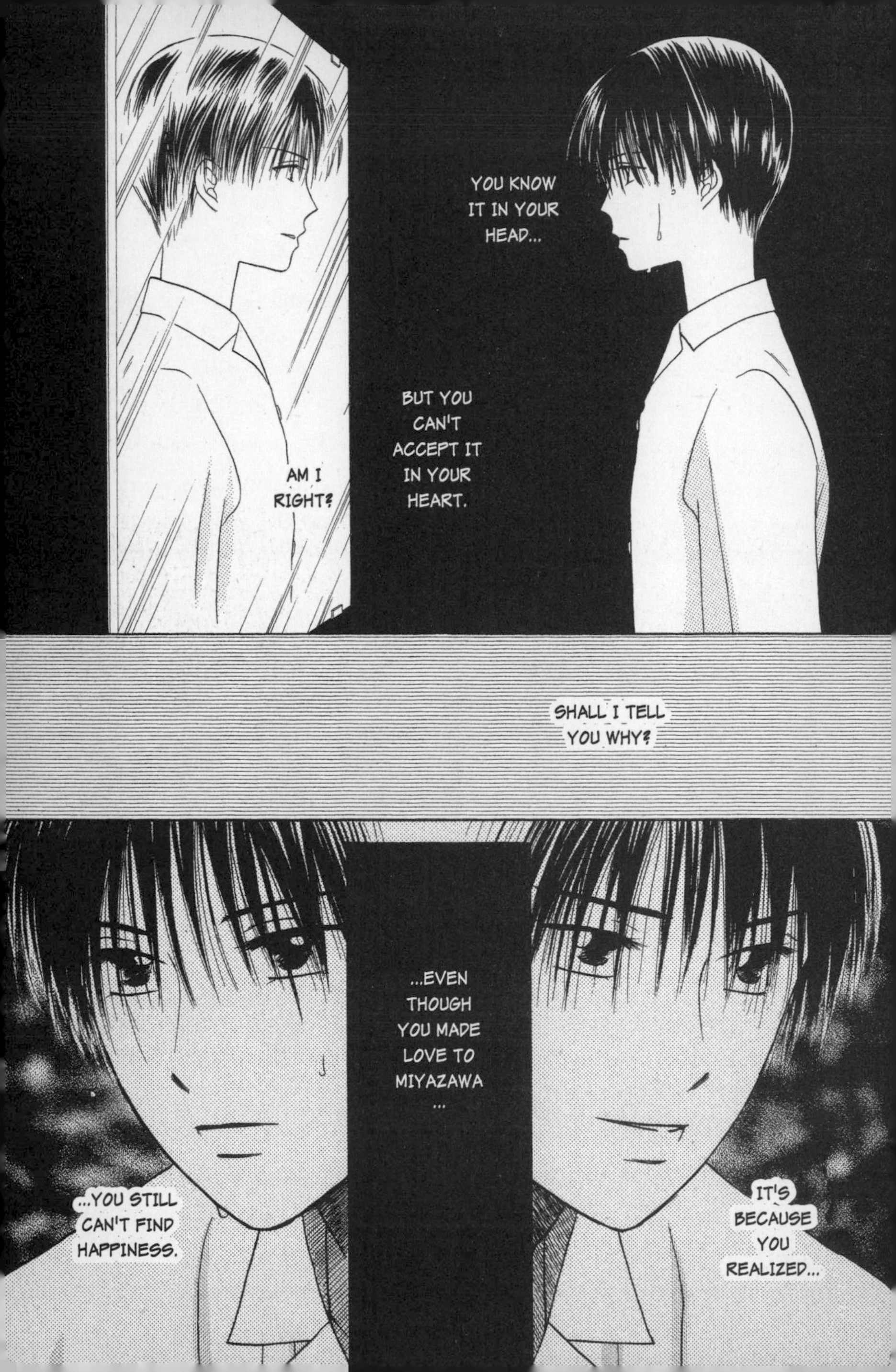

YOU KNOW IT IN YOUR HEAD...
BUT YOU CAN'T ACCEPT IT IN YOUR HEART.
AM I RIGHT?
SHALL I TELL YOU WHY?
IT'S BECAUSE YOU REALIZED...
...EVEN THOUGH YOU MADE LOVE TO MIYAZAWA ...
...YOU STILL CAN'T FIND HAPPINESS.

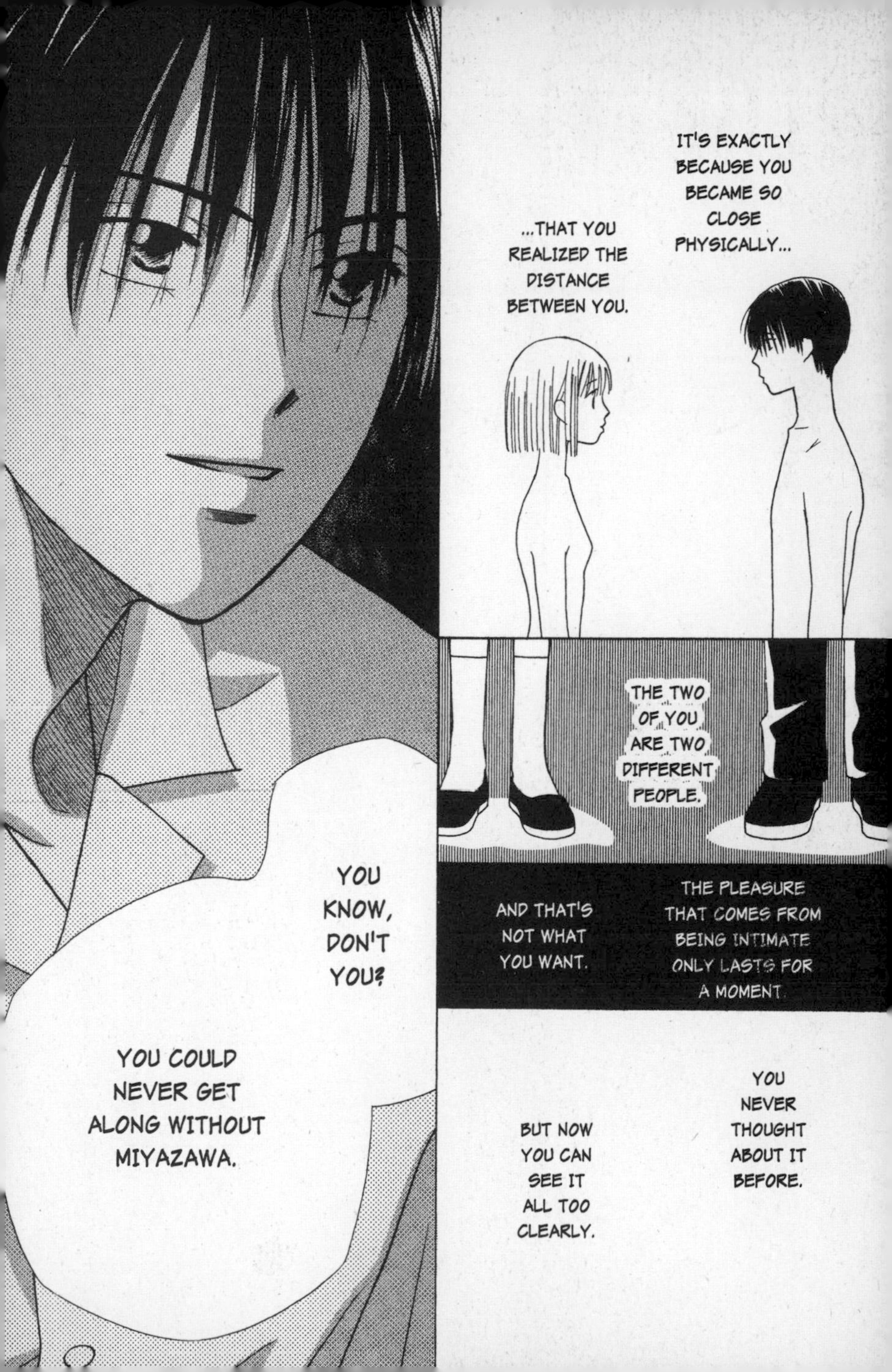
IT'S EXACTLY BECAUSE YOU BECAME SO CLOSE PHYSICALLY...
...THAT YOU REALIZED THE DISTANCE BETWEEN YOU.
THE TWO OF YOU ARE TWO DIFFERENT PEOPLE.
THE PLEASURE THAT COMES FROM BEING INTIMATE ONLY LASTS FOR A MOMENT.
AND THAT'S NOT WHAT YOU WANT.
YOU NEVER THOUGHT ABOUT IT BEFORE.
BUT NOW YOU CAN SEE IT ALL TOO CLEARLY.
YOU KNOW, DON'T YOU?
YOU COULD NEVER GET ALONG WITHOUT MIYAZAWA.

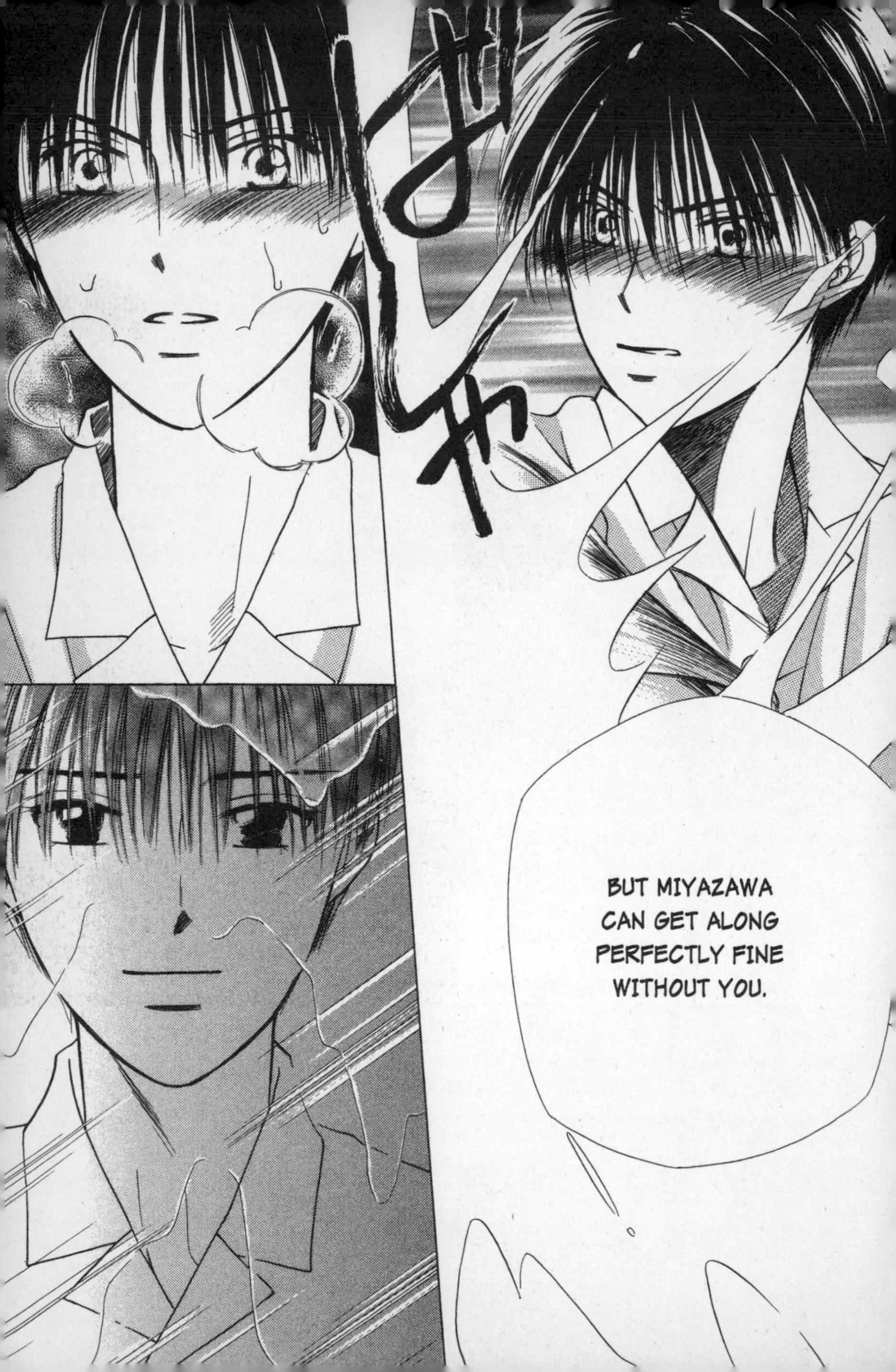
BUT MIYAZAWA CAN GET ALONG PERFECTLY FINE WITHOUT YOU.

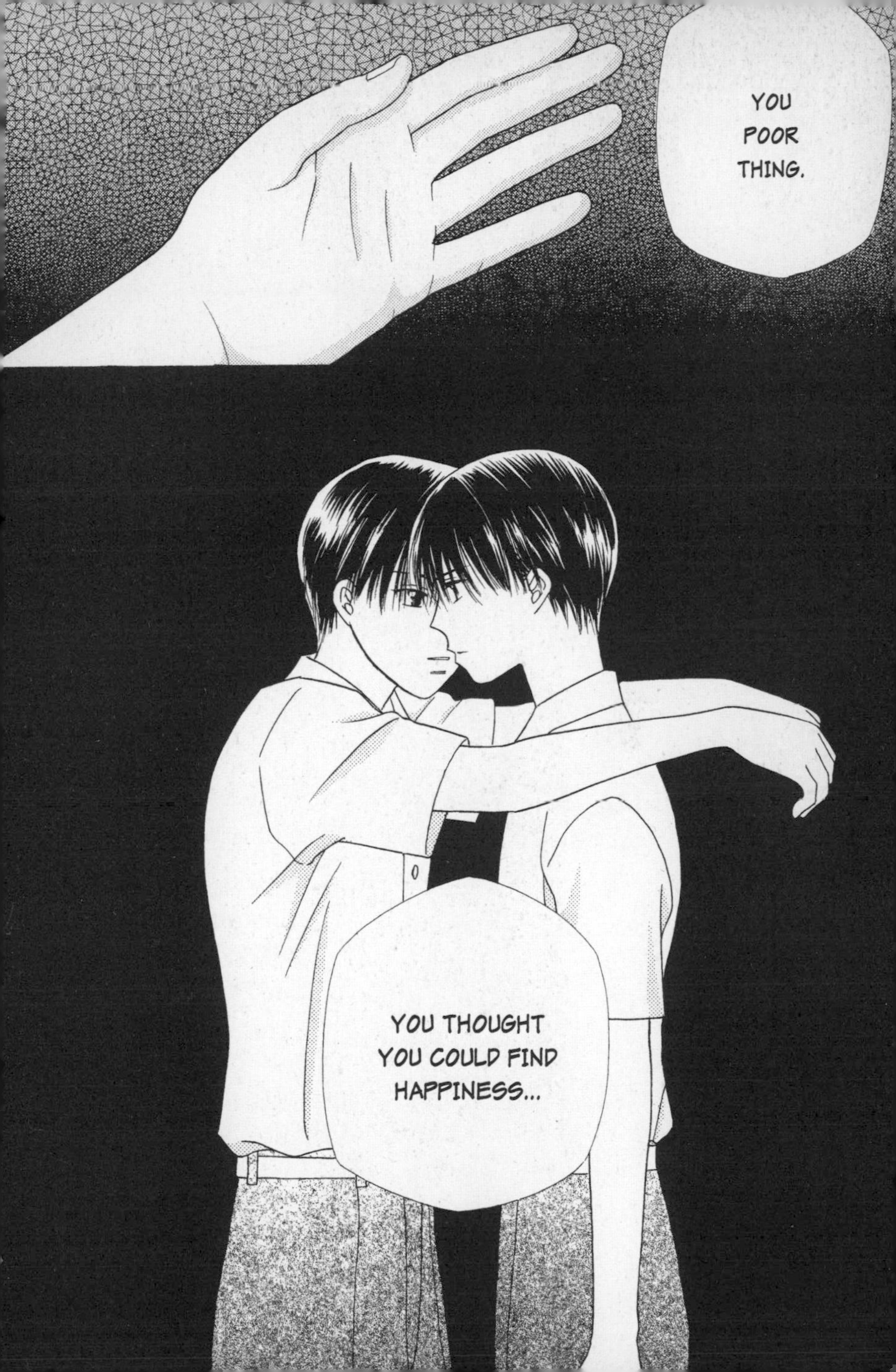
YOU POOR THING.
YOU THOUGHT YOU COULD FIND HAPPINESS...

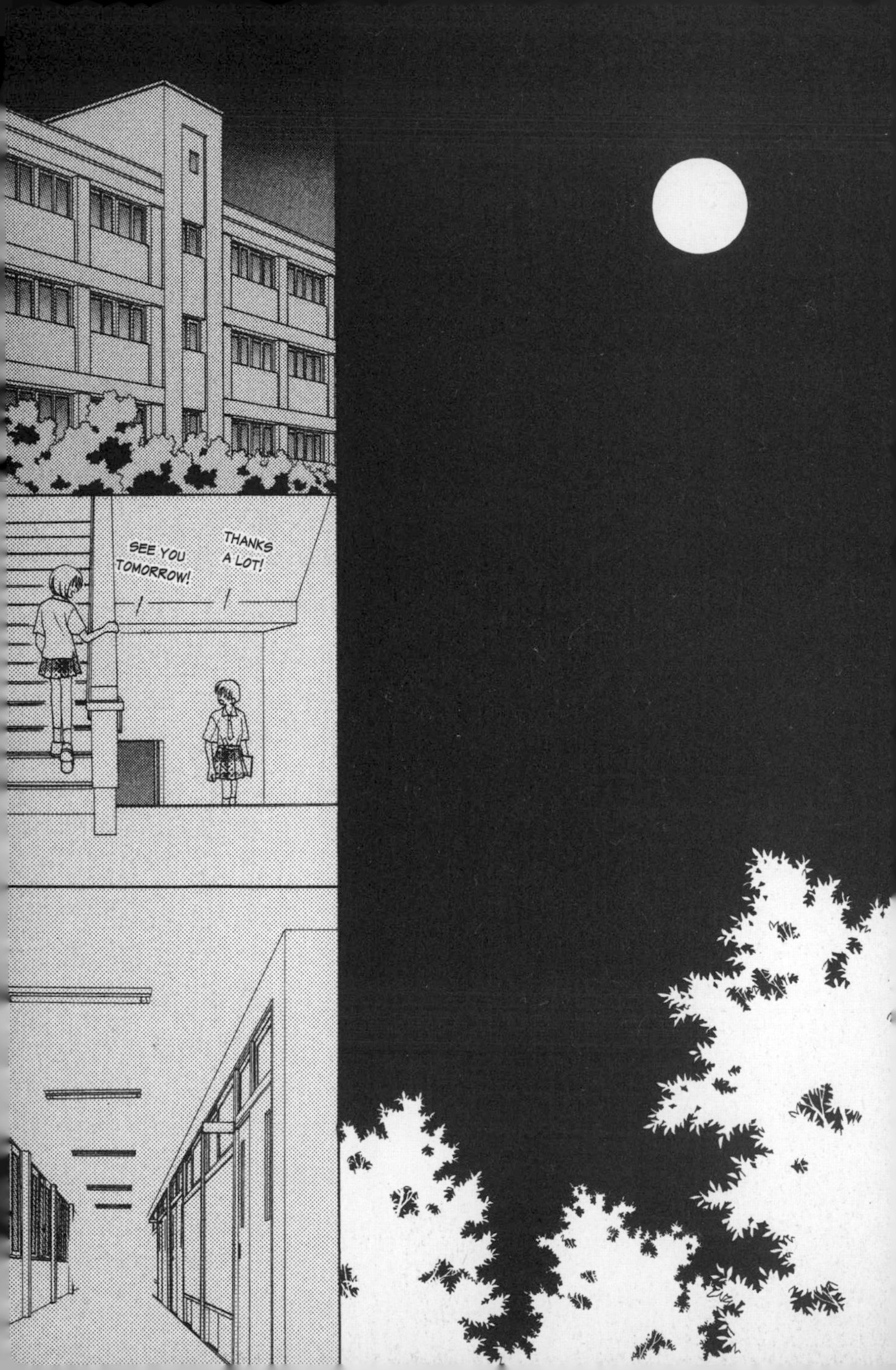
THANKS A LOT!
SEE YOU TOMORROW!

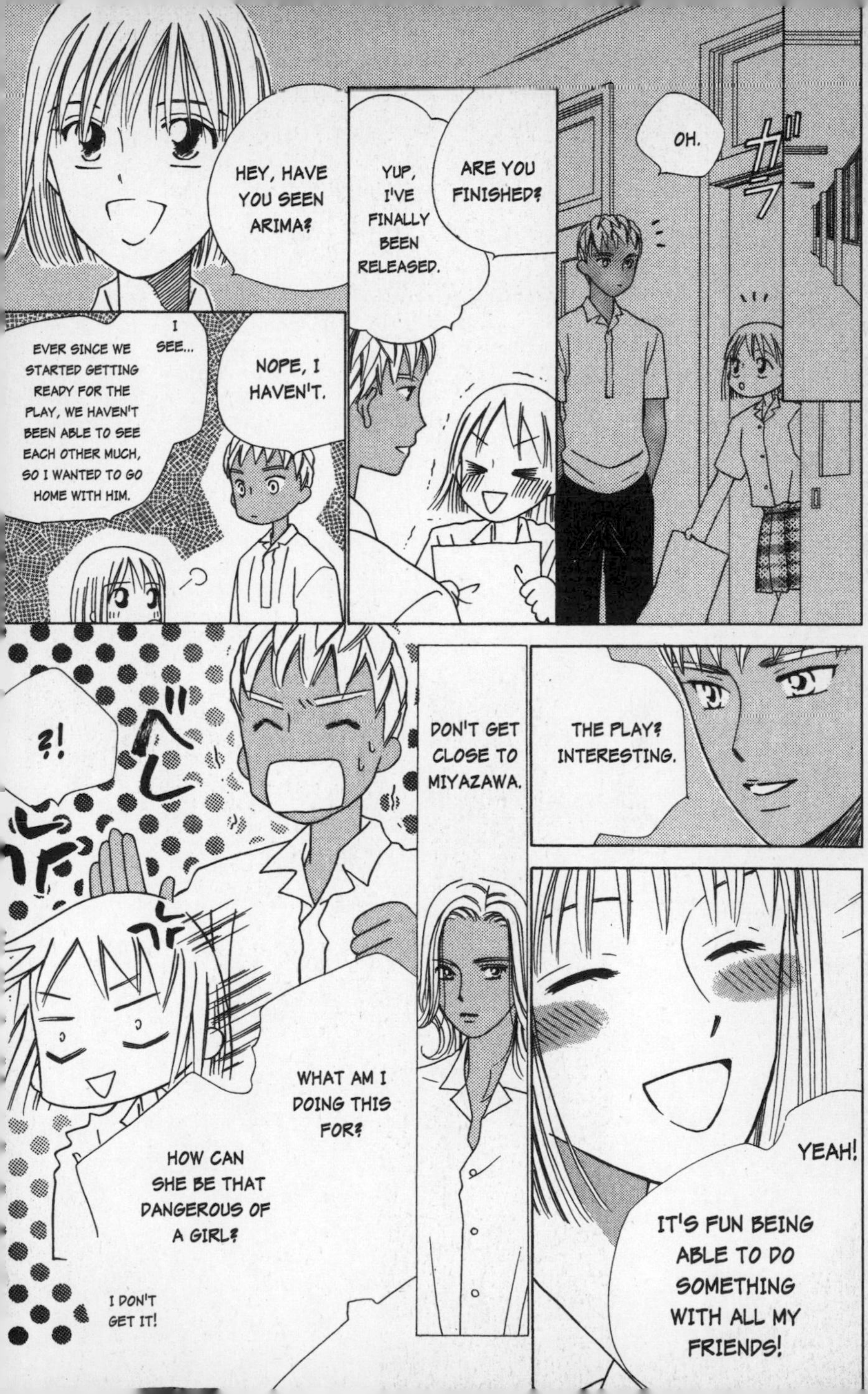
OH.
ガラ
ARE YOU FINISHED?
YUP, I'VE FINALLY BEEN RELEASED.
HEY, HAVE YOU SEEN ARIMA?
NOPE, I HAVEN'T.
I SEE...
EVER SINCE WE STARTED GETTING READY FOR THE PLAY, WE HAVEN'T BEEN ABLE TO SEE EACH OTHER MUCH, SO I WANTED TO GO HOME WITH HIM.
THE PLAY? INTERESTING.
YEAH!
IT'S FUN BEING ABLE TO DO SOMETHING WITH ALL MY FRIENDS!
DON'T GET CLOSE TO MIYAZAWA.
?!
WHAT AM I DOING THIS FOR?
HOW CAN SHE BE THAT DANGEROUS OF A GIRL?
I DON'T GET IT!

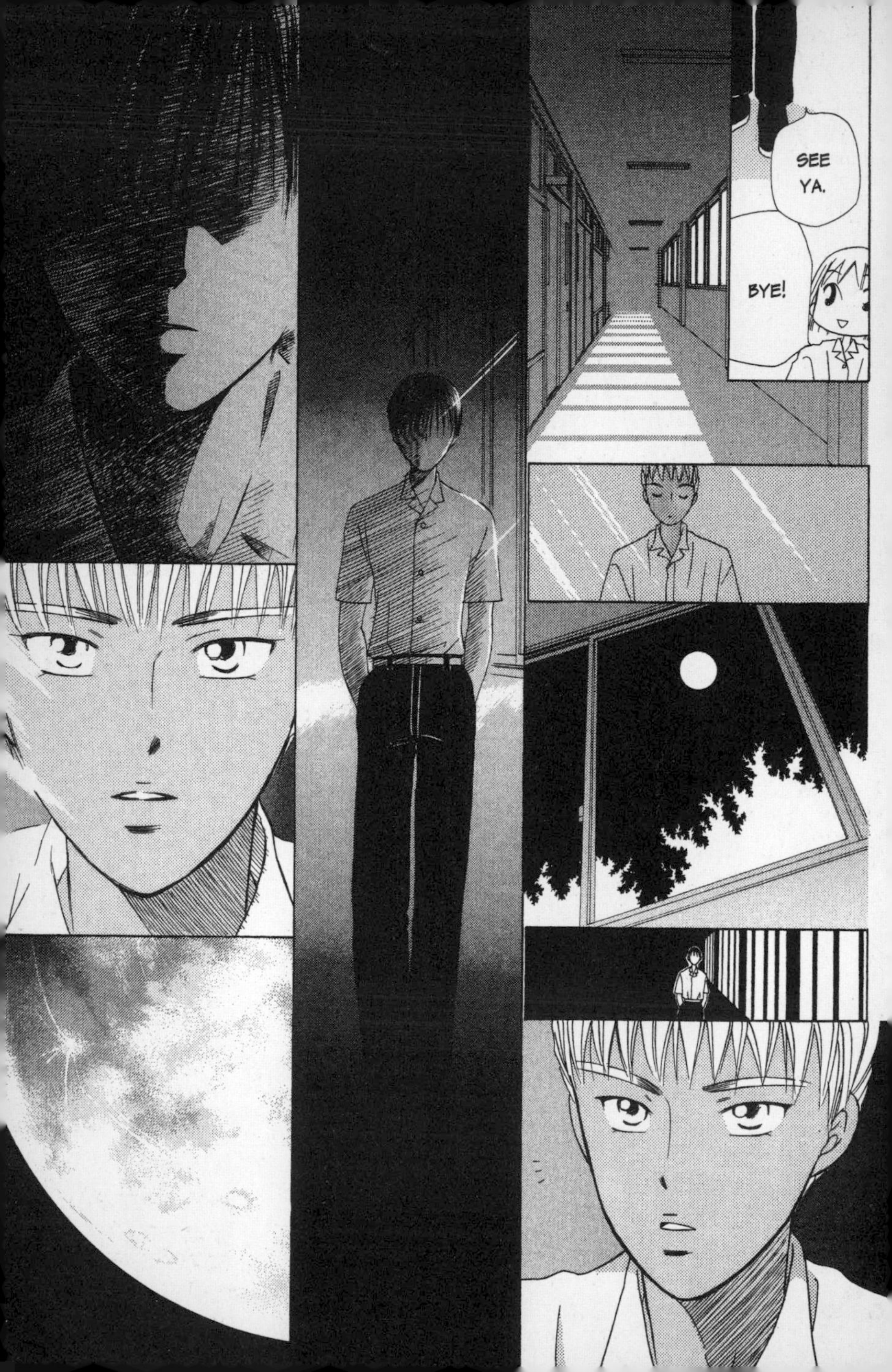
SEE YA.
BYE!

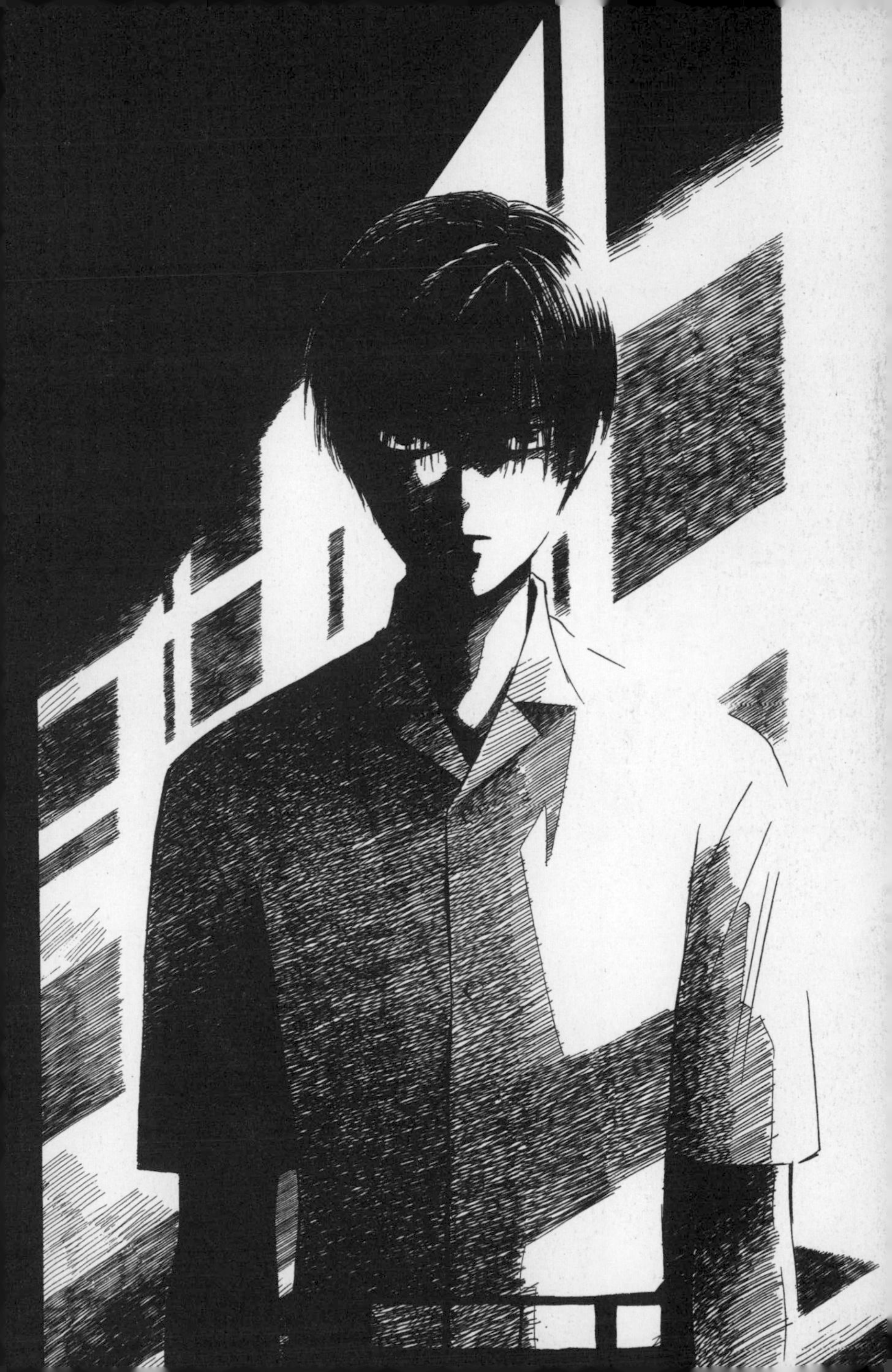

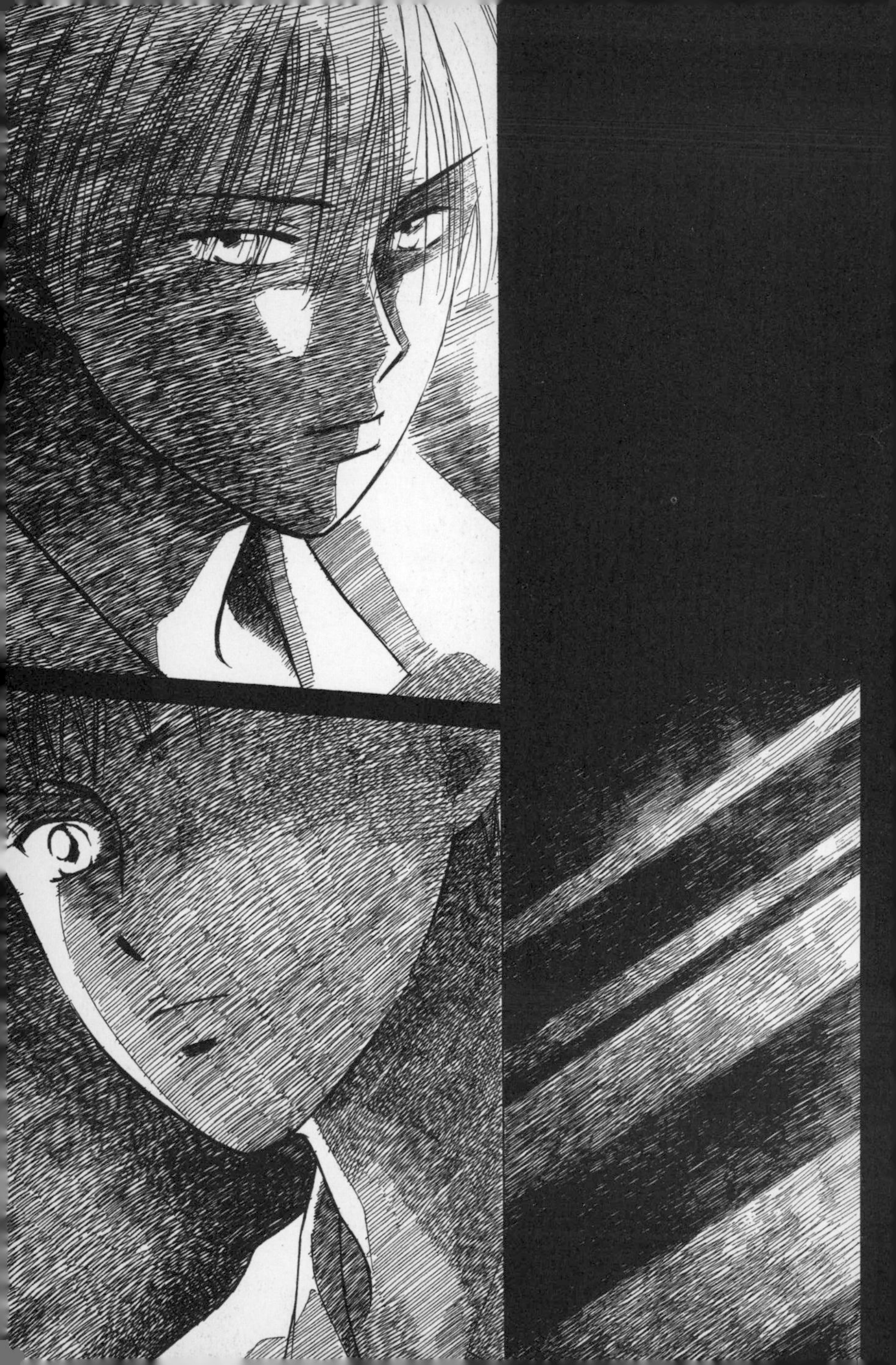

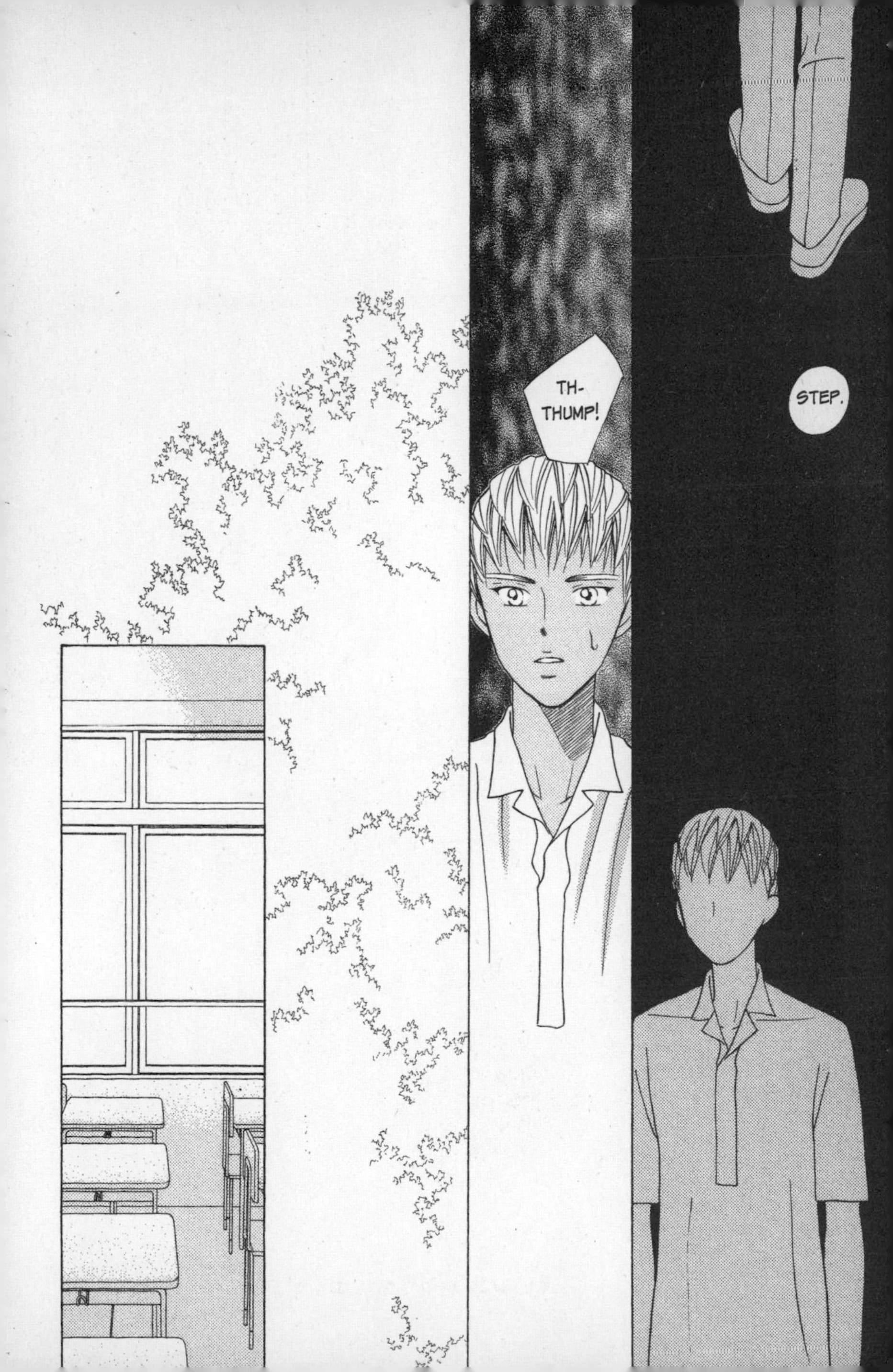
STEP.
TH-THUMP!

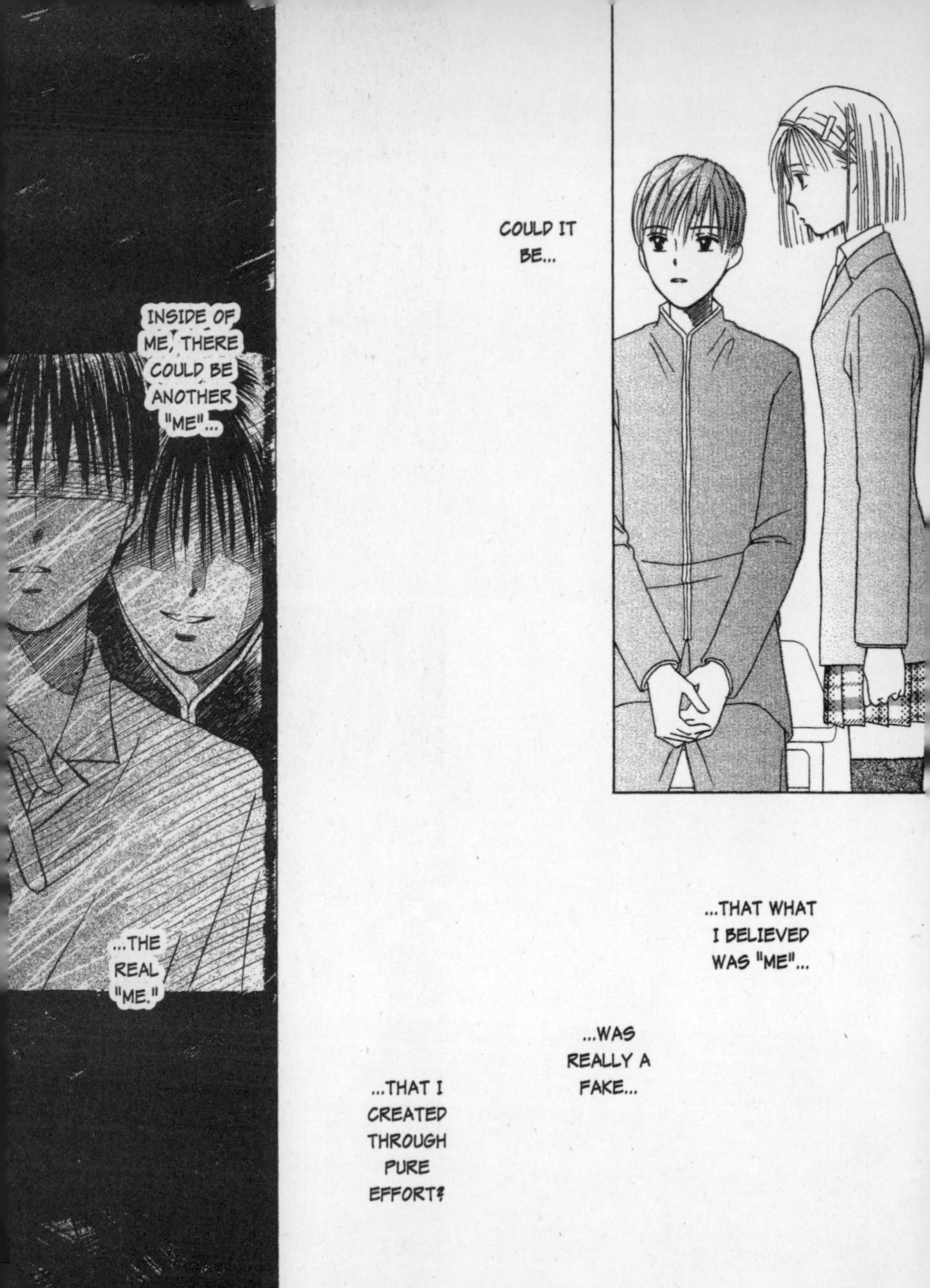
COULD IT BE...
...THAT WHAT I BELIEVED WAS "ME"...
...WAS REALLY A FAKE...
...THAT I CREATED THROUGH PURE EFFORT?
INSIDE OF ME, THERE COULD BE ANOTHER "ME"...
...THE REAL "ME."

ACT 32 ✱ 14 DAYS: SUNLIGHT AND MOONLIGHT —THE END

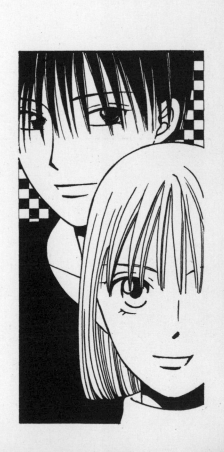

TSUDA DIARY

FROM THE READERS

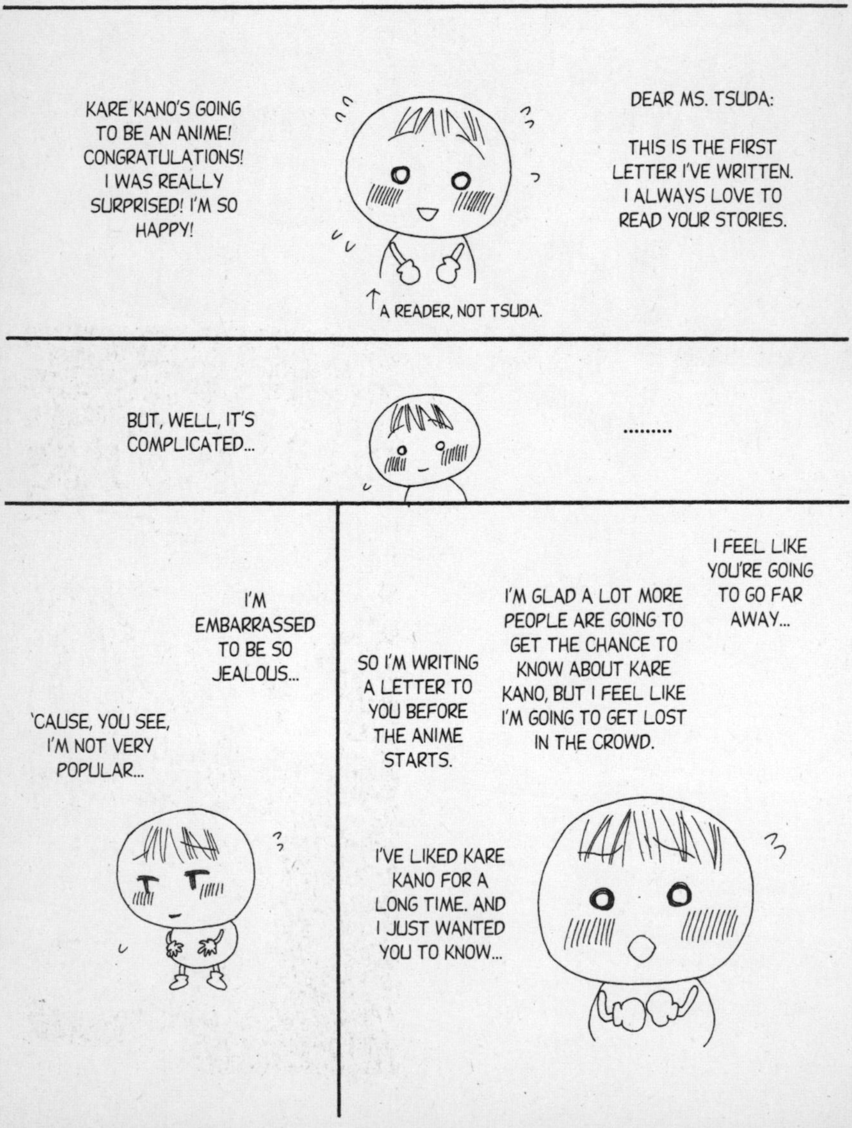
DEAR MS. TSUDA:
THIS IS THE FIRST LETTER I'VE WRITTEN. I ALWAYS LOVE TO READ YOUR STORIES.
KARE KANO'S GOING TO BE AN ANIME! CONGRATULATIONS! I WAS REALLY SURPRISED! I'M SO HAPPY!
A READER, NOT TSUDA.
....
BUT, WELL, IT'S COMPLICATED...
I FEEL LIKE YOU'RE GOING TO GO FAR AWAY...
I'M GLAD A LOT MORE PEOPLE ARE GOING TO GET THE CHANCE TO KNOW ABOUT KARE KANO, BUT I FEEL LIKE I'M GOING TO GET LOST IN THE CROWD.
SO I'M WRITING A LETTER TO YOU BEFORE THE ANIME STARTS.
I'VE LIKED KARE KANO FOR A LONG TIME. AND I JUST WANTED YOU TO KNOW...
I'M EMBARRASSED TO BE SO JEALOUS...
'CAUSE, YOU SEE, I'M NOT VERY POPULAR...

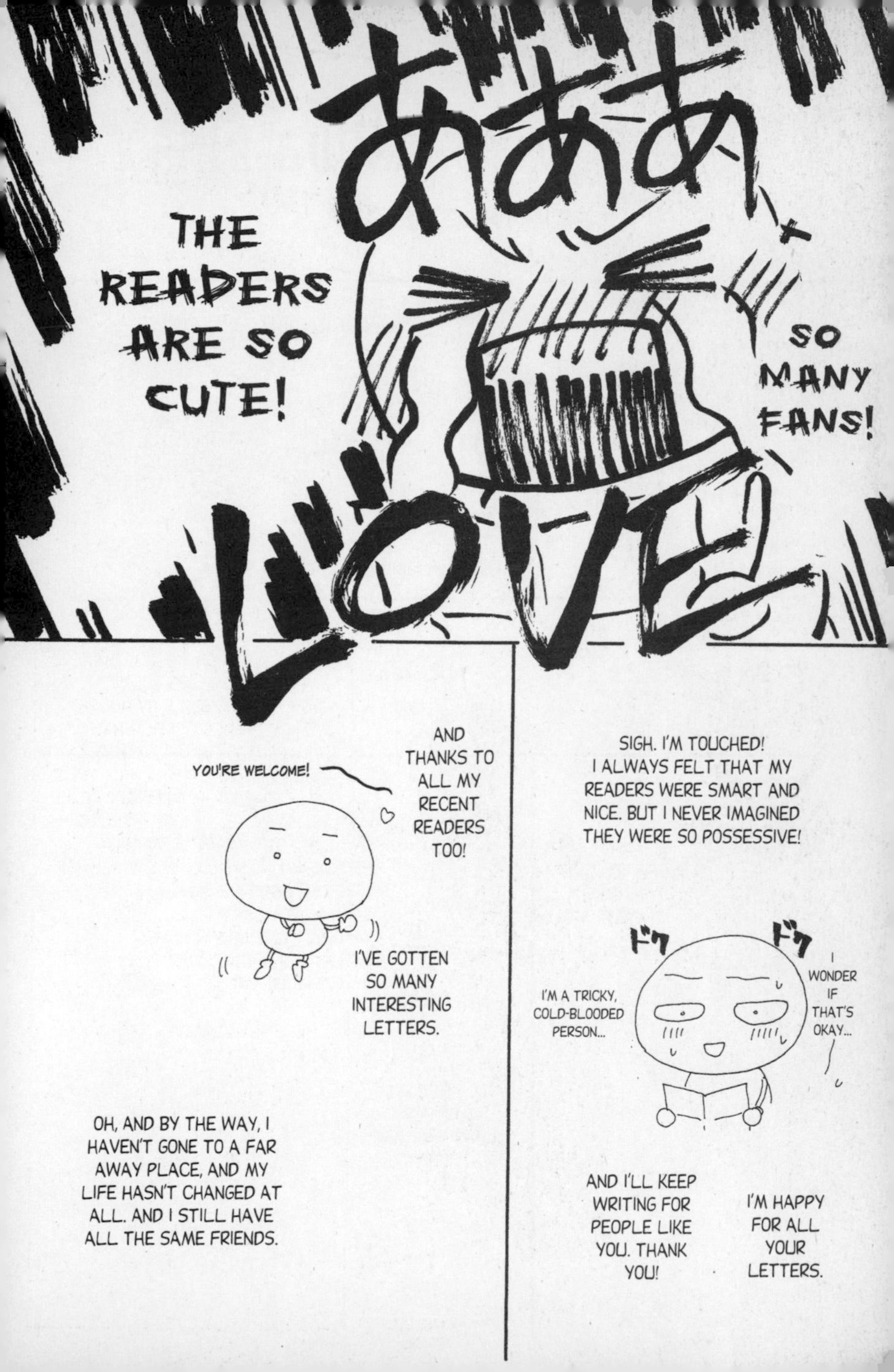

あああ
SO MANY FANS!
THE READERS ARE SO CUTE!
LOVE
SIGH. I'M TOUCHED! I ALWAYS FELT THAT MY READERS WERE SMART AND NICE. BUT I NEVER IMAGINED THEY WERE SO POSSESSIVE!
ドク
ドク
I WONDER IF THAT'S OKAY...
I'M A TRICKY, COLD-BLOODED PERSON...
I'M HAPPY FOR ALL YOUR LETTERS.
AND I'LL KEEP WRITING FOR PEOPLE LIKE YOU. THANK YOU!
AND THANKS TO ALL MY RECENT READERS TOO!
YOU'RE WELCOME!
I'VE GOTTEN SO MANY INTERESTING LETTERS.
OH, AND BY THE WAY, I HAVEN'T GONE TO A FAR AWAY PLACE, AND MY LIFE HASN'T CHANGED AT ALL. AND I STILL HAVE ALL THE SAME FRIENDS.

READER'S CORNER

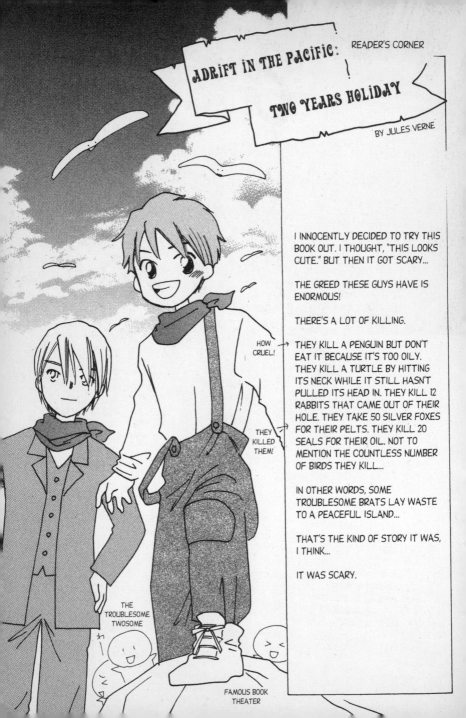

ADRIFT IN THE PACIFIC: TWO YEARS HOLIDAY

BY JULES VERNE

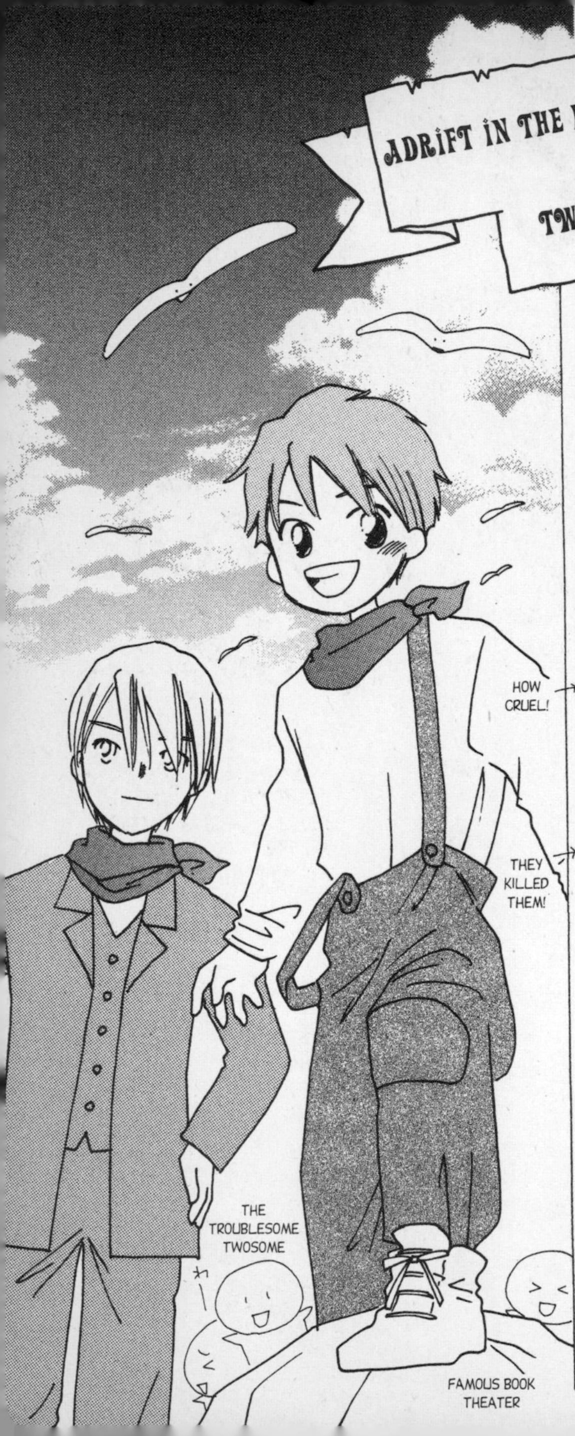
HOW CRUEL!
THEY KILLED THEM!
THE TROUBLESOME TWOSOME
FAMOUS BOOK THEATER

I INNOCENTLY DECIDED TO TRY THIS BOOK OUT. I THOUGHT, "THIS LOOKS CUTE." BUT THEN IT GOT SCARY...

THE GREED THESE GUYS HAVE IS ENORMOUS!

THERE'S A LOT OF KILLING.

THEY KILL A PENGUIN BUT DON'T EAT IT BECAUSE IT'S TOO OILY. THEY KILL A TURTLE BY HITTING ITS NECK WHILE IT STILL HASN'T PULLED ITS HEAD IN. THEY KILL 12 RABBITS THAT CAME OUT OF THEIR HOLE. THEY TAKE 50 SILVER FOXES FOR THEIR PELTS. THEY KILL 20 SEALS FOR THEIR OIL. NOT TO MENTION THE COUNTLESS NUMBER OF BIRDS THEY KILL...

IN OTHER WORDS, SOME TROUBLESOME BRATS LAY WASTE TO A PEACEFUL ISLAND...

THAT'S THE KIND OF STORY IT WAS, I THINK...

IT WAS SCARY.

LORD OF THE FLIES

BY WILLIAM GOLDING

THE SET-UP FOR THIS BOOK IS ALMOST THE SAME AS "ADRIFT IN THE PACIFIC: TWO YEARS HOLIDAY." A WAR BREAKS OUT, AND A PLANE CARRYING SOME BOYS WHO WERE BEING EVACUATED CRASHES, AND THEY END UP ON A DESERTED ISLAND.

I REALLY LIKE THIS BOOK.
IT REALLY CONVEYS A HOPELESSNESS TOWARDS MANKIND. HUMANS REALLY AREN'T THAT GREAT. (BUT THAT'S HARD TO ADMIT WHEN YOU'RE BEING TOUCHED BY GOOD ART OR AMAZING MUSIC.)

YOU KNOW, I WONDER IF IT REALLY WOULD TURN OUT THIS WAY IF PEOPLE TRULY WERE PUT ON A DESERTED ISLAND. (I MEAN, IF THEY WERE ADULTS.) I THINK IT DEFINITELY WOULD, EVEN IF THEY WERE GROWN-UPS. I CERTAINLY WOULDN'T WANT TO BE THERE TO FIND OUT!

MASAO HIRAI'S JAPANESE TRANSLATION FOR THIS BOOK WAS EXCELLENT! I REALLY LOVE READING JAPANESE, AND I LIKE HIS WRITING STYLE. IT'S KIND OF SEXY ALMOST. THERE WAS A SEXINESS RUNNING THROUGH THE WHOLE BOOK. IT WAS REALLY GOOD.

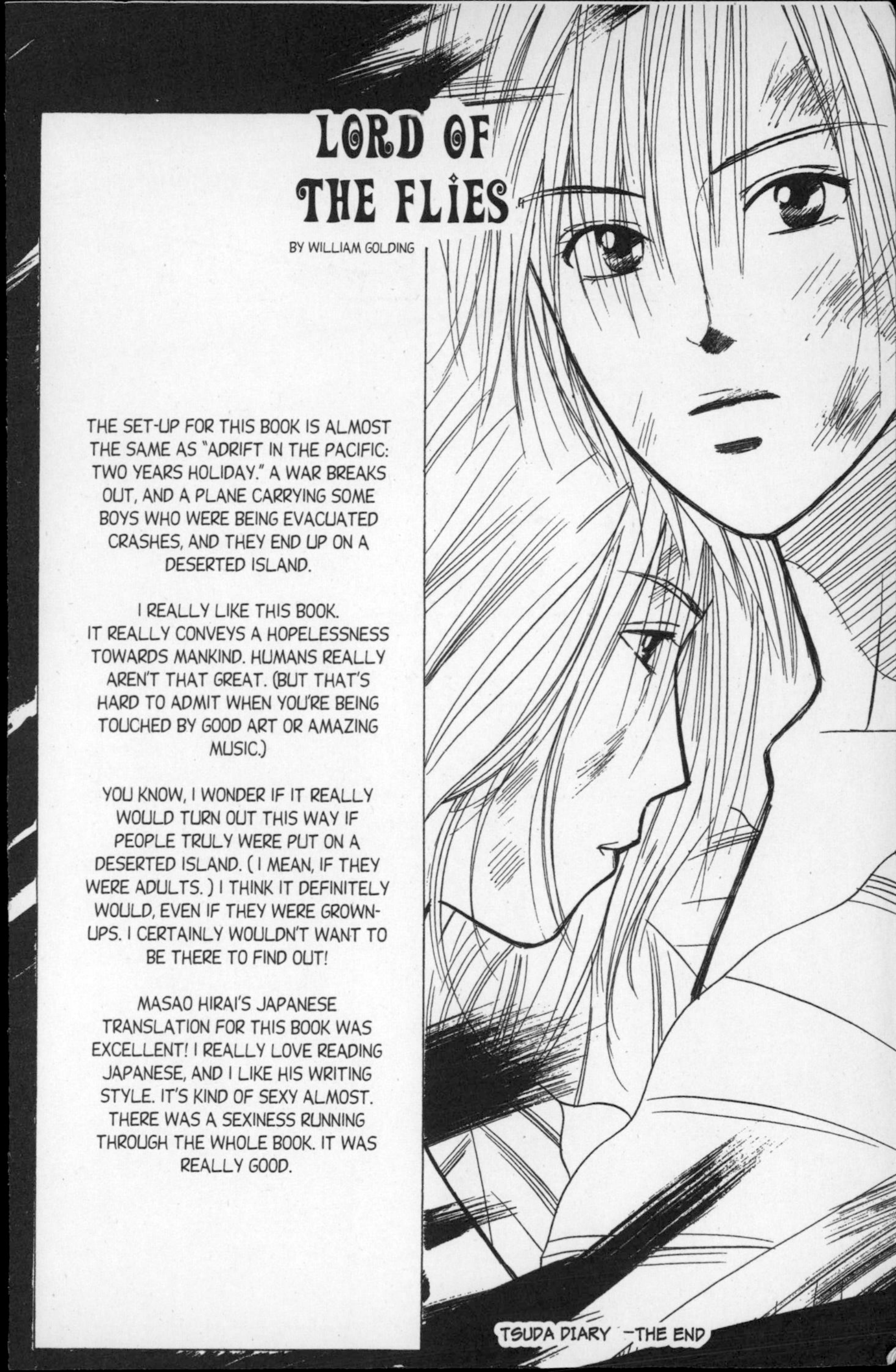
TSUDA DIARY —THE END

THANK YOU, AS ALWAYS.

S. TANEOKA

N. SHIMIZU

M. SHIBATA

R. OGAWA

AND MY MOTHER!

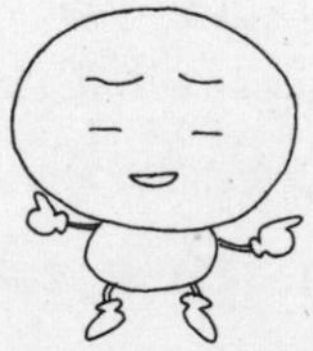

coming soon

kare kano

his and her circumstances

volume eight

Last minute preparations for the culture festival have shifted into high-gear and Tsubaki's play is really coming together! For his part, Soichiro continues to grapple with the two sides of his personality, particularly since one of them is a bit more violent and protective of Yukino than he'd like—a fact that has not gone unnoticed by Yukino, herself. Meanwhile, the bitter seeds of revenge begin to sweeten, as Tonami and Tsubaki finally come to the realization that they have fallen in love with one another.

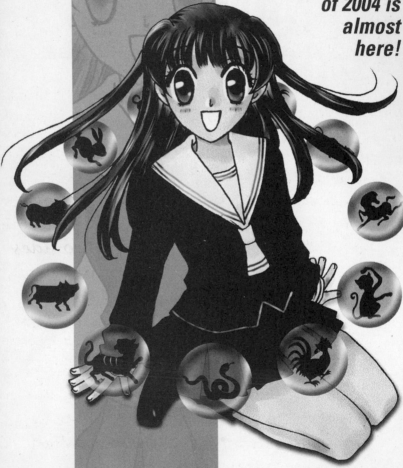

Fruits Basket

The most exciting manga release of 2004 is almost here!

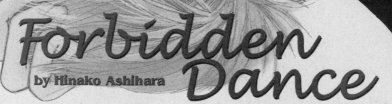

Dancing Was Her Life

Her Dance Partner
Might Be Her Future

TOKYOPOP®

Forbidden
Dance

by Hinako Ashihara

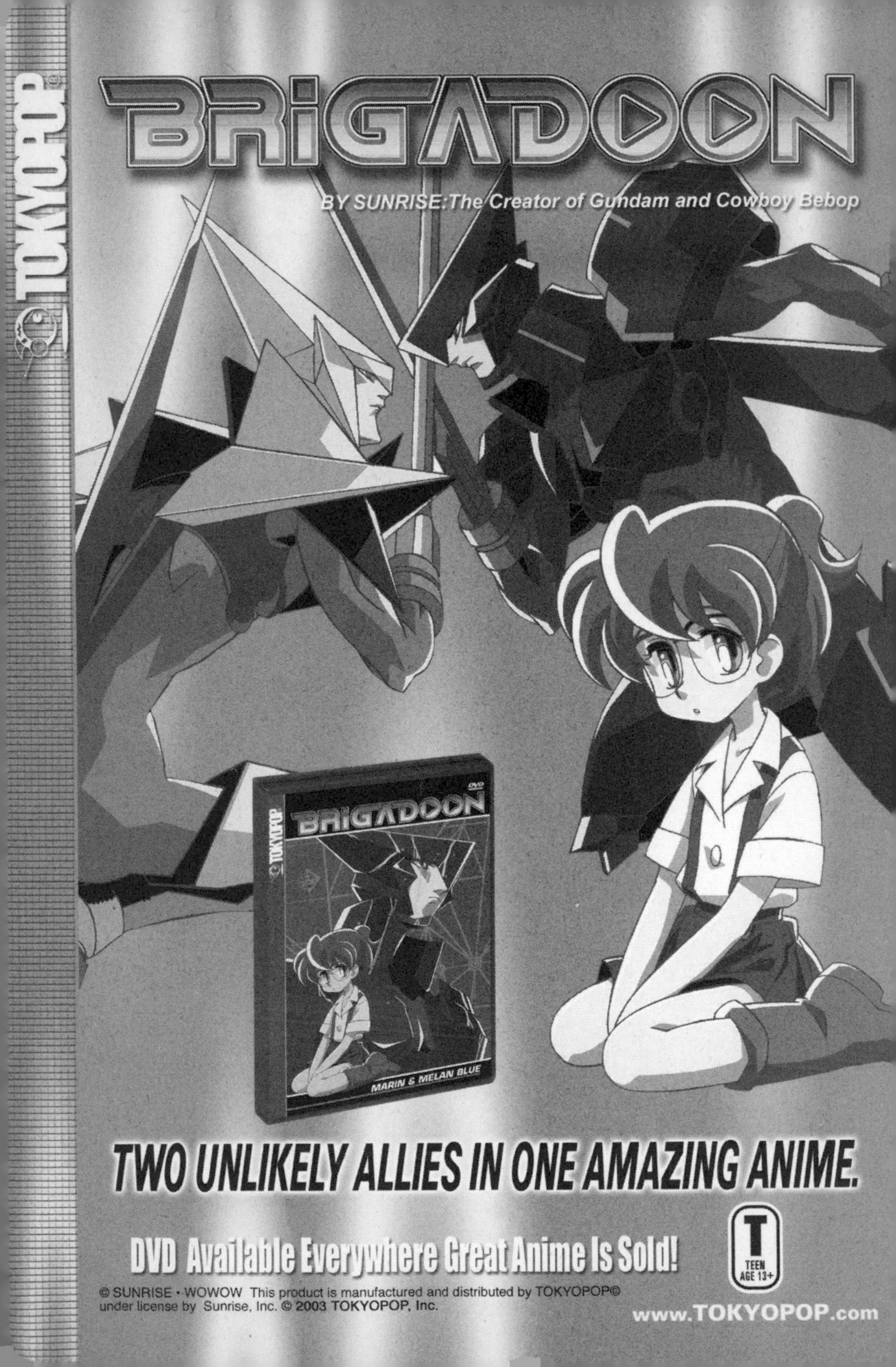
TOKYOPOP
BRIGADOON
BY SUNRISE: The Creator of Gundam and Cowboy Bebop
DVD
BRIGADOON
TOKYOPOP
MARIN & MELAN BLUE
TWO UNLIKELY ALLIES IN ONE AMAZING ANIME.
DVD Available Everywhere Great Anime Is Sold!
T
TEEN AGE 13+
© SUNRISE • WOWOW This product is manufactured and distributed by TOKYOPOP© under license by Sunrise, Inc. © 2003 TOKYOPOP, Inc.
www.TOKYOPOP.com

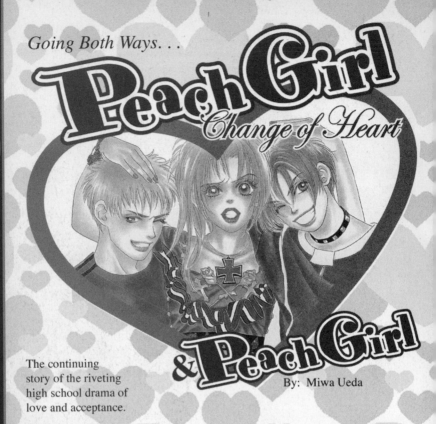

STOP!

This is the back of the book.
You wouldn't want to spoil a great ending!

This book is printed "manga-style," in the authentic Japanese right-to-left format. Since none of the artwork has been flipped or altered, readers get to experience the story just as the creator intended. You've been asking for it, so TOKYOPOP® delivered: authentic, hot-off-the-press, and far more fun!

DIRECTIONS

If this is your first time reading manga-style, here's a quick guide to help you understand how it works.

It's easy... just start in the top right panel and follow the numbers. Have fun, and look for more 100% authentic manga from TOKYOPOP®!

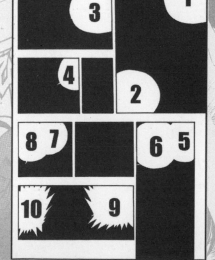

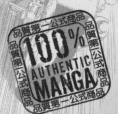